Makers of Democracy

Radical Perspectives: A Radical History Review Book Series

A series edited by Daniel Walkowitz and Barbara Weinstein

Makers of Democracy

A Transnational History of the
Middle Classes in Colombia

A. Ricardo López-Pedreros

DUKE UNIVERSITY PRESS
Durham and London
2019

Library of Congress Cataloging-in-Publication Data

Names: López, A. Ricardo, [date] author.
Title: Makers of democracy : a transnational his-
tory of the middle classes in Colombia / A. Ricardo
López-Pedreros.
Description: Durham : Duke University Press, 2019. |
Series: Radical perspectives | Includes bibliographical
references and index.
Identifiers: LCCN 2018033897 (print)
LCCN 2018042750 (ebook)
ISBN 9781478003298 (ebook)
ISBN 9781478001775 (hardcover : alk. paper)
ISBN 9781478002857 (pbk. : alk. paper)
Subjects: LCSH: Middle class—Colombia—History—20th
century. | Colombia—Politics and government—1946– |
Democracy—Colombia—History—20th century. |
Neoliberalism—Colombia—History—20th century. |
Social classes—Colombia—History—20th century.
Classification: LCC HT690.C6 (ebook) | LCC HT690.C6
L67 2019 (print) | DDC 305.5/509861—dc23
LC record available at https://lccn.loc.gov/2018033897

Cover art: Charles P. Fossum, Colombia aid mission
director, and Fabio Robledo, manager of the Colombia
Territorial Credit Institute, celebrating the construction of apartments for the middle class in Bogotá, early
1960s. Courtesy National Archives (photo no. 286-CF-
39-18), College Park, MD.

For **María Isabel** and **Valentina**

Contents

Abbreviations

ACEB	Asociación Colombiana de Empleados Bancarios
ACIA	Asociación Colombiana de Ingenieros Agrónomos
ACOPI	Asociación Colombiana Popular de Industriales
ACPO	Acción Cultural Popular
ADE	Asociación Distrital de Educadores
Alliance	Alliance for Progress
ANAPO	Alianza Nacional Popular
ANDI	Asociación Nacional de Industriales
ANEBRE	Asociación de Empleados del Banco de la República
ANUC	Asociación Nacional de Usuarios Campesinos
APUN	Asociación de Profesores de la Universidad Nacional de Colombia
ASDECOS	Asociación de Empleados de Compañías de Seguros
ASMEDAS	Asociación de Médicos al Servicio de Instituciones de Asistencia Social
ASPU	Asociación Sindical de Profesores Universitarios
ATSS	Asociación de Trabajadores de Sudamericana de Seguros
AVIANCA	Aerovías Nacionales de Colombia
BP	Banco Popular
BR	Banco de la República
CAFAM	Caja de Compensación Familiar
CARE	Cooperative for American Relief Everywhere
CAV	Corporaciones de Ahorro y Vivienda
CCAIM	Caja de Crédito Agrario, Industrial y Minero
CEDE	Centro de Estudios para el Desarrollo Económico

CELAM	Conference of Latin American Bishops
CFR	Council on Foreign Relations
CGT	Confederación General de Trabajo
CIA	Central Intelligence Agency
CINVA	Centro Inter-Americano de Vivienda y Planeamiento Urbano
CMC	Colegio Mayor de Cundinamarca
CNMH	Centro Nacional de Memoria Histórica
Colseguros	Compañía Colombiana de Seguros
CSTC	Confederación Sindical de Trabajadores de Colombia
CTC	Confederación Colombiana de Trabajadores
DAI	Departamento Administrativo Industrial
Davivienda	Corporación de Ahorro y Vivienda
DMCB	Dutch Middle-Class Bank
DNP	Departamento Nacional de Planeación
ECLAC	United Nations Economic Commission for Latin America and the Caribbean
ELN	Ejército de Liberación Nacional
ENC	Escuela Nacional de Comercio
ESAP	Escuela Superior de Administración Pública
FARC	Fuerzas Armadas Revolucionarias de Colombia
FAVI	Fondo de Ahorro y Vivienda
FECODE	Federación Colombiana de Educadores
FEDECAFE	National Federation of Colombia Coffee Growers
FEDEPROCOL	Federación de Sindicatos de Profesionales de Colombia
FEDESARROLLO	Fundación para la Educación Superior y el Desarrollo
FENALSTRASE	Federación Nacional de Profesionales del Estado
FENASIBANCOL	Federación Nacional de Sindicatos Bancarios Colombianos
FF	Ford Foundation

FN	Frente Nacional
FU	Frente Unido
IBRD	International Bank for Reconstruction and Development
ICBF	Instituto Colombiano de Bienestar Familiar
ICSS	Instituto Colombiano de Seguros Sociales
ICT	Instituto de Crédito Territorial
IFI	Instituto de Fomento Industrial
INCOLDA	Instituto Colombiano de Administración
INCORA	Instituto Colombiano de Reforma Agraria
INCP	Instituto Nacional de Contadores Públicos
ISI	import substitution industrialization
JUCO	Juventud Comunista
LMMC	Movimiento de Liberación de la Clase Media
M-19	Movimiento 19 de Abril
MOCLAM	Movimiento Aliado de la Clase Media Económica de Colombia
MOIR	Movimiento Obrero Independiente y Revolucionario
MUNIPROC	Movimiento Universitario de Promoción Comunal
OAS	Organization of American States
ONSC	Oficina Nacional de Servicio Civil
PCC	Partido Comunista Colombiano
PCC-ML	Partido Comunista de Colombia, Marxista-Leninista
PUJ	Pontificia Universidad Javeriana
RIAS	Rosca de Investigación y Acción Social
SENA	Servicio Nacional de Aprendizaje
SINTRASE	Sindicato de Trabajadores de la Rama Activa Aseguradora
SSROPU	Social Science Research Office of the Panamerican Union
UN	United Nations
UNAL	Universidad Nacional de Colombia

UNC	Unión Nacional de Contadores
UNCLAMECOL	Unidad Nacional de Clase Media Colombiana
UNEB	Unión Nacional de Empleados Bancarios
UNESCO	United Nations Educational, Scientific and Cultural Organization
UNIANDES	Universidad de los Andes
UPAC	Unidad de Poder Adquisitivo Constante
USAID	United States Agency for International Development
USOTA	US Office of Technical Assistance
UTB	Universidad Jorge Tadeo Lozano
UTC	Unión de Trabajadores Colombianos

Acknowledgments

This book has been long in the making. When I began to think about writing it, in the halls of academia, class as a category of historical analysis seemed to no longer matter. It was the beginning of this century, and the middle classes had yet again been deemed to represent "the end of politics." The catechism of democracy dictated that a society of one class, presumably a forever-expansive middle class, had made capitalism unquestionable. In 2008, at the very moment when I finished an early iteration of this book, a new global economic crisis ignited an intense interest in questions of class. Histories of capitalism took over the historiographical market, addressing what is usually defined as the major crisis of Western liberal democracies: the growth of material inequalities, the virtual disappearance of the middle classes, and the consolidation of a small global oligarchy.

This context made this book possible but also made its writing quite difficult, as the conjuncture posed pressing questions unreceptive to the critique that I wanted to offer about the historical formation of the middle classes. As neoliberalism dismantled democracy, I was often asked, who did not want to live in a society defined by an expansive middle class? Among some colleagues and interlocutors, I encountered either outright rejection or skepticism about the study's political importance. Some encouraged me to be politically wise and focus on the struggle between the bourgeoisie and the proletariat, the real class conflict of our times. Others invited me to take a more critical stand, in the belief that I was succumbing to the myth that the middle classes in fact existed in Latin America. I was supposedly imposing American or European realities on a region where the middle class had been at best a chimera, a desire that had been impossible to achieve. In disappointment, they often asked me how I could study—let alone write an entire book on—an illusion.

Such questions produced a degree of self-doubt, an occasional writer's block, and conceptual uncertainty. Yet they also invited me to think harder about why studying the middle classes produced such responses. I began to ponder how these interlocutors defined the middle class when deciding to ignore it as an object of study. How could I reconcile their admittedly difficult questions with my ethnographic work, in which a multiplicity of actors embraced—and defended—their belonging to a middle class? Was it possible that the defining of the middle class in Latin America as a chimera—a myth imposed by all-powerful oligarchies in their effort to consolidate rule—was part and parcel of the production of a middle-class identity? Did I have to ignore the fact that writing and teaching about the middle class have allowed me to earn a living as a member of this very class?

Certain authors suggested a way out of the rut that I felt stuck in. Stuart Hall's studies on identity proved crucial for understanding the role of the unconscious in class struggles. Tomás Gutiérrez Alea's visual masterpieces made evident how politically consequential the crafting of narratives about histories of class struggle could be. J. M. Coetzee's *Waiting for the Barbarians* highlighted the need for awareness of the paradoxes of democracy and power. Cedric Robinson's proposal to critically understand the roles of the petite bourgeoisie in revolutionary movements proved inspirational. And Gilles Deleuze reminded me to see teaching and writing as a way to become a traitor to one's regime, sex, and class.

I am profoundly grateful to those people who graciously allowed me into their lives in order to have difficult conversations about history, politics, society, family, and life. They let me into their homes and their archives. And they trusted me with their stories. I have told this history as I see it. Some will be disappointed. Others will disagree. I have done my best to remain true to their experiences and perspectives, but it is clear to me that we must question ourselves as members of the middle class in order to learn how to act, feel, and think differently in the world.

I want to thank friends, family, colleagues, and students who cheered me on, discussed extensively this book's ideas, and asked me difficult questions along the way. Daryle Williams lent support and encouragement at early stages of this process. Mary Kay Vaughan's scholarship, advice, and insights have always proved stimulating. Brian Owensby's exemplary study of the middle classes has influenced much of what I have to say here. Barbara Weinstein has been very generous. I believe that I have discussed every single idea in this book with her. She practices so well what Romand Coles calls "receptive generosity," a shared space in which both she and her colleagues are receptive to disagreements and open to being convinced by each other. It is a space through which both positions can be reciprocally transformed precisely because of those disagreements. Barbara's scholarship and friendship have been formative to my work as a historian.

I had the good fortune to present different parts of this book to engaged audiences at New York University, Princeton University, Humboldt University of Berlin, the Universidad de Antioquia in Medellín, the Universidad Nacional de Colombia in Bogotá, Tel Aviv University, the Colegio de México in Mexico City, the Universidad de San Carlos de Guatemala in Guatemala City, and the Centro de Investigaciones Sociales of the Instituto de Desarrollo Económico y Social, and the Consejo Nacional de Investigaciones Científicas y Técnicas in Buenos Aires. I have also presented drafts of sections of the book at multiple conferences. In particular, I want to thank the members of the Latin American History Group in the Northwest—Gabriela Aceves, Alejandra Bronfman, Ben Bryce, Anna Casas Aguilar, Alec Dawson, Bill French, and Stuart Parker—who read parts of the manuscript and offered perceptive comments. These experiences were a reminder that knowledge production is not an individual endeavor but rather a collective one. We carry along references, evoke conversations, and cite discussions with friends and colleagues as we craft narratives. Knowledge production should be defined as a labor of friendship and solidarity, not a competition over the ownership of ideas in a historiographical market. Thus whatever I have to say here depends on the work of those who have been writing about the Latin American middle classes with me: Ezequiel Adamovsky, Isabella Cosse, Iñigo García-Bryce, Enrique Garguín, Elizabeth Hutchison, Brian Owensby, David Parker, Claudia Stern, Sergio Visacovsky, Louise Walker, and Barbara Weinstein. I have also relied on those who have discussed with me various arguments about the histories of Colombia: César Ayala Diago, Mario Barbosa, Tania Luna Blanco, Viviane Brachet, Herbert Tico Braun, Lina Britto, Oscar Calvo, Valeria Coronel, Marta Isabel Domínguez, Matilde González-Izás, W. John Green, Medófilo Medina, Catalina Muñoz, Lida Núñez, David Orrego, Wilson Pabón, Mary Roldán, Manuel Ruiz, Eduardo Sáenz, Bernardo Tovar Zambrano, and Mónica Uribe. I am sad that Luz Gabriela Arango, my undergraduate adviser, whose scholarship molded my interest in the middle classes, cannot see this book in print. She is dearly missed.

I also acknowledge productive discussions about political economy and class formation with Susana Romero Sánchez. Claudia Stern has been a critical interlocutor and, above all, a good friend. Rob Karl has been a source of support along the way. We have remained engaged in discussions about archives, translations of historical documents, and arguments over the 1960s. Mauricio Archila Neira has been an intellectual companion. I have regularly turned to his friendship for feedback, guidance, perspective, and solidarity.

Mark Healey has been a wonderful reader of this manuscript, which he has gone through at least twice. He knows how to deliver an instructive critique, and the manuscript has greatly improved thanks to his generous reading. Others who were willing to discuss the challenges of writing while teaching include Leandro Benmergui, Herbert Brewer, Thomas Castillo, Shane Dillingham, Paula Halperin, Thanayi Jackson, Linda Noel, and Shari Orisich. I also want to offer special thanks to my dear friend Claire Gold-stene. Claire has been a trusted colleague whose collegiality, intellect, and integrity have supported me all along the way. Unspeakably important has also been her deep interest in theory, politics, and class formation.

I am grateful as well to the many archivists and librarians at multiple repositories. Without their work, this text would have been impossible. Research for this book has been generously supported by grants and fellowships from the Andrew W. Mellon Foundation, the American Council of Learned Societies, and the Library of Congress. The Department of History at the University of Maryland provided a year off for writing as well as financial support for a summer of research. The Research and Sponsored Programs at Western Washington University also provided funding for summer research and writing. And Western Washington's Department of History granted me a sabbatical, which proved crucial for finishing the manuscript.

My academic career has been possible thanks to public institutions across the Americas, which have provided spaces for critical and creative inquiry. I want to thank my students at Western Washington. So many of this book's ideas and arguments were tried out in my classes. And my students' questions often challenged me to be clear in what I had to say. In particular, Kelsey Gilman provided comments for the introduction and transcribed some interviews. Her work on neoliberal rule in Ecuador has also inspired me to think harder about power. I am indebted to my stimulating colleagues and friends, particularly Blanca Aranda Gómez García, Pedro Cameselle-Pesce, Kate Destler, Kristen French, Steven Garfinkle, Kevin Leonard, James Loucky, Ed Mathieu, Polly Myers, Johann Neem, Niall Ó Murchú, Shirley Osterhaus, Luis Gonzalo Portugal, Jennifer Seltz, Tamara Lea Spira, Joan Stamm, Maria Timmons Flores, and Verónica Velez. All of them have made this public institution of higher education a welcoming place for discussion about teaching, research, politics, and life.

I want to thank Sean Mannion, who edited this manuscript several times. Undoubtedly, his careful work has tremendously improved the text. Rafael Puyana worked diligently to produce several parts of the appendix and the illustrations. I am grateful to the anonymous readers who took the time to offer detailed comments, careful suggestions, and thoughtful criticisms that improved the manuscript drastically. It is a pleasure to thank Gisela Fosado for her support of the book. I must also thank her for our discussions about producing a concise manuscript and for her advice on how to get a teachable book published. Lydia Rose Rappoport-Hankins has guided me through the publication process.

Closer to home, Alex, Reyna, Wendy, and Julian have always made me feel at home in the United States, critical for those of us who are immigrants in the current political context. Their generosity is politically inspiring. Pedro, Jessyca, Nico, and Mateo have also provided perspective on what is important in life. My father, Abel Ignacio, would not be surprised to learn that, as for all of his other students, his teachings have proven foundational in my work as a historian. My mother, Myriam, has been a major inspiration in my life. She has continuously reminded me not to fall into an isolated academic life that promises the universal but delivers the particular. Teté, Juanita, and Gerardo have been enormously supportive. My in-laws—Matilde, Héctor, Sandra, Hernán, Felipe, and Sergio—have cheered me on along the way.

Last but not least, I owe deep thanks to María Isabel Cortés-Zamora, *una compañera de vida*. I am profoundly grateful for her candor, humor, solidarity, generosity, and intellectual creativity. Our shared commitment to teaching as a critical methodology for changing this world fills my life with hope, love, and meaning. Here I lack words to express how important she has been in this book's materialization. Not only did she provide economic support at a crucial moment of the writing, but her indefatigable belief in my ability to finish this study also proved pivotal. My journey with her has indeed been the pleasure—and the happiness—of my life. Valentina López-Cortés is my favorite daughter. Her enormous creativity, immense warmth, and unflagging commitment to making things different in the world have changed my approach to life. It is a joy to read her poetry and find that she too thinks that language is critical for social change. It is with a profound and unshakable love that I dedicate this book to María Isabel and Valentina in the hope that the history of the present can shed light on new futures through which all people of different genders, nationalities, religions, languages, ages, beliefs, races, ethnicities, and classes can fully participate in the equal distribution of the world's wealth. Con los Zapatistas decimos: queremos un mundo donde quepan muchos mundos.

Figure Intro.1 Charles P. Fossum, Colombia AID mission director, and Fabio Robledo, manager of the Colombia Territorial Credit Institute, celebrating the construction of apartments for the middle class in Bogotá, early 1960s. Courtesy National Archives (photo no. 286-CF-39-18), College Park, MD.

Introduction

"There Is No Other Class in Democracy"

The middle classes are the past, present, and future of democracy, or so we are continually told. Francis Fukuyama, who in the late 1980s proclaimed the triumph of Western liberal democracy as the end of history, has revisited his manifesto to declare the need for a new ideology "that could provide a realistic path toward a world with healthy middle-class societies."[1] As the middle classes have shrunk in the "developed world," and particularly in the United States, Fukuyama has critiqued the globalized economy for provoking de-democratization, through which societies across the global North have increasingly become divided into two homogeneous poles: elites and popular classes.[2] Contrary to what Karl Marx had predicted for his "communist utopia," Fukuyama contends, history has shown how "mature capitalism" generated "middle-class societies, not working-class ones." Marx's famous proletariat, the political scientist has proclaimed, became a global middle class.[3] But if the middle classes continue to decline, Fukuyama fears, the future of democracy is doomed. Thus, he calls for the reconstitution of "middle-class societies" that, although neither sufficient nor necessary conditions for liberal democracy, have proven crucial in averting the emergence of "oligarchic domination or populist revolution."[4] In a word, if at the Cold War's end the expansion of a middle-class society was seen as the unquestionable triumph of Western liberal democracies—that is, the *end* of history—now the middle classes must resuscitate themselves in order to secure the *future* of democracy globally.

Fukuyama is not alone. In the United States some scholars and policy-makers deem the US middle classes "the losers of globalization," which is already transforming an irresistible empire for democracy into a "third-world country" because of not only "unwelcome" immigrants but also the widening of economic inequality, political polarization, and class struggle.[5] This, some proclaim, brought Donald Trump to the White House.[6] It is indeed the vanishing middle classes, some argue, that are behind moral and political panic, as democracy is losing political currency in the so-called developed countries. Thus, some wonder whether the US government should stop setting up the "American way of life" as an example for the world and should instead focus on reviving the American middle class at home.[7]

And yet, in a seeming contradiction, US development institutions and international organizations position the middle classes as the bastion of neoliberal democracy throughout the world, the foundation for societies that will finally resolve economic inequalities, social instability, and extreme political belligerence.[8] Studies supported by development institutions provide extensive but mixed statistical evidence for how throughout the developing world—from the Middle East to Africa and Latin America—"new" middle classes have emerged to enhance democracy's prospects.[9] Amid a perceived threat to "the West," policymakers and commentators in the United States and Europe urge a "re-Westernization"—by invitation if possible or by military means if necessary—in which the expansion of middle-class societies could secure once and for all the superiority and distinctiveness of Western liberal democracies in the world.[10]

In Colombia, at a crucial moment when the Revolutionary Armed Forces of Colombia (FARC) and the government have reached a peace agreement, President Juan Manuel Santos has advocated Colombians toward a future—dubbed "the age of the postconflict"—in which all efforts are dedicated to strengthening an extensive middle class as "the driving force for a full democracy," a needed buffer between the rich and the poor.[11] Álvaro Uribe Vélez—former president, senator, and the most outspoken critic of the peace accords—cannot but agree with his "political enemy" that a "cohesive society" comes with an expanded middle class.[12] When Uribe categorizes the peace agreement as an antidemocratic takeover by communist forces, he evokes the destruction of middle-class society—grounded in foreign investment, private property, militarized social relations, and heteropatriarchal family values. Thus while differing on the means, Santos and

Uribe Vélez share the end: the middle classes should take the nation from a conflict-driven, violent, and antidemocratic past into a conflict-free, peaceful, and democratic future.

These discussions, far from mere abstractions, structure how certain people see themselves as part of a middle class and what role they play in society's democratization. Take Hernando Bahamón Soto, a professional for many years with the Departamento Nacional de Planeación (DNP), who assured me that "there is no other class in democracy as indispensable as the middle class."[13] Mobilizing these transnational discourses, he proclaimed, "No middle class, no democracy." After our conversations, he felt compelled to write an acrostic titled "This Is the Middle Class" to both describe the class to which he proudly belonged and claim democracy as the middle classes' exclusive possession.

Comunidad organizada del mismo grado (Community organized on an equal level)

Libre y con ideales definidos e iguales (Free and with defined and equal ideals)

Animada como población activa del país (Animated as the country's active population)

Sembrando bienestar, alegría y paz (Planting welfare, happiness, and peace)

En todos los lugares del mundo (Everywhere in the world)

Masa que surge a conseguir igualdad (Mass that strives for equality)

Entre todos los habitantes del país (Among all the country's inhabitants)

De acuerdo a las diferentes capas sociales (In accordance with different social strata)

Individuos de la tropa que marcha adelante (Individuals of the rank and file moving ahead)

Activado siempre con gallardía y arrojo (Always enabled by bravery and fearlessness)

¡Que viva la clase media! (Long live the middle class!)[14]

Long live the middle class? Most scholars would dismiss this acrostic as exemplifying how people such as Bahamón Soto remain unaware of their own true interests and therefore susceptible to an antidemocratic neoliberal order that only benefits what philosopher Alain Badiou calls "capitalist oligarchies."[15] In these accounts, the middle classes are treated as an "embodied lie . . . a myth . . . an act of camouflage" that disguises the true—and authentic—class struggle at the core of an undemocratic global order.[16] Others would add that amid growing material inequality, the important question is measuring whether the middle classes really exist.[17] Another group would counter that Latin American societies, in Göran Therborn's words, "have already learned through bitter experience . . . that there is nothing inherently democratic about the middle class, [as] its members actively oppos[ed] democracy."[18] Others, like James Scott, would urge that although "the petit bourgeoisie rarely, if ever, speaks for itself, [it] performs vital social and economic services under *any* political system."[19]

Despite their disagreements, these responses concede too much at the outset by assuming as self-evident the meanings and practices of democracy. They continue to ask how democratic—or undemocratic—the middle classes are at a given moment, thereby ossifying democracy as a transcendental evaluator to be used in a transhistorical manner. All these responses equally presuppose the existence of the middle classes as a reality through which the robustness of democracy can be measured. In the process, the putatively ontological relationship between democracy and the formation of a middle class readily goes unquestioned. What definitions of democracy, I ask in this book, do we often invoke but seldom specify when labeling the middle classes as anti-, less, or more democratic? What was the historical process through which we came to understand the middle classes as the normative foundation for democracy? How and why did different social actors—in particular, self-identified middle-class women and men like Bahamón Soto—participate in making the relationship between the middle class and democracy so appealing, to the degree that democracy now appears to be an "obvious" property of the middle classes?

Makers of Democracy is an attempt to historicize the material circumstances, discursive conditions, collective subjectivities, social struggles, and political battles through which a middle-class reality came to represent what democracy was supposed to deliver. The book does so by investigating how the transnational formation of the middle classes in Bogotá during the 1960s and 1970s both influenced and was shaped by the expansion of US power in Latin America, the implementation of development programs, the normalization of modernization theories, the growth of the service sector, increased urbanization, the reconfiguration of the state's role, the consolidation of radical politics, and the emergence of an early iteration of neoliberal rule. At the book's core are those professionals, white-collar employees, and small-business owners who engaged in multiple hard-fought political struggles, among themselves and against working-class groups and elites, over what shape democracy would take after the Second World War. In so doing, *Makers of Democracy* historicizes democracy not as an ideological chimera of total emancipation or a utopia without hierarchy but as an effect of political conflicts through which middle-class women and men attempted to at once question and naturalize class stratifications and gender hierarchies at the core of what democracy was supposed to do.

Democracy as a Question

As scholars have argued, the study of democracies has historically been associated with the experiences of Europe and the United States, from where democracy has long been understood as originating and then spreading to the rest of the globe.[20] Indeed, democracy is usually depicted as a selfless gift from "the West."[21] This has perpetuated a teleological narrative of an exclusively Western and universal democracy in which divergent historical realities can only be understood as deviations, failures, or, at best, derivatives.[22] Recent studies have criticized this normativity by examining the multiple experiences of democracy outside what is considered the proper West.[23] Although this has been a crucial move to challenge the triumphalist narrative of an exclusively Western democracy, scholars tend to particularize, even exoticize, those cases perceived to be outside a putative normativity of democracy. For example, in their pathbreaking collection of essays, Enrique Desmond Arias and Daniel M. Goldstein argue that "instead of viewing violence as indicative of democratic failure," one must see how a "violent pluralism" has been "critical to the foundation of Latin American democracies, the maintenance of democratic states, and the political behavior of democratic citizens."[24] This allows scholars to understand how "violent pluralism" was neither a social aberration nor emblematic of a state fallen from "the (implicitly Western) democratic ideal," which "even occidental democracies would have a hard time living up to." Rather, these multiple forms of violence have been fundamental "in preserving or challenging a particular form of lived democracy" that must be understood in Latin American terms.[25] In the wake of such reality, Arias and Goldstein invite scholars to recognize that "pluralist political practice in Latin America ... may very well depend on a tolerance for privatized violence and ongoing abuses of larger segments of the population ... unique forms of political practice, order, and subjectivity that need to be studied on their own terms."[26]

Although *Makers of Democracy* is part of this effort to deterritorialize the multiple histories of democracy, I would nonetheless argue that these studies tend to retain the dichotomy that has for so long rendered the world outside Europe and the United States alternative, vernacular, hybrid, and, in this case, violent. While US foreign policy toward Latin America has historically been crucial in perpetuating what Arias and Goldstein call "violent democracies," violence is too often historicized as a unique experience that must be understood in "Latin American terms." This leads Arias to conclude that "understanding politics in Latin America depends on us recognizing the limitations of applying the concept of democracy to the region."[27] Thus we reaffirm the imperialist histories that the United States and Europe want to tell about themselves, in which "Northern democracies" are original, superior, and more authentic because they are less violent or have incorporated a "legitimate" form of violence to enforce a social and political order.

It is through this framework that a normative idea of middle-class society serves as a barometer for democracy. The histories of democracies are hierarchically territorialized, with middle-class societies deemed properly democratic (superior, universal, global, exportable, class-harmonious, and legitimately violent) and those societies characterized by struggle between popular classes and elites deemed less, or anti-, democratic (inferior, local, alternative, class-antagonistic, and illegitimately violent). Because Latin America has often been understood as the latter, the middle classes are historicized as either absent or a failure, unable to democratize their societies—that is, make them more like the United States and Europe.[28] In the process, a middle class is defined as the barometer to measure the imperial *difference* between a global North (the West) and a global South (the rest of the world). Thus, the West is squarely located as the owner of—and original benefactor for—democracy as Europe and the US fully developed a putative exemplar middle class to be exported while other places in the world have historically provincialized the gift of democracy by trying to emulate those middle-class societies.

This assumption is at the core of how scholars understand the 1960s and 1970s in Latin America in general and its development programs in particular. Consider how we have historicized perhaps the most important development program of the twentieth century's second half, the Alliance for Progress. For some, the Alliance was a typical policy of containment, with US policymakers trying to export a ready-made middle class—"the American way of life"—as a way to push Latin American societies, in danger of succumbing to communism, toward liberal, democratic, and capitalist modernity.[29] And yet study after study argues that such development programs were, from their very inception, colossal failures, lost causes, or "the most portentous social experiments ... a grand design [that went] sour."[30] Despite their noble intention "to improve" the lives of the people of "the Third World" by making them middle class, the argument goes, US officials "misled themselves trying to apply dubious social science theories" alien to Latin American realities.[31] Echoing policymakers and intellectuals during the 1960s, these historians conclude that "Latin America was not Europe" and thus was inimical to US-style middle-class democracy.[32] Mired in two-class struggle, Latin American societies rejected US development programs, which further perpetuated political radicalization and social polarization.[33] For other scholars, the creation of a middle class in the Americas failed because policymakers did not put into practice the social polices they preached. Instead, US foreign policy turned from these development programs—or used them as smoke screens for "real" imperial policies—and weakened democracy by "fortif[ying] illiberal forces, militariz[ing] societies," and limiting the social definitions of democracy.[34] The Alliance was simply a manifestation of imperial hypocrisy.[35]

Such analysis is further reproduced in critical decolonial theorizations of the relationship between what are deemed the local (i.e., Latin American) experiences of modernity and the global (i.e., North Atlantic) designs of a modern-colonial matrix of power. And although my arguments in this book are inspired by this effort to decolonize histories of Latin America, such theorizations tend to dehistoricize power relations and systems of domination, thereby erasing any political or social role for the middle classes in "local" spaces.[36] Indeed, the local—or what is seen as outside a proper "Europe"—is thus subsumed into transhistorical "subaltern authenticity" positioned against a dominant—and perennial—Western colonial matrix of power. Any Latin American middle class is perceived as an inauthentic, "Americanized" formation, a deviation from what is considered a proper Latin American subalternity.

Thus, the problem is not so much that the formation of the middle classes has historiographically been elided.[37] As will become clear in this book, since at least the 1950s scholars across the Americas have discussed nonstop the middle classes in a comparativist narrative that frames them as failures, as lacking, as social and political actors unimportant to the histories of Latin America. This "enduring episteme" has trapped historical analysis of the middle classes in a quandary: either the middle classes are too Europeanized or US-influenced and thus presumably not exotic enough to be a worthy topic to understand the perceived radical alterity of Latin America, or the middle class is depicted as diverging from Europe and the United States and thus closer to a "subaltern" reality, which by implication means the consolidation of a two-class society where the middle classes as social or political realities are unimportant to historicize power relations in Latin America.[38] It is in this context that John Charles Chasteen writes in perhaps one of the most popular textbooks about Latin American history in the US that in this region "where the idea of a middle class majority is not a reality but, rather, a fond aspiration for the future" the prevalent free-market policies will only consolidate the division between "rich and poor. Conquerors and conquered. Masters and slaves . . . the old . . . conflict at the heart of Latin American history."[39]

Thus, despite the increasing amount of scholarship committed to critically examining the histories of the middle classes, to which this book contributes, the systems of domination are still framed via polarities: ruling classes and masses, oligarchies and popular classes, subalterns and hegemonic forces, local and global.[40] In his seminal works on the revolutions in twentieth-century Latin America, for instance, Greg Grandin, following José Nun's arguments in the 1960s, identifies among the Latin American middle classes a "susceptibility to manorialism" that propelled them to embrace the ideology of the oligarchy and "its heroes, its symbols, its culture, and its laws."[41] Thus the middle classes, "too structurally and ideologically dependent on the oligarchy," could not develop a universal ideology—or what Nun called "hegemonic vocation"—to transcend "an unsustainable model of exclusionary nationalism, restricted political institutions, [and] persisting rural clientelism."[42] Therefore, the middle sectors failed to become proper middle classes—hegemonic, democratic, Western-like—because for the most part they were co-opted by oligarchical rule. This co-optation soon translated into a key base of support for several dictatorships throughout the region in the second half of the twentieth century. This is why we have come to understand Cold War revolutionary politics and the global 1960s and 1970s in Latin America as a *dialectical* struggle between revolution and counterrevolution.[43] The former, originating mostly in Latin America, is historicized as vibrant, egalitarian, and collective, sustained mostly by subaltern groups and on a few occasions joined by certain middle-class sectors. The latter, emanating from the United States, is characterized as illiberal, antidemocratic, tepid, and backed by a coalition of the middle classes and oligarchies.[44] Thus, scholars still think of Cold War society as an already politically polarized space in which the middle classes, presumably removed from this polarization, were forced to side with either popular groups in support of a revolutionary project (usually categorized as a manifestation of democratization) or reactionary oligarchies in support of a counterrevolutionary one (often labeled an antidemocratic manifestation)—if they engaged in political struggle at all.[45]

This dominant narrative largely serves to protect an ideal account of democracy and middle-class development. In an influential Colombian history textbook, Frank Safford and Marco Palacios note that "despite the growth of urban middle classes during the twentieth century, profound social differences still can be observed in a continuing breach between the ideal of citizenship and political equality and the reality of continuing privileges and inequalities before the law and justice of the state."[46] This captures how many historians distinguish between an ideal middle-class democracy and the social reality of being middle class, a distinction put at the center of the middle class's historical formation because those actors who identified as middle class could never comply with the ideal of a middle-class democracy.[47] The ideal is therefore criticized for its incomplete enactment or distortion in practice. If this democratic ideal had been fully materialized, the assumption goes, then no dissonance, no hierarchies, and no contradictions would have existed. This argument also protects a fantasy of democracy by compartmentalizing class stratifications and gender hierarchies as in fundamental contradiction with democratic rule. More class hierarchies and gender stratifications imply antidemocracy; authentic, proper, or "democracy to come" is imagined as the overcoming of gendered and classed hierarchical rule.[48] Thus, we tend to treat democracy as a transcendental—context-free, nonhierarchical, and universally inclusive—fantasy of total emancipation presumably not yet materialized in practice. In the process, democracy, however idealized, remains unquestioned.[49]

Makers of Democracy conceptualizes democracy as contingent rather than preordained. It invites us to move from assessing where the middle classes could be more democratic to a historical critique of democracy itself.[50] It does so by historicizing the struggles over the meanings, subjectivities, practices, and rationalities of democracy. More specifically, *Makers of Democracy* offers a historicized explanation of how in 1960s and 1970s Bogotá middle-class women and men fought against working classes and elites to naturalize a hierarchical definition of democracy. Some struggled to couple the "legitimate" access to private property with middle-classness. Others emphasized that the right to represent "the people" in democracies needed to be associated with a professional competence central to middle-class status. Others tried to naturalize politics as the administration of hierarchical differences. Still others privileged economic success as synonymous with (masculine) middle-class entrepreneurial individual endeavor. Yet others defended affective labor in the tertiary sector as a commodity to be performed by those who could be categorized as middle-class women and men. And all of them saw education as an investment in middle-class status, fostering entrepreneurial individuality key to proper democracy. The book also problematizes how other middle-class women and men struggled to materialize different but equally hierarchical visions of democracy in which education was both a common social good and a central prerequisite for representing "the proletariat," economic success the result of a collective yet gendered project, access to land a question of labor, health a right, labor relations the product of conflict, public assembly fundamental to political participation, and social relations marked by solidarity. In so doing, *Makers of Democracy* historicizes how the first set of definitions of middle-classness—the one we now assume natural to a "global middle class"—began to gain transnational normativity and legitimacy while eclipsing other visions of middle-class democracy as unreasonable, impracticable, and disposable. The book demonstrates how competing class hierarchies, contested gendered stratifications, and conflicting forms of domination, far from exceptions to a true democracy, were constitutive of the multiple struggles for democracy during the twentieth century's second half.

An (Un)Avoidable Question

What is the middle class, anyway? This is the most common question asked of those studying the middle classes, a question that often precludes, rather than provokes, historical analysis. It is assumed that the middle classes cannot be clearly located in a sociological description of society between those who own the means of production and those who do not. While the elites and working classes, presumably because of their clear structural locations, represent homogenous, clear-cut interests, the middle classes are deemed too heterogeneous to constitute a category for rigorous historical analysis.[51] This invites us to understand middle-class identities and subjectivities as transparent reflections of social configurations, economic developments, and structural changes.[52] But if we accept this, we face a complicated and ulti-mately self-defeating task in which certain fixed assignations, attributes, and characteristics have to be found in different historical contexts in order to confirm—or disprove—our assumptions about what the middle classes are.

This does not mean, however, that the middle classes are discursive or metaphorical creations, floating signifiers, merely projects with no material purchase in reality. As Michel Foucault long ago argued, we can no longer sacralize "the social as the only instance of the real," with what people think, do, and say as less real.[53] This assumption sanctifies a hierarchical distinc-tion between objectivity (a hard, pristine, and thus finished reality) and sub-jectivity (a soft, messy, and therefore less important actuality).[54] Drawing on recent historical and anthropological studies on the middle classes, I seek to understand the middle class not as a descriptive, self-contained index, metaphysical category but as historical formations.[55] My fundamental premise is that "middle classes . . . are not real *because* they exist in theory but rather because people exist in classed ways that can be theorized."[56] This must account for, rather than neglect, the heterogeneous, messy, and contradictory practices through which women and men have historically experienced their middle-class lives.

With this in mind, I appropriate Foucault's concept of genealogy as a way to historicize the conditions and practices that allowed certain histori-cal subjects—and not others—to define themselves as middle-class women and men.[57] My main purpose is to historicize the formation of the middle class in Bogotá as a question of subjectivity. But such an effort, far from ig-noring what is perceived as the objectivity of class, requires understanding middle-class formation as simultaneously a structural condition, a rational-ity of rule, a material reality, a gendered social experience, a political claim, and a collective movement. Thus, my working definition of the middle classes encompasses three inextricable aspects and several subsets.[58] First, the formation of the middle classes in Bogotá of the 1960s and 1970s was an effect of specific structural conditions: the intensification of urbanization, the growth of the service sector, the reconfiguration of the state's role in soci-ety, the consolidation of small and medium industries as part of industrial-ization, the increase in educational opportunities for certain social actors, and the expansion of development programs in a context of radicalization and decolonization. These are the structural conditions of possibility that lead me to focus on three main social actors as representative of middle-class formation: professionals, white-collar employees, and small-business owners.

Second, such structural conditions were mediated by what I call gendered and classed rationalities of rule. On one level, such rationalities of rule are a product of knowledge/discourses—modernization theories (in the 1960s), left revolutionary theories, and neoclassical economic principles (in the 1970s). On another level, rationalities of rule are translations of those discourses into specific development policies, revolutionary discussions about social and political change, and neoliberal strategies that attempted to mobilize different but closely related "fantasies" about the social and political role of middle-class women and men in democracies.[59] Amid concern about the spread of communism, such fantasies, not to be mistaken for falsehoods, activated certain historical subjectivities and not others to think, do, and speak as middle class and, as such, empowered these subjectivities to perform as if they were the sovereign representatives of "the people" in democracies.

Third, the middle classes were also a product of subjective formation through which some women and men engaged in multiple practices to define what it meant to be—and live as—middle class. But rather than employing a notion of rational individuals who exercise agency as they please, I understand middle-class subjectivities as involving interrelated questions of identity claims, conscious interests, and unconscious desires that depended on but were not reducible to shared gendered and classed fantasies activated by those structural conditions and rationalities of rule.[60] Such an approach might help us overcome narratives of Latin American history in which the middle class is either a class for itself (true consciousness) or in itself (false consciousness).[61] Such readings acknowledge the social existence and structural consolidation of a middling group or even a middle-class identity but assume that middling groups did not coalesce as political subjects as they could not materialize a unified project, develop common social interests, and form a class consciousness.[62] I propose that even when subjects are unaware of their class interests, their practices of being middle class are part of a collective economy of desires/practices that constitute a sense of (un)conscious commonality against gendered and classed others. Here gender can be defined as "a historically and culturally specific attempt to resolve the dilemma of sexual difference, to assign fixed meaning to that which ultimately cannot be fixed."[63] Thus heterogeneous middle-class subjectivities were practiced through mutable, hierarchical antagonisms. Such antagonisms, I conclude, shaped a sense of middle-class political identity that, as part of a larger political mobilization, enabled certain middle-class women and men to make a claim to represent "the people" and struggle for a legitimate right to dominate in democracy.[64] It is through these struggles and relationships that middle-class women and men also challenged the very practices of what it meant to be middle class, redefining what democracy was supposed to do.

This approach relies on an eclectic array of newly uncovered archives and sources—from transnational-imperial and development organizations, Colombian state agencies, private companies, middle-class political organizations, and personal collections comprising diaries, teaching lesson plans, professional reports, and annotated readings. As Ann Stoler argues, scholars have developed sophisticated critical perspectives with which to read state and elite archival documents "against the grain" in order to shed light on how subalterns left evidence revealing how they resisted, appropriated, and negotiated systems of domination.[65] But when studying middle-class formation, this approach must be combined with a sustained engagement with those archives as both catalogs of hierarchical class rule in the making and ethnographic sites of disparate notions of what defined democratic practices and middle-classness. Following Stoler, I propose seeing archival activity not just as a process of extracting authentic middle-class voices but as an ethnographic exercise through which one can historicize power relations from the middle.[66]

I also conducted numerous interviews with self-identified middle-class women and men, not to reclaim marginalized voices—or to recuperate the role of a silent majority in democracies—but to critically engage with these historical actors' contested memories in order to illuminate why and how they think, act, and speak as they do. As Bahamón Soto's memories, cited at the beginning of this introduction, suggest, this reveals how certain women and men became convinced that middle-classness meant democracy and that democracy meant the consolidation of a middle class.[67] I discuss how these memories became gendered and classed claims through which women and men legitimized a specific way to remember the 1960s and 1970s that was intimately connected with competing hierarchized visions of democracy in the present.

Tragic Histories of the Middle Classes

While the middle classes continue to appear as a democratic or antidemocratic force, *Makers of Democracy* proposes, following David Scott's important arguments, a tragic narrative of middle-class historical actors in order to offer a historical critique of democracy itself.[68] The book's first part, "Conscripts of Democracy," describes how an idea of middle-classness became one of the most contested fields of knowledge in the late 1950s and 1960s. Global policymakers, Latin American state welfare program representatives, spokespeople for privately sponsored social programs, politicians, state policymakers, and elite university professors across the Americas tied the middle class to a hierarchical definition of democracy while demarcating popular groups and oligarchies as the bases for antidemocratic populism and feudal society, respectively. Such transnational discussions shaped development projects under the umbrella of the Alliance, which envisioned the middle classes as "the last democratic hope for the world." I demonstrate how these programs of community building, agrarian reform, education, housing, and financial literacy, crafted by intellectuals and policymakers across the Americas, supported by private foundations, sponsored by the United States' development offices, and put into practice as state policies during Colombia's National Front (FN), elevated this hierarchical vision of democracy to the status of common sense. In so doing, I historicize how an idea of the middle class, far from a false ideology intended to obscure the realpolitik of empire, legitimized the exercise of US imperial rule on a transnational terrain. Responding to the violence of the 1950s in Colombia and the Cuban Revolution, the Alliance sought not to weaken democracy in the region but to naturalize a particular classed and gendered definition of democracy.[69] I also show how during the FN in Colombia, a bipartisan coalition between the Liberal and Conservative Parties, this definition of democracy became an everyday reality for certain women and men charged with bringing a new era of peace after a decade of violence. Through meticulous yet contradictory processes of selection and schooling in state offices, universities, small and medium industries, and service offices, professionals, small-business owners, and white-collar workers were conscripted, and thus empowered, as transnational democratic subjects.

The second part, "Contested Democracies," proposes to understand the middle classes as a social movement of class politics. My arguments build on recent studies of the Cold War in Latin America and cultural approaches to the global 1960s, though such studies tend to take the middle classes' political roles as given and to sidestep what was particularly middle class about their political participation in revolutionary projects.[70] I ask what it was like to live through revolutionary/counterrevolutionary times, to make a political claim to middle-classness, and to struggle for a democratic society. I show how state professionals, white-collar employees, and small-business owners, in their struggle to become part of a middle class, partially consented to Alliance and FN social policies. Such consent did not, however, merely mean an "Americanization" of the middle classes in Bogotá, a reproduction of an elite master plan, or support for a counter-revolutionary project. Rather, these historical actors mobilized in disorganized yet meaningful collective action as a class in order to structure their vision of a democratic middle-class society.

Such collective action was rooted in three interrelated demands. Against perceived oligarchical elites, professionals demanded that hierarchies in a proper democracy stem not from lineage or blood but from effort, education, and competence, virtues squarely reserved for the middle class. Small-business owners demanded political recognition as representatives of an entrepreneurial state that could democratize the economy for everyone's benefit. And white-collar employees demanded recognition as society's productive class for promoting understanding and interdependence among employers and employees, the cornerstone of a democratic social order characterized by labor harmony. Yet these varied political demands produced what I dub a gendered and classed chain of equivalence through which these three middle-class actors aggregated their particular demands to struggle against "the oligarchs" and "the laboring classes" for material rewards hierarchically distributed according to gendered and classed notions of intellectual labor, professional competence, and economic productivity.[71] In so doing, they opposed the middle—disciplining—position in a three-class society prescribed by development programs and pushed instead to be hierarchically located *above* the elites, the working class, and the peasantry. In so doing, some joined a populist oppositional party, the National Popular Alliance (ANAPO), to claim sovereign representation of "the people." Gender featured centrally in these demands, with middle-class men joining forces to silence their female counterparts, who were increasingly participating in professional associations and white-collar unions. Indeed, these gendered claims fomented a certain degree of commonality among otherwise heterogeneous middle-class demands, strengthening the political call for a hierarchical, masculine, and classed vision of domination—and democratic representation—over those whom they considered feminized forces: elites, working-class unions, and middle-class women.

The book's second part also historicizes how and why some professionals and white-collar employees, both by deploying their conscription as democracy's representatives and through their classed and gendered encounters with a transnational left, challenged the sociopolitical order that had empowered them in the first place. This new radical petit bourgeoisie—as they consciously and unconsciously began to see themselves—reconfigured the meanings, practices, and rationalities of proper democracy by advocating education as a common good, knowledge production as a means of radical critique and the proletariat's revolutionary awakening, health as a fundamental right of modern society, economic success as a collective endeavor to own the means of production, and land distribution as predicated on labor. In this new democratic order, communal solidarity and generosity would typify social relations, and labor would be properly compensated. This radical petit bourgeoisie struggled to make public assembly a central aspect of democracy. Women contributed to this dismantling of patriarchal practices via equal pay, childcare services for professionals, gender solidarity at home, and sexual, economic, and bodily autonomy. Yet like their middle-class counterparts, this petit bourgeoisie endeavored to make dominant their particular classed and gendered visions of revolutionary change. As they questioned oligarchical elites, they simultaneously sought to erect a hierarchical vision of society in which they themselves, as petit bourgeoisie, properly represented "the proletariat" and thus held the right to dominate in a true democracy.

In the last chapter of the book the narrative shifts to discuss the historical emergence of an early iteration of neoliberal rule. It traces how, in response to middle-class oppositional movements and petit bourgeois radicalization, the administrations of the 1970s attempted to normalize a particular definition of democracy that we now call the "global middle class." In so doing, these administrations sought to further conscript a specific middle class as the exemplar of a postclass, postpolitical, and postideological society. And, unlike the second half of the 1960s, middle-class women and men consented to this by locating themselves in the middle of a socially cohesive three-class hierarchical society. In the process, a middle class was further associated with the primacy of private property, the holiness of economic individualism, the postpolitical management of classed differences, and the sanctity of the free market as the legitimate organizer of social hierarchies. This is the tragic, complex history that would allow us to historicize Cold War politics as a struggle between and among heterogeneous classed and gendered mobilizations, happening *within* revolutionary and counterrevolutionary movements, through which competing conceptions of class rule as well as opposing forms of domination were contested and legitimized.[72]

Deprovincializing Histories of Colombia

Rex Hudson, mobilizing a widely shared narrative, has claimed that the history of Colombia is "paradoxical." It is a country, he writes, with "a distinguished tradition of political stability" and "one of Latin America's longest-functioning democracies, with a lasting record of usually fair and regular elections and respect for political and civil rights."[73] Historians usually understand the second half of the twentieth century as the moment when Colombia secured this tradition of political stability, relative social and economic growth, and an expanded urban middle sector, all while avoiding a major military dictatorship or authoritarian regime. And yet scholars simultaneously characterize Colombia as fragmented, regionalized, polarized, and violent. Despite a formally civilian democratic government with presidential elections held every four years, the argument goes, during the second half of the twentieth century Colombia became home to Latin America's oldest and largest leftist guerrilla insurgency, paramilitarism, and illicit drug trafficking. It is these "genuine anomalies ... unusual [and] peculiar" in Cold War Latin America, that lead scholars to understand Colombian democracy as paradoxical, if not enigmatic.[74] Indeed, Colombia is often depicted as a country of "cities without citizens," "a nation in spite of itself," a "democracy without the people," a society in which modernity is forever "deferred," and an idiosyncratic political culture in which "modernization works against modernity."[75]

At the risk of overgeneralization, one might posit an overarching narrative employed by scholars to explain this "anomaly." Some have historicized the 1960s and 1970s as cementing an antidemocratic, exclusionary pact between the two traditional parties via the FN that defended the oligarchies' political and economic interests by excluding the majorities from political power. For this reason scholars historicize the state as a *failure*, unable to secure, following Antonio Gramsci's understanding of hegemonic rule, popular consent.[76] Other historians, evoking Max Weber's analysis of "modern societies," characterize the FN as a *weak* state unable to secure a full monopoly of violence to control social and political unrest. In this reading, the FN embraced development policies to mystify its *lack* of interest in improving the lives of the popular classes.[77] This oligarchical state turned instead to violence, coercion, and the co-optation of a politically *apathetic* middle class that did not play a role in correcting an exclusionary, elite-driven system. Indeed, since the 1970s scholars have defined the failure of the middle classes to become a democratizing force as the "critical fissure"

at the core of a *peculiar* model of modernity.[78] In such a model, modernization materialized different social sectors—strata, groups, segments—in the
middle of the society, but modernity/democracy was forever deferred since
the same middling sectors joined, rather than challenged, what Antonio
García called a "manorial republic."[79] In such a political reality, the argument goes, the country's "oligarchs did not *need* to call on crude military
dictators."[80] In this foundational narrative of the second half of the twentieth century, antidemocracy (particularity, tradition, exclusion) is coupled
with oligarchical rule, whereas democracy (universality, modernity, inclu-
sion) is intimately attached to a proper middle class.[81]

By historically critiquing what is usually celebrated as a democratizing
force but failed experience in Colombian reality—again the formation of
an urban middle class—*Makers of Democracy* contributes to deprovincial-
izing histories of Colombia.[82] It is an effort to tell the histories of Colombia
beyond nationalized narratives of failure, lack, and deficiency by critiquing
power relations and forms of domination from the middle so that we can
unsettle the way we think about histories of democracy. In so doing, it proposes that the meanings and practices of middle-classness have a bearing
on questions about democracy that cannot be approached through local
detail alone—although such detail is at the core of my analysis. The book
experiments with not only telling different stories but also telling stories
differently—stories of how a state becomes gendered and classed, the productivity of knowledge in the pragmatics of development programs, the
complex formation of class and gender subjectivities, and the making of
social and political legitimacy in democratic systems of domination. Thus,
Makers of Democracy highlights the contestations, accommodations, fragile
but durable pacts of domination, and inclusionary and exclusionary practices
engaged in by a middle class and constitutive of, rather than incompatible with, democratic rule. The stories told here matter not only to a place
called Colombia but also for a larger, universal question about democracy.
This allows us to understand those histories not as anomalies but rather as
contributions to how democracy was heterogeneously experienced in Cold
War Latin America. I historicize democracy not as a gift from the West to
the rest of the world but as a worldwide question over which different historical actors engaged in hard-fought battles over its meanings, practices,
subjectivities, and institutions.

Part I Conscripts of Democracy

*The Alliance for Progress, Development, and the
(Re)Formation of a Gendered Middle Class, 1958–1965*

Genealogy challenges conceits of purity: through it, particular democracies are revealed as enfolded within histories of imperialism, slavery, genocide, class dominance, or punishment and as saturated with these legacies in the present.

—**Wendy Brown,** *Politics Out of History*

1

A Bastard Middle Class

In 1962, photojournalist Marvin Koner published a photo essay in *Fortune*, a magazine targeted to a US middle-class audience. Titled "Neighbors Who Are Neither Rich nor Poor," the essay was "intended to introduce Latin America's large and expanding middle class" (figure 1.1). For "balance and comprehension," Koner warned, the images would need to "be filed in the reader's memory along with pictures of other Latin-American classes that have long been familiar: the poor Indian beside his llama, the white-jacketed playboy, the rack-ribbed children in Rio's *favelas* or Lima's *barriadas*."[1] This middle class, he emphasized, was becoming apparent everywhere, as US foreign policy had always hoped: "middle-classers stream[ed] early to work in tall office buildings, [ate] quick lunches, and skip[ped] the siestas that used to paralyze business for half the day." All this gave to the Latin American middle class a "configuration resembling the middle class in the US."[2]

Yet, the photographer cautioned, this resemblance could be deceiving, the photos concealing "the difference in thought patterns, attitudes, and reactions that sets the Latin-American middle class apart" from that in the United States.[3] This was what journalist Walter Guzzardi Jr. addressed in a companion analysis titled "The Crucial Middle Class." Like Koner, he criticized those scholars and policymakers who described Latin America as a place where "rich [were] rich and poor [were] poor," implying that "the perplexing and explosive restlessness stirring in Latin America" could be

NEIGHBORS WHO ARE
NEITHER RICH NOR POOR

A portfolio of photographs by Marvin Koner

Figure 1.1 Koner, "Neighbors," 88.

traced to a "polarized social immobility, which paralyze[d] enterprises, [froze] hope, and suffocate[d] democracy."[4] In contrast, Guzzardi wrote,

> The sharecropper and the peon, for all their misery, are largely outside their country's political life. . . . As for the very rich, while they are losing over and trying to resist change, they are hardly restless. The political significance of these two groups lies not so much in what they do as in what the man between thinks should be done about them. . . . The man pressing for change, generating the friction, and throwing off the sparks is the man in the middle.[5]

As part of a transnational discussion, Guzzardi mobilized a vision that was, in the Cuban Revolution's immediate aftermath, becoming common sense: because hopes for a democratic future in Latin America rested on the middle classes, a democratic system for the region was all the more "problematical." The journalist argued that "the middle-class man" in Latin

America was promoting not a democracy characterized by political stability, economic independence, and social harmony but rather "revolutionary
change" and social polarization.[6] Unlike the "North Atlantic societies," in
Latin America the middle class had developed a "spirit of restlessness."
Thus the journalist called on scholars and policymakers to adopt a sym-
pathetic understanding in grappling with a class that at its best offered the
only possibility for consolidating regional democracy but at its worst could
produce a "Fidel Castro type—restless, utopian, word-drugged, paranoid,
and possibly violent."[7]

These preoccupations capture what was often referred to, among scholars,
policymakers, and social reformers associated with development programs
such as the Alliance, as the middle-class enigma. Why, they asked, were
the Latin American middle classes acting so differently from the Euro-
American middle classes, to the point that a democratic system still remained unreachable for the former? What was needed to overcome this
middle-class enigma, foster a proper middle class, and therefore secure
a lasting democracy? In this chapter, my task is to demonstrate, as Ann
Stoler has suggested, a countercomparison that confronts the very comparative choices made about the relationship between democracy and the
consolidation of the middle classes during the late 1950s and 1960s in different geographical locations.[8] In so doing, I show how these comparisons
produced a transnational political rationality of rule that linked an idea of
a middle class with a hierarchical notion of democracy characterized by
the development of a politically proper corps of professionals, free-market
small-business owners, and a large stratum of white-collar office employees who embraced harmonious social and labor relationships. As a specific
response to a "politicization" in Latin America—from populist experiences
in Guatemala and Argentina to La Violencia in Colombia to the Cuban
Revolution—this rationality both shaped development programs and legitimized the United States' self-assigned imperial role of universalizing
democracy in Latin America. Policymakers and elite intellectuals across
the Americas produced a hierarchical geography of class through which
Latin America's middle class was politically, culturally, and socially defined
as illegitimate—in a word, a bastard middle class—and thus in perpetual
need of normalization by an irresistible democratic empire that supposedly
embodied a proper—and superior—middle class.

The Alliance for Progress: Toward
a "New Democratic Rule"

In 1939, the US government set up its first organized and systematic technical cooperation program with Latin America as a part of Franklin D. Roosevelt's Good Neighbor Policy. With the potential involvement of the Western Hemisphere's nations in World War II in mind, Roosevelt established via executive order the Office of the Coordinator of Inter-American Affairs. Nelson Rockefeller was appointed to this position, and shortly thereafter the US government established the Institute of Inter-American Affairs, a corporation authorized to carry out cooperative programs with Latin American governments to promote public health, housing, economic development, public administration, and agricultural growth. In 1944 a similar corporation, the Inter-American Educational Foundation, was organized to provide hemispheric cooperation in support of elementary and secondary schools. These prepared the US government to undertake the Point Four Program, a major effort to promote technical assistance, modern technology, knowledge exchange, and capital investment initiated shortly after Harry Truman's inaugural address of 1949. The Act for International Development, approved by the US Congress in 1950, supplied financial assistance to carry out many technical cooperation programs. Simultaneously, recently established international and transnational institutions— the Organization of American States (OAS), the United Nations (UN), the International Bank for Reconstruction and Development (IBRD)—initiated an integrated set of liberal economic development policies, technical assistance plans, social welfare activities, population improvement programs, and cultural management agendas.[9]

These programs reconfigured and reconceptualized the legitimate forms and methods for exercising imperial rule on a transnational terrain. Policymakers, consultants, experts, and politicians across the Americas debated how to overcome what Truman called in 1949 "the old imperialism," no longer an adequate basis for overseas expansion and influence because it was based only on "exploitation for profit." The new US political agenda needed to move away from European colonial rule because it had to spread democracy and invite those in underdeveloped areas of the world into a process of self-governance.[10]

If Truman believed that US involvement in Latin America could be distinguished from European colonial rule because of the United States' putative lack of interest in financial gain, several policymakers argued otherwise. Ward Hunt Goodenough, a professor of anthropology at the University of Pennsylvania, contended in 1957 that US foreign programs in the first half of the twentieth century had primarily been geared toward what he called "economicism."[11] Like former European colonizers, Goodenough argued, the United States had only been concerned to offer, at worst, bread and roads, and, at best, agricultural technology.[12] Furthermore, this imperialism was based on practices of "domination, imposition, and subjugation." These practices assumed that those in the underdeveloped countries were passive recipients of economic aid, unable to "think . . . act . . . feel by themselves."[13] In contrast to both European colonial rule and earlier US economicism, the United States now would develop an international role that would depend on "negotiation . . . social contracts . . . meaningful encounters, and understandings." If the old imperialism was based on imposition, the United States would now approach other regions "by being sensitive" to their "cultural differences." And if the old imperialism worked by subjugating and marginalizing the underdeveloped world, the United States would now lead based on inquiry into what the people wanted, restoring the "participation and autonomy of underdeveloped people to shape their own destiny."[14] In doing so, the United States would promote the "development [of] human welfare."[15]

Scholars, policymakers, and experts across the Americas defined themselves as living in a new transnational order characterized by economic insecurity, anticolonial unrest, and real and imagined concerns for the spread of communism. And to make sense of such an order, they sought answers to what they defined as pressing questions: What were the most effective and appropriate ways to govern in democracies? Who was able to be effective in the arts of governing, and who should govern whom? These were transnational questions that propelled development programs such as the Alliance during the late 1950s and 1960s. The Alliance, as an international development program, was neither historically new nor a unique creation of the United States. Rather, as a response to rapid political radicalization, the Alliance was the product of a transnational discussion about who embodied the legitimate right to rule in "proper" democracies and how such a right should be properly exercised and distributed throughout different societies in the Americas.[16]

Thus, despite the discourse critiquing the old imperialism, the first attempts at community development, agrarian reform, education, and housing by the Alliance drew heavily on the experiences of the British colonial administration with rural social projects in India; on community-based organizing prototypes in Mexico, Bolivia, Puerto Rico, and the Tennessee Valley; and on modernization programs in Colombia in the 1930s and 1940s.[17] But as transnational, if uneven, discussions evolved, different policymakers and intellectuals across the Americas disavowed these experiences because they imagined that the United States had already achieved a "middle-class society" and thus could represent, unlike any other foreign power, an empire for democracy. Thus in the late 1950s policymakers envisioned development programs as the first—and perhaps last—opportunity for Latin American nations to consolidate the very revolution that the United States had experienced almost two centuries prior. John F. Kennedy argued that the United States had to be "culturally sensitive" to Latin American realities.[18] He did not want the Alliance to be another imposed program of foreign aid but rather a comprehensive overhaul in which all nations of the Americas would unite to achieve "modern democracies." Kennedy contended that Latin America and the United States were not as different as they appeared. Simón Bolívar had desired to see the Americas fashioned into the greatest region that the world could witness, a region that, Kennedy added, had never been nearer "to the fulfillment of democracy." And yet, the president cautioned that such a possibility had never been "in greater danger" because, despite the desire for democracy, certain historical actors in Latin American societies were not ready to experience the irresistible gifts of modernity. It was indeed a political conundrum: how to spread the American Revolution to a region not ready to embrace such an advanced version of democracy. But it was not a moment for hesitation. As were others, Kennedy was confident that Latin America and the United States shared a colonial history. The difference was that while the latter had moved forward to achieve democracy, the former had remained frozen in history: feudal conditions still characterized the nations south of the Rio Grande. It was this shared colonial rule, however, that would allow the United States to finish what had been started in Caracas in 1811, by spreading to 1960s Latin America what had happened in Philadelphia in 1778. Kennedy envisioned the Alliance as a vast cooperative effort, unparalleled in magnitude and nobility of purpose, that needed to demonstrate to the entire world that man's unsatisfied aspiration for economic progress and social justice can be best "achieved by free men working within a framework of democratic institutions. . . . every American family will be on the rise, basic education will be available to all, hunger will be a forgotten experience, the need for massive outside help will have passed, most nations will have entered a period of self-sustaining growth . . . so that all, and not just the privileged few, share in the fruits of growth."[19] What was at stake in this determination to supplant the old imperialism, to claim a shared "colonial past," and to promote democracy at the very moment when US foreign policy was invigorating Latin American militaries, orchestrating military interventions, and supporting intelligence agencies? Was the Alliance an attempt by the United States to mystify imperial relations by promoting "lofty humanitarian goals"?[20] I want to study the rationalities underwriting development programs because what was at stake was *not* the suspension of imperial practices, as we tend to assume, but rather how to prolong imperial power through democracy.[21] In so doing, we can critically interrogate one method of rule in the large repertoire of US practices of domination during the second half of the twentieth century.

More significantly, I will demonstrate how the development programs of community building, agrarian reform, education, housing, and financial literacy—crafted by intellectuals and policymakers across the Americas, supported by private foundations, sponsored by the United States, and put into practice as expansive state policies during Colombia's FN—consolidated a specific hierarchical vision of democracy as common sense.[22] The Alliance—mediated by a transnational production of knowledge in cultural anthropology, social psychology, economics, administrative management theories, and rural sociology studies—galvanized a political rationality oriented toward interrelated projects of economic development, human welfare, and proper political preparation for "modern democracy."[23] These community development programs would incorporate, as President Kennedy said in 1961, a "cultural and socially sensitive approach" that considered how people in the underdeveloped areas of the world were "socially and culturally embedded human subjects."[24] US leadership would depend on constant encounters leading to social arrangements that allowed the communities of the underdeveloped world, through proper economic, political, and cultural guidance, to "best utilize the human capital and natural resources available in promoting the interests of their own communities."[25] In this way, the "poor populations of the world" could "learn to understand their own current situation, the disastrous effects of poverty for them, their families, and their countries."[26] Furthermore, this "new mentality" would enable a "society [in which] human beings" could "take care of themselves and others."[27] The Alliance would develop a new paradigm that would work within a "democratic framework," promoting "bottom-up social approaches" to create participatory and "democratic spaces" where the people would be able to develop their own ideas and cultures, enhance their own capabilities, and understand what economic goals they were able to reach.[28]

Thus, imperial governance was to occur neither by coercively imposing nor by marginalizing people's participation but through a process of schooling in proper forms of self-government and self-discipline that targeted "people's talents . . . people's actions, feelings, and beliefs." This imperial humanist rationality would target what was often called "human capital."[29] In short, this imperial humanist governance sought to make "the Third World" a society of governors, a society capable of governing itself.

The Role of the Middle Class

Central to this rationality was a (re)formation of a middle class. Imperial humanist rationality was to take place through a democratic middle class properly selected, guided, and disciplined to become competent in stimulating and distributing the necessary human capital for "national democracies to emerge."[30] It is in this specific sense that the imperial humanist rationality at the core of development programs, rather than weakening regional democracy, sought to legitimize a classed and gendered definition of democracy. As early as 1948, the Pan-American Union (soon to become the OAS) decided that it was imperative to develop a series of studies on the middle classes' role in Latin American societies. The Social Science Research Office of the Pan-American Union, a wellspring of modernization theory, defined this as "perhaps the most important political endeavor of the twentieth century."[31] Theo R. Crevenna, a sociologist in charge of this project, argued that studying the middle class was "the last hope for a democratic world" in a region so long displaying the undemocratic tendencies of a "two-class society." Thus, this research office contacted those whom they considered the most qualified intellectuals in Latin America and the United States to prepare ethnographic studies about the social structure and the political and economic roles of the middle class in Latin America.[32] The hope was that these studies would spark an "intellectual excitement" that would push Latin America, like the United States, to think of itself "in middle-class terms."[33]

In 1951 the Pan-American Union published a six-volume study with twenty-seven contributions on the role of the middle classes in Latin America (neglecting only Guatemala and Peru). In the first call for submissions, Crevenna outlined the critical implications for the future of the

Americas of studying "a social group that is unstable and so difficult to define": "A powerful middle class contributes to the social, political, and economic stability of society . . . to the future democratic progress of the American countries."[34]

Some years later, the UN's Economic Commission for Latin America and the Caribbean (ECLAC), the seedbed for Latin American structuralist economic thinking, echoed the hope of the Social Science Research Office of the Panamerican Union (SSROPU) that a middle class would transform the region away from a dual society. In 1963, when the Cuban Revolution was influencing a discussion about the region's revolutionary future and the spread of military rule was becoming too real, ECLAC was loudly telling policymakers engaged with the Alliance that the middle class needed to be taken into account. Evoking Max Weber and his studies on modernization, ECLAC published a report that asked,

> Who will be the social class capable of renewing Latin America's destiny? Could it be the traditional sectors, who in the past succeeded in their historical task but now find themselves exhausted in the face of the task of promoting economic development? Could this economic development be carried out by the popular classes, even if they are not squared within a rigorous discipline that replaces their historical shortcomings? Shouldn't the middle sectors be the class in charge of this political and economic development, given that they not only have a level of culture but also ample political experience? Does Latin America have a middle class with enough political will to achieve what other middle classes have achieved in other parts [of the world]?[35]

Certainly, ECLAC was not as unreservedly optimistic about the middle class as was the SSROPU. And yet both international institutions defined the holy grail of democracy as a consolidated, growing, and robust middle class against the politically exhausted and economically traditional oligarchies as well as the backward and politically inexperienced popular classes. As part of the Council on Foreign Relations (CFR), for instance, Lyman Bryson organized a roundtable in 1958 (published as a book a couple of years later) with several prominent anthropologists—Richard Adams, John Gillin, Allan Holmberg, Charles Wagley, and Oscar Lewis—on this debate over how to proceed with development programs. Despite their disagreements, the participants concurred on the need for a proper middle class, or a "class of 'operators,'" as Bryson called them.[36] These experts claimed, however, that US policymakers should bear in mind that sharing US "engineering and business know-how" would not automatically translate into "know[ing] how to vote."[37] Money would satisfy the laboring classes but would not create democracy, as they did "not want democracy" but material benefits. Bryson warned that if policymakers continued to assume that "poverty-stricken people" saw democracy and political values "in ready cash," all US foreign aid would be at best meaningless.[38] The oligarchies, conversely, were outside democracy's parameters, with their feudal and old-fashioned politics. Because of these conditions, Bryson concluded, Latin America needed the creation of a "middle group" that could do the more "skilled work of the economy, manage the machines as they [were] created, provide a hospitable group into which the gifted poor man could climb." Indeed, what was crucial was making Latin America home to a "democratic-minded and democratically ambitious middle group" who could mediate "between ignorant poverty and blind wealth, and get personal benefit out of increasing freedom and self-government."[39] In other words, at the core of the Alliance's development programs was a desire to sanctify a *proper* hierarchical democratic class rule centered on a normative definition of a middle class, a definition that wanted to equate democracy and the middle class by delinking democracy from popular groups and oligarchies.[40]

Reforming "a Bastard Middle Class"

Yet as those development program policymakers located their political hopes in the materialization of a middle class, they also worried that this Latin American middle class would not live up to such a democratic task. Experts from elite universities and intellectuals across the Americas told policymakers that if the Alliance were to succeed in bringing democracy to the region, it was also imperative to account for the region's cultural, political, and social particularities. "The middle mass was not a class in the usual meaning of that European word . . . [was] not yet fully self-conscious and . . . not rigidly organized," these experts insisted, a reality that had historically produced a fundamental distinction between "Latin American middle strata [and] the middle classes of the US and Western Europe."[41] This was due to Latin America's embedment in feudal relationships that provoked attitudes and values—personalism, kinship, stratification, materialism of a wrong kind, transcendental spiritualism, dependency, emotional expression, and fatalism—that prevented Latin America's middle *strata* from becoming proper Western middle *classes*.[42]

Colombia attested to this impossibility. Erupting a full decade prior to the Cuban Revolution, the experiences of La Violencia concerned the US government as well as scholars and policymakers.[43] They saw it as the worst political conflict in the Americas during the midcentury. During the late 1950s, the FN promoted study of this event by inviting certain scholars to explain the role played in it by the middle class.[44] In one of the first studies about La Violencia, Germán Guzmán Campos, Orlando Fals Borda, and Eduardo Umaña Luna pointed to the lack of a strong middle class and its tranquilizing political force as one cause for the spread of violence and party rivalry during the 1950s. According to Southern Illinois University professor Richard W. Poston, however, the problem was not the absence of a middle class per se but rather the persistence of a middle class characterized by what he called an "antihuman consciousness." This middle class, on the one hand, was "set off from the lower classes," for whom it expressed "disdain," and, on the other, was aspiring "to copy the way of life of the elites." This antihumanistic middle class, Poston continued, did not have a "productive relationship" with either the elites or the poor, the lack of which led some scholars to conclude that the middle class—with "no political competence of its own"—sharpened the conflict "by tending to increase the numerical strength of the enemies of the masses."[45] The Colombian middle class was neither a liberalizing nor a stabilizing element in the national struggle and thus could not have prevented a decade of violence in which over 200,000 people died.

Among policymakers, the Guatemalan case seemed further proof of the existence of a "middle-class enigma" in Latin America. Just one year after the 1954 Guatemalan coup d'état, social scientists in the US State Department blamed the lower middle class for leading the nation toward communism. According to their study, the Guatemalan Labor Party was composed of young middle-class schoolteachers, former university students, journalists, white-collar workers, and former employees of US and foreign enterprises in this country. These sectors were the most politically frustrated within the "archaic social structure of Guatemala."[46] This frustration, the State Department feared, had become not only the source of political radicalization but also the incubator of the post–World War II communist movement because these middle sectors were the social group able to intellectually digest such "foreign" influences. In a society supported by a backward, coffee-growing agricultural economy in which a small number of landlords controlled large groups of illiterate Indian laborers, these middle sectors since the 1940s had found communism quite appealing as a way to make substantial changes. It was these small-business owners, professionals, teachers, and technical workers who had the most intimate contact with the outside world and who became most aware of Guatemala's social backwardness.[47]

Yet why did the US State Department, along with other scholars and policymakers, find it imperative to stress middle-class participation in the Guatemalan communist revolution and silence any working-class or peasant participation at the same moment when development programs were exalting the middle class as representative of political, economic, and social democracy? The Guatemalan revolution proved beyond doubt the "ungenuine [and] particular nature" of the middle class in Latin America as well as the political equivocations embedded in it.[48] Unlike in Europe, the State Department observed, where the working class and peasants were capable of becoming "truly proletarians" and thus creating proper democracies, in Guatemala, as in most Latin American countries, those popular classes lacked political experience and social consciousness. And unlike the United States, where the middle class became the source of social harmony by rejecting extreme political dogmas, the lower (read, of lesser political quality) middle sectors in Latin America "represented virtually the only element in the social environment favorable for the cultivation of a Communist growth."[49] As communist leaders, these middle-class elements threatened democracy by giving away the right to rule to backward workers and peasants politically unprepared for the democratic tasks of the twentieth century. If the CIA's PBSUCCESS operation was carefully covert, the political justification for overthrowing the democratically elected government of Jacobo Árbenz Guzmán was not necessarily so. The improper political nature of the middle sectors in Guatemala, some scholars argued, gave the US government the right to end a revolution assumed to represent neither peasants nor workers.[50]

Elaborating on the subsequent US intervention in Guatemala, John P. Gillin urged those involved with US policy toward Latin America to turn from militarization and instead focus on a middle class that had made itself a political troublemaker. The CIA operation in Guatemala could have been avoided had the State Department realized in 1944 what became clear in 1954: that the middle class played an important role in consolidating the Guatemalan revolution. Military operations, he said, had to be accompanied by a (re)formation of the middle classes. A new foreign policy should recognize, concluded the anthropologist, "the seriousness of the shift in leadership . . . to win the confidence of the idealistic but inexperienced architects of the 'new Guatemala.'" It was crucial for US policymakers to promote development programs that would train these "ungenuine" middle classes to develop a "genuine" democracy.[51]

After 1959, when the Cuban Revolution epitomized political radicalization across the Americas, the contradiction between the Alliance's promotion of the middle classes in Latin America and their role in "communist revolutions" became even more pressing. Policymakers asked what would soon become a foundational question: What was wrong with the middle class in Latin America? During the early 1960s, Theodore Draper, a historian and adviser for the Alliance, thought it essential to examine how—in contrast to the myths created by the popular media and scholarly works focused on peasants and workers—the indispensable social group to the Cuban Revolution, in both leadership and social agency, was the middle sectors.[52]

The historian framed his critique in two specific ways. First, he described all important members of the revolution as coming from a "middle class background," as being "middle class in character," and as being raised in "middle class homes."[53] Second, he tried to prove that, contrary to a common sociological explanation of Cuba that portrayed the island's population as "squatted on the edge of the road in . . . filthy huts . . . a place of misery and illiteracy . . . exploitation and sloth," Cuba was, before the revolution, "one of the most middle class countries in Latin America."[54] Cuba's peasants had neither the political intelligence nor the social awareness to carry out the changes necessary to live in democracy. Thus, by definition the revolution could be nothing other than the product of a middle-class society that had the political intelligence and cultural capital to create democracies. But Draper wanted to show that Cuba was yet another example of the middle class's impropriety in Latin America, a middle "déclassé revolution."[55] It was déclassé—that is to say, undemocratic—because its middle-class leaders invoked middle-class values to overthrow Fulgencio Batista only to turn around and give away the legitimate right to rule to peasants and workers.

These sociological and historical realities, Draper argued, had no precedent in world history. This type of middle class was a "Latin American problem" and as such produced peculiar manifestations of political and economic systems: "bastard [and] spurious 'socialisms,'" on the one hand, and "unsuccessful capitalisms," on the other. The former, Draper asserted, were spurious because, unlike in Europe, in Cuba and Latin America workers and peasants were not yet ready to become a politically aware proletariat. Socialisms in Latin America could thus only emerge from the middle class, which generated a "bastard" democracy because the middle class was speaking not legitimately as a middle class but only on behalf of workers and peasants.[56] This produced a middle class so politically weak that, instead of perpetuating middle-class values, as in the United States, "the peasants and workers went up" while "the middle class went down," transforming itself into "the second-class citizens of the revolution."[57] Neither properly capitalist nor genuinely socialist, the Cuban Revolution was a middle-class revolution that had destroyed the middle class as middle class. This was what Lino Novás Calvo, a Cuban scholar, called "the tragedy of the middle class."[58]

Other scholars, however, offered a different answer for the Alliance's policymakers. As the Cuban Revolution became more associated with a socialist and communist future, these scholars challenged the argument about middle-class participation. For example, Hugh Thomas, professor of history at Queens' College, Cambridge, argued in the early 1960s that the revolution's most important participants were peasants and workers. He claimed that of the 165 men who participated in the attack on Moncada on July 26, 1953, only 7, apart from Castro himself, could be categorized as middle class—that is, highly educated, economically independent, and politically prepared. Furthermore, the majority of Castro's followers were not middle class but rather from "lower class origins" with a "less educated background."[59] If the revolutionary leadership's core was middle class, they were nevertheless surrounded by social actors with doubtful political experience who were able "to corrupt" whatever middle-class political positions the revolutionary cadre could have developed.[60] Had the middle class played a significant role, Thomas concluded, the Cuban experience could have entered the charmed circle of democratic revolutions—the American, the French, and the English.

It is amid these discussions that John J. Johnson, a Stanford University historian, developed his foundational arguments about the middle sectors in Latin America. Like so many other intellectuals who moved with relative ease between university halls and the policymaking arena, he became aware of the pressing need to study the middle sectors while working for the State Department, as acting chief of the South American branch of the Division of Research for the American Republics during the early 1950s.[61] Johnson, who published a book in late 1958 (to be discussed in the next chapter) arguing that the middle sectors would become middle class by bringing Latin America into the fold of democratic nations, in the early 1960s found it important to revise his previous work in lieu of what he considered a new political reality: the launch of the Alliance, with its promise of bringing democracy to the region, and the rapid wave of military takeovers. He did not lose faith, but the Stanford historian elaborated on the political justifications for believing that the middle sectors in Latin America would still be the democratic force even within military rule. He claimed that military rule emerged during the nineteenth century due to the development of a particular "middle class with [in]sufficient economic strength to control the new government."[62] After the colonial authority was destroyed, the economically weak, politically disoriented, and fragile middle sector could not cement a democratic role in Latin America, allowing the church and aristocracy to unite and rule through military means. During the twentieth century, however, Latin America's armed forces underwent major social and economic changes: army officers had improved their material conditions, had reached a significant level of professionalization, and had access to public education. This transformed the political role of military rule, as now most members of the military forces not only were controlled by "urban middle sectors" but also had developed a certain economic independence and professional neutrality that eventually would translate into democratic regimes.[63] This gave way to the "most striking development" in the twentieth century: the political alignment between "urban groups most anxious for rapid material progress" and a military professionally competent in matters of democracy.[64] By making a sharp distinction with an imagined nineteenth-century past, Johnson offered a sociological narrative of the twentieth century in which modern military officers had distanced themselves from an old-guard, politically retrograde oligarchy and adopted political middle-classness.[65]

Thus, argued Johnson, military rule, with the support of specific development programs, would in all probability become democratic. Writing in 1964, Johnson predicted that given Latin America's particular political conditions, the military would "on occasion" function as "the most reliable institution to insure political continuity," at least for the 1960s.[66] Indeed, the military had to intervene in politics because if they were passive, an "unsatisfactory" and "morally indefensible" status quo would remain in place, in which either the working classes or the oligarchy would claim the right to rule. The democratic rule of middle-class military officers, by contrast, would be based not on violence but on a consolidated political, economic, and social order reflecting the middle-class values of knowledge, professional expertise, economic independence, civic action, and political neutrality.[67] Military officers, as representatives of urban middle sectors, would become "effective intermediaries between [military] governments and [the] masses."[68] They would able to legitimize military rule by seeking the consent of those to be ruled. Johnson joined many others to argue that the most promising way to promote the professionalization of society was "to hold democracy in military tutelage."[69]

This link between democracy and middle-classness justified what Mario Laserna, one of the founders of the Universidad de los Andes (UNIANDES) in Bogotá, defined as "the dictatorship of development," a democratic need that could also legitimize military rule throughout the region and US rule over Latin America.[70] For these scholars, the intimate relationship—or blurred distinction—between military rule/dictatorship and democracy was neither a political oxymoron nor a misnomer because of what they considered an "undeniable" fact: Latin America was *different* from Europe and the United States. Hence, the democracy produced by the former's middle class would be not only particular but also of lesser quality compared to the putatively universal and superior middle classes of North Atlantic societies.

All these social scientists, politicians, and policymakers crafted a political rationality that asserted that contrary to the "global" middle class in North America and Europe, the "local" middle class in Latin America was too specific in its thinking, too particular in its political developments, too unique in its historical backgrounds, too déclassé in its social roles, "too bastard" in its political nature, and too distinctive in its cultural circumstances. And because of this, the Latin American middle class could only develop particular, incomplete, bastard, and imperfect democracies—in a word, a middle-class-oriented dictatorship. It needed political instruction, social regulation, and economic discipline if it was to create a proper form of democracy, characterized by state professionals in search of political tranquility, small-business owners promoting economic development independently of the state, and white-collar employees overcoming the traditional struggle between capital and labor.[71]

Thus, the Alliance's political rationality naturalized a hierarchical geography of middle-classness. Because the Alliance's development programs assumed that neither the laboring classes nor the oligarchies had the right to rule, societies with successful and proper middle classes should by definition enjoy the democratic—that is, imperial—right to rule over societies with absent or improperly developed middle classes. This right could be exercised through development programs, if possible, or military means, if necessary. Indeed, the idea of the middle class became the foundational legitimation for development programs and sanctified the intimate relationship between democracy and imperial politics: a middle-class society became the normal explanation for why the United States had the moral imperative and political obligation to "help" Latin America move away from a dictatorial dual society into a proper democratic three-class society, even if that society remained within military rule.

"A Middle-Class Revolution": Disciplining the Middle Classes

It was this political rationality, legitimized as "scientific knowledge," that the Alliance put into practice in several development programs. Perhaps unlike anybody else, Arthur Schlesinger Jr., a Harvard historian and adviser to Kennedy, translated this vision into policy. He was convinced that "the last hope for the world" was "a middle class revolution."[72] Such a call was the product not so much of political optimism but of the belief that Latin America was a "hopeless land for democracy." Echoing other experts in the Americas, Schlesinger saw Latin America as a land of feudalism, radicalization, and communism. Despite, or precisely because of, these conditions, the middle class could break the "agrarian, semi-feudal economic structure . . . and backward economy" that had only privileged "the so called landholding oligarchy." This adviser argued that the region needed "*a middle class revolution* [*sic*] where the processes of economic modernization carry the new urban middle class into power and produce, along with it, such necessities of modern technical society as a constitutional government, honest public administration, [and] a responsible party system."[73]

Schlesinger was also advising Kennedy that if democracy was to be a reality in Latin America in a decade, as the Alliance promised, the middle class would need to be taken into account, because this class could become déclassé and thus produce a society of two classes rather than three. Schlesinger had in mind Draper's political explanation of the middle class's role in the Cuban Revolution, which he told Kennedy was the best analysis of the event that he had ever read.[74] It offered an urgent political lesson: a déclassé middle class would give the right to rule to those with neither the preparation nor the desire to democratize society at large: the peasants and working classes. This made the middle class "the most dangerous class" in the region. In 1961, mobilizing a transnational field of knowledge, the adviser once again told the US president that "the pressing need in Latin America is to promote the middle class revolution as speedily as possible.

The corollary is that, if the possessing classes of Latin America make the middle class revolution impossible, they will make a 'workers-and peasant' revolution inevitable [*sic*]; if the middle class parties do not go over the goal line in the next decade, they will be finished, and the initiative will pass to parties committed to a drastic and violent radicalism."[75] As this advice makes clear, the Alliance and its expansive development programs sought to sediment a democracy in which a normative middle class could be hierarchically located in the middle of society to discipline the oligarchies and to pacify the working class and peasantry. One must emphasize that the Alliance did not create a middle class in Latin America. More accurately, in a moment of political anxiety and radicalization these development programs sought to discipline improper middle classes to materialize a specific hierarchical class rule. It was this hierarchical rule that policymakers, politicians, and experts usually baptized as modern democracy, middle-class revolution, or three-class society.

Such a vision of democracy was by no means a US imposition. In the late 1950s and early 1960s, the FN, the political pact between the majority of the Liberal and Conservative Party factions, sought to overcome a decade of violence and four years of military dictatorship by institutionalizing reconciliation efforts, "rehabilitation" programs, and numerous policies for peaceful coexistence—*convivencia*—among different social groups and between political parties.[76] Carefully validated by a plebiscite in 1957, overwhelmingly approved by Colombian voters, and eagerly formalized in 1958, the FN created "a sixteen-year period in which the presidency would alternate between Liberals and Conservatives and all positions in the three branches of government, throughout the country, would be distributed evenly between the two parties."[77] It sought to materialize a "stable and legitimate state . . . the development of state bureaucracy for planning and economic growth."[78] Alberto Lleras Camargo, the first president of the FN, defined it as an inauguration of a second republic.[79]

As a product of a transnational discussion on democracy, FN's social programs participated in shaping the Alliance's rationality in order to promote a middle class that could consolidate such a republic by overcoming what were considered the two main causes of La Violencia and economic underdevelopment: political partisanship and class conflict. Nowhere was this relationship more clearly stated than in the claims about the "need" to perpetuate the state of exception as a state of rule. During the FN's sixteen years, a state of emergency (the suspension of the rule of law) was declared in all or part of the Colombian territory almost continually in the name of protecting democracy. As several presidents and policymakers justified this from the late 1950s, "No sacrifice is too great for democracy. . . . We will have to do whatever necessary not to return to a decade of violence, dictatorship, and open conflict."[80]

One might see this as the FN perpetuating empty democratic rhetoric to implement antidemocratic policies. But I think that one also has to ask what specific definition of democracy the FN meant to promote. Such an approach allows us to see how development policies, sponsored by the Alliance and put into practice by the FN, worked in tandem—rather than in contradiction—with the "need" to perpetuate the state of exception as rule during the 1960s. In a transnational context in which a middle class was seen as central to a proper, hierarchical vision of democracy, the FN implemented policies to create the necessary conditions for such a vision to be fulfilled. The rule of law could be suspended in the name of forming a proper middle class that would prevent the return to power of social forces (traditional oligarchies and laboring classes) that had provoked violence, social conflict, and dictatorship in the first place. Hence, democracy could be sacrificed in the name of democracy because a state of exception would create the middle class that would, as Lleras Camargo put it, "make social relations right."[81]

Such rationality gained further political legitimacy, at least in the first half of the 1960s, from a cohort of Colombian intellectuals educated in Europe and the United States. As some elite intellectuals participated in crafting the Alliance, they addressed the pressing need to create a middle-class society in order to bring peace and democracy to Colombia. Before founding the Frente Unido (FU) and joining the Ejército de Liberación Nacional (ELN) in the mid-1960s, Camilo Torres Restrepo concurred with the FN's social policies by proclaiming a middle class the potential difference between a "violent and nonviolent path to democracy." As dean of social studies of the Superior School of Public Administration (ESAP), sociology professor, and chaplain at the Universidad Nacional de Colombia (UNAL), and member of the Colombian Agrarian Reform Institute's (INCORA) board of directors in the early 1960s, the Catholic priest declared that the success of these new development institutions founded and sponsored by the Alliance would depend on the consolidation of a "democratic middle class." Although not as pessimistic as Schlesinger but definitely echoing Kennedy's vision of democracy, Torres Restrepo argued that a "democratic . . . peaceful revolution will come neither from the oligarchies nor from the laboring classes but from the middle class . . . ready to change a society full of feudalism, bossism, violence . . . political division."[82]

Kennedy, Lleras Camargo, Torres Restrepo, and so many others, representing different positions across the political spectrum, linked middle-classness with democracy so closely that they became synonymous. This underwrote the distribution and allocation of the Alliance's financial resources and the FN's social policies. Colombia, the recipient of the most foreign aid in Latin America during the 1960s besides Brazil, received $761.9 million in US economic aid between 1962 and 1969.[83] By 1973, that amount reached $1,396 million, 90 percent of which was channeled as economic aid; the other 10 percent materialized as military aid.[84] Those economic resources translated into an unprecedented expansion of programs of political education, state rationalization, economic progress, community development, rehabilitation initiatives, financial literacy, labor reorganization, and agrarian reform. Elementary education expanded 100 percent between 1938 and 1964. In the same period, private education grew 500 percent.[85] Likewise, along with different international development institutions and private US organizations, the FN founded, consolidated, or sponsored technical centers, vocational schools, training institutes, universities, and institutions to train professionals in different areas of technical knowledge and social science. The FN's first two administrations launched several more programs through private national organizations such as the National Federation of Colombian Coffee Growers (FEDECAFE), while international institutions such as the UN, OAS, World Health Organization, and Cooperative for American Relief Everywhere (CARE) promoted or sponsored educational institutions, training centers, and universities in Colombia.[86] Lleras Camargo extolled the community development programs as state policy and officially founded the Division of Community Action in 1959. Also, following the example of the French public administration schools, his government supported, along with the Rockefeller Foundation and several US universities, the creation of ESAP to forge a democratic state government. The FN also promoted the further institutionalization of family compensation funds, founded in the early 1950s. The product of intense negotiations between industrialists and official workers' unions, these private but state-mandated agencies were first limited to monetary compensation but during the 1960s expanded to vocational training and social welfare programs. Finally, the FN, with the advice of several US universities, established business credit in the hope of growing a class of small-business owners. All of this produced an unparalleled growth of local and national states during the 1960s.

As we will see in the next three chapters, these Colombian development programs and the visions of democracy that they promoted, far from failures, were every bit as powerful as the better-known programs of US military imperialism. Development programs, through meticulous yet contradictory processes of schooling, conscripted and empowered professionals, white-collar employees, and small-business owners as democratic subjects par excellence.

2

An Irresistible Democracy

During the late 1950s, Colombian architect Alberto Valencia took a short trip to the small town of Anolaima, two hours from Bogotá. Trained at the Inter-American Housing and Planning Center (CINVA)—a joint project of the OAS and the US Office of Technical Assistance (USOTA)—Valencia was excited to arrive in this "remote but attractive place" where "a middle-class guy like [him]" could find "the reality of social life." After some days in the field, Valencia resolved to leave his books and city behind to put into practice what he had been taught at CINVA about democracy. He wanted to return to Anolaima soon to teach "how to build houses, how to live in community . . . how to live in democracy." He wanted to "know the Colombian peasants in person . . . their families . . . their lives . . . their souls" and to transform them into "modern citizens of the Colombian nation." The major obstacle to such an important task would be "the cultured Colombian elites." Nevertheless, Valencia called on his fellow professionals to be "committed to work for a democratic society . . . to be fully involved with those who [were] oppressed." In a moment of consciousness, Valencia defined himself as a privileged man born "in a beautiful class . . . a class that makes democracy irresistible."[1]

Valencia's story raises critical questions about the historical formation of a professional middle class in Bogotá during the late 1950s and the first half of the 1960s. What were the historical circumstances and discursive conditions that enabled Valencia to classify himself as a middle-class man? At a moment when development programs such as the Alliance were seeking a "middle-class revolution," what did it take to participate in such a revolution as a member of the middle class? In this chapter, I interrogate the discursive transnational conditions that knotted democratic state rule to a professional middle class. I explore how certain professionals became conscripted and empowered both as properly belonging to a gendered middle class and as quintessentially representing state rule. In so doing, I historicize how the Colombian state became classed and gendered through a transnational production of knowledge about democracy and the role of professions in society.[2] I detail how middle-class professional women and men were schooled—in their desires, sentiments, and rationalities—in the methodologies of state rule and on the practices of how to search for consent for a transnational hierarchical vision of democracy. I seek to explain why people such as Valencia thought that their role as middle-class professional men would make democracy irresistible.

Proper Politics: A Democratic Three-Class Society

In a transnational context in which the horror of Nazi racism was still fresh, and decolonization processes were materializing, the populism of Latin America of the 1940s and 1950s was understood as highlighting everything dangerous about democracy. Writing on 1950s Colombia from Bogotá, T. Lynn Smith, a sociology professor at the University of Florida, argued that the country's professional middle class "lack[ed] class consciousness," perpetuating a polarized, undemocratic society in which the oligarchies received "a free ride." Influenced by rural sociology, he described Colombian society as "highly stratified" between a small upper crust; a wealthy, highly intelligent, aristocratic oligarchy; and an "ignorant, illiterate, disease-ridden, malnourished, ill-clothed, poorly housed, poverty-stricken, landless, dissolute mass which simultaneously constitutes the bulk of the Colombian population."[3] This society was undemocratic because "prestige, wealth, income, political power, educational training, culture, and positions of honor" were monopolized by the upper classes. This provoked political radicalization, populism, and communism's appeal. Democracy was thus alien to Colombia's reality.

Like many others, Smith wanted to link democracy's political horizon to the formation of a proper professional middle class, which would foster an unstratified urban society of three classes ripe for democracy. He offered a gendered critique of the oligarchs to elevate a "genuine" professional middle class as the manifestation of functional and scientific democracy.[4] Drawing on a larger discussion about how the colonial legacy blocked modernity in Latin America, Smith argued that the oligarchies had functioned as castes, not classes, from time immemorial and that privileges and wealth had largely been distributed through "family names and birth status."[5] As landowners, the oligarchs were the descendants of white conquistadores who had perpetuated themselves in power through violence, force, and terror. Therefore, landowners on one side and campesinos on the other were bound together "ever since the conquest," allowing this "handful of Spaniards" to "set themselves up in their own new administrative centers as ruling oligarchies."[6]

Smith furthermore maintained that as members of a caste, Colombia's oligarchs had neither the professional preparation nor the abilities needed for state rule.[7] The colonial experience had left them "too feminine" for their democratic tasks. After "centuries of passivity," the oligarchs could only care for themselves while neglecting the nation's overall social development. Looking inward toward their "private matters . . . and interests," Smith asserted, the oligarchs acted like an "old woman" preoccupied with "her banal affairs" in her intimate "domestic circle." Historically feudal, psychologically feminine, politically outdated, and professionally unprepared, the oligarchs were able to occupy "the apex of the social pyramid" only by "birth [and natural] right privileges" and not "through the exceptional professional abilities and efforts" necessary to be "at the center of modern democracies." By feminizing the oligarchs, Smith envisioned a rational, masculine, professional, and legitimate class that could promote a "true democracy."[8]

Yet the main problem for Smith was that the Colombian middle sector was an impoverished "hanger-on" of this feminized oligarchy and, as such, an "un-genuine middle group" lacking the professional (masculine) consciousness shared with other middle classes in the global North. This class could potentially create more "professional" relationships among opposite social classes and thus become a "universal class," filling the great "void between oligarchies and lower orders." But to do this, professionals would have to become conscious of their democratic role and detach themselves from any particular "class interest." Only then, Smith reasoned, could professionals embody the universal right to rule in a democracy represented as "an environment free of politics." This professional middle class would transform the feminine tendencies of socially polarized traditional societies (sentimental, private, "domestic," inward looking, class particular) through their presumably masculine predispositions—rationality, public-mindedness, knowledge, and class-free, if universal, interests.

Smith's analysis provoked debate among some important scholars working in Colombia. In the mid-1950s, Gerardo Reichel-Dolmatoff, a European-trained anthropologist who had conducted extensive fieldwork in the country, published a reply.[9] Reichel-Dolmatoff, influenced by medical anthropology, contended that Colombia was not a "feudal society" in which a handful of blue-blooded families dominated a mass of "ignorant mestizos." Moreover, he contended that the existence of three well-established social classes—an upper class, a professional middle class, and a lower class—was obvious to those truly familiar with Colombian reality. Writing from Bogotá, he questioned colonialism's role in consolidating this social structure. The upper class—in contrast to oligarchs or castes, as Smith defined them—did not have their class origins in the colonial experience but rather in the nineteenth-century accumulation of "wealth, influence, and social manners." The anthropologist conceded that some of the elites were descendants of presidents and important groups and had thus taken advantage of "natural birthrights." But in most cases the elites consisted of families who had acquired material capital and now were concerned with providing "the appropriate [professional] education" to their descendants for the democratic tasks of the twentieth century.[10]

Why was it necessary to emphasize professional education in describing the elites? Why was it imperative to categorize Colombian society as divided into three, rather than two, social classes? Reichel-Dolmatoff replied that, given the forces of industrialization and modernization at work in several of Colombia's cities, these elites could be the legitimate source of a new middle class. While the elites were certainly experiencing downward mobility, this would translate into not a lack of professional middle-class consciousness but rather an expanded professional middle class with an inheritance of considerable material means who would detach themselves from any specific class interest. Since material constraints would not color their class interests, these professionals could pursue the necessary prerequisites for a functioning democratic society—objectivity, knowledge, and political detachment. They could form a class of professionals who would become the lawyers that democracy demanded, the engineers that modern infrastructure required, and the doctors that a healthy society needed. Thus, despite their disagreement, Smith and Reichel-Dolmatoff agreed that it was the professional middle class who could claim the legitimate right to rule in a democracy.[11]

Seymour Martin Lipset, a political scientist at the University of California, Berkeley (UC-Berkeley), attempted to demonstrate in several of his publications in the 1950s and 1960s how the most important requisite for democracy was not economic and material progress per se but rather the social development of a middle class, an argument that would be categorized as the "Lipset hypothesis." He was partially inspired by Aristotle, who had argued that the existence of numerous middle groups standing between the rich and the poor could secure a harmonious society. Those who possessed substantial economic means would find it difficult to "obey the rule of reason," while reason was beyond the reach of those who lacked such means.[12] A society based on the middle class, the philosopher argued, was the mean point between the extremes of oligarchy and democracy, defined as rule by the economically poor.[13] In contrast, Lipset argued that two-class societies could produce only two political possibilities, both of which fundamentally contradicted democracy: oligarchy (dictatorial rule of a small upper stratum) or tyranny (a populist dictatorship). In 1959 he concluded that there were plenty of modern examples easily fitting these descriptions: "Tyranny's modern face is Communism or Peronism; oligarchy appears today in the form of traditionalist dictatorships such as we find in parts of Latin America, Thailand, Spain, or Portugal."[14] Lipset linked a middle class with "true" democracy because this class would transform society from "an elongated pyramid with a large lower-class base, to a *diamond* with a growing middle-class . . . moderating conflict since it [was] able to reward moderate and democratic parties and penalize extremist groups."[15]

It is amid this transnational discussion that John J. Johnson published his influential book on the formation of Latin America's middle sectors. He researched more extensively than any other scholar how the middle sectors had shaped democracy in Latin America. Johnson argued that those of Argentina, Brazil, Chile, Mexico, and Uruguay had "contributed brilliantly to the fight for freedom and to the cause of liberalism" during the independence movements. Although unable to confront "reactionary elements" in the independence period's immediate aftermath, since the nineteenth century's second half professionals—along with entrepreneurs, managers, and scientists—had entered into a contestation "for power [against] the traditional ruling elites."[16] In this struggle, the professionals sought popular support outside their ranks.[17] Thus for the Stanford historian the middle professional sectors had played a fundamental role in moving their societies away from two-class feudal systems, despite the structural obstacles that they had faced: an oligarchy that consolidated power by exercising violence, and popular groups that participated in politics by following their "immediate material needs [rather than] reason."[18] The middle sectors emphasized "social rather than political equality" as "the prime requirement for social progress" as this allowed for "more equitable distribution of income, and in certain extreme cases, of wealth."[19]

For Johnson, such an interpretation was a powerful way to include Latin America within the charmed circle of modern democracies of North Atlantic societies. He sought to demonstrate that the political systems of the "more advanced countries of Latin America were opening up, and that new elements that were being incorporated into the political arena were bringing about fundamental changes in the socioeconomic life of the republics."[20] The middle sectors had achieved a political equilibrium by balancing a mass of political antagonisms, becoming "the stabilizers and harmonizers in society" after learning "the dangers of dealing in absolute postulates."[21] Thus, amid the political anxiety of the late 1950s and early 1960s, Johnson concluded: "The middle sectors' cultural experience may be their greatest political asset. . . . It gives them, more than any other group, faith that the golden age lies not behind but ahead. If it does, they may in the years ahead be up to the herculean task of providing the type of leadership requisite to advance before the fires they themselves lighted overtake them."[22]

Johnson's analysis narrated the Latin American middle sectors' democratic role through five historical processes beginning in the nineteenth century. One was urbanization, through which professional middle sectors helped develop democracy by transforming rural society and its constitutive two-class struggle. Second was the Latin American state's teleological development into a meritocracy in which teachers, bureaucrats, technicians, and managers planned their society's social, political, and economic future.[23] Third, Johnson framed the professional middle sectors as the universal and democratic group who could gain political consent from the urban "proletarians" who had filled the cities and factories amid industrialization and who, unfit for democracy, had succumbed to the "demagoguery" of radicals and polarizing populists such as Juan Perón and Getúlio Vargas. Fourth, this search for consent enabled the middle sectors to become a universal nationalistic force, as they would represent the interests of urban proletarians not yet ready to integrate themselves into the modernization process. Finally, the middle sectors developed as education became a central feature of modern societies, and it was the middle sectors who could spread this across the nations through public education. The urban middle sectors could be the future of democracy.

If in his discussion of legitimate democratic rule Johnson mostly compared a proper professional middle sector to the politically fatigued and socially archaic oligarchics, others preferred to discuss the role of popular groups in the political movements of twentieth-century Latin America. For instance, by making a sociological comparison between Europe and Argentina, Gino Germani, an Italian-born intellectual writing from Argentina in the late 1950s and early 1960s, sought to explain why middle-class professionals, and not the working classes, were the antidote to populist regimes. He questioned what he considered a shared Eurocentric political assumption that defined "fascist ideology as middle-class ideology." Only in Europe had the middle class consolidated itself as a fascist political force. In other parts of the world, however, it was the working class who legitimized such totalitarian movements.[24] Thus Peronism, theorized as a local version of fascism, drew its power from the support and participation of the Argentine proletariat, whereas the country's middle classes, in contrast to those in Italy and Germany, stood as democratic forces against the quasi-fascist movement.

According to Germani, this difference was due to certain social and political conditions that during the first half of the twentieth century had transformed the European middle classes into an antidemocratic and fascist force. With rapid industrialization and urbanization, the popular and middle classes had emerged concurrently as results of mass society. The popular classes, composed of industrial workers, had joined forces with the left in attempting to foment socialist or communist revolution. By contrast, white-collar workers and small-business owners feared that they were losing their class privilege to proletarianization and the emergence of a powerful working class. Due to "class irrationality [and] . . . blindness," the European middle classes found in the nationalist fascist movements the only political possibility for maintaining social and political class distinction vis-à-vis the working classes.[25] In the Argentine case, the middle class suffered neither materially nor psychologically from proletarianization because, as a historical creation of the twentieth century, they did not need to create a class reputation in relationship to the working classes. The Argentinean middle class could not be politically co-opted, because they were able to participate in a democratic politics—the Radical Party—that sought the popular groups' consent and participation.

Popular groups, however, did not follow middle-class democratic leadership. The incomplete process of modernization in pre-1950 Argentina developed "irrationality" and aberrant politics amid the popular groups.

Inexperienced in matters of modern politics and unprepared for the realities of an urban society, this proletariat was politically manipulated by Peronism's fascist demagoguery. A new middle class could actively undertake the "de-Peronization"—Germani's term for democratization—of Argentine society, reclaiming the right to rule from the working classes by signaling a fundamental contradiction between populism and democracy. De-Peronization would occur only when the nation's middle class created the necessary conditions for "the masses" to have political options other than Peronism. In this way, Germani, along with several other scholars, linked the right to rule with a professional middle class who would transform Latin America from a two-class, rural, and populist-driven society to a "proper," democratic, three-class urban social order.

The Cultivation of Middle-Class Rule

Drawing on these transnational discussions, the FN's social policies sought to legitimize its rule by portraying the Gustavo Rojas Pinilla dictatorship (1953–1957) and the previous decade's violence as products of conventional party rivalry, class struggle, populism, and political bossism.[26] If this violent past was imagined as a two-class dictatorial society, the future had to entail a peaceful three-class society, with the present defined as belonging to a professional middle class who could make the transition from violence to peace, from dictatorial government to democratic rule. Thus in 1960 President Lleras Camargo composed a long letter addressed to several state institutions and private organizations describing the democratic undertaking to which these bodies' new generation of professionals should be committed.[27] Advised by the Colombian sociologist Orlando Fals Borda and French priest J. L. Lebret, who had recently completed an important study on Colombian social conditions, Lleras Camargo told "the professionals of Colombia" to actively embrace the "task of the twentieth century": to turn Colombia "into a democratic society comparable to those industrialized nations of the world." Given their class preparation, these middle-class professionals had been chosen to "activate every human capacity of society."[28] Reproducing the language of political negotiation between Laureano Gómez, the Conservative Party's leader, and himself, a representative of the Liberal side, over the creation of the FN in late 1956, Lleras Camargo wrote that professionals should be concerned with "forgetting La Violencia, reconquering the liberty . . . and the interests of the great majority . . . [and] thus achieving political stability for the whole nation." Furthermore, the president urged professionals to engage in "closing the abyss between a small enriched social class and a great mass of an impoverished class." Their "preoccupations and passions" as professionals should aim at "harmonizing the social relations between these two classes . . . their mutual understanding, their peaceful coexistence."[29]

To achieve this, the FN's policymakers thought it necessary to implement what they deemed an impartial, rational, scientific training system for those who would potentially be working for—and representing—state rule. Along with the institutionalization of the National Civil Service Office (ONSC) in 1958, an unprecedented process of workshops and job orientations in state development offices, lectures and classes at Bogotá university campuses, and international conferences, students and professionals became everyday experiences for those who found jobs with a development state.[30] They were schooled in the democratic gendered dispositions and classed capacities necessary for state rule. A cohort of elite intellectuals—trained in Europe and the United States, employed by US development offices, the OAS, and the UN, and in constant dialogue with several North American and European universities and the Catholic Church—were pivotal in materializing what the Alliance defined as middle-class revolution. Héctor Abad Gómez (medicine); Carlos Escalante Angulo, Orlando Fals Borda, Germán Guzmán Campos, and Camilo Torres Restrepo (sociology); Ernesto Guhl (geography); Virginia Gutiérrez de Pineda and Roberto Pineda (cultural anthropology); Gerardo Molina and Eduardo Umaña Luna (law); María Cristina Salazar (sociology/social work); Alberto Hernández Mora and Guillermo Nannetti (public administration); and José Joaquín Salcedo Guarín (religion), among several others, invested significant political work to craft the emergence of a new professional, which they considered imperative.

Nowhere was this concern clearer than in the development of Escuela Superior de Administración Pública (ESAP). Founded in 1958 by Law 19, ESAP was the product of intense transnational exchanges between US, Colombian, and French universities as well as international institutions such as the UN and the OAS. The *escuela* followed some of the proposals of Rudolph P. Atcon, a UN Educational, Scientific, and Cultural Organization (UNESCO) consultant, in his mid-1960s report on the Latin American university. For him, the development of "*the local* human factor" was pivotal for independent societies.[31] Latin America, Atcon wrote, needed "specialized men in great numbers, men with initiative, imagination, and know-how . . . more desperately than it needs machines."[32]

Sponsored by the Alliance, ESAP sought to institutionalize a public administration program to develop what was suggestively referred to as a "consciousness of state for a democratic society."[33] Such consciousness would create a need to move away from an antidemocratic state—"antihumanistic, antitechnical, despotic, and trampled under the pressure of political interests of the privileged few"—and toward one that represented a "vertiginous . . . methodical force to realize the goals of social justice, peace, and liberty in society."[34] It was this task of "public salvation" that the middle-class professional would undertake. The foundational classed assumption in this model of democratic government was that both laboring classes and oligarchies, representing a particular set of class interests, could not claim any universality within democratic rule. Middle-class professionals could exercise state rule by politically preparing oligarchies so that their interests could coexist peacefully—and hierarchically—with the interests of working-class peoples in a three-class society. Professionals could move society away from party rivalries and class struggles by developing what were considered unquestionable features for crystallizing consciousness of state rule's importance: technical preparation, discipline, self-control, and an apolitical stance.[35]

This is why both students at ESAP and development program professionals were taught to think of themselves as middle class in distinction from the laboring classes and oligarchs. *Escuela* professors as well as invited lecturers from international institutions and US universities repeatedly told professionals that they could demonstrate to the world that, as John F. Kennedy had argued at the Alliance's 1961 inauguration, the unsatisfied human aspiration for economic progress and social justice could only be realized through democratic institutions. As Eduardo Mora y Mora, dean of training at ESAP, put it in his lesson plan for a 1963 lecture on public administration and human relations,

> You are part of a state that seeks the progress of the nation. . . . You will make sure that not only basic education is available to all but also that education works for democratic institutions. You will make sure not only that hunger will be a forgotten experience but also that the poor can become productive members of the nation. You will make sure that those in most need receive help but also that they can help themselves to reach progress and democracy. You will make sure that they not only have access to health but also can become healthy members of the nation.[36]

In other words, the political rationality at the Alliance's core—economic development, human welfare, and proper political preparation—had to be put into practice by middle-class professionals working for the state. But to do this, as Mora y Mora reiterated, these professionals needed to build the conditions for "democratic government," one that eliminated any form of "class resentment . . . or aggression" by universalizing the particular interests of those classes in struggle and thus ameliorating potential forces of political radicalization.[37]

Such education shows how the Alliance's protean development programs, far from merely decorative aspects of imperial politics, were woven into the everyday lives of Colombian middle-class professionals as they came to represent a "middle-class revolution." There were at least four shared lessons with which these middle-class people became familiarized. First, drawing on modernization theories, students and state professionals were educated in matters of "state ethics." Second, following theories on management and leadership studies, international consultants and elite Colombian intellectuals schooled this new generation of professionals on how to exercise state rule in a "modern, rational, and egalitarian" way in order to persuade others to participate in democracy's lasting benefits. Third, drawing on notions of cultural anthropology, professionals were also instructed in the politics of sentimental education, because it was through "the matters of the hearts and minds" that this new democratic state rule could achieve consent. Finally, the new professional cadre learned about those whom they needed to change—and how that change should happen—so that the democratic system of domination could at last gain proper legitimacy.

Curricula at ESAP, UNAL, and the Pontificia Universidad Javeriana (PUJ)—as well as minutes of job orientations at INCORA, the Instituto de Fomento Industrial (IFI), and the Instituto de Crédito Territorial (ICT)—suggest that these four shared teaching interests were further divided into several dispositions that any state professional should embody. The question of "state ethics," for instance, included four classed and gendered dispositions. First, the proper state representative needed to cultivate "professional honor," a predisposition to claim recognition not through monetary interest or compensation, as "elitist professionals" had in the past, but rather through the democratic acknowledgment granted by "the people." This honor defined the professional's work as "a calling that only few would be able to perform." Catholicism shaped this ethics, the professionals' job as state representative deemed an "act of faith," part of a "social apostolate" in which the only recognition that could be expected was the "emergence of a new democratic society." Gabriel Isaza, the ICT's general manager, conveyed this sentiment at a 1965 seminar about social problems in certain Bogotá slums. He invited the attending professionals to understand that, as representatives of the state, they would be engaged in an unacknowledged task fostered by a "love for your neighbor . . . a love that will be both the guide and the purpose for everything."[38]

This love, then, was thought to lead these professionals to embody a second disposition—"administrative ethics." Middle-class professionals were often told that they needed to remain politically neutral, their main task to "administer," rather than politicize, the multiple demands from society's different groups. They could do this by devoting themselves to "the public interest [or] the common good," which in the early 1960s was equated with peace and *convivencia*. Given that administrative ethics was always couched as apolitical, professionals also needed to develop a third predisposition— "ethics in public service." As representatives of state rule, professionals could not be loyal to either political parties or class interests because this would jeopardize the hierarchical coexistence of classes. Rather than "choose sides" in the political struggles of the twentieth century, they would be properly political, that is to say, "loyal to a democratic state . . . and comply [with its] development programs."[39]

This loyalty also implied—and this is the fourth disposition—"the ethics of probity," which entailed professionals cultivating, following their own initiative, their intellectual skills and moral capacities to remain "the most valuable members and moral authority in society." As state representatives, they would have to set the example for "moral integrity, honesty, and respectability" through "impeccable behavior at home, in the street, in the field, and in the office." Personnel offices in state development agencies were packed with manuals of good behavior advising professionals not to engage in "less-than-honorable activities" when working for the state because this could jeopardize their ability to embody state ethics. These manuals are vague as to what such activities might be, but scattered evidence suggests that the personnel offices worried that professionals were getting "too close . . . to their clients" not only in terms of political positions but also "in questions of love and sex." It seems that professionals were asked to maintain their "professionalism" so that they could avoid the "relaxation of polite manners."[40] State ethics meant that these professionals, in order to represent and exercise state rule, should maintain the necessary class distinctions between themselves and those they were serving. These manuals sought to police the boundaries between those defined as having the right to rule in democracy and those seen as having the right to be ruled.

"Egalitarian Leaders"

During the late 1950s and 1960s, on campuses across Bogotá and in state development offices, elite intellectuals also taught these professionals how to be "egalitarian leaders" to achieve legitimate consent among those whom they needed to rule over if a proper democracy were to emerge. This was a shared teaching discourse, but Fals Borda played a pivotal role in its materialization. As a director of the Ministry of Agriculture in the late 1950s, a founder of UNAL's Faculty of Sociology in 1962, an active member of CINVA, and a lecturer in several state development offices, this sociologist, who worked with Lowry Nelson, professor of rural sociology at the University of Minnesota, and later with T. Lynn Smith at the University of Florida, envisioned middle-class professionals as "egalitarian leaders" who would know how to distribute "rights, obligations, and opportunities" for society's different members.[41] In one of the first seminars for state professionals laboring for INCORA's agrarian reform initiatives in the early 1960s, Fals Borda wanted professionals to understand that there were legitimate and illegitimate forms of leadership in democratic societies. He insisted that a traditional form of what he called "feudal" leadership, defined by "heritage . . . favoritism, politics, and violence" rather than "meritocracy and mutual understanding," could have devastating consequences for democracy.[42]

Other consultants for state institutions soon joined Fals Borda. Caroline Ware, a consultant for the Alliance through the OAS, gave a talk at CINVA to an audience of professionals working for several state institutions. Following the typical pattern of the time, Ware narrated stories of imagined yet specific professionals performing their jobs. She appealed to her experience working in Puerto Rico by citing "frustrated cases" in which she could detect what she called an autocratic professional.[43] This professional would not allow the people to express their opinions about social problems that they faced in their own communities.[44] It was the professional's obligation to make decisions, assume responsibilities, and know what was good for the people.[45] But by acting in an "authoritarian way," he ignored or even sought to elide the poor's interests. This authoritarian leader, whom Fals Borda called the "feudal leader," not only intimidated people to participate in democratic processes but also produced "fears, resistance, and rejection" from the people toward progress. And when faced with these rejections, he had no option but to use violence to force the people to obey what he thought their interests should be.[46]

Elite intellectuals also criticized a second type, the paternalist leader. Unlike the feudal/authoritarian leader, who was easy to detect, the paternalist professional could be difficult to discern because of his pretensions to be democratic. With the best intentions, he would quickly seek to please peasants and workers without pondering their real "felt needs."[47] He was willing to work with the people but was confused because he preferred to think for, rather than like, the peasants and workers. As a consequence, this leader could get interested in people's lives as long as he could "keep the [real] authority in his hands." And the people themselves would not develop awareness of their own problems, because they would expect the leader to make the decisions for them. This paternalistic relationship created dependent, unaware people striving for short-term and immediate material benefits without becoming conscious of their own social situation. Neither interested in profound transformations nor able to "inculcate desires for change and democracy," the paternalistic leader was bound to be forgotten, because the people had experienced no change as a result of his presence.[48]

In contrast, elite intellectuals imagined for the development programs a gendered, egalitarian leader who would be a hybrid product of what Max Weber identified as the bureaucratic and the charismatic leader. As a member of a bureaucracy, this democratic leader would have to develop professional knowledge in order to "substantiate his actions more in persuasion and social catalysis than in coercive power."[49] And, as a charismatic leader, he would secure state rule via personal merit, sympathy, and guidance. Only then could a "true professional man" become a representative of a democratic government claiming a legitimate form of domination.

To exercise this legitimate state rule, a new form of classed masculinity was needed. As dean of ESAP's School of Social Research, a sociology professor at UNAL, and a member of INCORA's *junta directiva*, Camilo Torres Restrepo advocated for this new egalitarian man who—unlike the traditional leader, who carried "a big stick around" to legitimize his dominant position in society—could lead via a "gentle personality . . . tender character, [and] trustworthy temperament," masculine dispositions that allowed him to exercise a "democratic capacity" for understanding the people's needs and wants.[50] It was necessary to create "an authentic and realistic professional" who, as a proper man, would leave any manifestation of "femininity behind" and embark on discovering "the reality of Colombia." In 1961,

Torres Restrepo lectured at ESAP for INCORA professionals on the inauthentic and the authentic professional. The former harbored an irrational desire—defined as a "feminine obsession"—for securing a diploma and thus "moving up the social ladder." Preoccupied with mastering "sophisticated language," camouflaged as scientific objectivity, inauthentic professionals could not take a masculine position toward real social problems. Such feminine obsession not only made these professionals "the most cowardly members of society" but also "castrated [their] virility" needed to face the popular classes' hard realities.[51] Torres Restrepo instead invited his audience to be authentic professionals—that is, to "leave [their] girlishness at the office" and embrace the most important task of all: "to discover the nation . . . to go out there, to observe Colombian reality, and to produce democratic change."[52]

As the main director of Popular Cultural Action (ACPO), a state-supported but privately controlled Catholic agency for social welfare, Monsignor José Joaquín Salcedo Guarín echoed Torres Restrepo's vision of state rule as the masculine task par excellence in his job orientations to agronomists, rural specialists, and sociologists working for ICT, INCORA, and ACPO in the early 1960s. The monsignor invited these professionals to overcome any fear and "get [their] hands dirty with the poor."[53] Applying his Christian beliefs, Salcedo Guarín saw this masculine task as part of a mission of salvation through which, with proper scientific preparation, these professionals could bring democracy to those who barely had any experience with it. Here science and religion worked in tandem to imagine a proper, masculine professional. As he told professionals in his orientations, "Your science must be put in practice for the benefit of the people. . . . You are a mystic force . . . practitioners of popular redemption. . . . God calls on you to bring democracy."[54]

Cultural anthropology and rural sociology were pivotal in defining the professional's role as a representative of state rule. Elite Colombian intellectuals at various university campuses and state offices in Bogotá taught a new cohort of professionals to move away from "racist . . . thinking . . . and actions," from a natural and fatalist understanding of classes in which groups behaved according to unchanging, biologically inherent values. Perhaps unlike any other intellectual, anthropologist Virginia Gutiérrez de Pineda crystallized—in her classes at UNAL, her consultant work at CINVA, and her countless job orientations at ICT and INCORA—a culturalist explanation of Colombian social reality. Educated at the Escuela Normal Superior and UC-Berkeley, as a social anthropologist, she argued that society in general should be defined as a learned culture, as a "way of life" in which "behaviors, customs, and social institutions" could be passed down—and thus were changeable—from generation to generation.[55]

If this was true, then the monumental task of professionals would be to transform the major obstacles to progress and democracy in Colombia: an "oligarchical culture" and "the culture of the [average] Colombian man."[56] Gutiérrez de Pineda claimed the former was marked by an "innate belief" that class status was associated with landownership, which had produced a privilege wrongly based in birth and "class ancestry." Unlike in Europe and the United States, where a middle-class society had destroyed the oligarchies via democratic revolutions, in Colombia such an oligarchical culture still reigned.[57] In a 1962 seminar at CINVA, the anthropologist said that this oligarchical culture, the product of an almost immovable "colonial legacy," had produced a "feudal culture" in which social classes were defined by "blood, biology, family names, and personal influence," and material resources were believed to be more important than the "human capital" that could make those material resources economically productive.[58] Fals Borda was convinced that state professionals—as charismatic, egalitarian, and democratic leaders—could transform these oligarchies into modern elites who "could build a new society, not to destroy it, to enlighten the path of democracy, not to close it." He thus invited professionals to see as central to their job the renovation of this "oligarchical culture."[59]

At the same time, other transnational experts elaborated on the "problems of the Colombian man," in reference to laboring classes. They began by arguing that La Violencia had been a product of "classist thoughts and feelings." To reach peace, professionals needed to understand that the laboring classes were not a "homogenous mass of ignorant and miserable people."[60] In other words, professionals had developed in the past an "elitist" disposition to understand the people as only composed of "biologically inferior" human beings.[61] Professionals were told not to think of the poor as "native, primitive, or inhuman," because these descriptions could constitute social prejudices that must be excluded from the actions, thoughts, and feelings of a democratic professional.[62] Instead, the poor had be regarded as "peasants and working people, [as] the dispossessed," who behaved according to learned cultural patterns.

These professionals were also told that these peasants and working people were culturally driven to believe that their economic and social situation was "unchangeable." Professionals needed to understand what Fals Borda called the cultural ethos of passivity, an ethos so powerful that in some cases certain beliefs, values, and habits appeared, if not "as second nature," then at least as "God's mandate." In contrast to the oligarchies, these laboring classes had been brought up with the belief that their poverty was caused by the oligarchies themselves. The poor had a culture in which liberal values were lacking, as they did not take "individual responsibility for their own situation." These laboring classes developed what Gutiérrez de Pineda and Roberto Pineda called in a 1963 ICT seminar "the contempt . . . the disdain for wealth, human resources, and property." Following Weber, these elite professors argued that the poor had developed a culture of lacking: "a lacking of a vision of the future, a lacking of a drive to improve oneself, a lacking to be somebody in life . . . no initiative, no notion of economics, no individual incentive." It was a "cultural heritage," product of centuries of colonial domination, that had made these laboring classes "unaware of themselves."[63]

But as overwhelming as this cultural heritage was, the task of professionals was to transform that culture so that the laboring classes could govern themselves. This transformation had to materialize not through imposition but rather through persuasion and negotiation. The democratic role of the middle-class professional was to "remove the cultural obstacles among the laboring classes," to guide peasants and workers to self-awareness of their own talents and innate potentialities so that they "could discover democracy [by] themselves."[64] They were also to be guided to become aware of their "own interests, needs . . . [and] social situation" in setting out "their own goals."[65]

Although all these elite professors, consultants, and experts would soon part ways in how they defined democratic rule, during the first half of the 1960s they shared a belief in the intimate association between middle-class masculinity and legitimate state rule. They imagined a proper, masculine middle-class professional located between two improper, and thus illegitimate, forms of state rule: a traditional, feudal, and oligarchical rule associated with violent virility, and a paternalistic, if not elitist, professionalism, a feminized rule distant from the poor. Between these two gendered and classed forms of rule, the proper middle-class professional would help the oligarchies to renew themselves as elites and assist the laboring classes to become proper economic and political subjects.[66] Thus the professional was constituted as the keystone figure in a hierarchical and classed redistribution of tasks.

"Profesionales Queridas"

The policies forwarded by the Alliance and put into practice by the FN were shaped by a concern to educate sentiments, aspirations, and attachments, imagined as required for democratic state rule. Although professional women and men worked with both the oligarchies and laboring classes, there was a tendency to assume that professional women were especially suited for work with the oligarchies, who should be educated sentimentally in order to become likeable, desirable, and trusted. Alternately, it was often assumed that professional men should work with laboring classes, as they were seen as unmodernized and thus more difficult to work with. Thus, transnational experts argued that that which was considered "feminine weakness"—a professional career dictated by sentiment rather than rationality—could be professional women's "most powerful tool" in exercising state rule. Some of these transnational experts asserted that if a proper democratic leader exercised leadership through persuasion rather than violence, professional women were well positioned to seduce the isolated oligarchies.[67]

This is why Lucrecia Tello Marulanda and Matilde González Ramos, pioneers in women's education in Colombia, appropriated religious ideas, modernization theories, and sociological studies in advising the ONSC that middle-class women could represent the state in its main tasks of "harmoniz[ing]" social interests and "administrat[ing] justice."[68] "Intellectualism, rationality, and male-centered interests" had produced a decade of violence. Professional women could bring "sentiments, emotions, and feminine instincts" to bear on making the democratic state efficient and seducing oligarchies into the belief that the nation needed "democratic coexistence" among social classes. Able to see beyond party lines, professional women could transform oligarchical feelings of hatred into productive sentiments for democratic leadership. As González Ramos and Tello Marulanda concluded in their advice to the ONSC—advice that was reproduced, in different language, by state personnel offices throughout the 1960s—women "have been made to love in society."[69]

State offices imagined the relationship between professional women and the male oligarchs as heterosexual seduction. Oligarchs were often described as difficult men with violent tendencies who did not want anybody to disturb them in their own business. Professional women were imagined as democratic leaders because of their capacity to sway this group. Women, Tello Marulanda told a group of professionals in the early 1960s, "would modernize [and] democratize society from one end of the social ladder to the other." By cultivating the oligarchs' "politeness, sympathy, spontaneity, and spirituality," professional women would achieve what "men had not . . . in over a century": a "society without violence, a society without conflict."[70]

Thus, in job orientations and workshops state development offices taught how to carry out this heterosexual seduction. Carmen Torres Medina, with the advice of Eleanor Southerland from the US Agency for International Development (USAID), told social workers at several workshops at IFI that "human relations [was] the art of seduction and persuasion . . . the art of making others want to do what you need them to do."[71] And as part of this heterosexual seduction, it was imperative that professional women become *simpáticas*. They needed to use their "feminine powers"—beauty, delicacy, touch, and patience—to be liked and desired by the oligarchies and to make them interested in their own self-renovation. The key point of the seduction and persuasion, then, was that professional women had to "feel, think, act, and speak in relation to what the other wants," to create "affinity bonds." It was women's "delicacy" that could play a fundamental role not only in their being simpática but also in their ability to create those bonds of mutual understanding among social classes. Citing Sigmund Freud, Torres Medina claimed that professional women would have to work with oligarchs who by definition tended to see themselves as "the most important people in the world." Yet unlike professional men, who would engage these oligarchs in a "fight of male egos," professional women would use their feminine tranquility to make oligarchical men "feel important" and thus persuade them to end up doing what the professional women wanted. With appropriate doses of sentiment and emotion, these professional women would seduce these oligarchs to embrace what Fals Borda defined as their task for the twentieth century's second half: to renovate themselves as elites in order to "enlighten, rather than obscure, the path to modernity."[72] But for female professionals to successfully perform such heterosexual class seduction, they needed to "remember to eliminate any sentiment or tendency to engage in discussions, as the only argument you win [was] the one you avoid[ed]." Professional women were advised to "keep in mind that you convince another not by consolidating individual prestige but by the application of psychological . . . feminine powers of convincing, trust, and fondness."[73]

In contrast, professional men tended to be seen as those who could discover "the felt needs of the poor." Those felt needs were not to be identified by imposing "foreign ideas" on the popular environment or by producing knowledge about the poor from a distance. Rather, it was necessary to structure a hierarchical relation of fondness and negotiation between these democratic professionals and those who needed them the most: "peasants, working people . . . and [the] economically deprived." In this way, professional men would become trusted sources of identification and inspiration for the people.[74] Male professionals needed to develop "democratic emotions . . . affective concerns" for the people's difficult cultural conditions and social situations.[75] True middle-class professionals could find gratification and enjoyment in an "attachment" to the poor, willing to get their "hands dirty," develop a social sensibility for how they lived, get into rough places to listen to people's voices and to sympathize with their wants and needs.[76] By experiencing the conditions of the popular groups, democratic middle-class professionals could build a democratic and intimate rapport with them.

In sum, the very notion of democracy at the core of development programs was to be implemented through a process of hierarchical *class*ification between those who were supposed to rule in the service of the state and those who were supposed to be ruled by the state. The historical intelligibility of the democratic professional working for state rule depended on a hierarchical constitution of the laboring classes and oligarchies as the others in dire need of being guided on how to live in democracy according to their particular cultural conditions. Neither too proximate nor too distant, the masculine middle-class professional could achieve his democratic role insofar as he could govern and maintain the very hierarchies and categorizations that made the laboring classes and oligarchies stay in their own culturally specific places minding "their own business." Likewise, professional women were demarcated as seducing the oligarchies through proper affections and desires. The main assumption behind these positions was that professional women and men could not themselves belong to the working classes or the elites, because without a vertical, hierarchical relationship of class, democratic recognition could not take place: there would be no laboring classes to be attached to, or oligarchies to be seduced. There would be no others to provide fascination, satisfaction, and pleasure—crucial desires and sentiments imagined as required of professional woman and men laboring for state rule. Only then could a peaceful—and hierarchical—coexistence of classes called democracy emerge.

3

The Productive Wealth
of This Country

During the 1950s and 1960s, Colombia witnessed important growth in small
and medium industries. This was part of structural changes taking shape
since at least the 1930s, when the state acted to respond to the economic
consequences of the Great Depression.[1] But it was also the product of specific economic policies that, as part of development programs, sought to
propel small and medium industries as a condition for industrialization in
what was referred to as an unprecedented economic democratization. Alejandro Hurtado, a small-business owner, experienced these changes firsthand. Hurtado had finished his studies at the National School of Commerce
(ENC), a technical school founded in 1905 that prepared its graduates for
financial pursuits. Soon after finishing his degree in the late 1950s, Hurtado
was ready to put into practice the knowledge that he had learned. "I was a
practical guy—I wanted to be a businessman," he keenly told me. In 1960,
with a family loan in hand, he founded Casa Hurtado, a small business that
manufactured *ruanas*, sweaters, and other clothing. He recounted how
after three or four years he "was barely able to keep the business afloat. . . .
[There was] not much excitement in terms of growth or profit." He owned
a small shop in Chapinero, a business locality in Bogotá, but did not have
enough capital to purchase raw wool and additional equipment to "move
the business forward."[2]

In the mid-1960s, another small businessman informed him about a state-sanctioned but privately sponsored program for the promotion of small and medium industries at the Caja de Crédito Agrario, Industrial y Minero (CCAIM). He remembered this as one of the most important moments in his life because it catapulted him as a small businessman. His personal archive attests that he applied for a fifty-thousand-peso loan. After verifying his eligibility, CCAIM sent its industrial extensionist to evaluate both his small factory shop and his "family environment." As CCAIM delayed its final decision, Hurtado feared that he had been rejected. Yet his fears were ungrounded: CCAIM granted the loan, albeit for a lesser amount (forty-five thousand pesos), to invest in the necessary equipment. According to the final decision, CCAIM had recommended a lower amount because, upon evaluating the case, they found that Casa Hurtado was facing "production capacity."[3] Regardless, the businessman was happy because his "business took off," and he was now able to expand his market, hire more workers, and secure a "comfortable position in society." He later wanted to sell his clothing in a US market, but this never materialized, and instead, in the late 1970s, Hurtado decided to sell his business, turning instead to the food industries.

Throughout our conversation, Hurtado considered himself a small-business owner. When I asked him why that was, he replied: "Well, look at me, I am a middle-class guy.... That is why." When I inquired what he meant by this, a rather interesting conversation developed:

AH: Look around this house! I do not have enough money to be a *gran industrial* like Arturo Calle or Carlos Ardila Lülle or [Luis Carlos] Sarmiento Angulo, but I have enough money to live pretty well. I have worked hard so that my family can live comfortably. Those gran industriales have always been rich. . . . Their companies are huge and they can do pretty much whatever they want. All my life I have had to worry about money because I do not have a lot of it. . . . I succeeded in life all by myself. . . . I did not need anybody to help me. I just needed opportunities. And I conquered them all. . . . I embraced them, I exploited all the opportunities available. . . . And with my business I put two kids through college and my wife never had to work outside the home. . . . She took care of the kids. . . . That is why they turned out to be outstanding . . . productive people for society.

RL: Did you make it all by yourself? The state loan helped you get off your feet, and your parents loaned you. . . .

AH: Money is not the only thing you need for a successful business. That money could have been wasted had I not known how to do good business. . . . You need the will, the strength, the adaptability, the endurance, and knowledge of the market. . . . It is people like me who have moved this country forward. . . . We have developed the country economically, we have generated jobs, foreign exchange, boosted exports that are critical for the economic development. Imagine a country just with *grandes industriales*. . . . We are the productive wealth of this country.[4]

These seemingly contradictory memories and understandings raise important questions about how the political rationality and political economy of development programs played out. Why did Hurtado's memories oscillate between a recognition of the importance of state financial and educational programs for his success as a small businessman and an assertion that only he made possible his successful business and concomitant gendered middle-class status? Why did the *grandes industriales* feature centrally in Hurtado's understanding of himself as a middle-class man? And why did Hurtado see men like himself as the embodiment of economic democracy or the country's wealth?

Since at least the late 1970s, historians have argued that in Colombia, as part of a larger Latin American pattern, the state attempted to promote domestic manufacturing via trade protectionism, financing, and public involvement in the growth of large industries.[5] This process, referred to as import substitution industrialization (ISI), was supposed to support protectionist tariffs, endow public agencies with resources for direct industrial promotion, skew the exchange rate toward appreciation to facilitate the substitution of industrial imports, and ensure that manufacturing firms enjoyed extensive access to credit at beneficial rates.[6] Although historians concur that the Colombian state attempted to use ISI as a development strategy from the late 1930s through the late 1960s, most historians claim that it failed, as the Colombian state had neither the resources nor the political will to spur industrialization.[7] More recently, other economic historians have instead argued that the Colombian state—at worst economically fragile and at best financially anemic—never envisioned "pro-developmentalist policies." "Industrialisation proceeded apace," these scholars conclude, "but this was chiefly a market- or private-led phenomenon."[8]

Often, these studies see the political economy of industrialization and development as macroeconomic realities isolated from other social spheres. Economic development is historicized through the experiences of large and major industries. Such economic analyses usually presuppose a clear-cut, teleological transition between three historical moments: First was export-boom industrialization (during the late nineteenth century and 1920s).[9] Next came ISI (from the 1930s through the 1970s).[10] Finally, there was the period when the state took (or failed to take) an active role in promoting industrialization through market-driven neoliberal development, with the free market as the only player in the political economy (from the 1970s to the present). In a word, we often assume that, historically, political economies have traveled from state-led development to free-market absolutism, from regulated economies to deregulated ones.[11]

This chapter rethinks these assumptions by looking at the political economy and political rationality forwarded by development programs such as the Alliance during the late 1950s and 1960s. I focus on the politics of educational and development counseling services for financing programs supported by a combination of state and private (national and international) institutions to promote small and medium industries as the engine of economic industrialization. By examining the interlocking relationship between economic realities, discourses, and subjectivities in these policies, I argue that the expansion of small and medium industries—and the intertwined political rationalities—was not an ephemeral by-product of a failed political economy. Rather, at this time the economic growth of small and medium industries generated productive discourses about middle-class democracy. Simultaneously, those discourses—legitimized in a transnational field of knowledge—substantiated new economic policies empowering small-business owners as the representatives of a gendered and classed notion of economic democracy.

Closely following ECLAC's advice, the Alliance and the FN sought "economic democratization" by promoting small and medium industries because, it was believed, such industries could not only compete with large ones but also propel an "unstoppable" materialization of a middle class, an economic subject that would allow productivity to expand across the country.[12] In so doing, development-program-affiliated policymakers and experts across the Americas neither proposed nor imagined deregulating the state's role in industrialization. Rather, the state, along with private credit institutions, sought to allocate public capital—including financial support, financial literacy, and schooling in management—to small businessmen who purportedly could *reconcile* a proper state with a free-market economy. Through the politics of selection and training, state credit programs for small and medium industries conscripted—chose and educated—middle-class men as legitimate economic subjects for a market-driven democracy. In short, small-business owners such as Hurtado began to think of themselves as those who, as the "productive wealth of this country," could, unlike *grandes industriales* and working-class people, legitimize private property and unequal distribution of ownership rights as "obvious" features of a proper democracy.

The Middle Class as the Wealth of Nations

As several historians have argued, Colombia witnessed important economic changes during the late 1950s and 1960s. Although fluctuations in the world coffee market affected GDP during the mid-1950s, by decade's end Colombia enjoyed unparalleled economic growth. Gross national product increased "5.6 percent annually between 1946 and 1955, and 5.15 percent annually during the quarter century after."[13] Along with the intensification of political struggles in the countryside, the 1950s also witnessed what some historians have called the "Golden Age of Colombian industry."[14] These structural changes generated new enterprises in the manufacture of investment goods and other import substitutes—from metal products and electrical machinery to transport equipment and clothing. According to the Departamento Administrativo Industrial (DAI), by the end of the 1960s small business and industries accounted for 53 percent of the net increase in industrialization. Likewise, other reports contended that during the 1960s the number of small and medium factories increased by eighteen hundred.[15] State offices also published statistical reports suggesting that around 3,613 small and medium factories accounted for 38 percent of the persons employed, 27 percent of the value added, 22 percent of the horsepower installed, and 22 percent of the new fixed investment in all manufacturing industries. Similar studies argued that small and medium industry plants provided over 44 percent of the net increase in manufacturing employment from 1959 to 1969.[16] It is clear that during these years small and medium industries substantially increased their participation in creating jobs, boosting exports, and generating foreign exchange to further finance industrialization.

This is when the state and the Alliance's different programs began to celebrate small businesses as engines of economic democratization and industrialization. Statistical reports were accompanied by fervent prophecies that the expansion of small and medium industries would augur an "unparalleled new phase of a true Colombia's industrial revolution," in which not large industries but rather "small and medium factories [would] assume a democratic role in the nation."[17] No matter how late in history, these state reports insisted, the growth of small and medium industries could uplift the Colombian economy into the charmed circle of the "most important revolutions" and create the necessary conditions for a middle-class man, whose economic role had "made the Industrial Revolution in England . . . the French Revolution . . . and the US revolution" possible.[18]

Yet if the so-called underdeveloped world needed to experience the different stages of economic development already undergone by the West in order to reach a superior economy, it also needed to develop unique "human values and motives." It was these values, not just the structural conditions, that could materialize a man who could "shape his own [economic] destiny [by] exploit[ing] opportunities [and] taking advantage of favorable trade conditions."[19] For instance, Everett E. Hagen, an economist and political scientist then teaching at the Massachusetts Institute of Technology (MIT) and an active economic adviser in Colombia in the 1960s, deemed "purely economic theories . . . inadequate" for explaining underdevelopment, economic stagnation, and the absence of growth.[20] Claims that economic growth would result from underdeveloped societies following the West's structural conditions—namely, technological advancement or injections of capital— were "ethnocentric and incorrect."[21] The West's superior economic development and democracy instead depended on a "human uniqueness" lacking in societies outside Europe and the United States.[22]

What was this "human uniqueness" that, once identified and cultivated, could move underdeveloped societies toward modern industrialized democracy? Scholars across the social sciences offered competing answers, but all insisted that the missing component had to be found in what David C. McClelland, a Harvard psychologist, defined as "a 'need' for [economic] achievement," a variable as measurable as GDP.[23] This meant that the wealth of nations should be quantified also by the quality of a *Homo economicus*, who would make economic progress possible. Thinkers such as Theodore W. Schultz, a University of Chicago economist and 1979 Nobel laureate, insisted that economic development depended on the accumulation of human capital—intelligence, creativity, innovation, and all the "attributes and competencies embodied in the human body that formed economic value and growth."[24] Schultz concluded that the West, particularly the United States, enjoyed wealth because it had produced an economic subject who could own, develop, and accumulate his own human capital to the benefit of himself and society.[25]

Such stances soon entered debates on economic culture taking place in Latin America since at least the Second World War to produce a new classed and gendered language explaining away material inequalities. The discourse on human capital would help consolidate what Marisol de la Cadena has called "racism without race"—the belief in the unquestionable intellectual and moral superiority of one group in society over others based on notions of "culture, the soul, and the spirit."[26] During the late 1950s and 1960s these discourses naturalized culture as embedded in bodies while defining the human qualities needed to produce a desire for economic achievement. Via this combination of discourses on culture, human capital, psychology, and entrepreneurship, scholars across the Americas located economic democratic subjectivity neither in the popular classes nor in the oligarchies but rather in the middle classes.

Delegitimizing the Oligarchies

A member of the Chicago school of economics, Schultz considered human capital the most important discovery of the twentieth-century economy. Criticizing Marx's understanding of economic relations within a classical tripartition of land, labor, and capital, Schultz argued that the "presumed dichotomy between labor and capital" was anachronistic in the twentieth century because in "proper" contemporary economic development *labor was part of capital*. The very existence of the human being should be understood as an individual economic reality, and thus economics, the science that studied such reality, needed to investigate the conditions through which human beings could develop and accumulate their own human capital. Because labor was not an abstraction of, or alienated reality from, capital, as Marx had argued, but rather a concrete experience of capital accumulation, the problem of economic growth and achieving economic democracy could not be resolved by restructuring the relations of production or by a revolutionary change of the mode of production, as Marx had insisted. Instead, Schultz argued for reconceptualizing the very notion of an economic human being in society at the core of a proper economic democracy. Economic self-exploitation could in and of itself be a source of individual capital accumulation.

This economic democracy, Schultz continued, would not be defined by a dialectical relationship between labor and capital, elites and workers, peasants and landowners—relics of the nineteenth century—but rather by the emergence of a presumably new historical economic subject: the middle-class entrepreneur who would develop society's human capital and wealth for greater economic productivity. To legitimize such a vision, policymakers, intellectuals, and scholars across the Americas studied the oligarchs of Latin America and their putative failure to transform into entrepreneurial elites. Schultz, for instance, called to "rid our societ[ies] of indentured service and to eliminate all vestige of feudalism with its lord and vassal relations" because they were obstacles to fostering the human capabilities and potential for true economic development.[27] He viewed them as signs of "slave societies" built on the unproductive dependency of one class on the other instead of "free men."[28] A traditional two-class society could not achieve the productivity of a proper economic democracy because its population could not cultivate their human potential for competition, innovation, and achievement.

According to these studies, Latin American oligarchies acted and thought exclusively in terms of the past and fatalistically accepted the idea that nature dictated life's material conditions. Economists and psychologists highlighted certain cultural traits embodied in the oligarchies' way of life as the main obstacles to developing a society of entrepreneurs. Fixated with land as a measure of economic productivity, Latin America's oligarchs were feminine because they conquered nature not through creativity and innovation—presumably the masculine traits of entrepreneurship—but by passively "contemplating" it. These oligarchs were too close to nature, and thus feminine, because they claimed to deserve their role in society as a "natural thing" rather than as the result of "built and hard accomplishments." Instead of a "doing orientation" toward economic life, they developed an "economic being" through which they wanted to defend the natural order of things. Toward this end oligarchs deployed traits associated with nature—physical prowess, brute strength, bodily endurance—in a way that made them improperly masculine, perhaps even feminine.[29]

These studies also cast Latin America's two-class feudal oligarchy as inimical to a democratic economy of entrepreneurship. In one edited volume containing several analyses from the late 1950s and early 1960s, Seymour Martin Lipset and Aldo Solari explained why "a competent elite, motivated to modernize their society," was critical for economic development and growth.[30] Lipset argued that one of the main reasons for Latin American oligarchs embracing a "gentleman complex" instead of entrepreneurship stemmed from the cultural distinction between the Protestant ethic and traditional Catholic society. The former had produced a "universal elite" of a middle class who could achieve elite status—that is, become proper democratic rulers—because they had reached their social standing through entrepreneurial efforts; the latter developed economic dependency on inherited family privileges in a rural feudal system. Drawing on Talcott Parsons, Lipset deemed Latin American oligarchies particularistic and ascriptive fixed cultures focused on kinship and family relations, which deemphasized larger centers of (masculine) authority such as the state and the market. Oligarchs were "in poor condition" to develop an "entrepreneurship culture," as they privileged expressiveness over pragmatism, sentiments over rationality, and immediacy over long-term planning. Several scholars across different disciplines concerned themselves with this "feminine tendency" among the Latin American oligarchies to defend family interests at the expense of a larger, and presumably more masculine, preoccupation with market competition.

Thus several scholars appropriated Gilberto Freyre's "gentleman complex"—a term originally coined to explain Brazilian oligarchs and their preoccupation with accumulating material capital as fast as possible—to define a broader "cultural problem" of the oligarchies throughout Latin America that established them as anathema to proper economic democracies. This was what the economist Albert Hirschman termed the oligarchs' "ego-focused image" of economic change: "Although seemingly reflecting a desire to get ahead, this orientation, which inhibits efforts to advance by cooperation with others, is inimical to economic development" since "success is conceived not as a result of systematic application of effort and creative energy, combined perhaps with a 'little bit of luck,' but as due either to sheer luck or to the outwitting of others through careful scheming."[31]

Thus, these studies defined the Latin American oligarchies as socially *deviant* because, as Lipset put it (following Bert Hoselitz), "the dominant culture [was] not supportive of entrepreneurial activity."[32] Researching the elites' economic role, Aaron Lipman, a US sociologist affiliated with UNAL's Faculty of Sociology, and Orlando Fals Borda argued that the few entrepreneurs in Colombia were "non-Latin in their ethnic origins."[33] Following Weber's theories on economic development, Lipman and Fals Borda blamed Colombian elites' lack of entrepreneurial "drive" on ethnic heterogeneity and Catholic roots, which had created a cultural environment in which achievement, competition, and innovation were seen as, at best, exotic and, at worst, evil. The Colombian entrepreneur existed "in spite of and often at odds with his cultural milieu," deviant in relation to an ideal democracy, alien to his own culture and society, and incongruent with the existing traditional order.[34]

Why did Latin America's oligarchies lack what David McClelland labeled "the achievement motive," a real yet intangible trait that he deemed essential for democracy? McClelland's globally comparative research sought to discover why Western societies developed entrepreneurial democracy while other societies were ruled by economic oligarchies. In *The Achieving Society*, he extended Weber's argument on economic development by proposing that the achievement motive resulted early in life from sequential education in certain specific values and from child-rearing practices that stressed independence, self-reliance, excellence, maternal warmth, and low paternal dominance. In this he agreed with Everett Hagen, who, based on several interviews with elites across the globe, argued that oligarchs were raised to see the world as given, fixed, and thus the result of powers greater than themselves.[35]

This is why scholars across the Americas elevated the middle class as the sovereign subject of democratic economic change, a "normalizing class" who could create the conditions necessary for generating the human capital fit for a market economy.[36] The middle class could become the legitimate force for economic change because they would base their class status and privilege not on nature but on reason, not on a naturally ascribed position but on a culturally constructed one, not on family prestige but on socially achieved status, not on feminized tradition but on masculinized innovation, not on feminine passivity but on masculine risk-taking, not on authority but on negotiation, and not on family influence but on competition.[37]

Here Virginia Gutiérrez de Pineda played a foundational role. After extensive ethnographic research starting in the mid-1950s, she published two hefty volumes in which she regionalized both biology and culture as a way to hierarchize subcultural and regional differences within the Colombian nation.[38] She fused anthropological concepts (family values, culture, biology) and economic ones (development, growth, human capital) to describe a normative economic democracy, associated with an unmarked notion of middle-classness, against Colombia's indigenous population, Hispanic oligarchs, and Afro-descendant families. Oligarchs and the laboring classes, anathema to economic democracy, needed to democratize by embracing "cultural," "biological," and "social" middle-class qualities.

The anthropologist did all of this by dividing the Colombian nation into four "peculiar" cultural complexes: Andean (American), Santanderean (neo-Hispanic), Negroid (coastal/riverine/mining), and Antioquian.[39] Each regional complex contained, Gutiérrez de Pineda argued, certain unique human traits—produced by specific cultural environments, "demographic-biological" makeup, family dynamics, male-female relationships, sexual behaviors, experiences of masculinity and femininity, household formations, labor patterns, land tenure systems, religious influences, personality development, and child-rearing methods—that could foster or thwart economic development. Andean individuals were not prepared to rule in a developed economy because their cultural complex contained a small "biological makeup of white upper class" and a large "lower-class indigenous group." The region thus perpetuated a two-class feudal system in which *minifundios* and *latifundios* predominated. Elite landowners delegated tasks to overseers, while a large group of landless indigenous peasants remained dependent on the landowners for survival. This backward system of colonial rule created fragmented communities, isolated autarchies, or subsistence economies that only satisfied family consumption.[40] The Santanderean cultural complex, in which the basic "ethnic denominator [was] Hispanic blood," likewise promoted a "rigid class system." It made land the most important source of economic privilege.[41] This system simultaneously produced a "social quietism" because social status was based only on nature rather than achievement in the ever-expansive economic market. The Negroid complex, dominated by a "black biological denominator," was closer to nature than to reason and thus lacked the entrepreneurship required for a market economy.[42]

Gutiérrez de Pineda, however, proposed the Antioquian complex, with Bogotá as an urban center, as the answer to the economic obstacles perceived in the rest of the nation. The region marked by this culture was home to a universal society that could consolidate proper economic democracy. Antioquia's land tenure system had historically been defined by "private small-scale landownership."[43] Only weakly connected to Spanish colonial traditions, Antioqueños developed a natural strategy and mentality of small-scale landownership. This produced two of the most important social conditions for a market-driven economy. First, social relationships were defined not by wage labor but by independent landowning entrepreneurs who relied on not the elites but their own human and material capital. Second, land in itself was not the yardstick of wealth and status; hard work, economic initiative, and innovation were the means to achieve and maintain social prestige. This culture therefore developed a notion of entrepreneurship tied to individuals who could freely enter into the market and thereby define themselves as economic beings. This Antioqueño culture produced a rare yet universal case of economic democracy in a land dominated by "the traditional Latin latifundio."[44]

But if all these social actors belonged to the same nation, she pondered, why did only specific actors and regions want economic democracy and middle-classness? For the anthropologist, the answer lay in the dialectical relationship between the economy, cultural conditions, and biological traits that shaped each region. Culture had foundational powers to explain the economy, and the economy had foundational power to shape culture. Gutiérrez de Pineda associated distinct notions of masculinity and femininity within geographical regions with the conditions "productive" of an entrepreneurial economy. The anthropologist argued that in the economic system of the Andean complex, men from the laboring classes with an "indigenous background" developed a "frustrated machismo" that, at best, alienated them from economic productivity and, at worst, destined them to an eternal, feminine passivity in the pursuit of wealth. This cultural situation, furthermore, produced economic stagnation, masculine quietism that linked economic success to religious mores and thus placed it beyond human action.[45] "When you go and see these peasants seated under the shadow in the middle of the day without a job," she wrote, "they are waiting for the corn harvest to come. . . . as an individual excuse for their immediate economic problems such as the lack of food on the table, they answer stoically: 'God does not want us to eat today.'"[46] Such dependence on religion produced a "cultural reluctance" to searching for wealth and accumulating human capital, perpetuating instead an unmasculine "anorexic desire" averse to economic and social change.

But the oligarchs also lacked proper masculinity. A masculine quietism blocked economic and entrepreneurial democracy in both the Andean and Santanderean complexes; as a legacy of colonialism, economic rights and privileges were inherited rather than accomplished. The neo-Hispanic men of Santander possessed a "physical machismo"—a "Latin machismo, Mexican machismo"—that destroyed the human capital of rationality and planning needed for economic development. This machismo, the "genesis of underdevelopment" that became increasingly accentuated the further down one went on Santander's social ladder, promoted irrationality, violent defense of authority, and "unproductive" rebellion.[47] The men in Santander were closer to nature than to culture; as a consequence, they developed a physical machismo that represented only an "imminent force of a brutal primitivism."[48]

Such physical machismo was problematic, but it was better than the "sexual or biological machismo" of the "Negroid complex." Here, Gutiérrez de Pineda theorized, religion was so loose that rules of discipline, organization, productivity, and planning were absent. Religion celebrated a lazy masculinity, and it was only in carnivals that black men released their "natural instincts." The historical black resistance in the region, the isolation of black cultures, the lack of education and teaching, and the lack of contact with Western culture meant that these men could develop only an economically unproductive masculinity. Black men, as improper men, were conquered and driven by natural and sexual desires. Their masculinity was antieconomic, even anticultural. Whatever human capital their bodies possessed—desires, intellect, physical energy, emotions—was wasted in sexual gratification.[49]

In contrast to these improper masculinities, Antioquia and Bogotá were the hope for consolidating proper economic, masculine, and entrepreneurial democracy. Unlike the Andean complex, the Antioqueño region lacked a strong indigenous element. A struggle between indigenous groups and "white blood" had led to the former's decimation, in both number and culture. Likewise, black "culture and biology" were only marginal and waiting to be incorporated into the dominant culture.[50] Therefore, the region had developed an economic identity defined by a "subculture" of "white blood."[51] This biological and cultural situation both explained and was explained by the region's particular historical and religious development. Antioquia had left behind the "natural stage" that still marked the Negroid complex sometime during the late colonial period and the early nineteenth century. And Antioquia, even if people in both regions presumably believed in the same god, lacked the enervating religion of the Andean and Santanderean complexes, instead creating men with "a blind faith in the individual, freedom of the human being, and development of human capital." Revising Weber's theories of religious and economic modernity, Gutiérrez de Pineda linked this historical development of middle-class qualities to Catholicism, not Protestantism. This Catholic work ethic viewed economic success and power as a way to secure a place in society and heaven.[52]

One of the most important cultural reasons for this positive religion was the Antioquian complex's "cathartic machismo," which could regulate the "cultural imperfection" and "primary [natural] desires" that drove the machismos elsewhere in Colombia. It could also energize and "sublimate" the productivity of the masculine body, whose "natural aggressiveness" Antioqueño men developed not to destroy but to conquer and dominate their environment.[53] This cathartic masculinity allowed middle-class men to engage in industrialization, mining, and entrepreneurship in search of wealth.[54] The right to rule in economic democracy should be exercised, Gutiérrez de Pineda concluded, neither by feminized oligarchs nor by improperly masculine indigenous popular classes but by an economically productive middle-class man who—thanks to his cultural, biological, regional, and psychological conditions—could generate a properly masculine entrepreneurial democracy.

A State for a Market-Driven Economy

These transnationally shared social classifications and hierarchical definitions of democracy were potent discourses pivotal for the political economy and political rationality promoted by development programs such as the Alliance during the late 1950s and 1960s. The FN administrations sought to implement a series of development policies to strengthen the small and medium industries thought necessary to industrialize the nation. Although among policymakers in the United States and Colombia there were major differences about how to pursue agrarian reform, during the early 1960s ECLAC and FN policymakers agreed on the need to promote a state-led industrialization framework via trade protectionism, financing and direct public involvement in industrial ventures, and affordable credit for small-business owners.[55]

Thus ECLAC advised FN policymakers to expand credit programs in order to create the conditions for the small-business ownership that would act as the engine of industrialization and democratization. Small-business owners would move society away from the feudal, antimodern, and technologically backward economy of the latifundio while avoiding the urban, modern, technologically advanced, yet economically isolated large industries. Contrary to what they counseled in other countries, ECLAC contended that in Colombia large industries would not be able to offer employment to those peasants who migrated to cities in the hope of finding better opportunities, which would further expand the chasm between society's two extremes. Small and medium industries would be able to employ these migrant peasants, integrating them by fostering a proper social equilibrium while simultaneously shifting industrialization away from monopolization by the privileged few.[56]

Furthermore, small and medium industries could promote better standards of living and new consumption patterns.

The commission and the DNP wrote the ten-year plan for economic development adopted under the Alliance in 1961 with these notions of industrialization in mind. Earlier that same year, the Popular Bank (BP) and DNP had initiated conversations with US development offices to launch a coordinated credit program for small and medium industries. In November, these two Colombian institutions contracted the Stanford Research Institute to develop a detailed study of small and medium industries and recommendations for the role that these industries could play in Colombia's economy. Eugene Staley, Robert Wesley Davenport, and Richard Morse, experts whom Alliance development offices often hired, met several times with Colombian government representatives and public and private credit institutions.[57] They agreed that Colombia needed "special development programs to accelerate the growth of modern, efficient, and competitively viable small and medium firms in appropriate manufacturing lines."[58] After over a hundred visits and extensive field surveys of small and medium industries throughout the country during the early 1960s, the consultants reported that, unlike any other country in Latin America, Colombia presented the ideal economic conditions for further development of said programs. They concluded that the small and medium industry sector was an integral and dynamic element in the nation's economic growth.[59] Such good news, the consultants told the FN's policymakers, should serve to further strengthen the role of small and medium industries in achieving not only industrialization—by diversifying productive activity, meeting product demands, substituting imported manufactures, and providing new employment opportunities—but also the economy's democratization, by encouraging entrepreneurial talent as the engine of a middle-class society.[60]

And yet Staley, Davenport, and Morse also issued a warning. They informed Eduardo Nieto Calderón, the BP's general manager, that these favorable conditions could make creating such a middle-class society all the more "problematic."[61] In an epistolary exchange that accompanied the production of their report, the Stanford economists told different high-level officials at Colombian credit institutions that, although financial support could be available for the country, Colombia was perhaps not ready for a democracy defined by the entrepreneurial values key to an economy centered on small and medium industries.[62] In their factory visits, they encountered small-business owners who had developed "traditional, anti-innovative economic attitudes." Invoking countless transnational studies, the Stanford researchers voiced wariness as to whether Colombian small-business owners could develop a "democratic financial literacy." Staley, Davenport, and Morse contended that a "spirit [and] talent for entrepreneurship" were underdeveloped. Thus the Colombian entrepreneur's personality and psychological makeup could potentially jeopardize the whole effort to give a greater economic role and more vigorous impetus to small and medium industry. Colombia's small businessman, the Stanford economists insisted, had neither the preparation nor the willingness to become a "market-driven man."[63]

These preoccupations shaped the recommendations offered by the US government, private international foundations, Colombian state and private institutions, and international universities and led to the expansion of at least four major financing and counseling initiatives (what soon would be referred to as industrial extension programs) during the 1960s. First, from 1962 on the BP developed a program offering financing and training opportunities for small and medium industries. Second, CCAIM, which since the early 1930s had focused on rural and mining financing programs, opened an industrial credit program for small and medium businesses, combining credit and technical assistance. Third, these two programs worked in tandem with already existing financing programs that earlier had focused only on large-scale industries but now, with pressure from the FN and the Alliance, focused on providing credit to small and medium industries. Fourth, the Central Bank of Colombia (BR) and IFI opened credit programs for small and medium industries.[64]

Of particular importance was the National Service of Learning (SENA), a state educational institution founded in 1957 that provided financial training and industrial schooling to those selected as beneficiaries of state financial support during the 1960s. Likewise, the Colombian Institute of Administration (INCOLDA)—a private, purportedly "apolitical" organization started in 1959 and sponsored by the National Association of Industrialists (ANDI), the OAS, and USAID—provided seminars, workshops, and orientations in management theories to those who, by receiving financial support and creating new industries, were becoming the nation's "economic leaders." The Institute for Technological Investigation and the Latin American Institute for Agricultural Merchandising were important in providing small-business owners training material on marketing strategies.

Through a detailed selection process, these state offices and private institutions wanted to allocate public resources to those who could develop "the entrepreneurial talent." It is clear how those discourses discussed across the

Americas, particularly the cultural arguments forwarded by Gutiérrez de Pineda, were practiced in the state institutions' selection processes. Howard Volgenau, a representative of the US government development office, advised both the BP and CCAIM to assess not only the viability of the small and medium industries but also the specific "economic future" envisioned by the applicant. US and Colombian policymakers advised financing institutions to use their selection processes to discover an "economic conquistador . . . a man of merit and value . . . who could be pioneering, competitive, a creator, a risk-taker."[65] They must select only those proper, masculine small-business owners who had the potential to discover their own "economic desire" and then develop their "natural aggressiveness" not to destroy but to take advantage of all the opportunities offered by "pretty much a virgin market."[66]

To be eligible for state credit, applicants needed to demonstrate that they owned a small or medium industry. With some variations, these programs defined a small industry as one with gross assets below 500,000 Colombian pesos, a medium industry as one with gross assets between 500,000 and 2 million Colombian pesos. Anybody owning an industry grossing below or above these amounts would be considered, respectively, a "laboring person" and a "big businessman."[67] Thus from the outset these credit loans targeted those whom policymakers considered middle class: those who could both demonstrate "creditworthiness" compared to an imagined working class defined as lacking not only assets but also "modern financial literacy" and prove "a manifest need" for assistance, unlike the big entrepreneurs who had the economic means to develop an industry.[68] After receiving notices of candidates' initial approval, industrial extension agents, trained by US consultants, scheduled visits to family homes and factories to get a "firsthand view of the environment where the applicant develop[ed] himself."[69] These visits were meant to assess whether the applicants had the elements most important to entrepreneurship. Then the industrial extension agents wrote a report to be attached to the main application. The final decision rested with state agencies but usually followed the agents' recommendation.

Through such a selection process the state agencies, with the support and advice of US development offices and private institutions such as the Ford Foundation (FF) and the Dutch Middle-Class Bank (DMCB), wanted to discover the industries' "potential growth and viability" and evaluate small-business owners' administrative capacities, experience with credit, sense of productivity, and potential for economic success. A careful reading of the reports and recommendations suggests that transnational development programs, far from failures or smoke screens, as we tend to argue, further consolidated a classed and gendered notion of economic democracy, one that sought to materialize a middle-class small businessman as a democratic ruler in market-driven economies.

At the heart of the selection processes was the tautological legitimation of this democratic rule and its concomitant unequal distribution of resources—that is, distributing resources to certain historical actors was legitimized, allowing these subjects to think of themselves as middle-class entrepreneurs and as thus entitled to economic resources from the state. After long closed-door meetings, high-ranking state officials, US development advisers, and industrial extension agents drew on the belief that, following modernization theories, selection interviews and factory visits should evaluate the "social environment, the ecological aspects . . . the distribution of human capital, the values and attitudes, the social norms, and the social organization that encompass[ed] the behaviors and codes of conducts" of these small-business owners.[70] By identifying certain "social environments" as "economic impediments," industrial extension agents legitimated the gendered and classed distribution of resources, as all applicants were already categorized as in need of support and thus eligible for credit loans. For example, industrial extension agents argued that some applicants should not receive state monies because, although they owned small or medium industries, they had developed "an overwhelming mentality of a poor person."[71] Such a mentality encouraged the small-business owner to behave as an "economic victim," passively waiting rather than actively searching for individual improvement opportunities. Such an attitude was a cultural and psychological problem, precluding the development of an "economic ego through which men would find satisfaction in investing in their human capital to secure profit." Sentimentality drove the economic choices of these improper small-business owners, who lacked the "habit" of rational decision-making, quantification, and economic calculation. Despite their material conditions, these small-business owners were "behaving, thinking, and feeling as working-class peoples" and as such lacked the qualities of free enterprise and entrepreneurship.[72]

A second impediment was a passive, feminine attitude that manifested as a predisposition to regard financial assistance not as an economic investment in the development of new market practices and capital accumulation but instead merely as "a measure of social welfare." This feminine passivity and hesitation in the face of market forces was the product of a "socially inherent statism," an abandonment of the economic rights that small businessmen should embody in pursuit of economic productivity within the market. Such small businessmen behaved not only as working class but also as women, or at least as less than "true men . . . jeopardizing and wasting state resources" because they lacked a "new economic . . . democratic attitude."[73] Industrial extension agents lamented how some of these small-business owners, oriented more toward life's worldly pleasures, celebrated state dependency and viewed hard work, dedication, and independence as immoral, illegitimate, and antiheroic. This produced an almost indescribable type of "confusing . . . puzzling virility." These small businessmen had no economic virtue because culturally and socially they lacked "the classic trinity of economic success: innovation, risk, and competency."[74]

This feminized masculinity and déclassé behavior would provoke a third impediment: small-business owners could potentially block national industrialization and economic democratization. As economic subjects, these small-business owners, given their class deviation and gender abnormality, would act as "dependent members of society." Or as Simón González, a member of INCOLDA, put it in 1963, these small-business owners would behave as "economic victims" waiting to be helped by others rather than as entrepreneurial forces in society. As such, González insisted, these business owners looked more like working-class people because they lacked initiative, wasted their human capital, and assumed a position of "economic servitude."[75] Raised in an environment of dependency, these feminized small-business owners, troubled personalities lacking the spirit of enterprise, envisioned the state's financial support as a way to secure "immediate and quick profit," which produced perpetual economic insecurity and passivity.

We can compare these negative reports with those that celebrated certain gender and class traits embodied by those small-business owners deserving of state credit. Banco Popular and CCAIM officials described the refreshing qualities that they encountered during some of their interviews and evaluations in the field, reporting that the "entrepreneurial spirit" abounded and was manifest for all to see in several small and medium industries owned by true men.[76] These proper middle-class men actively applied their "economic will . . . and desire" by taking risks in the market; following their "economic ego," these small businessmen wanted to "conquer and dominate the market." Various reports and recommendations described such men as owners of their own economic paths, planners of their own futures, savers of their own capital, and independent masculine producers who, with audacity, bravery, and fearlessness, anticipated economic opportunities. These "true men" could develop "that masculine trait" that produced a "burning need to depend on no one but themselves." Such economic subjects would rule in a "democratic market" in which only "the best, the most capable, the most independent" triumph. As Rafael Pardo Vuelvas, one of the directors of CCAIM's financing programs, wrote in a 1965 report: "They are risk-takers par excellence. They insist on the centrality of their role. They are economically bold. They struggle every day, they overcome all odds . . . they are always willing to risk who they are to make economic development possible."[77]

Other reports elaborated on how these entrepreneurial men deserved financial support because they experienced their labor as human capital internal to their masculine self. This attitude would produce an entrepreneurial assertiveness toward life in which labor exploitation could take on a more economically productive meaning. Drawing on transnational discussions on entrepreneurship, agents described these proper, middle-class, and masculine small-business owners as the manifestation of a market-driven economy, in which the roles of exploiters and exploited would disappear with a new entrepreneurial attitude that redefined labor as a capital investment in a larger enterprise. In this market economy, labor and capital could become synonymous because small-business owners could be neither the bosses of anybody nor the workers for anybody, only "the bosses of themselves." They would accumulate capital for development not by exploiting others' labor but by investing in their own labor. In that sense, these small-business owners were seen as "the most important manifestation of democracy the world will ever see," the "missing link" between the market and democracy.[78]

Such policies and resource allocation delinked the working classes and elites from economic democracy, linked instead with a gendered notion of middle-classness. Although some of these applications are incomplete, it is clear that middle-class men, not women, were the main recipients of credit loans for small and medium industries. My research suggests that during the 1960s few, if any, businesswomen were directly granted state support for growing a small business. These disparities sprang from how economic development programs such as the Alliance further naturalized middle-class masculinity as foundational for proper economic democracy while reiterating that womanhood fundamentally could not be associated with entrepreneurship, a market-driven economy, and democracy. According to the selection policies, women embodied many feminine (or at least unmasculine) traits that would militate against the development of entrepreneurial talent. Invoking cultural explanations, some high-ranking officials argued that women harbored an "economic insecurity" that prevented them from anticipating economic opportunities created by the market. In a "social environment" in which a "vacillating personality" had been established for their gender, women could exercise neither "economic agency nor sound judgment" in the market, acculturated as they were to sentimentality rather than knowledge.[79] While recruitment policies for state professionals had categorized sentimentality as a positive feminine trait, in the selection practices for credit loans it was considered potentially fatal in moments of uncertainty and scarcity, as it prevented women from envisioning different economic choices offered by the market. This would preclude capital accumulation and, more worrisome, paralyze market forces altogether. Rather than embodying a "market personality," women would further develop a passivity and a "perpetual statism." Thus, it was argued, they were economically and culturally unfit to receive state credit loans.[80]

A Classed Market-Driven Man

As for professionals and white-collar employees, a process of schooling accompanied the allocation of credit support. The United States Agency for International Development, the UN special funds, the FF, the DMCB, Stanford University, the International Labour Organization (ILO), INCOLDA, and SENA all participated in this aspect of resource allocation presumed inevitable. USAID argued that only foreign experts should train the industrial extension agents, who would not only allocate resources but also train those small-business owners receiving state monies. After the credit was granted, state offices sent their representatives to factories to supervise on monthly or bimonthly intervals, depending on the needs of each case. In addition, small-business owners were required to participate in workshops and seminars, usually held at SENA, INCOLDA, or state credit agencies. The scattered training materials for these suggest that the most important task was creating a "market consciousness"—"to elevate the awareness of the unavoidable existence of market competition for industrialization"— among small-business owners. This task included three main educational narratives that sought to reinforce the gender and class assumptions that had led to the selection of these small-business owners in the first place: management (how to be a democratic economic leader), economic choice (how to anticipate and allocate opportunities produced by the market), and technological investment (how to use technology in service of the market).[81] Through these seminars the state sought to convert "economically dependent beings into creative and independent entrepreneurs" with passions, predispositions, and desires that ensured a properly functioning market-driven economy.[82]

This was not an attempt to release these small businessmen from state power, as one might assume, but rather an effort by the state to prepare these entrepreneurs to consent to a market-driven society, one that high-level officials, US advisers, and industrial extension agents called economic democracy. Often, these seminars began with general statements about economics, which small-business owners were told was "a matter of liberty, freedom, and choice." In evident contradiction to their selection policies, high-ranking state officials argued that "anybody in society possessed that entrepreneurial talent." But only "true men" could develop it to the market's benefit. These small-business owners were told that they, unlike elites and working classes, were economically free for two major reasons. First, and despite the fact that they were paying a state credit loan, small-business owners were seen as economically independent because "nobody"—neither the state nor society—could tell them what to do. Second, only by becoming aware of the market's existence could they develop their full potential, their economic wills and desires entering into competition for the opportunities produced by the market itself. They needed to prepare for such a market-driven society because only "the best, the most prepared, and most valuable in society" would prevail.[83] Competition would democratize economic pursuit because the market itself would create the conditions for choosing those who deserved to be chosen. In the process, the market, these small-business owners were told, could measure the qualities of democracy.

Pedagogical stories and questionnaires provided a similar political and moral narrative: intervention in the economy was unnecessary because all men possessed entrepreneurial talent, but only through democratic market competition would those most economically fit conquer economic opportunities and secure a better future. Such profits, unlike those secured by elite oligarchies, were legitimate because they were earned through (masculine) competition. One such pedagogical story, for instance, depicted the experiences of Captain Courage, who, as a small businessman, embarked on economic adventures across the sea, here a metaphor for the market.[84] Endowed with motivation, knowledge, and opportunity, Captain Courage wanted "to control the sea . . . to have the sea at [his] service," to struggle with other men, overcome obstacles, and make the right economic choices. Such manly conquest would secure a "golden prize," which in this allegory was an economic profit that only those who were "truly men" could enjoy. At first, the sea's waters were calm and thus decisions were easily made. But suddenly Capitan Courage encountered obstacles at sea, which like the market behaved unpredictably. His motivation, economic will, enthusiasm, and knowledge would be tested to "conquer" the sea again. Both his masculinity and social distinction were at stake. But such challenges needed to be embraced because Captain Courage knew that, through competition, he could master the opportunities provided by the market. Captain Courage, unlike lesser men, had as his final goal becoming somebody in life, the pleasure produced by securing a legitimate profit. In such masculine competition, Captain Courage would prevail by focusing on himself to develop self-discipline, self-governing attitudes, and self-confidence. He needed work tirelessly, to invest all the human capital available without losing sight of the competition.[85] The story's end is quite predictable. Captain Courage—practicing audacity, bravery, knowledge, and resolution—not only conquered the market but also defeated others who, perhaps due to improper masculinity, could not face the market's challenges. After all, the market, like the sea, was an uncontrollable natural force mastered by true men. From it economic profit would be earned not by family legacy, as with the elites, or as a gift, as for laboring classes, but through masculine middle-class competition, in which small-business owners would concentrate capital unequally but legitimately.

In this romance, small businessmen were economically sovereign also because they were expanding the market's role in democracies. Unlike the big-business owners—who sought to monopolize economic profit, become rich, and thus paralyze market competition—these small-business owners were schooled at perpetuating rivalry through market forces and thus providing a "paramount opportunity" for economic equilibrium. In contrast to elite reliance on ample material resources, this market competition emphasized a desire "to get better and better."[86] It was a circular proposition. The market created the conditions for competition through which "the best, the most prepared, the fittest" would prevail over those who lacked entrepreneurial talents, economic will, and self-discipline to take advantage of the market's opportunities. And yet the small businessmen needed to prevail because, unlike the economically undisciplined popular classes and the market-paralyzing elite, they secured the very conditions for a market to remain in place via their democratic self-interest. In this tautological form of legitimation, these small-business owners were taught to think of themselves as the sovereign manifestation of economic democracy.

In conclusion, the notion of the middle-class entrepreneur was imagined not as a question of wealth redistribution but rather as a way through which private property and capital accumulation could be hierarchically legitimized. A productive middle-class entrepreneur or small businessman would create the conditions for a better standard of living, better purchasing power among the laboring classes, and more labor opportunities.[87] If small-business owners secured economic profit, it was because they, as masculine entrepreneurs, had competed economically against others amid objective market conditions. They were the winners in—that is, the legitimate representatives of—the unequal distribution of wealth called democracy.

4

Beyond Capital and Labor

As several historians have demonstrated, one of the most important structural changes of the twentieth century's second half was the expansion of the service sector and its concomitant tertiarization of the economy.[1] In the late 1950s and 1960s, recent graduates from private and public universities created by these changes found new job opportunities with better salaries and new kinds of affective labor. Some such white-collar employees remember these years as the moment when they became aware of who they were, a formative experience that allowed them to become part of a middle class. Jorge Ortiz, a former white-collar employee at Compañía Colombiana de Seguros (Colseguros), recalled his luck in getting "such an amazing job." After majoring in accounting at the Instituto Nacional de Contadores Públicos (INCP), he realized in his new job that he was a "true member of the middle class," as he found "people like [himself] who had the same interests, preoccupations, and goals." He then expanded on why laboring in offices meant "mov[ing] society forward." He was eager to say that he secured his job not by luck but by "preparation . . . hard work, effort . . . [and] intelligence." Speaking in the early 2000s, when Álvaro Uribe Vélez had recently come to power via an antiunion discourse, Ortiz also felt that people like himself—white-collar employees who had "worked all [their] lives"—represented "democracy at its best." In contrast to an imagined bureaucratized union member who gained material benefits with *palancas,* he, a middle-class man, had prepared himself to be somebody in life. To prove this, Ortiz proudly told a story about how he conquered fear, difficulty, and the always-present possibility of failure to secure "a well-deserved position in life."

> I would not be middle class without Colseguros. . . . I loved getting up in the mornings and going to my office. . . . People looked at you when you entered those beautiful buildings. . . . We were hardworking people . . . people from a good class. . . . [In] companies like Colseguros, only the best made the cut. . . . My philosophy in life is this: you work hard every day, you do not bite the hand that feeds you . . . and you stay out of trouble. That is why I do not like unions, they make a mess. . . . They want everything handed to them. . . . My philosophy of life does not allow me to side with unions. . . . Unions are antidemocratic.[2]

These classed and gendered memories raise critical questions about white-collar employees during the late 1950s and 1960s. Where did Ortiz find inspiration for his philosophy of life? Why did he think that an office job could secure a gendered middle-class status? Why was the contrast with labor unions so important to his story of individual success? And why did he think that his classed and gendered experience during the twentieth century's second half epitomized democracy?

As historians and social scientists of Latin America have relocated historical explanations to the realm of the political and cultural, class as an identity linked to labor has become nearly obsolete as a useful category of analysis. Indeed, when labor is reclaimed as legitimate for historical interpretation, it is usually coupled with an effort to historicize the industrial sector's consolidation and the working classes' social experiences. We continue to assume that labor must be located in the formal relations of production between the proletariat and bourgeoisie.[3] James P. Brennan contends that it is important "to widen labor history beyond the issues of identity and political culture," though "the object of study should be nothing more and nothing less than the many industrial worlds of modern Latin America."[4] Therefore, historians tend to deem the middle classes residual in questions of labor because of their ambiguous relationship with what is considered from the outset as the objective structural conditions of economic production. Or else the middle classes appear as proper topics of labor history when experiencing proletarianization. Meanwhile, most recent studies of the Latin American middle classes have focused more on consumption than on labor. We see middle-classness and labor almost as

Figure 4.1 The gendered tranquility of the office. Ca. 1960s, Colseguros Offices, COLARCH.

irreconcilable because we assume that the working classes *labor* while the middle classes *consume*.[5]

But as Rachel Heiman, Mark Liechty, and Carla Freeman have argued, we need to expand what counts as labor to include what these anthropologists call, following Michael Hardt and Antonio Negri as well as a critical genealogy of feminist theories, affective labor.[6] Drawing on their approach, this chapter offers critical insights for understanding one of the labor market's major structural transformations in post-1950 Bogotá: the expansion of the service sector, with its implications for the intimate relationships between service as labor/commodity, class subjectivities, gendered hierarchies, and a dominant definition of democracy. The chapter locates the service sector at the Alliance's core to elucidate the pivotal role that its new labor and management practices played in shaping Cold War politics in Colombia. I examine the experiences at four service companies in Bogotá—Colseguros, an insurance company; Caja de Compensación Familiar (CAFAM), a family compensation fund; Aerovías Nacionales de Colombia (AVIANCA), an airline company; and the BR—during the late 1950s and 1960s, when the FN sought to usher in a new era of labor peace through social, economic, and labor programs.[7] By reading management theories, hiring policies, job requirements, and training workshop documentation across these service companies, I demonstrate how "productive" these programs were in linking the service sector to a specific gendered middle-class subject. I read the technology of classification that these policies produced to unearth different class rubrics and normative gender notions that established office service as an "obvious" manifestation of middle-class labor and thus a representation of democracy. In the process, new forms of affective labor were defined as part of middle-class subjectivities, while physical/material labor was yet again associated with working-class "realities." These social policies, sponsored by the Alliance and put into practice by private service-sector employers, empowered certain historical subjects to think of themselves as middle class and representatives of a specific definition of democracy.

The *Empleado:* "The Most Valuable Individual in Modern Democracies"

The Alliance's political rationalities of rule mediated the service sector's expansion with new labor relations policies, just as the sector's expansion generated new discourses shaping hiring policies, training ideas, and managerial strategies. In a context of political anxiety, social scientists provided an explanation for why labor relationships were moving from factories (industrial sector) to office spaces (service sector). Some policymakers and scholars insisted that the fundamental struggle between capital and labor needed to be rethought. Mental labor (associated during the twentieth century's first half with office work) would democratize labor relationships and triumph over "dual societies," with their struggles between labor and capital, factory worker and employer, and peasant and landowner. If the entrepreneur would restructure the very relationship between capital and labor, and the professional would harmonize it, the service sector's expansion would exemplify proper modernization. These structural changes would, scholars and policymakers hoped, change Colombia from a society of workers and peasants to one of independent white-collar office employees. Neither workers nor capitalists "in the traditional nineteenth-century sense," these office employees would represent democracy because their labor was a form of capital and their capital a form of labor. By defining capital as everything that could become a source of future income, these policymakers and scholars framed office employees as those who could make labor a question of investment in human properties. These modernization thinkers argued that Marx had it all wrong: capitalism would not "impoverish and expropriate until nothing [was] left but vast masses of the 'exploited proletariat' and a mere handful of 'exploiters.'"[8] Rather, the service sector would strengthen an "educated society" in which independent office employees invested in their own human resources, the most important source of capital accumulation. Because their labor was fundamentally a form of capital investment, office employees could not be exploited by outside capitalists. Thus they were not, by definition, workers. Rather, they were capitalists themselves, in perpetual need of investing in their own labor. In this circular argument, scholars imagined a social democracy in which office employees would not be alienated from their own labor, as workers had been in the past, but rather would be at the same time exploiters and laborers in accumulating their own human capital. It was such "growth of human capital" that according to Theodore W. Schultz—the original theorist of the concept, who, as we have seen, was intimately involved in Alliance development discourses—had transformed laborers into capitalists, generating the "productive superiority . . . of economic systems" in "technically advanced countries" by freeing employees from the "hard, manual work" that rendered them dependent on income based on property.[9] Thus, during the 1960s some modernization thinkers associated a notion of the democratic labor relationship with the structural changes in the tertiary economy, the consolidation of white-collar labor, and the superiority of the West.

It is tempting to accuse these scholars of ignoring the realities of the capital-labor struggle in the Americas in their effort to stop communism's spread and political radicalization. In a way, they did. The productivity of their ideas, however, proved pivotal in US policy toward Latin America in development programs as well as the hiring and training of those women and men laboring in the service sector. This body of scholarship produced a teleological notion of democracy based on a hierarchical stratification between the economy's three sectors.[10] Atop this hierarchy—which all societies would have when they became democratic—was a consolidated service sector, associated with the office as a place of labor/capital accumulation. Second was the industrial sector, with the factory as its milieu. This sector was viewed, in part, as an obstacle to democracy because its constitutive labor relationship was an everlasting struggle between workers and capital. At the hierarchy's bottom was the agricultural sector, whose paradigm was the hacienda system, the fundamental colonial relic. This sector was democracy's antithesis, the hacienda reflecting the most unproductive labor relationship of all: a two-class system marked by unending struggle between landowners and landless peasants.

Thus these scholars made the service sector and tertiarization synonymous with democratization because of their new labor relationship, within which the white-collar employee was neither capitalist nor worker but a kind of *laborer-capitalist* who owned his own human capital by privileging knowledge over physical energy, mental work over unproductive manual labor, and constructed intellect over inherent physical features. Luis Ratinoff, a sociologist based in Bogotá and Buenos Aires, argued in the mid-1960s that "in Latin America the source of modernization [had] by definition been from without," which meant that "the social structure of the economy tend[ed] to employ preferably the physical effort in the agricultural and industrial sectors . . . and only in a very marginal way the development of other human intellectual potentialities for the accumulation of the human capital."[11]

Because of its putatively democratic character, the tertiary sector was defined as a social terrain in which a particular gendered and classed subject would become the laborer-capitalist. The sector thus had to be reserved for "only the intellectually fittest, most economically productive, mentally competent human beings of the society."[12] Robert C. Williamson, a sociologist at Lehigh University affiliated with UNAL's Faculty of Sociology, undertook field research, sponsored by various international institutions and US universities, to demonstrate why the white-collar employee represented "the least known but most valuable individual in modern democracies."[13] In his ethnographically detailed yet unpublished notes on Colombia, Williamson argued that although appropriate human resources were lacking, white-collar office employees represented a new "Colombian reality" that could first overcome traditional labor relations and then restructure the appropriate "utilization of the intellectual capacities" in a country overwhelmed by violence. Interviewing male and female employees in offices, homes, and places of leisure, the sociologist classified only those with a "middle-class background" as "the type of persons" who would "find [themselves] at home" in the service sector. This was because, on the one hand, the oligarchs had historically identified intellectual pursuits with leisure time rather than labor and, on the other, mental labor had no place in peasants' and workers' experience of work.[14] The peasantry's methods were archaic and simple, and the unskilled laborer could survive in a factory job with "little education." For a poor Colombian, furthermore, "excess of knowledge [did] not immediately contribute to his well-being and could actually prove to be detrimental . . . unnecessary and costly to carry around."[15] For these cultural and social reasons, peasants and workers were by definition unfit to participate in the democratization of labor relationships.

Other scholars further developed this classification of the service sector as epitomizing social democracy. Explaining the structural tension between agricultural development, industrialization, and service-sector expansion, Aaron Lipman argued that only the most intelligent and masculine could "survive" in a service-driven economy. The sociologist attempted to demonstrate how mental labor and not physical labor, white-collar office employees and not factory workers, intellectual virility and not physical passivity would be required to produce a more "masculine . . . muscular economy."[16] By comparing rural and urban places, he tautologically argued that a "muscular democracy" was possible through the normalization of intellectual labor, and that intellectual labor was only possible by consolidating such a muscular democracy. At the center of this tautology, he located the white-collar office employee as the historical subject who could link masculine democracy with intellectual labor.[17]

Lipman attempted to understand why, unlike in the United States, where everyone was presumably searching for an office job, in Colombia some historical actors preferred to identify as peasants and workers. Through seemingly contradictory comparisons, he wanted to demonstrate how, unlike white-collar office employees, peasants were passive, perhaps even feminine, men whose "labor attitude" was alien to intellectual labor and, by definition, the service sector. Unfamiliar with urban settings, almost feminine in their dependency on land and landowners, and yet culturally driven by violent masculinity, peasants would be "out of place [in the] orderly office." Peasants emphasized physical prowess, their "masculine role" consisting of the ability to manipulate "concrete entities such as tools and animals" and thus privileging "brute strength, toughness, and physical endurance."[18] This peasant idea of society, Lipman concluded, was fundamentally opposed to the urbanized service sector, where "a masculine tenderness" among white-collar employees was paramount in a society in which intellectual skills were consistent with democratic labor relationships.[19]

Other scholars argued that office labor provided opportunities for an ideal family, in which men and women could perform specific roles equally important for democratic society's emergence. Some anthropologists and sociologists—particularly María Cristina Salazar, Virginia Gutiérrez de Pineda, and Lucy M. Cohen—argued that (as Salazar put it) such "balanced and harmonious social relations" could create the conditions needed to overcome La Violencia.[20] Office labor could also generate equality among the sexes. Men in this labor displayed "manly values" through "taking care of the family . . . wife and children." They avoided unproductive activities such as gambling and other "rough masculine pursuits" and instead favored the productive "manliness" of an orderly family life. Therefore, office employees were seen as belonging to a proper masculine space—the service sector—that could develop social democracy by moving society away from unmasculine tasks such as factory work and land labor.[21]

This preoccupation with gender also shaped the discussion of female office women. Social scientists saw the service sector as the ideal place for not only creating new labor relationships but also constituting harmonious relations, a middle ground, between home-work and office-labor. They compared peasant and working-class families, typified by antidemocratic male-female relationships, to white-collar, middle-class ones, elevated to represent the gender ideal of the democratic labor relationship. Labor studies, statistical analyses, and ethnographic work emphasized the need for middle-class women to participate in the service sector, the area of the economy ideal for them. For instance, María Cristina Salazar, a Catholic University of America–trained sociologist and a representative of the ILO in Colombia, reported to her labor organization that, after her research in certain public and private offices, it was clear that "the future of the Colombian woman [was] in [those] offices . . . in this sector where women [were] particularly more active." Indeed, Salazar went so far as to declare the office sector "the future of democratic relations among the sexes."[22] Women were able to be "exceptional [office] workers . . . next to the great men" while at the same time working at home to ensure clean homes, well-fed families, and morally upright children.[23] They were thus fundamentally different from peasant and working-class women, who had "extremely dysfunctional families" in which there was either "too much female authority . . . or too much masculine [authority]"; such families were marred by the growing realities of common-law unions, single mothers, and male irresponsibility. In contrast, Salazar asserted that the new reality of women working next to men in offices created a middle point for shared authority among the sexes, both at home and at work. It is clear, therefore, that participation in the service sector enthroned women's moral authority. In a word, white-collar women embodied values that would lead society away from the antidemocratic and violent struggle between capital and labor.[24]

The Expansion of the Service Sector

In a context of political anxiety about the radicalization of society and potential labor unrest in the late 1950s and early 1960s (some bank and airline employees had sporadically protested), policymakers, private employers, and scholars alike worried that the expansion of the service sector would bring "the vulgarization of the office" into a place where "dubious, old-fashioned, and traditional influences" would want to organize labor relations and society according to a "rivalry of interests, divisions, and disagreement."[25] Thus as the service sector expanded, private service-sector employers increasingly appropriated the transnational discourses on the relationship between the middle class, service labor, and democracy to respond to these political preoccupations.[26] As an executive director of Colseguros anxiously put it in 1961, "Unless [the vulgarization of the office] is soon to be taken care of . . . productivity will be a reality of the past, efficiency will vanish, expertise will be difficult to find [and] social disharmony will return. . . . workers bound in traditionalism will fill offices across the nation, producing a cataclysm of major proportions. . . . Our empleados will look like workers."[27]

At first blush, one could argue that this political preoccupation was another example of how certain service employers wanted to "protect" the office from communist infiltration. In one sense, that was the case. But reading against and along the grain of the records for the service companies Colseguros, CAFAM, AVIANCA, and the BR—executive board minutes, personnel CVs, job entrance exams, personality tests, psychological interviews, and training material—also suggests that a political rationality underwrote service employers' larger effort to implement a form of scientific and administrative management as well as theories of labor relations.[28] Private employers further embraced what they considered pathbreaking scientific ideas about how to organize "democratic office places where men and women serve the interests of national progress."[29] Service companies took advantage of the Alliance's labor programs; they forged close ties with US development offices, Colombian universities, and a number of international institutions. In 1963, for instance, the UNIANDES economics department received funds from USAID to contract the University of Minnesota to provide advanced training for its faculty members to develop graduate programs in business and economics. The Instituto Colombiano de Administración contracted Syracuse University for a similar program.[30] Harvard, Stanford, Syracuse, PUJ, INCOLDA, and UNIANDES worked in tandem with several service companies to apply a diversity of theories on human relations and administrative management.

Across the four service companies under study, the sources of inspiration for these theories were quite eclectic. Chester Barnard and his theories of cooperation and loyalty in organizations, proposed in the 1930s, became an inspiration for thinking through labor relations beyond conflict and struggle.[31] Abraham Maslow's hierarchy of psychological needs, offered in the 1940s, would be applied to measure "job satisfaction" in service companies.[32] The Systems School of the 1960s was used to see companies as bureaucratic families in which each member performed a specific, gendered role. Early iterations of total quality theories became common currency in those companies, which began to follow the motto "The customer is always right."[33] These administrative management theories were joined to behavioral studies, labor psychology, psychoanalysis, cultural anthropology, and the sociology of affective and service labor. Psychology and psychoanalysis would provide the tools to discover "what [was] behind the human mind."[34] Sociology would help to understand how "the human man . . . [was] a social animal [and] thus behave[d] according to specific social norms in which he [was] raised."[35] Political science would explain "the interests at heart among human beings" to predict how "new elements of the organization" would behave. And anthropology would provide a "cultural approach" to uncover behaviors according to "family patterns, upbringing arrangements, [and] childhood education."[36] In this way service-sector companies sought to create recruitment policies that revealed the ideas, values, sentiments, and understandings of those applying for office jobs. The overall task was to discover "the best qualities in all future members . . . [and] servers in our company." Following the advice of experts from the OAS and the UN, recruiters aimed to dissect "people's propensities for conflict . . . inclinations to disorderly behavior . . . and tendencies to disagreement," traits that could potentially "vulgarize office spaces."[37]

It was this combination of new management theories and social science knowledge that produced detailed yet contradictory processes of selection and schooling in service companies. These new processes worked as a technology of classification and discipline through which private employers sought to materialize a specific gendered and classed definition of who was best suited to labor—or to *serve*, following the language of the moment— in the service sector. Indeed, through these new recruitment policies and discipline practices, the service sector—and the office as the foundational spatial symbol of this labor—was cordoned off as belonging to an "adequate" people with specific class and gender traits.[38]

Who, then, was to be selected to be part of the service sector and save the office from becoming a "vulgar" (i.e., factory-like) labor space? Who was to embody the so-called laborer-capitalist and thus represent social democracy? Who was to redefine labor relations away from that of capital and labor? Although these new human resources offices were confident about the "scientific value" of this selection process, they struggled to select those they thought "adequate people."[39] Service employers preferred men and women with an "urban upbringing," who they believed would be more familiar "with the modern world."[40] That urban upbringing was usually associated with formal university preparation for the candidates and their immediate families. Service companies, unlike state recruitment offices, privileged candidates from private rather than public universities, as they believed that those who came from the former developed "understanding as a philosophy of life" while those from the latter had "strong tendencies" for involvement in social conflicts. Graduates from public institutions tended to follow "demagogic and foreign ideas," which made them unsuitable for overcoming the divide between capital and labor: rather, as representatives of a "working-class background," they had "appetites for social conflict" and thus most likely would promote "class struggle in peaceful offices."[41]

Service companies tried to avoid the office's vulgarization by hiring "capable women."[42] Although men increasingly participated in the service sector, women's participation in the tertiary sector significantly expanded compared to other sectors of the economy.[43] Unlike the exclusionary policies for credit loans to small-business owners, service companies believed that female employees could well represent social democracy because they could overcome the tensions between labor and capital. Replicating María Cristina Salazar's arguments about female office employment as a manifestation of equality of the sexes, job advertisements invited women to apply to the service sector as "the best place for women to be."[44] One journalistic account intended for an unnamed major Colombian newspaper described Colseguros as not only a pioneering insurance company in the country but also a job creator, one that had opened countless opportunities for "young, accomplished . . . well-prepared women . . . ready to enter into the workplace."[45] Carlos Echeverri Ángel, the company's president, argued that Colseguros had long foretold women's emancipation in Colombia (women had gained the right to vote in 1957). For Colseguros, argued the president, "women [were] capable of doing whatever they want[ed] to do." And

Colseguros, as a service company, had opened the labor market to Colombian women because

> our women have been the consciousness of economic progress and modernity. . . . Long before women were granted the vote, Colseguros knew that women had to be main participants in progressive labor relations . . . in new places where people find themselves serving a nation. We are the first service company to allow women into the office. [Women] generate a consciousness about the importance of service. . . . they have the human wit, the creative imagination, and the audacity to carry out all the services we provide.[46]

On its surface, this account would lead us to conclude that, as a result of modernization, occupational diversification, and educational opportunities, women began to play a more visible role in the service sector, particularly in office labor. But Echeverri Ángel's account also raises two interrelated questions: In the context of the Alliance, why did service companies celebrate women as those who could embody the laborer-capitalist and remove the office from the struggle between capital and labor? And what specific definition of women did private employers have in mind when linking the service sector with democracy?

All human resources offices spent time discussing women's role in the service sector. They all agreed that it was "the problem of modern life," which they had to treat with a "soft touch."[47] Some private service companies insisted that they should hire young single women because serving in offices should supplement, rather than interfere with, women's main task: the creation of a family, the "most important societal institution of all."[48] But this could also open opportunities for "working women" to take over office jobs. According to Colseguros's, important but unnamed anthropologists and sociologists had demonstrated how working-class women in Colombia had developed neither attachment to nor affection for "family dynamics." Among them family "as an institution [was] of no importance," and thus their happiness did not depend on "familial values, and home-driven concerns." Therefore, Colseguros's human resources office concluded that for working-class women it was less difficult to leave their "children alone . . . and their husbands unattended" to secure a job.[49] Colseguros reasoned that if they hired married women, then most likely working-class women would apply for office jobs, women from different social backgrounds (i.e., the middle class) finding it difficult, if not impossible, to abandon their families.[50]

As a product of these discussions, service employers tended to privilege single, young, and presumably middle-class women to defend society's "moral, spiritual, and family values." For these service companies, hiring married women with children was "inconceivable," as this could mean abandonment of the women's domestic responsibilities.[51] Recruitment policies conversely underscored the "need" to hire married men, meant to associate the service sector with a vision of social democracy represented by the heterosexual middle-class family. Once again anthropological and sociological studies came in handy, used to legitimize working-class men's exclusion from the service sector. If working-class women had less difficulty leaving their families unattended, working-class men would follow suit because "there [was] no woman to go . . . to visit . . . to protect . . . to take care of." Therefore, for working-class men it was "normal . . . and common" to have "disorganized families [in which] wives and husbands" left children unattended. In contrast, society's "educated and cultured" members were wise enough to negotiate the "realities of the modern world" and protect the family's sanctity. Thus human resources offices assumed that married and educated men, raised in an environment where family values mattered, would protect their families. And, presumably unlike working-class men, they could dedicate themselves to supporting their families without needing "women's work."[52]

These human resources offices also privileged married men because they were thought "more responsible" than single men, who tended to be "less productive, less loyal, and more inclined to labor conflicts." But service companies also privileged married men because, it was assumed, they needed a job to support a family. Thus as employees they would exercise "self-restraint, productivity, and organization." Furthermore, hiring married men—as the representatives of a proper masculinity in the service sector—would dissuade women from entering the labor market. As Colseguros described the benefit of this, "behind a successful man . . . there [was] always a beautiful woman. Behind that associate, there [was] a married man, behind that associate [was] a father. An associate in our company can have it all—a family, a great job, and tranquility in life."[53]

This classed and gendered vision of the office—and more broadly of the service sector—as a heteropatriarchal space was further legitimized through the constant association of service and middle-class femininity. A cursory reading of the psychological exams and entrance tests for the four companies under discussion here suggests this clearly. Religious discussions, "cultural arguments," and "scientific" opinions on biology were combined to assign a classed and gendered role to middle-class women. Some service companies—such as CAFAM, with its Catholic background—argued that service—or what the company called the task of "assisting others"—was women's "God-given attribute." As such, middle-class women were chosen to contribute to this service company's mission to "protect and defend the Colombian family."[54] Other companies assumed that women's "innate . . . burning need to serve others" was the product of nature. Colseguros argued that middle-class women exemplified service to others because "that service thing . . . being a servant, being attentive to others . . . to exercise great care of others" was more suitable to "delicate, fine, and caring female bodies."[55] Other companies, such as AVIANCA, thought these "feminine traits" not innate or biological but rather culturally and socially formed.[56] All the same, women, as part of a proper cultural upbringing, had learned to "care for others . . . to serve others . . . to have patience . . . to offer sympathy."[57]

As women increased their participation and visibility in the service sector during the late 1950s and early 1960s, these associations between middle-class femininity and office service perpetuated a hierarchical definition of social democracy through which middle-class women became the classed and gendered superiors to working-class women. Through this hierarchization private service companies erased the labor of middle-class women because, unlike working-class women, they were serving rather than working. They were investing the gendered human capital they owned as "service talents" in the office. They were capitalizing their female human properties accumulated in years of proper gendered education. They were serving, rather than working, because their work in the service sector was an extension of their "obligations and duties"—whether God-given, biologically distinctive, or culturally created—within heterosexual families. The "natural impulsiveness" of mothers to take care of children at home could be capitalized into "unparalleled spontaneity" in the service of company clients. The daily "problem-solving talents" needed to manage a home could be invested into "managerial talents" when serving in the office. And that sense of "recovery" that women felt at home after an exhausting day of child-rearing could be converted into an "endurance quality" for facing difficult challenges in the office. The "sacrifices" that women made at home for family survival would be capitalized into "endurance . . . patience . . . [and] knowledge" in performing the most important task of all in service companies: satisfying the customer, who was "always right."[58] Or as an entrance workshop brochure for CAFAM put it in 1965, "when women offer their services it seems that they are not working, they do it almost effortlessly, as they just want to satisfy a demanding client."[59]

Middle-class women could thus become a laborer-capitalist and represent democratic labor relationships in the service sector. Middle-class women were associated with specific gendered traits that would prevent the office from becoming a place of "disagreement . . . struggle . . . divergence." Cultural approaches legitimized a vision in which, as described in recruitment employment policies, women, unlike men, were defined by "submission . . . and little interest in political questions." Such gendered attributes would help "democratize" the workplace because women would never "say no to an order given by a superior" because "disrespect for authority [was] not part of a woman's anatomy."[60] Despite worry that hiring married women would vulgarize the office, some service companies contemplated hiring them in the belief that they, unlike single women, could be more submissive and loyal. Here we see an important contradiction. Service companies thought that hiring married women meant the destruction of the middle-class heteropatriarchal vision that the service sector should represent. Yet that notion of social democracy—or, in the language of service employers, democratic labor relationships—needed to be safeguarded by married women, who, according to the "latest psychology treatises," were more "reliable . . . responsible and less guided by politics."[61] Despite this seeming contradiction, or because of it, service companies were preoccupied with discovering and measuring the compliance that middle-class female employees would presumably bring. The task was clear: to find "the feminine submissiveness . . . and docility" necessary to prevent the emergence of a capital-labor relationship in the office.[62]

Becoming White-Collar Employees

During the 1960s, this economy of classification was further institutionalized in the service sector through a meticulous process of schooling. Companies' archives are packed with training material: advising manuals on how to be female and male collaborators, handbooks on theories of human relations in office spaces, stories of successful team members, and multitudinous minutes for workshops on how to be "democratic members of families devoted to service." Archives also contain a plethora of company management theory slogans, stickers describing the pride of belonging to a company, tapes recording ideas about office service, and countless Christmas cards issued to the "true owners of the company." At first blush, one might say that the existence of such documentation speaks to how comprehensive and calculating this process of schooling was. It was no doubt intense. But it was because both recruitment practices and schooling efforts were fragile that service companies kept offering more training. This process was as much about disciplining as it was about empowering certain historical actors as gendered and classed representatives of social democracy.

This teaching material shared certain narratives. The factory and its working-class laborer were delineated as the other to the "collaborator in office spaces." Fictional stories in such training materials contrasted collaborators who served in "clean ... harmonious offices" with workers laboring in "dirty ... grotesque" factories with "rebellious, undisciplined, and discordant" labor relationships. Such comparison meant to demonstrate a point that these human resources offices thought imperative: "the privilege to serve, not to work, in offices." Human resources offices also welcomed "new collaborators" by telling them how the service company, unlike the factory, would function as a community of shared interests. That community was simultaneously imagined as a family in which each collaborator had gendered obligations and classed responsibilities. The company was a "home" where male collaborators would be loyal to a "family enterprise" that allowed them to be "the best men in society" and female collaborators would dedicate themselves to "keep[ing] the family enterprise alive."[63] Take, for instance, what AVIANCA, following the guidelines of Pan American World Airways, told a group of flight attendants in 1964 about their space of work: "You must be as meticulous in the care of your cabin as you are in the care of your own home. You must be as courteous and pleasant with the passengers as you are to your family. You must be as happy and devoted to your job as a flight attendant as you are in your role as a housewife."[64]

As this advice suggests, teaching narratives offered much more than family analogies. Rather, they were powerful ways to legitimize the office as a place where the struggle between labor and capital could be overcome and where unions would be unwelcome, if not unnecessary. Service companies invited their employees to see themselves as collaborators, associates, teammates, and colleagues, but not as workers. After all, they were not working but rather investing their labor into a shared "family enterprise." If this were so, the struggle between capital and labor could be overcome, because all collaborators were benefiting from a universal community of shared interests. To put it quite simply: to optimize one's labor in a company was to invest in oneself.

Influenced by labor psychology, these training programs presented male collaborators with stories of hypothetical situations to evaluate their reactions. Most of these succinct stories took place in office settings. They followed a teleological development of labor relationships from conflict to harmony, the participants in these relationships evolving from less-than-men into proper men, from workers and employees into collaborators. Such stories would begin with union-driven workers, usually described as unaware, in perpetual conflict with their bosses and thus impeding democracy. Then these workers would become aware of who they were, transforming into collaborators who resolved any labor conflict in a rational and peaceful manner. These stories usually would have a "happy ending" in which the office is described as a panacea for labor relations because workers realize there that they can exercise their social agency and become collaborators with the company.

One could dismiss these teaching efforts for their evident political naïveté. Or one could note how much they ignore the reality of labor relationships. Yet through these efforts private service companies sought to delegitimize unions as exotic—radically exterior—to the service sector. Working under the assumption that middle-class women were "apolitical and docile" while middle-class men could be driven by "interests in politics . . . conflict . . . and disagreements," human resources offices believed that gendered training was necessary.[65] The task was quite specific: to eradicate "male inclinations" to union politics and to cultivate a moral economy through which male loyalty to, respect for, and identification with company values could emerge. It is telling that during the late 1950s and 1960s, all four companies studied here repeated, in different language, that the task was to identify those "subjects that have a low rate of obedience, subjects that have no sense of authority or responsibility . . . those subjects that have inclinations for unionism."[66]

This teaching material articulated a distinction in the office between a proper masculinity, associated with the democratic collaborator, and another, feminized masculinity, correlated with the unionized working-class member, usually defined as an "autocratic worker." The former was the possession of "modern . . . educated men" accustomed to living in "democratic environments."[67] The properly masculine middle-class collaborator was antiunion because he defended not "just particular benefits" but the interests of a larger community, the company as a whole. He was destined to succeed in life not through alien influence but through "individual hard work . . . personal effort . . . and solid professional preparation." In moments of difficulty and disagreement, this collaborator would have a strong tendency to "negotiate" rather than differ, to discover shared ground rather than disagree, to compromise rather than confront. Violence, conflict, and struggle were outside his "manhood."[68]

These human resources offices contended that this proper middle-class masculinity stemmed from a specific family upbringing and cultural environment in which conflict had never been routine. This developed men who could trust themselves and thus had fewer "propensities . . . susceptibilities . . . [and] proclivities toward unionism." They would be "loved, trusted, capable, [and] optimistic."[69] As a proper man, this democratic collaborator embraced obedience, discipline, and productivity "spontaneously." He was a "self-obedient personality" who, in contrast to the feminized autocratic worker, was aware of the need "to receive and follow orders." This self-obedient personality was based on the willingness to overcome feminine values such as "personal vanity, futility, desolation, and emptiness" and to embrace a masculine "democratic sentiment" to put the community's interests first. The democratic collaborator would by self-critique become aware of his own mistakes so that the community would not suffer. With his "active and positive attitude" he would develop a "moral and intellectual power" to cultivate self-discipline so that he would act properly without needing outside discipline or instructions. In a word, he would manifest "democratic self-government" because he, barring any foreign influence, would discipline and rule himself.

In contrast, human resources offices demarcated the other of this democratic collaborator as the working-class feminized man driven by "private self-interest." Brought up in an environment of conflict, he would not compromise his self-driven private interests for the company. This worker would not take an active role in the company because, as a product of tradition rather than modernity, he would always be "in a passive position . . . waiting to be told what to do." Embodying female passivity, these men would not represent themselves but rather expect to be represented by others (i.e., unions). The problem was not only that these workers were susceptible to communist ideas but also that they did not have "male . . . liberal agency" and could therefore not speak for themselves. This traditional worker lacked loyalty to a community of shared interests, self-discipline, and self-obedience. Without "that masculine value" to accommodate oneself to "a social order," he lacked the capacity to coexist in "ranked organizations." He found happiness in the "pleasure of struggle," which made service-sector organizations "unbearable" for him.[70]

Usually, the human resources offices prefaced these training materials by asking three interlocking questions: "To what type of person do you think you belong? To what type of person would you like to belong? Are you happy with the type of person that you are?" Although I have not found any responses from participants in these training workshops, such questions allowed human resources offices, informed by labor psychology, to create a hierarchy of personalities that further disassociated masculinity and middle-classness from union participation, defined as a symptom of psychologically abnormal feminized masculinity from which the office needed protection. Union-driven workers developed "problematic personalities": they were "the lesser men . . . the gloomy ones" who isolated themselves and had the hardest time being "part of a team." Their "fatalistic attitude" and "hostile sentiments" made them antiliberal individuals who blocked the interest of the group; "easily impressed characters," they were susceptible to outside ideological beliefs.[71] These less-than-men, it was argued, were not liberal enough, as their "lack of male agency" prevented the rejection of an all-oppressive unionism.

That Sixth Sense: A Service Mystique

Although middle-class women in the service sector participated in seminars that sought to delink unionism from office labor and middle-classness, the assumption was that union participation contradicted "women's nature." A major theme in the teaching material was that—as an executive director of Colseguros argued in 1961—women had developed an "intangible" yet fundamental human capital for making the service sector function properly and thus could not be driven by unions. Human resources offices celebrated an "indescribable" disposition to serve as a "sixth sense" that only women with "certain particularities" could develop.[72] This "imperceptible . . . exceptional female nature" was described as a "service mystique" because it was difficult to explain why middle-class women embodied those qualities that made "service a feminine task par excellence." This sixth sense—typified in "service beauty: smile, attractiveness, charm appeal, patience"—could make the office a place where "tranquility . . . and peacefulness" reigned.[73]

But because this sixth sense was imperceptible, service companies sought to cultivate it among female collaborators, with "experts" hired to give training sessions and sponsor retreats in which women would become familiar with service theories. Middle-class women were taught four connected ways for exploiting this sixth sense as cultural capital in an office environment. First, these "good women" would have to please the companies' clients. No matter what—said Fabiola Vallejo, an expert in service with a graduate degree from the Catholic University of America, at one Colseguros seminar—the mission was to fulfill the clients' desires. To achieve this required the self-exploitation of a feminine quality that only appropriate women possessed: patience. Unlike men, burdened by calculating rationality, these women would demonstrate their sixth sense by always putting the client's interests before their own. Second, these good women would capitalize this service mystique by pleasing themselves through others. Unlike working-class women, who displayed masculine selfishness, these women would find "feminine satisfaction" in serving others, derived not from a quest for "profit" but rather from the "enjoyment of being useful for society, love of complying with the female's duties, and a desire for progress." Women's "natural disposition" to sacrifice material interests made them ideal collaborators in the service sector.[74]

This sacrifice led to the third element of this "imperceptible service mystique": loyalty to the company. Seemingly in contradiction to the second element, this loyalty was based on women's "respect and obedience" toward those who provided their "material welfare." Unlike the ungrateful, unappreciative, and masculinized working-class women who joined unions, women with the sixth sense were characterized by trust and mutual respect. They would not join unions, because by doing so they would only be serving their own interests. Instead, women would have an "unparalleled human capital" to develop one of the most difficult elements of this sixth sense: discretion, a feminine quality that allowed one to know "when to speak to others . . . and when to silence oneself." This "superior attribute" allowed good women to avoid "rivalries, disorganization, [and] struggles . . . in the office space." As the BR's human resources offices advised in 1963,

> Modesty, reserve, and restraint are the base for the moral strength for women in the office. Women must place themselves in a high standard of respect. . . . Women must use polished and delicate words to express themselves. . . . If they descend into vulgarity, it is certain that nobody will respect them as women. . . . Take care of your human attributes, mold your actions every day, shine like a flower. To serve is to progress—smile![75]

This intense, if contradictory, schooling proved quite productive because it put into practice the Alliance's rationality, cultivating sentiments, dispositions, and desires so that an antiunion, gendered, middle-class sub-jectivity could materialize in the service sector. As we will see in the book's second part, these notions mediated—and gave substance to—the experi-ences of women and men who found jobs in the service sector and their identification as part of a middle class.

Part II Contested Democracies

Classed Subjectivities, Social Movements, and Gendered Petit Bourgeois Radicalization, 1960s–1970s

Identification always generates this paradox. It is one of the cruelest of ironies that, in trying to position oneself as different from what one has been made to be, one is condemned unconsciously to repeat elements of the old self one is trying to surpass.

—**Stuart Hall with Bill Schwarz,** *Familiar Stranger*

5

In the Middle of the Mess

Along with the intensification of political struggles in the countryside, the late 1950s and 1960s witnessed important structural changes: urbanization, major economic growth, the service sector's expansion, substantial increases in formal opportunities for education, and new development programs. Historians concur that "since the time of independence Colombian society had not experienced a change so charged with consequences as the partial capitalist modernization that occurred after World War I."[1] These interlocking changes diversified the labor market, renovated labor experiences in the service sector, altered the urban landscape with skyscrapers, and created new development offices. Such changes proved pivotal for both the materialization of a country of cities and, above all, "the rise of new urban middle classes."[2]

But as this book's first part demonstrated, the formation of the middle classes in Bogotá was not a unidirectional sociological reflection of these changes. Rather, these structural changes worked in tandem with a transnational totemization of a middle class fundamentally tied to a specific hierarchical definition of democracy. In this chapter, I ask what happened to flesh-and-blood professionals and white-collar employees when they carried out their tasks as conscripts of democracy: moving society away from labor-capital struggles, promoting peaceful class dynamics, and safeguarding democracy. I seek to think critically through the class and gender

Figure 5.1 Carlos Restrepo Personal Archive (CRPA), *The American Dream—a Play*, 1972.

subjectivities of those who, as Alberto Valencia put it in one of our conversations, found themselves "in the middle of the mess."[3]

Most scholars have concluded that the FN, along with the Alliance, "cultivated . . . and co-opted the middle classes with special care" to avoid political radicalization and communism's spread in Colombia. After all, the middle classes were the FN's "favorite social group."[4] This chapter pushes back against these arguments. The problem with such narratives is that they render the middle classes a politically passive, if apathetic, social group readily available to political co-optation. And because it is assumed that the Alliance was a US creation seeking to combat communism by making the region in the United States' image, scholars confidently conclude that middle-class people were preordained to embrace, or even become the pawns of, a grand imperialistic plan supported by a "golden age of [elite] gentlemen's agreements."[5]

Thus the fundamental goal of this chapter is to attend to class and gender subjectivities in ethnographic terms as a way to offer concrete stories—in service company offices, the rural settings and poor urban neighborhoods of professional field visits, and private factories—of those conscripted and empowered by development programs. In so doing, I discuss how these professionals and white-collar employees appropriated these programs' political rationality to secure better material conditions for themselves and thus claim belonging to a gendered middle class. Indeed, middle-class women and men offered a degree of legitimacy to the FN's social policies precisely because the political rationality underwriting these provided the grounds for collective identification as middle-class women and men. Such legitimacy—fragile and contradictory as it was—naturalized the relationship between democracy and middle-classness as common sense. Yet as these historical actors carried out their assigned tasks, they began to question such political rationality in order to redefine themselves as middle class, promoting in the process a different but equally hierarchical vision of democracy (figure 5.1). If policies, teaching discourses, and selection practices placed the middle class at the center of society as the negotiating force for a peaceful future, the very same middle-class people sought to locate themselves *above*, and in struggle with, the laboring classes, the peasantry, and the elites.

Professionalized Memories

In the late 1950s and 1960s Colombia experienced a twin process of rapid urban growth and geographic redistribution of the population.[6] Whereas 61 percent of all Colombians lived in the countryside in 1951, only a third did so a generation later.[7] By the late 1970s, 75 percent of the population lived in cities. Bogotá had 350,000 inhabitants in 1938; by the mid-1960s, it had almost two million. Although the statistics have always been disputed, most historians agree that the late 1950s and 1960s brought a substantial increase in formal opportunities for education. James D. Henderson, for instance, has argued that during the 1950s and early 1960s there was "a 111 percent increase in public primary education and a 537 percent increase in private primary schools"; according to him, "secondary education grew by 209 percent, with well over half of that expansion occurring in private colegios."[8] With the growth of private and public institutions (both universities and what were usually called *institutos superiores*), enrollment in higher education increased by 309 percent. By 1964, 84 percent of all school-age children were attending class. And illiteracy began to decline during the 1950s, falling to 27 percent during the 1960s.[9] Yet only few would gain admission to higher education, as most of the changes in education took place in primary and secondary schooling.[10] Likewise, access to higher education varied regionally, by gender, and by economic sector. The expansion of public universities and the recent opening of private ones mostly took place in cities.[11] As appendix figure 3 shows, women's participation sharply increased from the early 1950s to the early 1980s. These unprecedented changes were also accompanied by the economy's tertiarization and significant expansion of state development programs.[12] In fact, the service sector's contribution to the GDP increased from 28 percent in the late 1940s to almost 50 percent in the late 1970s.[13] And women's workforce participation increased to 30 percent of persons active in the labor force by the late 1970s. Most of this participation was concentrated in the service sector.

These interlocking structural changes provoked new professional, labor, and educational experiences. Some professionals remembered the late 1950s and 1960s as formative moments. Some recalled that their parents had migrated to a city either because of La Violencia or in the belief that the city, unlike the countryside, would offer the material conditions to achieve, or maintain, a middle-class status. Marta Jaramillo, for instance, remembered that her parents—her mother from the north of Tolima, her father from eastern Antioquia—decided to live in Bogotá because they were "preoccupied with being part of the middle class." Her father, Pedro, worried that after many years working the land his family could end up "wearing sandals." Jaramillo remembered that her father was forward-looking: "He knew that progress was in the city, not in the pueblo. He was well advanced for his moment. He wanted us to succeed." Her mother, Magdalena, left the countryside because of party rivalries between Liberals and Conservatives. Pedro and Magdalena arrived in Bogotá sometime in the late 1940s to "try their luck in the city." Her father, "a liberal . . . a *gaitanista*," called in some family favors, collected some personal savings, and started a small transportation services business. Her mother stayed at home and took care of the kids. "To tell you the truth, we were neither rich nor poor . . . well maybe we were lower middle class," Jaramillo remembered. But her parents wanted a bright future for her and her seven siblings. And the only way to guarantee that was, according to Jaramillo's parents, by providing the opportunities needed to prepare oneself for life's challenges. Jaramillo recalled her parents' lectures on how education was "the best inheritance a father could leave to a daughter."[14]

As the FN's and the Alliance's development policies celebrated a notion of middle-classness as the representation of democracy, such ideas and programs found a breeding ground among future professionals and their parents, who had recently left behind what they saw as the manifestation of a traditional and backward rural life. They wanted to achieve progress by "entering into contact with the city . . . by professionalizing and urbanizing themselves."[15] Yet future professionals and their parents soon disagreed on what else democracy could mean. Jaramillo "did not want to be like [her] mother . . . too dependent on [her] father . . . too submissive." But it was her mother, Jaramillo clarified, who supported her "to go all the way to college and find jobs." Things with her father, however, proved to be more vexing. Jaramillo recalled that, albeit forward-looking, he tried to control her; he thought the city could also be "too modern for a true woman." Indeed, her father harped on Jaramillo to find a "good husband . . . one with class." This provoked disagreement in the family. While attending UNAL during the late 1950s and early 1960s, Jaramillo faced repeated threats from her father to withdraw financial support because she was "becoming too liberated." Because of these threats, Jaramillo, still a student at UNAL, secured a job at INCORA as a *socióloga vivencial* for development programs in agrarian reform. Perhaps complying with her father's expectations, she wanted a professional job to "overcome herself in life, to progress, [and] to be a solid middle-class woman."[16] But this opportunity also allowed her to achieve a certain degree of economic independence from her immediate family.[17]

Jaramillo was not alone. During the early 1960s, thanks to the expansion of development programs, it became almost commonplace for women and men to find jobs in state offices. Thus professionals remembered the Alliance as formative in their lives. Development programs opened "a world full of modernity," a path toward "liberty, autonomy, and independence." As Jaramillo detailed that specific historical moment,

> I did not have to rely economically on my family [or] my father. . . . I did not have to get married right away. It did not make sense to me . . . to work hard for a professional degree and just get married and stay home. I became conscious of who I was. I became a professional woman. I had my money and although I had to help my brothers I had my economic independence. I felt I was doing something important.[18]

In other cases, the FN's social policies and the development programs were experienced as an "opening of new forms of knowledge to see the world."[19] Most of the middle-class professionals whom I interviewed remembered the elite intellectuals who championed the importance of a middle class as the most influential people in their lives. As we shall see in chapter 7, some of these professionals would become critical of this knowledge, but during the first half of the 1960s modernization theories became foundational sources of inspiration for getting to "really know" Colombian society. Marta Flórez, a sociology student at UNAL at this time, passionately explained why such encounters with development programs shaped her generation of professionals:

> Fals Borda opened the world for me. I graduated from my colegio and I didn't know anything about my own country. . . . I was middle class and I lived in Bogotá. What could I know about the realities of Colombia? I discovered the truth of the nation. Eduardo Umaña Luna . . . showed us that nothing was absolute, not even the law. Torres Restrepo didn't teach those classes in the classroom but in the field, the realities of the poor *barrios* and the rural parts of the country . . . the stories of the pueblo, the way they dressed, the way they thought, the way they felt, the structure of society.[20]

Thus, some professional women supported the development programs' gendered and classed assumptions because they allowed economic independence, gender autonomy, educational opportunity, and access to knowledge. Yet these middle-class women also rejected the assumption that their jobs were less professional, compared to those of men, and thus less valuable to state rule.

We see this paradoxical experience in Alicia Perdomo's story. Like many other professional women, Perdomo recalled how soon after finishing her degree in social work, at the Colegio Mayor de Cundinamarca (CMC) in 1963, she got a job at IFI. One of her first assignments was, she remembered, a challenging one: to give lectures about human relations, leadership skills, and modern forms of management to *grandes empresarios* in private firms located on the outskirts of Bogotá.[21] Although quite nervous, she was nonetheless excited about this classed and gendered encounter with an elite other because it gave her "professional status and importance." Imagine, she told me, a woman in front of "*machista* men who perhaps had not seen a professional woman in their entire lives." Performing her job well would demonstrate how professional women like her were unique, as only "true women could perform a job as social workers."[22]

Perdomo appealed to her rather disorganized but extensive personal archive as a way to authorize her classed and gendered vision of the past. She showed me several deteriorated copies of pay stubs from her years at IFI. As an "expert in social relations," she received an average monthly gross income of four thousand pesos in the first half of the 1960s, which at the time she thought a good amount of money "to live well." She had recently married Rafael Santana, an agronomist working for INCORA, and their combined household income of ten thousand pesos a month allowed them to achieve a solid "middle-class status . . . to live comfortably." While information about incomes during this period is rather incomplete, what is available suggests that this was slightly below the average salary for government jobs yet well above the regular salary for work in the industrial and agricultural sectors.[23] Perdomo insisted that it was her income that provided the extra economic push needed to maintain a certain class status: "Had I decided not to pursue my professional career and stayed home . . . we would not have been able to do much. . . . kids came later but [m]y income made the difference."[24] Perhaps because of such gendered and classed distinctions, Perdomo kept monthly household budget sheets, the contents of which suggest that the labor and educational opportunities offered by the Alliance and the FN allowed some professionals like Perdomo and her husband to claim middle-class belonging, able to live a comfortable life in which "there was not a lot of money, but money was enough to get by fine."[25]

Such belonging included decent salaries, health coverage, and social benefits. But development policies also enabled professional women such as Perdomo to define themselves as middle class, a claim she felt compelled to make while perusing through her personal archive. Perdomo found it important to emphasize that she, as a true woman, had been "the best representative in society" and thus entitled to work for the Colombian state. She also thought that, no matter her professional responsibility, she had developed "that feminine necessity" for taking care of their home. She remembered that she had "always tried to be an impeccable wife" because "true women . . . with that feminine touch could make a difference in life." Such balance provided a gendered and middle-class distinction.[26] She claimed that her labor could not be performed by those referred to as "any woman," a description associated with those she called "frivolous women in society . . . women with neither any serious purpose in life . . . [nor] female value," ladies in the upper social spheres "unconcerned with their life or the life of others" who "assumed that everything [could] get fixed with money."[27]

And yet such acceptance of development policies coexisted rather contradictorily with refusal. As Perdomo and I read together the ethnographic notes that she had been required to submit to her supervisors at IFI, a central complaint emerged. Her work as a professional woman usually went "unacknowledged" among her male peers: "They think I am just any woman," she wrote in one report.[28] She protested that nobody valued what she did because her job was seen as a "part of women's feelings." And because of that, "they [thought] anyone could be a social worker. . . . They [thought] you need[ed] neither professional preparation nor skills to do what I do. . . . It [was] just a woman's job."[29] This is why she felt the need to read out loud from her notes about what she found to be the most important part of her job: "to sensitize and raise the consciousness of the Colombian privileged classes," necessary for guiding those privileged classes on how to be compassionate regarding Colombia's social problems.[30] She showed allegiance to the Alliance and FN's shared political project while resisting the belief, central to development programs, that she was able to represent the state merely due to "natural characteristics of womanhood."[31]

As more professional women such as Perdomo and Jaramillo participated in state jobs, professional men experienced development programs as a gendered challenge to what they considered, in line with transnational discourses on democracy, the masculine task par excellence: exercising state rule. Professional men appropriated the association between state rule and middle-class masculinity to position themselves as better governors than their female colleagues, who by their very "feminine presence" could "trivialize and deprofessionalize the task of a true state."[32] José Tarazona, a rural specialist working for ICT on community development programs in Santandercito, a small town eighteen miles from Bogotá, wrote lengthy letters to the director of the social services office complaining about professional women. Tarazona blamed them for his failure to perform his class assignment as a true professional. For some time, he wrote in 1962, he had been working with Santandercito's peasant families, by whom he had succeeded in being accepted.[33] He was immersing himself, his letter implied, in their class environment.[34] Yet he complained that ICT had made a "pointless decision" by sending to work with peasant families women, who were never prepared for the "toughness of the rural setting."[35] It was a job for "real professional men," not for those "little girls [niñitas] who [had] just come from their luxurious city houses." They were becoming obstacles to the transformation that he, as a true man and thus a representative of state rule, was about to effect in the lives of these peasant families: since these "little girls" had come to the town, most families associated him with them and had become distrustful of his role as a professional man.[36]

Professional men such as Tarazona infantilized their female colleagues to delink middle-class womanhood, state rule, and professionalism: as "little girls," women could not exercise state rule over those who needed to be ruled (i.e., peasants and workers). Tarazona concluded that "these girls [did] not know how to approach the poor, how to listen to them, how to immerse themselves in their environment. . . . They knew little about democracy."[37] Yet Tarazona conceded that these "little girls" could become his true colleagues by shedding their "female arrogance," which prevented them from learning from professionals like himself with "more experience in the question of progress."[38] In a word, these women needed to be properly masculinized and professionalized before they could exercise the right to rule others.

Professional men further debated how and on whom their democratic task should be performed.[39] Heeding the teachings of Camilo Torres Restrepo, these new professionals wrote in their field notes that they wanted to rediscover the reality of the laboring classes, which had been hidden in complicated statistics and dry reports. Unlike those categorized as ancient professionals—described as performing "feminine behaviors" and stuck in their secluded offices—these new professionals wanted to "get out there" and face the "social reality of the nation." They saw themselves as embracing the public and masculine role of "experienc[ing] the country firsthand and chang[ing] society." In so doing, they would gain the knowledge and real experience—that is, male authority—to speak on the realities of the laboring classes. Evoking Virginia Gutiérrez de Pineda, these new state professionals further distinguished themselves from those ancient and feminized professionals who believed that class realities were biological destiny and thus impossible to change and who saw the laboring classes as living "in darkness, in economic hopelessness . . . with no agency of their own."[40] It was the task of the new professional to shed any "slight trace of girlhood" and to embrace man's true labor, to "get out there, to discover the social truth . . . and to change cultures . . . to penetrate into the nature of those at the top [as well] . . . as those at the bottom."[41] Thus professional men mobilized, and hence legitimized, their role as state representatives as a way to posit themselves as "true professionals," democratic subjects endowed to rule gendered and classed inferiors: laboring classes (peasants and workers), "little girls" (infantilized professional women), and ancient professionals (feminized male office professionals).

This gendered legitimacy proved productive as professional women and men embraced what they thought the task of the twentieth century: to prepare the elites and laboring classes to coexist harmoniously so that Colombia could become a democratic society comparable to the world's industrialized nations. Professionals thought that the policies of the FN and the Alliance—as Torres Restrepo had taught at ESAP, INCORA, and ICT—could make the difference between a "violent and nonviolent path to democracy." At least during the 1960s' first half, these professionals thought it possible to eliminate the abyss between the "small enriched social class and a great mass of an impoverished class" so that Colombia would become a "sterile ground [for] dictatorship . . . conflict, class hatred, and violence."[42]

Disciplining Capital: Making the Oligarchies into Elites

As part of the Alliance-sponsored development programs during the FN, IFI—a state financial corporation founded in the 1940s that worked closely with ICT, CINVA, the Ministry of Labor, the Ministry of Agriculture, ESAP, Cafeteros, CAFAM, and the OAS Permanent Technical Committee on Labor Matters—established a series of disjointed yet important initiatives to oversee private companies' compliance with labor rights hard won by different working-class social movements, such as family monetary compensation funds, minimum wages, overtime compensation, health coverage, vocational-training opportunities, transportation allowances, appropriate labor conditions, and industrial security. The Instituto de Fomento Industrial penalized several industries in Bogotá and surrounding areas for not complying with some of the labor laws guaranteeing these rights. Additionally, IFI and the labor minister mandated that factory owners receive lectures on human relations and labor conditions. This is why, empowered by human relations discourses and their roles as state representatives, professionals from different disciplines went to factories, big industries, and major private firms, charged with reaching "those who rule in factories and [have] no social contact with national life . . . industrialists, presidents of companies, high-level bureaucrats, managers, and administrators, factory owners, entrepreneurs, businessmen, and bosses."[43]

Professional women and men consented to disciplining the proper distribution of sentiments and desires among the oligarchies so that they might develop *sensibilities* fitting for progress, *aspirations* appropriate for democracy, and *dispositions* suited for social peace.[44] It was this sentimental education that produced so many reports, inspection minutes, field

notes, and lecture outlines. Preparing presentations, writing notes on factory visits, crafting reports, submitting evaluations, planning lectures, and
visiting factories became everyday practices through which professionals
attempted to transform "oligarchs" into modernizing elites. In 1963, for
instance, a group of female social workers, nurses, and home economists
working with IFI were sent to several factories throughout Bogotá and surrounding areas to gain through social surveys a general idea about the interests and desires of their "bosses and owners."[45] The IFI team wanted to
evaluate how motivated *patronos* were to participate in the government's
education programs on human relations and labor conditions. Deploying
human relations discourses on the need to seduce "resistant groups," these
professionals sought to know how patronos felt about their "brothers and
sisters of the lower classes."[46] To persuade patronos, the surveys needed to
avoid being either too specific, which would "hurt some [class] feelings,"
or too general, which would cause patronos to be disengaged. Mobilizing
human relations discourses, these professional women argued that the
patrono could represent "violence, tradition, [even] machismo" by assuming
a confrontational attitude with those "working on the factory floor."[47] They
needed to become *hombres de empresa*, a term for peaceful men who could,
as true leaders, coexist with workers in a democratic environment. Using
such language, these professionals concluded, could seduce those who were
to be educated in matters of democracy.

Presentations became crucial to this pedagogy of class persuasion. Most
began with professional women explaining "the hard facts [that] could not
be questioned because [they were] scientifically and statistically beyond
doubt." The professionals then described the conditions of the different social classes and concluded with lengthy suggestions about how to approach
particular social situations.[48] The political content of these presentations
came in demonstrating what the oligarchs did not "want to see . . . hear,
or feel: the social situation of the laboring classes." Following what they
learned in classrooms and state development workshops, the professionals
sought to explain "how the peasants and their families live, how their workers worked, what they were able to do during and after working hours."[49]

To give one concrete example of such presentations, in 1963 Lilia
Sanabria and María Eugenia Santana, professional nurses for IFI and ICT,
respectively, were assigned to offer a series of talks about labor and human
relations at a factory in the south of Bogotá.[50] They recounted a story with
a familiar trope: the teleological class transition of a "traditional patrono"
into a "modern hombre de empresa" who could promote, rather than limit,

progress and democracy. The story, based in a factory, aimed to unpack the "conceptions of the world" hidden within "patronos' minds and spirits."[51] By comparing the story's class descriptions with their real-life experiences, patronos would gain context and self-knowledge.[52]

The traditional boss, Santana and Sanabria instructed potential hombres de empresa, was unaware of his important social role and lacked sentimental attachment to the "social problems of the peasants or workers," since he did not want to know them intimately. Lacking a truly masculine disposition, this traditional boss had only "ancient stereotypes" about the lower and laboring classes, who were at best "objects of production" and at worst "beasts of burden, dirty, sick, malodorous, unable to take in what [was] new . . . and unable to leave their position as a serf of a demesne."[53] This traditional boss, a lesser man given his unsentimental conceptions of the social world and lack of manly action, cultivated a paternalistic relationship that, by expanding the "chasm . . . and misunderstanding between the oligarchs and the laboring classes," prevented both from taking an active role in national development.[54]

In contrast, Santana and Sanabria lectured, the hombre de empresa was an "active man" willing to momentarily set aside his privileged status to encounter peasants and workers for what they were capable of doing for the nation's development. Fighting his feminine tendencies—his inherent desire to isolate himself from social realities—the hombre de empresa was willing to develop a "social spirit" and thus sympathy for the laboring classes' role in national growth. In so doing, he eagerly recognized how an "intimate relationship between those who work at the factory . . . [those who] cultivate the land, and those who rule" was necessary for a mutual goal: a peaceful democratic society.[55] The virile hombre de empresa knew—and felt—that multiplying human capital required seeing "the members of the laboring classes as total men" who desired to be part of progress and development.[56] In other words, the hombre de empresa needed to develop an affective judgment allowing him to see the laboring classes' agency. Yet whether such judgment could translate into material benefits for those laboring classes did not enter, at least during the first half of the 1960s, into the sentimental education carried out by these professionals.

It was equally imperative to take advantage of the "oligarchy's latent human capital." Because they occupied a "superior rank in the nation," several professionals lectured, the oligarchs somehow owned an innate masculine authority that could be profitably utilized to change their own "oligarchic ethos."[57] Professionals were to make use of elites' "superior authority as oligarchs . . . their human values as leaders" to instill what was most needed for democracy: an active sentiment to serve the nation's larger interests and society's larger good. Professionals saw themselves as becoming middle class by disciplining these effeminized male oligarchs— passive, insensitive, and mentally underdeveloped, yet bearing a latent male authority—into wholly masculine elites who could serve the nation at large.[58]

It is critical to underscore here that for the most part it was professional women who were supposed to masculinize the feminized oligarchies. As these professional women put it, their task was to effect a "change of . . . heart" among the leading classes.[59] They were to educate the sensibilities, dispositions, and attachments at the core of the oligarchies' "cultural ethos" so that, as Gutiérrez de Pineda had envisioned, the oligarchical milieu could be critically renewed and modernized.[60] Professionals argued that democratic education should be tailored to each class's cultural norms, which historically for the oligarchs had entailed "materialistic desires and egoistic competitiveness," "the oligarchic motto of life" being "to own more material objects . . . for personal satisfaction." Thus, the professionals' assignment as members of the middle class was to emancipate oligarchs from their sentimental attachment to material artifacts. In so doing, they would educate oligarchs to become "socially driven men," men who could "care for the society they live in."[61]

Yet as development programs put professionals in intimate contact with those perceived as oligarchs, those encounters simultaneously provoked unforeseen contradictions and class struggles. Some of the so-called hombres de empresa critically resisted the role assigned to them in development programs. Hombres de empresa filed lawsuits and complaints to avoid state-mandated fines and penalties. Some also criticized professionals' "lack of professionalism, competence, and skills" as well as "problems of character [and] dubious intellectual capacity." The factory owners protested that some professionals had developed "suspicious" political positions preventing them from doing their jobs objectively; they acted as the workers' advocates and thereby risked their "impartial and respected tasks."[62] Hombres de empresa found troubling the idea at the development programs' core: the possibility of the *"convivencia de clases."* For some, this ideal was a clear manifestation of communist infiltration into state rule, which was supposed to be neither liberal nor conservative but merely professional. This fear gave hombres de empresa a handy legitimation for resisting these development programs. These professionals were "difficult people," feminized men, because they showed "a natural flaw" in being easily influenced and corrupted by "foreign [and] confusing ideas."[63] Such professionals, hombres de empresa protested, were the ones who would undermine social peace and bring another wave of political violence, since they were taking workers' side. They requested that the state be more careful in selecting and preparing professionals for the tasks of what these hombres de empresa called a democratic state.

For other hombres de empresa, gender dynamics were the more threatening aspect of these professionals. In one short but telling letter, Jesús Antonio Toro and Gabriel Millamarín, presidents of a metal manufacturing factory in Bogotá's outskirts, protested that "women went to [their] company to tell [them] what to do."[64] They complained that these professional women showed arrogance, "a spirit of intrigue," a "violent attitude," a "neglectful manner," and a "desire to annoy," seeking to disrupt these directors' "usual way of doing business." Such complaints were couched in the language of professional preparation and reveal the gender anxiety produced among elite men by the presence of women. As hombres de empresa often asked: "Who do these women think they are?" The presence of professional women was not only "uncomfortable to deal with" but also "disturbing."[65] It was uncomfortable because, Toro and Millamarín insisted, women listened not to them but only to the factory-floor workers, undermining the masculine authority that directors needed in order to "make business work." It was disturbing because of the women's tendency to embrace "foreign ideas." Thus, Toro and Millamarín hoped that IFI's supervisor of factory visits would understand their masculine situation: "We are writing this letter from a man to another man," they stated in the letter's opening sentence, hoping that the supervisor would understand as a man how difficult it was to have "women who [did] not listen to you and pretend to boss you around."[66]

These class frustrations and struggles were productive because—as an unintended consequence of development programs such as the Alliance and the social policies of the FN—professional men and women recast the meanings of middle-classness and their political role as democratic representatives of state rule. They began to think about their own project of classed and gendered rule, a project that, as we will see in the next chapter, would politically resonate with—and be shaped by—one of the most important oppositional populist movement of the 1960s: ANAPO.

Educating the Laboring Classes

By partially consenting to development programs, professionals also attempted to educate the laboring classes into the experience of "modern democracies." This project materialized on at least two overlapping and competing fronts. First, professionals sought to transform the laboring classes into gendered and classed economic subjects so that they would learn how to utilize their human capital as well as their insufficient material resources to benefit their communities and, by extension, the nation. Second, professionals saw themselves as guiding those laboring classes on how to participate properly as political subjects in a democracy so that they could see themselves as "fully self-determined people" acting according to their own interests.

Many professional men and women remembered working with development programs as foundational. Alberto Valencia recalled it as his most important opportunity for democratizing Colombia, as the FN and its social policies allowed him to encounter the country's peasants. For him, this encounter was a gendered experience. "There was a turning point in my life when I went to work with peasants," he reminisced; he was forced to leave his "class naïveté and political virginity behind" and become a truly "conscious man."[67] Although committed to working with the peasants, he felt at the time that he was "still a privileged city boy." To face those "remote but attractive places" like a man would help him overcome the "fears and weaknesses of city life" and enter into a more rewarding and masculine existence in which he could be recognized by his professional commitment to democracy.[68]

Valencia's story captures the complexities of a middle-class rule, which required thinking as the other in order to educate that other to consent to a specific notion of democracy in which professionals could legitimately—and hierarchically—rule. Working during the late 1950s and 1960s with several urban and rural development programs dedicated to agrarian reform and housing, Valencia decided to live with families in rural areas for periods of three to four weeks just to be recognized as a true professional man. As an active participant in the University Movement for Community Development (MUNIPROC), founded by Torres Restrepo in 1959 for students and development program professionals, Valencia was convinced that knowing and experiencing "the class ethos" of the laboring classes was needed to create social peace. In his field notes, he wrote that although he was hesitant to ask "difficult questions," since he did not want to sound sophisticated, he could not help but begin to wonder about "the peasant life."[69] Valencia wrote in his reports about how he was attempting to establish some "rapport with the people in order to be accepted by them."[70]

Unlike the careless oligarchs, Valencia wanted not only to preach and work for the good of the peasant families but also to celebrate—even sanctify—all their labors and pleasures, gestures, tools, and tasks. In several field notes to CINVA and ICT, he described his strategies to become "unnoticeable" among peasants. It was essential not to be seen as "excessively superior or different."[71] He dressed not to impress but to mask his class origins. He decided to wear a poncho, use the pickax, and even get his hands dirty "by working the land." He wanted to participate in the "darkness of the drinking places," sit on the floor when visiting peasant families. Valencia proudly read his field notes to remind me that he never asked the peasants to "remove their hat." And in his commitment to portraying himself as not excessively superior, Valencia ordered the peasants "not to address [him] as doctor."[72] This anonymity would help establish professional class authority and its concomitant class rule because it would allow him to have proper influence over those who needed education in matters of democracy.

What was at stake was a hierarchical rule by homage, which allowed professionals to educate peasants and workers on how to utilize their available human capital and material resources as proper economic subjects in a market-driven economy. Professionals argued it was time to take into account, rather than waste, "the human capital of those who have been ignored" and to guide them in how to invest in their human capital for their economic benefit.[73] Professionals would guide, rather than impose, the restoration of the poor's "economic agency."[74] Professionals thought that by tolerating and celebrating the class difference of peasants and workers they could become not only a productive part of the nation but also proper capitalists—owners of their own human capital who knew how to, under their specific class conditions, produce, accumulate, invest, and maximize that human capital for their own "family enterprises."[75]

It is crucial to emphasize that the Alliance's agrarian reform initiatives, health programs, educational policies, and housing plans were not merely promoting an abstract economic distribution that failed to materialize; what was at stake was, in an effort to expand capitalist growth, the formation of new economic subjectivities. Here, as in other strands of development discourse, the home was the economic unit through which a productive family could be created and where new children—prospective capitalists—would know how to optimize their own human capital. And this raised the question of gender. To prepare the environment for true capitalists to emerge, it was argued, "the mothers and wives of the laboring classes" would make the home an economic unit for the consolidation of a free-market economy. "Without a happy home, money does not matter," professional women told working-class mothers. Professionals urged working-class mothers to become competent at "the art of dealing with scarcity of material resources," using their imagination and female skills—their human capital—to obtain "satisfaction and happiness in the midst of limited income."[76]

Thus, development programs targeted not wealth or distribution of material resources but rather teaching how to become economic subjects who could accumulate human capital and deal independently and efficiently with a precarious existence. Professionals thought this a democratic project because they were respecting, if not praising, the cultural ethos of the working classes—their beliefs, thoughts, and customs—for dealing with scarcity of resources. It was almost as if access to material resources could in practice violate a putative working-class cultural ethos that needed to be respected. Only when the laboring classes detached themselves from this cultural ethos—and instead became middle class—could they access more material rewards.

It was in such efficient grappling with scarcity, furthermore, that working-class women's femininity would be tried and proved. The fate of working-class children and the productivity of laboring-class men depended on how mothers and wives invested "those feminine attributes or virtues" that belonged to their sex—such as sacrifice and the art of dealing with scarcity—to prepare the proper familial environment for the accumulation of the whole family's human capital. For professionals, laboring women were the head of the home and as such assigned gendered roles to each family member. Luz Eugenia Correa, a nurse and social worker assigned in early 1963 to Quiroga, a working-class neighborhood in Bogotá, advised mothers that they needed to prepare a welcoming environment for husbands to stay at home and join in the family enterprises. She offered advice on hygiene, nutrition, child development, and household budgeting; she urged working-class mothers to keep a clean house where their husband would happily spend time with his family and provide not only monetary satisfaction but also love, responsibility, and attention. Those activities were a capital investment in the future, as they would result in children with "economic independence, self-confidence, and self-discipline." "The cultural inertia" that made working-class children think that it was "society that needed to support them" could be overcome if the heterosexual family provided the right amount of love and responsibility. Working-class children would then see themselves as active members of a nation because they could capitalize their "working-class pride" in order to reach their own economic goals.[77]

Because a great deal of political hope was invested in these projects, professionals complained in their reports about the impossibility of achieving their classed assignments. Although claiming "sympathy and understanding," these professional women griped that working-class wives showed no "interest in bettering their situation."[78] Professionals found it frustrating that, despite their services, these mothers were still unable "to help themselves."[79] Here we glimpse how some laboring women interpreted these forms of development to mean that they should get more respect, autonomy, and economic independence from their husbands. Working-class and peasant women complained to professionals that their husbands were uneasy with their constant contact with "city women." But for professional women, at least during the first half of the 1960s, these forms of resistance meant that working-class women were reluctant to assume their assigned role. Professional women contended that working-class mothers only wanted "food on the table"; unaware of their own "cultural ethos," "all they want[ed]" were "material benefits."[80] This was the language that these professionals used to characterize the fact that working-class women were also working outside the home. A social worker wrote in a memorandum to the ICT's social service office in 1963 that while she was trying hard, working-class women were perfectly content to have "absent husbands who can provide money for the household."[81] It was illegitimate, or so these professional women thought, that working-class women associated democracy with some form of material equality.

Working-class men took this gendered economic partnership to mean male entitlement to access to women's labor, supportive wives, and better homemakers. Some of the working-class and peasant husbands complained that these professional women were giving too much power to "their" women participating in workshops and seminars and distracting "their wives from their duties at home."[82] Despite the fact that these seminars sought to create a notion of economic partnership in which women were economically dependent on men, laboring-class men told professional women that they should "mind [their] own business" and not infringe on men's right to "rule in [the] privacy of the home." After all, these laboring-class men told professional women, "one has to respect the independence, intimacy, and sanctity of the home."[83]

Increasingly by the mid-1960s, professional women deployed Gutiérrez de Pineda's arguments about economic progress and cultural beliefs to respond to some of these complaints. They wrote in their reports that the most challenging part of their job was transforming "the machismo of the working class," a major obstacle to working-class women's active preparation of homes that would foster properly trained economic subjects.[84] It was this working-class machismo that alienated men from pursuing human capital and economic progress, encouraging instead a male quietism that reflected a working-class economic passivity and that simultaneously provoked the waste of "latent, dormant, hidden and . . . human capital at their disposal."[85] Because they wanted to remain workers, not to become capitalists, working-class men refused to learn how to exploit their own human capital.

If peasant and working-class women were mostly targeted as economic subjects, peasant and working-class men were directed as those who could bring an important political change for reaching social peace and political stability. The task was much more than depoliticizing peasants and workers or moving them away from communist tendencies. Rather, professional men saw themselves as those who could consolidate peasants' and workers' "natural democratic political potential" by guiding them into the "participatory process." Professional men wanted to awaken the laboring classes' political power to recognize their active role in national development and progress. In the process, professional men sought to create a new sense of the political self, a transparent, self-possessed subject who could think about and feel his enormous capabilities for acting on himself and others. Indeed, by appropriating modernization theories, professional men reimagined politically passive peasants and workers as autonomous and self-enclosed subjects able to exercise "political agency" by organizing their life, improving their situation, and helping to solve the problems created by underdevelopment. They would be "free . . . virtuous, self-disciplined," democratic, and socially conscious subjects who could be guided in how to exercise self-evaluation, self-motivation, and self-criticism to learn how to "desire progress and democracy."[86] In so doing, professional men, as proper, masculine representatives of a development state, hoped that these peasants and workers would remove the "burden of development" from the state and put it instead on their own shoulders.[87]

The everyday lived experience of this political education triggered class struggles and confrontations between professional men and the laboring classes. Professional men working for multiple development programs both embraced and rejected their role as conscripts of democracy forwarding their own class and gendered rule. They wrote about what they considered to be peasants' and workers' resistance to this rationality of community action. Although it is rather difficult to decipher the specifics of this putative working-class resistance, professionals complained that despite their best efforts, peasants had developed apathy for politics, as "every individual expect[ed] the worst from his fellow men." Peasants and workers wanted not to "help themselves" but rather to find the "daddy state" as the only source of economic and political participation.[88] The laboring classes' political capital, they said, remained feminine, politically passive, and economically dormant; members of this class preferred to stay at local bars drinking beer and playing *tejo* instead of joining their community for social and political action.

In further response to this putative resistance, professionals made a sharp distinction between politicking and politics. Politicking was "dirty, dishonest, pointless in society," the outcome of a "violent past" in which oligarchies had ruled "with a stick and with no national interest in their hearts." Politics was what professionals exercised, allowing them, in a "civilized and democratic nation," "to organize things to happen": "we need physicians to work in hospitals, we need teachers to teach at schools . . . we need architects to build houses . . . we need a government and the government is the center of politics."[89] Following Fals Borda and Gutiérrez de Pineda, professionals argued that Colombia's laboring classes manifested a "female submission . . . [and] docility in politics," to the degree that democracy had become a chimera. Professional men saw themselves as those who could awaken and masculinize what they thought was asleep and in a feminized stage among peasants and workers: their democratic attitudes.

Thus during the first half of the 1960s, most professional men and women found themselves frustrated and disappointed, as they could neither become a true professional middle class nor construct a democracy because they were unable to educate workingmen to own their political capital or to guide traditional women to become modern wives who prepared their environment for the emergence of new enterprises that would improve their families. This collective class frustration and disillusionment perpetuated middle-class professionals as class superiors whose dire democratic obligation was to rule those beneath them not yet ready to experience the pleasures of democracy. As was true for their work with the oligarchs, professionals structured democracy as a project of class and gender rule constructed through hierarchical bonds in which professionals, in the process of becoming middle class, found themselves in a tragic conundrum. While the class assignment for these professionals was to produce the conditions for class harmony and political stability so that democracy and peace might emerge, in practice the formation of middle-class identifications created hierarchical antagonists (the not-yet-modern wife; the working-class machista; the unprepared, submissive, feminized peasants) as the included other in constant need of guidance. As we will see in chapter 7, these frustrations proved quite productive for a political radicalization in the second half of the 1960s.

White-Collar Employees: Gendered and Classed Memories

Female white-collar employees remembered working in office jobs during the 1960s as a "democratizing experience." Clemencia Casas, a graduate of ENC in Bogotá in the late 1950s, recalled how grateful she was to get a job with Colseguros, as it allowed her to "enter in these beautiful offices, serve in one of the most important insurance companies in Colombia, and become somebody in life."[90] She associated her class status with the opportunities offered by this service company: "I was lucky to find this job. I finished my high school, got into the ENC, and then got the job at Colseguros. The woman that I am is because of Colseguros. My life, my marriage, my kids, my education, my house, my car, the education of my children, my husband, I mean everything is because of Colseguros."[91] She had to be grateful, Casas insisted, because she was able to move up the social ladder in this private firm. After a decade as a receptionist, she took advantage of a student loan offered by Colseguros that allowed her to receive a degree in accounting in the early 1970s from PUJ. With degree in hand, Casas applied for internal jobs. By her retirement in the late 1990s, she held an important position in the company's accounting offices. "Hard work, a little bit of luck, and a wonderful company" was the right combination to become part of "the middle class . . . where everyone wants to be."[92]

While male and female white-collar employees shared their class distinction, their memories part ways on questions of gender. Jorge Ortiz, for instance, remembered the expansion of the service sector as the opening to become a middle-class man, "the head of a home, the breadwinner." He recalled with masculine satisfaction how, after some years working at Col-seguros, he was able to tell his wife that "she could stay and take care of the children." "I know," he continued, "that was a privilege. But if we wanted our children to be good members of society, we could not leave them with a maid."[93] As he recalled her role with satisfaction: "Margarita [his wife] did a fantastic job. I took a risk because there is an age difference between her and me . . . but she was a well-behaved family woman. She sacrificed her goals in life for the larger good of the family [because] . . . behind a great man there is always a great woman. I would add, without a great mother there is no great family . . . with no mother the family becomes poor."[94] By contrast, although Margarita Delgado de Ortiz believed that being at home was important, she remembered this moment with frustration. She had been working for mul-tiple banks in Bogotá and surrounding cities, but once she and Jorge had their first son, she had to give up her work as a secretary. Yet she also demanded recognition because the family's middle-class status depended on her sacri-ficing her work as a white-collar employee: "This is what I have done in my life . . . raising children, but I hope they recognize what I have sacrificed. . . . Without me here at home this family would have fallen apart."[95]

But for other female and male white-collar employees, the service sec-tor's expansion meant the crystallization of a "gendered partnership." As did professional women working for the state, female white-collar employ-ees remembered their personal lives as critical in maintaining their middle-class status. Without their income, they would have been unable "to stay just right in the middle." In our conversations, they argued that they tried to balance all their obligations because such middle-class women were not easy to find in society. They took pride in saying that they had made pos-sible what their families had become, "a solid middle-class." These women narrated their classed and gendered experiences in the early 1960s as a combination of four main roles: "middle-class mothers . . . middle-class wives, middle-class students . . . and middle-class office women."[96] But it was possible to succeed in these roles, they remembered, because of the partnership that they built with their husbands. For these women, forming a family enterprise was essential to "move the whole family forward." Some of the female white-collar employees narrated their gender distinction and class stratification as linked to the "kind of man [they] wanted to get mar-ried to." They shifted gender assumptions about the relationship between men and women in the family home when declaring how "behind every successful woman there was always a wonderful and supportive husband."[97] And unlike for Delgado de Ortiz, who saw her decision to stay at home and raise her children as central to middle-class distinction, for other female white-collar employees it was their husbands who made such distinction possible. A specific combination of masculinity and femininity was remembered as required for maintaining middle-class distinction:

> We did it together. We had a partnership. I remember that I finished my shift in my office, ran to the university at night, and then ran home. . . . I sometimes had help around the house. I felt I was free. . . . I am lucky to have had such a supportive husband. He is not a guy from a bad class. He was not . . . scared because I was working. And that was what I taught my daughters . . . find somebody to work with you as a partner, not a poor guy who does not support them.[98]

Yet other female white-collar employees begged to differ. Isabel Delgado de Téllez, a nurse who found a job at CAFAM in the mid-1960s, remembered this new experience as a question of gender hierarchization. While the expansion of the service sector meant educational and job opportunities, she also remembered these days as "triple labor shifts. . . . I had to work, I had to study, I had to take care of my family."[99] Guillermo Téllez, Isabel's husband and also a white-collar employee, never complained about her participation in office work. This did not mean, however, that he was willing to participate in family obligations. But no matter how difficult this triple shift was, Isabel's role, as a middle-class woman, was to balance these three labor spheres. After all, unlike the "uncultured and uneducated women of the popular classes," Isabel had the needed experience and preparation to be part of the middle class. As she narrated her story to me: "[Guillermo] and I had to work hard, but the difference was this: he had to work, he had to study and . . . he had to party with his friends. I had to work, I had to study . . . I had to take care of the children, and I had to take care of the home."[100] These white-collar employees' stories share a foundational gendered and classed silence: the so-called help that made possible middle-class status and gendered distinction.

The Rule of Class and Gender Difference in the Service Sector

These memories open a window onto why and how white-collar employees consented to FN development programs through which the service sector and office labor became associated with middle-classness. There are different ways to unearth this process, but perhaps the way to go is to examine how during the 1960s these women and men participated in internal competitions to encourage productivity, contests to choose the "collaborator of the month," workshops on customer service, weekly seminars on teamwork, monthly retreats to promote "healthy" working environments, and yearly conventions to celebrate holidays, among several other activities. Such experiences became very much part of their everyday lives as white-collar employees of the service sector.

Colseguros, for instance, wanted its collaborators to engage in monthly competitions over who could be most productive (secure the most insurance policies). Participation was not mandatory, but the competition encouraged collaborators to join the "struggles of the twentieth century, struggles for productivity . . . a struggle for a better, happier, and brighter future."[101] At stake, it seems, was these collaborators' proper masculinity. An advertisement from 1963 for the competition read, "How many insurance policies have you sold this month? . . . Are you beating your fellow contestants? Are you man enough? If so, prove it in the struggle for productivity."[102] And the material rewards were indeed an incentive: a salary bonus for the next three months and a brief interview published in the company magazine. And if this was not enough, the winners—referred to as "exemplary collaborators"—had the opportunity to give a speech at a monthly celebration. Finally, the winner's name and picture were posted throughout the offices for "all the members of the Colseguros family to admire."

The competition was defined as a struggle among (unequal) gendered partners. To register for the competition, male collaborators had to select a "godmother," who was supposed to protect her "godson" while he was "away selling insurance policies." Indeed, the godmothers stayed in the office, now imagined as a home, and took care of any problems that might arise there in the men's absence; if necessary, they would cover some of the tasks that the men had left unattended because of the "pressure, demands, and obligations that the competition imposed."[103] The task was to "work as a team" to reach "the goal that could benefit them both."[104]

These competitions show how most male white-collar employees embraced the political rationality linking masculinity, service work, and democracy.[105] In a context in which women were participating more in the service sector, these employees also appropriated the gendered and classed discourses of these competitions to confront the association between the service sector and women. Thus, some white-collar men understood female employment as an "inexplicable . . . perplexing" reality or as "counterproductive," because women could jeopardize productivity. Male white-collar employees wrote in their competition victory speeches, for instance, that women had developed a "lack of agency" that prevented them from "achieving whatever they set their mind to." Furthermore, women could not be ready for competition unless true men masculinized them; women needed a "male orientation" to succeed in the "roughness of the competition." They needed to learn "bravery, perseverance, determination, boldness . . . and power of decision," attributes that these white-collar men thought to be masculine.

Thus, male employees insisted that women should perform tasks "according to their sex."[106] In one of the few instances when a woman collaborator was a finalist in the competition, in 1963, the winner, Julio Vaca, felt compelled to explain why "women [did] not look like women in an environment of competition." Vaca wrote that women who became too competitive would squander their "femininity . . . sweetness, and tenderness." He asserted that there were "exquisite female sensibilities" to be celebrated that allowed women to play "outstanding roles as supporters" rather than "leaders." Women avoided recognition instead of seeking it. They shirked ambition instead of promoting it. In a word, for Vaca women were at odds with their own "female interests" if they decided to enter "the ruthless and unfeeling competition." Instead, he concluded—appropriating discourses of service firms as communities of shared interests—that women should support the endeavors of their peers to reach a reward that would benefit "everybody as [part of] a service company."[107] Furthermore, unlike women, men found competition "unavoidable," as it kept their "virility alive." After all, "in the struggle and in the competition, one could know who the true man is": the middle-class man who, thanks to his "male desire and virility," could succeed in any endeavor because success was "the first, the last, and the only goal in life."[108]

These white-collar men thought that it was this virility that distinguished them from those defined as feminized men—"lesser men" in some cases associated with the upper classes, in others with the laboring groups, who had "few male characteristics . . . men who look like women" and were at odds with the masculine requirements for competition. Like women, they were insecure, dependent, and thus unable to do anything but follow others, instead of becoming the leaders and winners of society. For example, Jorge Franco, the winner of a competition in February 1964, wrote a speech and letter to the CEO of Colseguros in which he defined three classes of men. The first he categorized as of "poor virility" because, amid a wealth of opportunities, they did not want to compete for a better future. These men, imagined as those of the laboring classes who released their "masculine power" in less-than-productive pursuits such as "factory labor," waited for success "in the competition of life." The second class of men were feminized men who, while having "ample education, money, and talent," only achieved success through "old money."[109] In contrast to these two classes of feminized men, Franco imagined himself in a third category: men who succeeded as a result of "education, self-consciousness, masculine drive . . . desire, determination, and ambition." It was this combination that made Franco a "victorious man" who could enter in "duels among gentlemen" and always win. In this schema, Franco imagined himself in a gendered and classed triangular social order in which he—as the most capable, most masculine, and most conscious—should legitimately and logically be at the top of the social hierarchy, above the other two feminized men, who should follow his example because they did not have the right combination of masculine preparation and self-awareness.[110]

White-collar men used these competitions to legitimize a rule of class and gender difference—what they called "democratic success"—that naturalized material inequalities between men and women in the service sector. Furthermore, some white-collar men employed in the service sector in Bogotá partially consented to development programs, the expansion of the service sector, and the new discourses on human relations because these consolidated their middle-class masculinity, which translated into material rewards. It is no accident that despite—or precisely because of—women's increasing participation in the labor market and in service companies such as AVIANCA, Colseguros, CAFAM, and BR, most of the winners of company competitions were men. Male employees mobilized the discourse that white-collar women, given their natural and "exquisite female tenderness," should play a supportive role in a heterosexual office to legitimize men's higher salaries.

This hierarchical division of labor, however, did not mean that female white-collar employees passively received these discourses. Although during the first half of the 1960s a political rationality that defined service jobs as properly female social tasks obscured, if not erased, women's increasing participation in the service sector, women themselves embraced, confronted, and rejected such political rationality to demand classed and gendered recognition in the workplace. In the participatory meetings promoted by service companies, for instance, women discussed how they, as white-collar employees, were different from those who worked in factories or did not work at all outside the home. According to them, factory labor led women to "flexibility in their morals, dangerousness in their health, and confusion in their lives."[111] Factory work was, furthermore, for "tough men," and because of this some office women saw female factory workers as too masculine and in fundamental contradiction with the most female task of all: serving others. Alternately, female office employees contrasted themselves, as "productive members of a democratic nation," with "rich . . . elite women" who stayed at home "*vegetando* an unproductive life." Like their male counterparts, office women placed themselves at the top of a triangular social hierarchy, above both the elites and the working class; unlike any other area of employment, the service sector was inhabited only by "true . . . exceptional women."[112]

But as these female employees embraced the association between femininity and service, they simultaneously confronted it. If service companies and male white-collar employees saw women's participation in the service sector as a natural outcome of their "feminine mystique," women themselves saw their task as a product of professional preparation and as a legitimate form of labor. Women questioned whether men were the only ones able to represent service labor. In some cases, women even argued that masculinity was at odds with service because "traits [such as] patience, tolerance, [and] nurturing" were lacking even among the "most tender . . . compassionate, [and] caring men."[113] In one seminar on customer service in 1964, for instance, Estela Correa, a graduate with a technical degree in health services working for CAFAM, discussed how women were "professionally prepared to serve customers better." She contended that although service was very much part of what a "true woman" was, it was "one of the most difficult jobs a true woman could ever do." Correa, with an evident sense of frustration, advocated for seeing customer satisfaction as the product of "hours of training on how to talk to clients, how to convince them, how to treat them well." She asked her peers, "What would happen if men were to be the ones providing service?"[114] The answer, she said, was clear: "a company characterized by broken communications, unsatisfied clients . . . and with no business."[115]

The Service Sector Must Be Defended

During the first half of the 1960s, most white-collar women and men joined forces to define the office as a heterosexual space in which the struggle between capital and labor should not germinate. They saw themselves as part of a community of shared interests in which there were "neither bosses . . . nor workers but collaborators serving for the same objective."[116] They were convinced that the "progress of the company [was] their personal success." Indeed, as some white-collar employees discussed in weekly "participatory meetings," all employees, no matter their specific job, were "united by the same interests, part of the same company, and tied to the success of the company." In fact, male white-collar employees in service companies across Bogotá were "masculine enough" to recognize that, unlike factory workers, they did not need bosses to dictate what they needed to do in their jobs. Rather, they wanted to "follow, obey, and respect" what they considered the most democratic boss of all: economic success.[117] Others went even further in their belief that they, unlike working-class laborers, were free to exercise their agency. They owned their own destiny because white-collar employees would bring another type of labor relationship that would overcome the struggle between capital and labor and in which these white-collar employees, as collaborators and not workers, would be "the boss of themselves."[118]

Yet the ever-present possibility of unionization exacerbated class and gender anxieties among some white-collar employees. They mobilized the belief that positioned unions, the service sector, and middle-class identity as incompatible. They wanted to protect the office from its "vulgarization" and "obrerización" because, as Jorge Pineda said in one of those "participatory meetings" at the BR, the unionization of service offices "would be the end of the world as [he knew] it."[119] Or, as José Ramirez contended in one such meeting at Colseguros, almost terrified by the prospect of unionization, "if people are known by the company they keep, it says a lot if we are keeping company with union members."[120] Thus, white-collar employees across several service sectors defended the notion of office labor as a classed and gendered space where unions should not exist. And in order to do this, they supported "apolitical" meetings called "supportive collectives," which regularly met to discuss "important issues about the office" and, with the service companies' ample support and sponsorship, released a series of publications celebrating how democratic the service sector was.[121] They methodically sent letters to major national newspapers to make sure that "public opinion" knew that service-sector unionization was carried out only "by a minority of misfits [who did] not even know that they [were] members of a democratic society."[122]

For some male white-collar employees, this was a question of religion and spirituality. Hernán Pulido argued in a 1965 participatory meeting that those who joined unions were "a-religious girly men who preoccupied themselves with basic material needs such as food, clothing, shelter, and erotic experiences."[123] Such girly men, furthermore, found themselves dissatisfied because their "lowest and unspeakable desires" led them to see material rather than spiritual rewards as the answer to their social problems. In contrast, Pulido defined himself as a "true man" who found "masculine satisfaction" in serving the "larger democratic good." His preoccupation with work, society, and family would bring him happiness because in heaven "true men" could find "honesty, justice, and equality." A white-collar unionist, Pulido concluded, could become "a spiritual killer . . . a killer of virility."[124]

Other male white-collar employees stressed gender even more in their critique of unions. For them, participation in unions was "the disease of the twentieth century" that presented itself in the form of "wom[e]n with hysterical outbursts."[125] Middle-class masculinity and union participation were to be understood as irreconcilable. In Colseguros, for instance, a group of collaborators argued that white-collar employees "who [had] a tendency to cause trouble in labor matters" could not control themselves and developed "anxieties, frustration, dissatisfaction, paranoia, and selfishness." As "potential hysterical women," they reacted violently to "normal development in society . . . and common facts that everybody knows, such as that some groups in society have money and others do not." These feminized men defined their role in society through "hatred, class discordance, and resentment," sentiments that made them waste their energy causing trouble rather than focusing on what proper men should do: "succeed in life, form a family, and . . . satisfy a woman."[126] After all, according to this diagnosis, white-collar union members showed a "lack of proper performance in matters of sex." Thus such demasculinized hysterical men could hardly represent social democracy in the service sector. As so many said in the participatory meetings and antiunion collectives, union members "are sterile men who do not help themselves. Their virility vanishes and . . . they are not productive members of society."[127]

Some white-collar women also participated in delegitimizing unionization in service companies. For them, white-collar union members were "very poor fathers." In fact, just participating in unions could destroy "happy homes," as fathers preferred to go to union meetings instead of spending quality time with "children and wives." Union participation provoked "internal dissension among married couples," as unionists needed to sacrifice family time in order to comply with union obligations. As a result, these women concluded that unions were the source of social disintegration.

Families headed by white-collar union members would resemble "poor and working-class families, [in which] the husbands [became] violent, *despotas*, intolerant, and violent." By participating in unions, these men, if men at all, became infected with "working-class interests and values."[128]

By the mid-1960s, male white-collar employees embraced development programs and FN policies to further hierarchize themselves as the representation of social democracy. They sought to constitute several gendered and excluded others—the girly and hysterical union member, the feminized elite man, the abnormal working-class man—to define themselves as part of a masculine, competitive middle class located above these others. While female white-collar employees also associated social democracy with their middle-class service work, they redefined their jobs as a product of professional preparation and labor rather than a natural result of their femininity. In so doing, they also established several gendered and classed others—masculinized working-class women and unproductive elite ones.

6

A Revolution for a Democratic Middle-Class Society

In the late 1950s and early 1960s, a group of state professionals, white-collar unionists, and small-business owners began a series of meetings that would, as the minutes recorded, "change the future of the middle class and the Colombian nation."[1] Régulo Millán Puentes, a graduate of the ENC, a member of the recently founded National Union of Accountants (UNC), and a major activist for the creation of the Allied Movement of the Colombian Economic Middle Class (MOCLAM), argued that it was essential to form an organization to "defend the intellectual, moral, economic, and social interests of those who [were] neither capitalists nor proletariats."[2] Mobilizing their transnational conscription as middle class, MOCLAM asserted that they merely wanted to found a "strictly apolitical organization."[3] And it was an apolitical movement because, as MOCLAM's first manifesto, published in 1963, insisted, it would take place through neither "dramatic or spectacular public rallies" nor "grandiloquent yet empty speeches" but through "professional debates, intelligent discussions and peaceful deliberations."[4] The movement aspired "to have a change of guard in society." Some members asserted that they, as middle-class individuals, were entitled to hold the highest offices in the state, as "new people in society could arrive to those positions thanks to their professional merits rather than family connections."[5] Others claimed that it was their democratic duty to fill "the void of power [left] in society" to prevent the return of a new era of "fanaticism and class hatred."[6] These middle-class people reclaimed a "revolution . . . for a democratic middle-class society" through which they could become "a new governing . . . class."[7]

To be sure, one might brush these demands away as part of an ephemeral, politically irrelevant movement that uniformly supported the exclusionary, anticommunist, and oligarchy-led policies of the FN because we still harbor the assumption that the Latin American middle classes had little, if any, political associative life.[8] Scholars tend to historicize any politicization of the middle classes as alien to its very class formation, as middle-class people merely appear as emissaries who support or reject what is mostly considered somebody else's political project. Thus, the middle classes could at times ally with the working classes' political projects to participate in revolutionary politics and at other times reproduce oligarchical interests and thus become a reactionary force.

In the histories of Colombia, such understandings have translated into foundational arguments about the FN.[9] Depoliticized and unaware of their own class interests, the FN's administrations, historians argue, summarily co-opted the middle classes by satisfying their immediate material needs—"house, car, and scholarship." In exchange, the middle classes abandoned formal political struggles and advocated the FN's restrictive political order.[10] As a result, a historical picture emerges of middle classes with externally determined political interests; they, as social actors, continue to be conceptualized as having no political horizon of their own.

By discussing the political mobilization of the middle classes in Bogotá during the 1960s, this chapter proposes a different interpretation. I work on three levels. First, I historicize how middle-class people, in response to the frustrations produced by development programs such as the Alliance and the FN's social policies, put forward an ample repertoire of associative organizations, political demands, and rituals to materialize a "democratic middle-class society." Second, I discuss how these heterogeneous demands produced a gendered and classed "chain of equivalence" through which small-business owners, professionals, and white-collar employees aggregated, but not homogenized, their particular demands to speak as a class. Third, I demonstrate how, as they struggled against elites and popular groups for the right to rule in democracies, professionals, white-collar employees, and small-business owners joined a populist oppositional party—ANAPO—to claim sovereign representation of "the people." I conclude that, far from being left out of political struggles because of their alleged political inertia, by the second half of the 1960s the middle classes played a pivotal role in dismantling the legitimacy of the FN leaders, and its development programs, even if, or precisely because, those middle classes depended on those programs to speak as a class.

Struggling for Recognition

As part of an expansive politicization of everyday life in the 1960s, the middle classes in Bogotá began to establish their own political organizations.[11] Yet, in a context in which anxious transnational policymakers, concerned FN politicians, and nervous employers in the service sector defined the middle classes as an apolitical—that is to say, proper—democratic force, professionals, white-collar employees, and small businessmen could not avoid discussions on whether they were entitled to set up political organizations to represent the middle classes. The movement argued that the middle class needed political redemption, a rallying cry to respond to the uncertainty about who belonged to the middle class. For MOCLAM, there were at least three interconnected "demoralizing political mistakes" that the middle classes had made in the past. The middle class's failure to form a political identity was due to a "social unawareness" about who they were. The middle classes in Colombia had suffered political oblivion, having developed neither their own voice nor representation in front of the nation. More worrisome, they had lived in a perpetual state of crisis because they did not know where they belonged.[12] Thus the task was as simple as it was challenging: the middle classes now needed to undergo a process of redemption through which they could reclaim for themselves the role of "the most important class in society."[13] Addressing the nation, Colombian society, and the FN, MOCLAM eloquently proclaimed in its 1963 political manifesto that

> because of our own guilty indolence, nobody takes us seriously as a middle class. Big capital is represented by its own organizations, and because of its influence and prestige it is able to have a political say regarding public affairs. The workers [who] are organized around the powerful labor unions have the capacity to deeply affect the nation. Until now, the middle class has always labored in favor of the insatiable ambitions of the capitalists and the assertions of the rural and urban working class. And we, despite the power we represent, are destined to be left aside. . . . It is inevitable that we join together to have our own

political platform. . . . We must be ready to vindicate and obtain greater social, economic, and political affirmation, and defend our rights and the rights of our sons.[14]

This was not empty rhetoric. Nor was it a decorative aspect of the political mobilization of society during the 1960s. The movement engaged in several interrelated tasks to mobilize the middle class and to struggle for its political visibility. They wrote letters to major newspapers in Bogotá to reach out to "those who [were] middle class" so that they could become aware of "how important the middle class [was]."[15] They carried out social surveys and sporadic research endeavors to demarcate who was part of that class. They founded a *radio periódico* through which they engaged in pedagogical strategies of persuasion to raise "middle-class consciousness." They traveled around the country in political campaigns to recruit more members for this middle-class organization. They promoted neighborhood committees in Bogotá to listen to what middle-class people had to say about what the movement should advocate for. Finally, they lobbied presidents and several leaders of the FN during the 1960s to establish a middle-class attaché office in the presidency, through which they envisioned organizing the middle class nationally.

Who belonged to the middle classes? Who was entitled to speak as and for a middle class? These questions became critical in MOCLAM's attempt to obtain political recognition. As early as 1962, for instance, MOCLAM's executive committee agreed to commission Rafael Viera Moreno to develop a general census of the Colombian middle class. Viera Moreno, an accountant with experience in social statistics, was in charge of providing a "good idea of who, in social terms, compose[d] and [made] up Colombia's middle class."[16] He crafted a letter to be sent to state offices, bank agencies, small industries, and private companies asking potential readers detailed questions about their "profession, specific job, position in the office, education, instruction, and previous position held in other companies or state institutions . . . residence, and family composition."[17] He sought to address what he called the political limbo of the middle class because socially everyone wanted to be middle class and thus potentially no one could have the right to politically "speak for the middle class."[18] Therefore, Viera Moreno argued that the way to gain political visibility was by determining socially who was truly middle class and naming those who could speak in its name. Such a survey could "unite, communicate, and raise awareness among the members of the middle class" to the point that it would show a "precise plan of action and appropriate orientation."[19]

Although it has proven impossible to find a tabulation of these surveys, Viera Moreno, based on the information that he collected along with some censuses published by the government, produced a statistical description of who belonged to the middle class. He grouped together small-business owners, white-collar employees, and professionals as the occupations most representative of a "democratic middle class." He reported to MOCLAM's executive committee that during the early 1960s, the middle class comprised 45 percent of the Colombian population.[20] He, as an accountant, was convinced that "numbers rule." Thus the "scientific description" he delivered before the executive committee could provide the grounds for the political legitimacy of deeming a specific version of the middle class as a "central class in the nation." As he asked in his report, "Could 45 percent of the Colombian population not participate in the most important decisions of the nation?" But if statistical weight was important, Viera Moreno claimed, a "flawless" delineation of who belonged to a middle class was also needed. Hitting a point that he would reiterate throughout the 1960s, the accountant noted that the middle classes were a "group composed of people generally illustrious, entrepreneurial, calm, worshipers of the law whose voice is heard neither in *la banca* nor in the street riots."[21]

Once statistically defined and socially delineated, the middle class needed their consciousness raised. Nowhere was this political preoccupation clearer than in MOCLAM's radio periódico, suggestively titled *The Middle Class Hour at Your Service*.[22] Viera Moreno, Jorge Rodríguez Pérez, and Octavio Arias Laverde lobbied hard in the House of Representatives and the Senate to secure support for this radio program, which it received when Guillermo León Valencia came to power as second president of the FN. While Valencia would withdraw this support by the end of his administration in 1966, Régulo Millán Puentes felt compelled to show me a brief but important epistolary exchange with Valencia soon after he came to power. In one of those letters, Millán Puentes and Vasco Vejarano, another member of MOCLAM, effusively thanked the president for his "unconditional support . . . for the causes . . . initiatives, and interests of the middle class."[23]

Such support soon translated into the founding in 1962 of MOCLAM's radio periódico, which was broadcast on two radio stations, Radio Continental and La Voz de la Víctor, on the weekends. The FN supported it because MOCLAM made the case for defining this radio periódico as properly political—that is, it would not be a manifestation of "dramatic or spectacular public rallies," just a tool for lifting the middle class away from its social unawareness. It was thus a pedagogical effort. Jorge Méndez Calvo and Francisco Ricaute, professionals laboring in a private service company, volunteered to host half of the hour-long program on February 19, 1962, during which they called upon middle-class listeners to become committed to their class.[24] "Let's work together ... join the middle-class cause," Méndez Calvo announced. "We are ... the middle-class family ... that needs to discover and find solidarity among its members to reach our common interests," Ricaute echoed. "It is true," both insisted, that "we have thus far been indifferent to knowing who we are and what we are capable of, [and because of that] we have fallen into solitude, in which every member of this class lives by forgetting the interests of those akin to him."[25]

How could the middle class overcome such political indifference? They needed to reach out to "the ordinary and busy middle-class man ... the man in the office ... the man in a state organization ... the small-business owners who care about their business ... and all the women at home who make things happen in life."[26] They crafted and read short stories on-air that could resonate with these middle-class people. Often, these stories consisted of three main parts: the presentation of a problem that an imagined member of the middle class had to face in his daily life, a celebration of the middle class's role as a democratic force in the nation, and the solution to the problem presented in the first part. At the core of these stories, MOCLAM located women as key players in raising middle-class consciousness. Moreover, women would emancipate their men, who, once properly masculinized, could likewise redeem the middle class. For example, Alba de Millán, a professional woman and stay-at-home mother who participated in several broadcasts between 1964 and 1966, invited "middle-class women like [herself]" to support their husbands so that they, as proper men, could stand up for "middle-class homes."[27] With her vision directed to Colombia's future, she invited "all those middle-class women" to join forces with their husbands in democratizing society. Speaking on the radio—which one might see as a public role par excellence—Millán made sure that middle-class women remained intimately associated with a private sphere. But what women could do in this private sphere was deemed fundamental because it would prepare their men to politically secure middle-class visibility in front of the nation. It was women's job to tend to the home's material conditions so that middle-class men could dedicate themselves to the hard political labor of uplifting their class from its "lethargy" and facing "the challenges of democracy." It was thus the task of middle-class women to break this passivity by making the home a place where "men could reenergize themselves" to work for other political endeavors.[28] It was this sacrifice that distinguished middle-class women from other women in society who, egocentric and insensitive, put their interests before everybody else's. Thus the middle class's political recognition and class consciousness depended on a gendered distribution of tasks. Women would sacrifice themselves as professionals and workers while their husbands would work to achieve political recognition for a middle class as a whole.

Perhaps because MOCLAM had difficulty determining how effective these radio programs were, the organization invited listeners to send missives commenting on the stories or making suggestions about the radio periódico as a whole. The movement received few but telling responses. Small-business owners, white-collar employees, and professionals participated in MOCLAM's programs for raising middle-class consciousness. Sharing the need to overcome a middle-class tradition of passivity, these respondents— mostly men—wrote about the past to search for a gendered visibility of a middle-class collective self in the present. By mobilizing transnational discourses on modernization theory, these men imagined an undemocratic middle-class past and tradition—constructed by selfish, feminized social climbers and unconscious lesser men—to define who could speak democratically for the middle class in the present and how political recognition should be sought via an organization like MOCLAM. In some of the first radio broadcasts, Francisco Ricaute responded to some missives by explaining how belonging to a political organization that would speak for the middle class depended on breaching the divide between individual life and the social sphere, developing a class consciousness linking each middle-class individual to those belonging to the same social space.[29] Employing a teleological, gendered narrative, he envisioned recognition as and identification with a middle class as a move away from a "middle-class undemocratic legacy . . . and a past of cowardly behavior" and toward a "virile . . . present [and] future."[30] He defined the class as "socially conscious and politically active."[31] In this new middle class, men could utilize their "knowledge and professionalism to give opinions about society and political matters of the nation." Indeed, in contrast to an imagined, feminized past tradition, the middle class had to be integrated by manly men who could speak for their own class, which could be done by creating an organization that could confront "those who [were] the owners of the capital, which [was] a minority, and those who [did] not have anything, which was the mass of workers and peasants."[32]

This search for gendered and classed visibility infused MOCLAM's demands as a political organization. Millán Puentes remembered, for instance, how he risked his job as an accountant in a private company to promote a campaign for the middle-class cause. He recalled those days with excitement as he visited several cities in Colombia.[33] He felt "as a true man . . . doing something important [as] these middle-class people paid attention to what I had to say. . . . Middle-class people wanted to make a difference. They wanted to be part of the middle-class cause . . . and redemption." Imagine, he continued, "I was telling middle-class people that a forgotten . . . voiceless class could play a role . . . that without them a democracy could not exist." But most importantly, Millán Puentes recalled, he realized that there was "a middle class . . . that wanted to join forces and do something for themselves. . . . Going to those rallies changed my life: people chanting 'long live the middle class,' imagine that!"[34]

For these political rallies, Millán Puentes and other members of MOCLAM's executive committee wrote sophisticated, if repetitive, speeches.[35] Millán Puentes invited audiences to ponder "difficult questions" about their role in the nation's democratization. Drawing on the discourses shaping the development programs, he asked audiences where "the human capital . . . the energy, and the organization" would come from to "carry out the necessary democratic transformation for Colombia." He answered by comparing "two old traditional groups," the oligarchy and the mass of rural and urban workers, to a "young group" looking forward to moving the nation onto the democratic path, a dynamic group that had emerged inevitably, not as part of "relations of production" but rather as a product of scientific and technological changes in society, and whom the other two traditional classes needed to look up to.[36] Millán Puentes invited middle-class audiences to embrace their role in this democratic transformation by asking two more questions: "Are we really letting the members of the working or peasant classes be the leaders in democracy when they have barely had any experience with it? Are we really letting the static . . . stagnant groups have the say in democracy when they are already falling behind the democratic changes that we are experiencing?"[37] This was the most important call made in this struggle for political visibility: in proper democracies, MOCLAM claimed, "the middle classes [were] the people."[38]

In another speech, given presumably in Cali in 1964, Millán Puentes further elaborated on this political call. He invited the audience to join MOCLAM so that the organization could become powerful. Indeed, Millán Puentes, perhaps unaware of the obvious connections to a famous cry in

Marx and Engels's *Communist Manifesto*, finished his speech by exhorting the audience: "Middle-class men of Colombia, please unite! . . . We have a passive past to overcome, a productive present to embrace, a virile future awaiting us and a revolution to make. . . . The future is the middle class."[39]

When I asked Millán Puentes about this speech and its political language, he assured me that there was no connection whatsoever with "communist tendencies." He swore that this was neither his intention nor MOCLAM's political objective. "I am a middle-class guy . . . don't you see it? MOCLAM struggled for a middle class," he told me, emphasizing what he thought was quite apparent: the middle class, as "the people in democracies," were at odds with "communist tendencies." The movement wanted a "society of administrators not proletariats. . . . We wanted progress and democracy, not backwardness."[40] My question, however, did ignite difficult memories, because Valencia and his administration saw these speeches as a manifestation of the middle class's potentially improper politics. As MOCLAM tried to institutionalize in the mid-1960s by requesting that Valencia's administration advocate for a "middle-class agency" attached to the presidency, Valencia's initial support for the organization soon dissipated. This was a major political disappointment, Millán Puentes recalled, as MOCLAM thought that it was only through the state's support and recognition that the Colombian middle class could be represented. Thus, while Millán Puentes first supported the FN and Valencia's bid for the presidency, as a "supporter of the middle-class cause" he later considered Valencia a representative of "the traditional oligarchies" who was against "the true people of democracy."[41]

The movement also established committees in "typical middle-class neighborhoods" in Bogotá—Centro Urbano Antonio Nariño and Los Alcázares, in particular—to receive suggestions on what it should advocate for. The organization used these suggestions to request from the president in 1964 a state agency that could address "the material and spiritual needs" of the middle classes. The movement made three main demands. They argued that the middle class, given its cultural and social beliefs, required a certain level of material comfort—comfortable houses, consumption, and quality education—that the working and peasant classes, accustomed to "simple clothing, disorganized houses, and general education," did not.[42] The second and third demands were ones that MOCLAM had been discussing since the late 1950s: the political representation of the middle class as "the people in the consolidation of democracy," and the expansion of "quality education" so that "middle-class children [could] become the future of the nation."[43]

Valencia's administration dismissed MOCLAM's demands, and the middle-class office never materialized. In what seems to be a response to the proposal, Valencia wrote few but quite telling words. In a context in which the middle class was linked with democracy, Valencia argued quite the opposite: a middle-class office "would not collaborate with the progress and modernity of the country."[44] Why? To be sure, the political moment of the mid-1960s did not help, as there were several working-class protests and salaries began to fall. Valencia thought MOCLAM's demands "too political." It is no accident that several MOCLAM missives submitted after the proposal's rejection elaborated on why they, as an organization defending the middle class's interests, were not only apolitical but also quite different from those organizations that created "chaos, anarchy, and poverty in the nation."[45] Their movement, MOCLAM insisted, sought a "social equilibrium of economic forces . . . not a class struggle." They claimed that they "never . . . in a thousand years" would think of "getting rid of private property."[46] They wanted "a professionalization of the nation, not a *campesinización*," "a nation of owners, not of proletariats." Yet given the political struggles, MOCLAM found it wise to remind the president of the political implications of his lack of support for the middle-class office. Evoking the Alliance, MOCLAM warned Valencia in 1965 that "if we do not find the solution . . . we will find ourselves in a social disequilibrium. . . . It is time to preserve the democratic institutions. . . . It is time to do something for the forgotten middle class. It is time to sacrifice the little to save the whole."[47] This warning is quite telling because, as we will see later in the chapter, MOCLAM, along with other middle-class organizations, would find in ANAPO a critical space to see some of its demands recognized.

The Right for Professional Self-Determination

Radio periódico and neighborhood meetings of MOCLAM opened crucial spaces for further politicization of the middle classes, even if that politicization departed from what MOCLAM was initially advocating for. During the first half of the 1960s, for instance, almost every professional occupation—dentists, accountants, physicians, agronomists, social workers, teachers, and physicians—established or expanded their own political organizations: Federación de Sindicatos de Profesionales de Colombia (FEDEPROCOL), Federación Nacional de Profesionales del Estado (FENALSTRASE), Federación Colombiana de Educadores (FECODE), Asociación Médica Sindical

Colombiana (ASMEDAS), Asociación Colombiana de Ingenieros Agrónomos (ACIA), and professional unions in ICT and INCORA, among several other organizations. These professionals simultaneously joined forces in what came to be known as the Movimiento de Liberación de la Clase Media (Middle-Class Liberation Movement [LMMC]). Indeed, if the FN saw MOCLAM as too political and thus unworthy of state recognition, the LMMC saw it as "very close to the government . . . [as it was] being bureaucratized with no real consequences for the middle class."[48]

It is crucial to emphasize that the LMMC emerged within the FN rather than against it, as one might be tempted to argue, because it developed from an intense discussion spurred by the frustrations that state professionals working for development programs such as the Alliance experienced as they attempted to educate both the elites and the laboring classes on how to coexist with each other peacefully and hierarchically. Fernando Agudelo, a member of this movement, recalled how he began coordinating meetings to talk about "professional issues" with several friends from ICT and other local state institutions such as INCORA.[49] Usually after work and field trips, he remembered, they started organizing political get-togethers in downtown cafés and at colleagues' houses. Sometime during the first half of the 1960s, these informal meetings became institutionalized "roundtables" that published newsletters demanding the materialization of a middle-class democratic society.[50] To create this society, it was imperative to initiate a manly struggle for reclaiming "the national professional sovereignty."[51] Drawing on the teachings of Torres Restrepo, professionals argued that for a democratic state to exist, it was important to become professional middle-class men liberated from "professional colonialism," which had destined the middle class to a state of "undemocratic perpetual dependency on the United States with respect to the affairs of the Colombian nation" and prevented them from having "Colombia's interest in their heart" when exercising state rule.[52]

As state representatives, they demanded ownership of the professional sovereignty of the nation. In one of the first newsletters issued as a result of these roundtables, Israel Guerrero, an architect and member of MUNIPROC and later FEDEPROCOL, wrote an editorial discussing the United States as a central force in what role professional men should play "in a changing society." He detailed how the role assigned to middle-class professionals— "to be the conscience of the nation . . . to defend the national future . . . to speak for [and about] the nation . . . to alert others of the dangers to democracy . . . to guide the destiny of the people"—had been hindered by professional colonialism.[53] Guerrero argued that "naive . . . and cowardly professionals" could not understand that the United States influenced how professionalization in Colombia was taking place. The United States wanted to "influence and control" what professional men did and thought because of "what the middle class [was] able to do for the nation." The United States wanted the middle class, Guerrero concluded, to follow "certain models" that could benefit "North America's interests" at the expense of the interests of the Colombian nation.[54] Thus LMMC, as a movement demanding "state democratization and professional advancement," would fight for the liberation of the middle class from any "colonial bond" or "US professional colonialism." In this way, Colombian professionals could exercise their national intelligence, technical preparation, and professional values in the service of the Colombian nation.

The Movimiento de Liberación de la Clase Media was also demanding the right to "professional self-determination," a democratic right that needed to be fought for "in a true and manly fashion" because the FN administrations were giving away the nation's "professional sovereignty," forcing these professionals to either live in *ostranticsmo* or leave the country in search of a better future.[55] Professionals complained that their preparation was seen by the state as of lesser quality, as the FN preferred to hire "foreign experts who [had] no idea of the realities of Colombian society." Nowhere was this demand clearer than in the consolidation of annual transnational professional conferences during the first half of the 1960s. Professional men started traveling to various countries in Latin America and, when possible, creating alliances to advance their political demands, so that the Colombian middle class's concerns could be heard on an international scale.[56] With the financial support of the OAS and UN, a group of accountants who were active members of the LMMC organized in 1964 the Congreso de Contadores Bolívarianos. The first meeting of this congress took place in Quito, Ecuador, and although it was organized as an occupational conference, at issue was the situation of professionalization. As one of MOCLAM's central figures and actively involved with the LMMC, Germán Giraldo played a critical role in organizing this conference and following up on transnational contacts produced as a result of such an international meeting. For the first meeting Giraldo, along with Clodomiro Rodríguez, another member of the LMMC, wrote the inaugural speech, which was recited by Rodríguez in front of Quito's Bolívar monument on Friday, July 24, 1964. For Rodríguez, the speech had to center on questioning the "giant of the north."[57] He thought that being a professional middle-class man meant defending the command of the nation's technical, scientific, and professional knowledge. Giraldo himself asserted that if such a liberation movement was to have some political resonance, it needed to go beyond these complaints. Thus Giraldo contended in the speech, and still insisted when he discussed its drafting with me, that the task was to call on professionals to draw on what I would call a homosocial past: "the past of those who were truly men," through which professional men could learn how to proceed with their movement.[58] He also spoke of their being able to articulate political demands for the constitution of a middle-class society in which the "democratization of Colombian society, professional independence, and intellectual sovereignty" could work together.[59] To make this point as clear as possible to the middle class, Rodríguez and Giraldo remembered, they needed first to give examples that tapped into the experiences of the middle-class professionals.[60] They then had to move on to what could be done "for the liberation of the professional middle class from the Yankees' control."[61] Rodríguez thus began the speech by asking a presumably male middle-class audience, "How many cases have you seen where the gringos get hired by the government to write an opinion about the future of your country? How many of you have seen gringo experts supposedly working for your country? These are two-bit experts that only want to write reports, with no knowledge of [our] national reality to benefit their country, and so we are in perpetual dependence."[62]

The time of allowing "gringos and oligarchs to monopolize the professional decisions about the future of the country" was over. And, as many professionals argued, Bolívar was close at hand to offer political guidance on how to assume this "manly posture." Bolívar became central to a homosocial past—or "the stories of those men and their organizations, their political and social relations, as well as the lives of those men who have united to liberate our countries from the foreign burden"—that offered political guidance for changing the situation of middle-class professionals.[63] They should embody those "virile and liberating standards of Simon Bolívar" to create a democratic middle-class society with independent, liberated, and intelligent professionals representing the state and leading the Colombian nation.[64] Just like Bolívar, these professional men wanted to become "middle-class liberators" of the vast and progressive expanse of America. Once Bolívar's masculine traits—"strength, energy . . . impartiality, professionalism . . . [and a] strong drive toward justice and democracy"—were recuperated and performed, a new political and social order could come into existence and the professional would be liberated to exercise his proper national role.

As Rodríguez proclaimed under the male gaze of Bolívar's statue: "With our professional intelligence as our only weapon, we are a force to specify the demands of the middle class.... Professional independence, justice, and democracy and Bolívar from the heights of your position enlighten us to take the right path to democracy."[65]

White-Collar Employees: Redefining Proper Politics in Democracy

Some female and male white-collar employees remembered the service sector's expansion as opening the possibility of forming unions and political associations (figure 6.1). Guillermo Ramírez, a former employee of Colseguros, recalled how this insurance company, rather than promoting of its own volition the economic well-being of its employees, was forced to negotiate educational opportunities, cooperatives, and housing initiatives, among other privileges and rights, due to the role played by unions and political organizations. As he was eager to say in our conversation,

> With other colleagues we founded or joined unions in Colseguros....
> For the company, we ... unionists were almost criminals. This never happened to me, but sometimes Colseguros visited future employees' houses just to avoid unionization.... We faced the company that did not want a union.... It was for true men, you know, there were so many colleagues who were afraid.... They just wanted enjoy the benefits of our struggles. I was among those who were man enough to speak up.... My family, my education, my house, everything is because of what we did back then with the union.[66]

It is no accident that the directors of service companies and so many other female and male white-collar employees assured me in our conversations that unions had not existed in the service sector. Others argued that former union members not only would give me the "wrong version of [their] history" but also would "make up stories that never happened."[67] Still others claimed that "the type of company" for which they worked and "its culture" made unionizing unnecessary: "the main reason to form a union was the quality of the salaries, and we did not have any problems with this.... There was something about the kind of people here that they were just not union-driven people because we did not have interests contrary to the company."[68]

Figure 6.1 The Right to Unionize. ANEBRAR, ca. early 1970s.

But some white-collar employees in the service sector experienced during the 1960s a process of politicization. The second half of the 1960s witnessed the formation of important unions in the service sector. The ACEB and UNEB were consolidated among bank employees. In private service companies such as Colseguros, white-collar employees founded organizations such as the Sindicato de Trabajadores de la Rama Activa Aseguradora (SINTRASE) and Asociación de Trabajadores de Sudamericana de Seguros (ATSS). And these employees also attempted to establish a general association across all insurance companies, the Asociación de Empleados de Compañías de Seguros (ASDECOS). In BR, white-collar employees founded the Asociación Nacional de Empleados del Banco de la República (ANEBRE) in 1964 and then joined forces with other banks' white-collar employees to found the Federación Nacional de Sindicatos Bancarios Colombianos (FENASIBANCOL).[69] Indeed, in service companies like CAFAM, white-collar employees began "clandestine" meetings to organize themselves in informal groups to voice their dissatisfaction with different company policies. Women in the service sector organized as Mujeres de Oficina—or Oficinistas—although women also did participate in this politicization through unions mostly led by men.

As the FN delegitimized middle-class union participation, along with the support of female and male employees, one of the major political demands among those who decided to found or join unions was that unions be defined as logical features of middle-class lives in the service sector. Union publications reveal, furthermore, class and gender anxieties about the need to explain why, as Jorge Santos Vallejo, a white-collar employee in BR, said, a union would "make a lot of sense" and represent "the most important manifestation of democracy."[70] He conceded that a union in the service sector would not look like those in factories, as an association of white-collar employees should epitomize "the democratic role of the middle class" and, as such, exemplify a "union of intelligence."[71] That classed union, he insisted, could be seen neither as an "exotic plant" in the service sector nor as a "dangerous organization" against the service companies' interests but rather as an association seeking to benefit those who serve in an "office, use a pen as a labor tool, and defend the understanding among social groups." Should the need for a strike arise, these organizations would not support the use of "any brute force or turbulent agitation on streets" but would rather take to the streets using the "power of persuasion, merit of dialogue . . . and argumentative talent" to earn their rights through democratic means.[72]

In the 1960s, these white-collar employees appropriated discourses about affective/service labor and middle-classness to demand a new definition of labor relations. It was neither a total reproduction of nor a radical departure from the discourses that placed the service sector beyond capital and labor and thus beyond union membership. Employees complied with the idea that the service sector was not defined by class conflict. But they simultaneously confronted the idea that the service sector was a labor space where unions could be discounted as if the relationship between employers and employees did not exist. Rather, the service sector was characterized as a labor relationship in which employers and employees would enter on equal and cooperative terms. Yet again, these white-collar employees explicitly wanted to make clear that their "middle-class unions" did not call for "following an outdated Marxist tradition," the end of democracy, but rather the democratization of a "waged economy" in which they could "get what [they] deserve[d]."[73]

These white-collar employees demanded political recognition by claiming that "unions of intelligence" would help foster cooperation between employers and employees and reduce labor conflict by helping service companies to promote their goals of teamwork, efficient communication, and mutual understanding.[74] In fact, these new unionists contended—almost mimicking the human relations discourses used by service companies to exclude unions from the definitions of office labor—that if service-sector employees were more satisfied with their jobs, which was the main purpose of "modern . . . democratic unions," then they could concentrate on their jobs and thereby increase both their productivity and, by implication, the company's profit. Thus these recently founded unions promoted among their colleagues a "double loyalty," the idea that there was no conflict between "being loyal to the company and being faithful to the union" because both "democratic attitudes" complemented each other in consolidating a service sector that defined itself as a community of shared interests.[75]

This demand for political recognition as union members was gendered. In contrast to those who saw union participation as a manifestation of a lack of middle-class masculinity, white-collar unionists demanded to be recognized as proper middle-class men. These unionists argued that they, "true men who stand up face-to-face with companies," should represent the service sector against other social groups. Unlike the "feminine . . . passive, kneeling positions" of "false white-collar employees" who did not want to join unions, unionists were man enough to develop their own "agency, think by [themselves], and become whoever [they] wanted to be."[76] Democracy depended not on white-collar employees who let themselves "be humiliated . . . demeaned, and dishonored" but rather on men who, by putting their virility to use for the benefit of a larger good, would embrace any challenge to improve the material circumstances of the "most important class in history."[77] It was up to "true men," they claimed, to defend the service sector from contamination by "irrationality, struggle, violence, and resentment," values associated with working-class unions. But "feminine, cowardly, and passive postures" would not do the trick. Rather, it was necessary to assume "active and masculine" visions and attitudes to protect the service sector as a space where "unionized men of work . . . unionized intelligent men [did] not vacillate to create the conditions for all of [them] to achieve success and improve democracy."[78] Unlike elites, these middle-class unionists would know how to lead. Unlike working-class unionists, they would know how to listen. As members of the middle class, they would be able to "choose [their] own destiny . . . joining forces together, walking the path not of cowardice but of courage and virility to reach the final goal: democracy and the freedom necessary to do our work well."[79]

Small-Business Owners: Making a Productive Fatherland

As the story of Alejandro Hurtado, described in chapter 3, suggested, small-business owners experienced development programs like the Alliance as an opportunity to "become somebody in life." But as development programs celebrated them as central to democracy, middle-class small-business owners both embraced and questioned that particular vision of democracy. Hurtado recounted, for instance, how his life as a small businessman oscillated between moving his business forward and actively participating in the Asociación Colombiana Popular de Industriales (ACOPI). Although he emphasized how his economic success was a product of his own individual effort, he also remembered those years as a formative time when he "got together with men like [him] to make things happen for us" to fight for the "rights of small businessmen like [himself]."[80] The association made him realize that he "was not alone"; "there were men like me stressed about all the things one had to do to get a business afloat." It was through ACOPI, Hurtado emphasized, "that I became aware of who I was as ... middle class ... discussing our concerns and interests."[81]

Although small-business owners founded ACOPI at the end of 1952, the organization became more politically active during the 1960s. Like other middle-class organizations, ACOPI had to put a lot of labor into legitimizing it as a proper political force and as representatives of a democratic middle class because the FN saw it as an apolitical influence, which precluded its members' participation in engagement in class struggle or embracing of "foreign ideologies." Thus ACOPI, mobilizing MOCLAM's political programs for raising middle-class consciousness, called on its members to overcome the "taboo toward politics" among small-business owners.[82] Echoing MOCLAM's account of a feminized and depoliticized middle-class tradition, ACOPI asserted that such a taboo was quite unproductive, because it allowed tradition to reign in the realm of politics. "Permissible ... passive ... tolerable," and hence feminized, beliefs among small businessmen had prevented the organization from engaging in the masculine task of defending what was rightly theirs and had allowed "traditional politicians ... to penetrate the organization" with interests unbefitting ACOPI's pursuit of "development, democracy, and happiness for the nation."[83] It was time, ACOPI invited its members, to "man up" and embrace the challenges of the twentieth century. Rather than perpetuating individualistic concerns, ACOPI claimed that it was time to join forces, in a "united effort and class solidarity."[84]

The association also made clear that this united effort did not mean to "get to the streets, use violence as a weapon, proclaim irrationality . . . speak of exploiters and exploited, or convince people whose simplest minds lead them to believe that the transformation [was] around the corner."[85] Rather, ACOPI's members embraced their role as representatives of an economic democracy to claim that they would pursue politics as a matter of "administration . . . management, and supervision." Yet they also questioned the FN's political rationality by claiming as their most important political effort the shifting of Colombia away from traditional politics, associated with an unproductive pact that the Liberal and Conservative Parties had promoted to stay in power, and toward modern politics, in which "a higher and more democratic form of political organization" could prevail. Furthermore, ACOPI demanded political recognition as members of the middle class dedicated to society's democratization who could "maximize scarce resources, valorize human capital, and generate economic opportunities for the nation."[86] In such a higher manifestation of democracy, politics would be a question of administration rather than ideology, management rather than bureaucracy, and negotiation rather than conflict.

Members of ACOPI drew on Jorge Eliécer Gaitán's famous populist discourses of the 1940s that divided the nation into the political country (the oligarchies) and the national country (the people) in order to formulate a classed definition of democracy. The association claimed that Colombia had suffered a sharp split between "the political country"—composed of "oligarchies, professionals of politicking, and the simplest people (i.e., the laboring classes) who had been co-opted by the very same oligarchies"— and "the productive country"—consisting of members of "the most productive class in the nation." The main political demand of ACOPI, one that resonated with ANAPO, was the formation of an organization through which its members, as leaders of "the productive country," would be able to take over—and rule—"the political country."[87]

For small-business owners, there was a fundamental difference between economic growth and development. The former was the product of economic policies that only benefited "the big industrialists," while the latter advanced "the national economy as a whole." According to ACOPI, the FN, as the manifestation of an "oligarchical pact," had been promoting certain policies that worked on the assumption that "the moneyed classes" tended to "save capital in order to invest it in further industrialization of the country."[88] But ACOPI contended that the opposite was true, for the savings rates among those classes were minimal, if present at all. The association claimed that the best argument for allowing the productive country to take over was the "feminine ways" of these moneyed classes, who behaved like "obsessive women in need of consumption" who instead of investing profit back into the national economy, as would a presumably masculinized and proper economic subject, "consume[d] luxury goods such as giant houses, fancy memorial stones, and concentrated capital for their own benefit."[89] For this reason small businesses charged the FN with perpetuating policies for "economic growth" rather than development, policies that took income and capital as the only measure of a society's industrialization. Income and capital, they admitted, were important to introduce industrial changes or even to capitalize the economy of a country like Colombia, but measures focusing solely on these ignored that Colombia was "an underdeveloped economy" and that therefore economic growth only increased the concentration of capital "in few hands." Such policies promoted an "anticapitalist democracy" benefiting only "the political country" of laboring classes and oligarchies.[90]

Small businessmen envisioned economic policies for a "democratic development," associated with the consolidation of the "productive country." The association also demanded that the FN promote development policies for further expanding the "production of wealth," sanctifying competition, mandating employment growth, expanding the capacity of work, and maximizing human capital. Drawing on transnational discourses on democracy and development, ACOPI insisted that the economy included much more than industrial growth because, following Gutiérrez de Pineda, true economic change equally required transforming "the values, qualities, and virtues" into those suitable for a capitalist democracy.[91] Thus, ACOPI demanded that the FN support those groups who could not only, given the realities of underdevelopment, diversify and maximize the economy but also expand the values and virtues needed for an "advanced economy" to emerge. Unlike the "political country," small-business owners—the "productive country" of "reasoned middle-class men"—would put the economy at the service of the nation and usurp the political country and its vision of "antidemocratic capitalism."[92] As ACOPI claimed in their annual conferences, economic studies, and political missives to the FN's presidents, the task was to make capitalism "an instrument for a democratic middle-class society." If oligarchies promoted monopolies, small-business owners would implement competition as "the most important democratic feature of advanced economies." If oligarchies encouraged monoproduction, small-business owners would diversify the economy. And if oligarchies concentrated capital for themselves, small-business owners would incentivize market competition by putting whatever capital was gained in their small and medium industries back into the national economy. The small-business owner would create a democratic capitalism characterized by free enterprise and competition, as they were able to produce more, better, and at lower cost in an underdeveloped economic environment of scarce material resources. And as they engaged in competition, small-business owners would expand exports to neighboring countries, reduce the balance of payments, and multiply employment opportunities. Or as they put it in their conferences and publications, they would create, "if not a capitalist democracy, at least a social market economy."[93]

It was amid this intense debate over the political role of small businessmen that Guillermo León Valencia issued Decree 2351, later formalized as law in 1968 by Carlos Lleras Restrepo. In response to a potential general strike by labor unions in 1965, the FN decided to provide this labor reform to expand social security, institutionalize laws about better labor conditions, protect certain labor rights, and provide access to health services. The decree furthermore established that fixed-term contracts for all industrial workers could not be for less than a year. It prohibited employers from terminating contracts without just cause; if workers could prove that they had been thus terminated, they had the right to proper compensation. This decree also mandated holiday pay for workers, double pay for overtime hours, and pay for days of rest. Occasional benefits (such as health) were also included as part of a worker's wage. The decree made state arbitration mandatory for labor conflicts.

The association vehemently protested every single aspect of this decree, claiming that it threatened the harmonious development of a capitalist democracy. In so doing, they rallied for more "reasonable" labor policies in small and medium industries that would deregulate the state's role in questions of labor rights. They demanded much more "productive" fiscal policies and public expenditure for stimulating economic competition. And they requested more expansive state credit and loan opportunities. Small-business owners elaborated these demands at ACOPI's annual conferences in 1966 and 1967. Some members contended that the FN was giving in to the laboring classes' pressure; instead of using "legitimate violence" to prevent "chaos in the nation," the government was offering too many "gifts" that benefited particular interests. Other members of ACOPI complained that a "weak" government, rather than defending capitalist democracy, was succumbing to "the pressures of the simplest minds in society who [did] not know how democracy work[ed]" and who, by "participating too narrowly [and] too actively" in matters of democracy, were forestalling the nation's achievement of modernity.[94] The association therefore demanded that the FN understand that small-business owners were not against laboring peoples. Rather, small-business owners wanted to create the conditions for a "productive nation" in which each member of society participated in democracy according to his or her specific functions.[95] "Who," ACOPI asked in one of its multiple editorials, "move[s] the economy forward, workers or small-business owners? Whose main concern is the productivity of the country, so that employment opportunities are in place for those who really need them? Who cares about the public good?"[96] The association wanted to make clear that the FN was surrendering to "the excesses of democracy" by allowing workers to make economic decisions for which they were neither prepared nor equipped. The FN was disturbing the "social harmony" required for capitalist democracy, a hierarchical relationship between workers—defined as "the sweat of the nation," who cared about their own individual and private economic interests—and those small-business owners demarcated as "social investors and wealth producers," who worked for the nation's economic interests. Small-business owners defined their own activities as a public good, as masculine and democratic, while deeming those of workers particular, private, and feminine. Thus, for capitalist democracy to coalesce, workers needed to respect a hierarchical (unequal) distribution of human capital, dedication, and occupations according to "the conditions of each and every member of the society."[97]

It is in this context that ACOPI complained that workers and unions more specifically were becoming obstacles to Colombia's productivity. Those privileges given to—rather than rights earned by—workers endangered small-business owners' role in defending the public good. Those particular privileges would "undemocratically increase the cost of production" among small and medium industries. They would demolish the possibility of offering more employment opportunities, as capital, instead of being invested back into the national economy, would be concentrated among, and likely wasted by, those "privileged workers" being paid "more than what they deserved."[98] These high wages would increase inflation, thereby preventing consumption, and threaten the fragile struggle to rationalize human capital and maximize scarce resources, as any potential profit by small and medium industries would be misused for "labor costs . . . among fewer and fewer workers" instead of being invested back into the nation as a whole.[99] Small-business owners begged workers to understand that such burdens

made the cost of "the labor factor" not only very high but also antidemocratic, as "the privileges" implemented by different labor codes since at
least the mid-1960s prevented the liberation of "democratic capital" and
stymied both the diversification of the economy and the expansion of employment opportunities to "more and more workers." For these reasons,
business owners supplicated the nation's working masses to play a "more
democratic role" by setting aside "pointless strikes or far-fetched lists of
demands," such as for better real salaries, so that "more people like them"
would have employment.[100] That unions did not do so proved that it was
the antidemocratic, antimasculine, antieconomic, and anticompetitive attitude of the working classes that was the main source of high unemployment rates and high inflation.

As a result of these complaints, ACOPI began as early as 1966 to demand
what it called a "unified or integrated salary" for workers in small and medium industries, which would allow small-business owners to save capital
by having workers assume responsibility for paying some of their own labor
benefits, including health coverage and retirement plans. These owners
called for lowering the "intolerable . . . unmanageable, and excruciating"
cost of social protection and private privileges. An integrated salary would
redirect the capital "wasted in the labor factor" to fostering employment,
competition, and economic productivity, which small-business owners
claimed could have "a democratizing element" by allowing both owners and
workers to "equally" contribute to diversifying the economy and expanding employment opportunities.[101] Yet for this integrated salary to function
as a source of economic productivity, "human capital" would have to be
maximized and rationalized—in other words, exploited and alienated—as
intensively as possible. The entrepreneurial state had to protect those with
"small and modest capital" because their exploitation of workers, presumably unlike the self-interested exploitation practiced by big industrialists,
could translate into profit invested in a larger democratic good.[102]

This is why small-business owners, unlike any other middle-class group,
mobilized what would later be defined as neoliberal discourses to exoticize
and delegitimize working-class unions as a radical other to democracy. The
demand was clear: they wanted "more employment opportunities [and]
less unions." Small-business owners thought that unions represented a
"working-class aristocracy," a "dictatorship of the few," and "tropical *cau-
dillismo*." Small-business owners wrote that unions were quintessentially
antidemocratic because they behaved like women who, thanks to their
"aristocratic privilege, happily vegetat[ed] and passively expect[ed] an

income." Union members were "old-fashioned women" awaiting their "sugar daddies"—in the parlance of small-business owners, the state. In a word, working-class unions produced "economically castrated men" who could not become productive members of the nation.[103]

What ACOPI wanted was a democracy based not on "distribution of wealth" but on the production of more wealth through democratic exploitation. It wanted to include as many people as possible in an exploitative process. It submitted countless scientific studies to prove their case. Alejandro Hurtado, for instance, kept several papers that he had presented at ACOPI conferences as well as letters that he had sent to different FN presidents. In them he complained about how state intervention in labor matters was counterproductive because "Colombian workers [were] getting used to leisure rather than work" and could now disguise their leisure as labor. As he wrote in one of his papers, all these "privileges," camouflaged as rights, were promoting among workers a loss of appetite for effort and a lack of love for work because there was no motivation to "get better and gain some dignity for themselves."[104] Small-business owners' imagined democratic capitalism required a rationalization and maximization—their terms for exploitation and alienation—of the labor factor, because if workers "feel secure . . . or feel that nothing [was] at stake when laboring," economic productivity was put in jeopardy.[105] What happened, Hurtado asked the audience of a congress for small-business owners in 1967, when "everything is fine and workers feel no threat to their labor conditions?" He answered: "They are not as motivated and hence productivity is low." And if productivity was low, then capital could not be saved and invested back into the economy, and employment opportunities would by definition decrease. Thus, in this hierarchical vision of democracy, unions were counterproductive not only because they prevented the exploitation of labor but also because they created an economically counterproductive sense of security among workers. Hurtado argued that a healthy measure of insecurity, along with a labor's rationalization or maximization would make workers think that their job, and hence their social well-being, was at stake and therefore make them economically productive and innovative.[106] The right amount of exploitation, Hurtado declared, would provide the conditions for workers to enter into (masculine) competition, which would cause their human capital to appreciate (or at least not depreciate) and allow them to earn, rather than passively receive, the material dignity that necessarily comes with labor. Workers could therefore develop virtues and values such as honesty, a sense of achievement, eagerness for competition, sacrifice, personal effort, innovation, economic aspirations, and, above all, tolerance for exploitation as long as they were under the right amount of material insecurity. Workers themselves needed to learn how to be democratic and to care for the nation's wealth by sharing among themselves the exploitation and alienation of their own labor.

There were two other demands that ACOPI pushed for during the 1960s: a tax reduction and the expansion of credit opportunities for owners of small and medium industries. As the FN increased sales and income taxes during the second half of the 1960s, ACOPI complained that these measures were "antidemocratic" because they worked against the public good by forcing small-business owners, not big industrialists with "fat bank accounts," to sacrifice capital that they could otherwise invest in the economy. In what they considered an obvious argument, ACOPI demanded that taxation be done democratically, or according to what each member of society could contribute to the public good. And because small-business owners saw themselves as job creators and wealth producers, it was only democratic to reduce their taxes. Hence the Colombian state was becoming "undemocratic, paternalist, *cantinero*, and antipatriotic" by burdening those who promoted economic productivity by stimulating competition and free enterprise.[107] The association used the same logic to demand a more protective state in matters of credit for small and medium industries, industrial production, and imported goods. Small-business owners, at least during the 1960s, partially defended ISI because it would create the conditions for them to compete in the market and to thereby become representatives of a capitalist democracy. The association lobbied hard to secure credit opportunities, which they complained were currently only allocated to the privileged classes with "friends in the domestic and foreign financial system."[108] In a word, ACOPI wanted a state that "look[ed] like a small industry," that intervened to produce, reproduce, and perpetuate the competition that would benefit the class that would bring capitalist democracy.

"We, the People": ANAPO and the Classed and Gendered Right to Rule in Democracies

In the late 1960s a group of middle-class professionals working for the state, white-collar unionists laboring in private service companies, and owners of small and medium industries founded yet another political organization seeking to speak for the middle class—the National Union of the Colombian

Middle Class (UNCLAMECOL). Joining forces with MOCLAM, UNCLAMECOL forwarded as its main objective the unification of different middle-class sectors through neighborhood programs, radio stations, *carnetización* (production of IDs), and platforms for raising middle-class consciousness. The union spent most of its energy in organizing four congresses of Colombia's middle classes during the late 1960s and 1970s. In the early 1970s, Aristobulo Forero, an economist working for the DNP and a cofounder of UNCLAMECOL, presented a paper at one of these congresses inviting President Misael Pastrana to understand that for a "true democracy to exist" there must be new "leading classes."[109] Forero insisted that UNCLAMECOL needed to work "toward the conquest of a more just state and . . . the conquest of a democratic system, which follows the simplest but most important doctrine of any middle-class society: a democracy must be a government of the people, for the people, and by the people."[110]

Forero was mobilizing the different demands of the middle classes as well as the populist language of ANAPO, a movement founded in 1961 by Gustavo Rojas Pinilla, the former dictator (1953–1957) in response to whom the FN had emerged. Made at a moment when this oppositional party gained momentum and the FN began to lose legitimacy for its development programs, UNCLAMECOL's political call invites us to think through four important questions. For these professionals, white-collar employees, and small-business owners, what did it mean to take power to consolidate a "middle-class society" and simultaneously claim to strengthen a democratic system of the people, for the people, and by the people? Which people were they imagining to embody democracy? How did gender and class intersect when these middle-class men and women made a claim to represent "the people"? And how did ANAPO respond to—or shape—these demands for representation of the people?

By way of conclusion, I want to show how, as middle-class women and men engaged in politically heterogeneous demands to redefine democracy, they simultaneously produced a "gendered and classed chain of equivalence" through which particular demands were aggregated for the materialization of a shared hierarchical vision of society in which the middle class, as a political movement, could rule over oligarchies and laboring groups. By claiming entitlement to sovereignly represent "the people," middle-class women and men legitimized their role in the consolidation of ANAPO—the most important populist oppositional movement of the second half of the 1960s—and, by extension, in dismantling the FN. The task, then, is to historicize both the political process through which the notion of "the people" got *class*ified as a representation of a proper middle class and how a classed and gendered right to rule in democracy, associated with that representation, got sanctified in the name of "the people."

As ANAPO leaders opposed the FN with discourses about democracy, such opposition soon resonated with different middle-class political groups. And as middle-class political organizations partially but increasingly opposed the FN, ANAPO's discourses opened space for middle-class demands. It was at the center of this dialectical relationship that middle-class women and men mobilized the populist notions of "the people and the oligarchy"—imagined in multiple ways—to classify themselves as superior to both laboring classes and elites and thus entitled to the right to rule in democracies. Members of the middle class, for instance, criticized the oligarchies as no longer authorized to continue "commanding the nation," as they had become unfit for such a "democratic task."[111] For professionals, oligarchies began to represent "privileged castes" who thought "God . . . blood . . . tradition and good family names [had] given them the rights in democracy." This "democracy of blood," as they called it, had forced the middle class to play the role of "transfer relay" between the "rich who want to become richer and the poor destined to become poorer."[112] As Juan Vargas, a member of ASMEDAS, wrote in an editorial in the LMMC's newsletter in 1964, "the democratic direction of the nation has gone off track" because it was in the "hands of the few."[113] Referring to the FN and its "lack of common sense," Vargas categorized this derailment as the result of a "democracy of the few" in which oligarchs were concerned only with themselves, ignoring the productive efforts that the rest of society put forward so that "development and progress could take place."[114] Vargas argued that this democracy of the few had produced difficult hardships that had forced the laboring classes to search for a "democracy of the many," which would produce "disharmony and regressive political instability."[115] If the middle class took the path of the democracy of the few, they would have no choice but to join "the backward and traditional parties" and would likely as a result become feminized and "dependent on the oligarchs." If the middle class took the path of the democracy of the many, they would undergo another form of feminization: "social and political anonymity." In contrast, Vargas demanded the building of "a democracy of the several" through which the nation's direction would be at the service of both the few and the many.[116] In a true democracy, a middle-class society, or a democracy of the several, the right to rule stemmed not from lineage, blood, wealth, or femininity but from knowledge, effort, experience, and preparation, virtues squarely reserved for a middle-class masculinity.[117]

The Alianza Nacional Popular was indeed receptive to these demands. As early as 1964, for example, MOCLAM invited Alberto Ruiz Novoa, former minister of war under Valencia, an outspoken critic of the FN, and an ANAPO leader, to speak to a middle-class audience at the Hotel Tequendama in Bogotá. He proclaimed the need for a "new movement for the change of political customs . . . [and for] the substitution of governing castes."[118] Almost repeating what middle-class political organizations had been demanding, Ruiz Novoa argued that for a democracy to function properly, the members of "the people" needed to be hierarchically divided into those who, given their professional and intellectual pedigree, could lead "great working and peasant masses" and those masses who, as part of the people, would "move the movement" from below. Thus the army general imagined a struggle between a manly professional vanguard fighting for "the national interest," followed by the laboring classes, against the oligarchies, with their "amoral . . . plutocratic state."[119]

Small-business owners heard and echoed this political call. As they demanded an entrepreneurial or managerial state, they also complained that the oligarchies were "terrible administrators who [knew] how to waste the resources of the nation." Behaving like "their women, who spen[t] money on the luxurious [and] sumptuous," oligarchies and big industrialists were taking the nation down the road of perpetual underdevelopment by promoting "backwardness and antidemocracy."[120] It was just to defend a middle-class society in which the capacity for work, the creation of wealth, and the proper exploitation of labor were the "most important virtues of democratic government." Such legitimation allowed these small businessmen to make one of the most important political demands of the second half of the 1960s and early 1970s: that the proper democratic state, imagined as a masculine force, represent neither "popular rule" nor "elitist government" but rather "the entrepreneurial people," who would provide every member of society a chance to enter the ever-growing middle class as "men of work" and "private property owners."[121]

Again ANAPO echoed these middle-class actors, making it clear that the party understood social justice not as a promotion of "communism, casteism, or chaos" but as the celebration of "the social function of private property."[122] Rojas Pinilla, when running for president in 1970, presented in his economic program what had been clear to so many small-business owners: in any democracy "private capital must jealously be respected." He argued that he could not "fall into a demagogic illusion of speaking out against private capital." The leader of ANAPO made a sharp distinction between "good and bad capitalists" that resonated with small-business owners, who could see themselves as legitimate representatives of an economic democracy, could create "private capital as an essential factor . . . for progress and develop labor opportunities, new sources of employment, establishing capital not for exploitation but for competition." But the distinction was also cherished by small-business owners because it allowed them to identify as part of "the people" against the oligarchies, the "outlaws of the economy" (as Ruiz Novoa called them) who were illegitimate capitalists because they "used and abused private capital in an effort to anguish the working classes."[123]

Some male white-collar employees also claimed a place in ANAPO's vision of the people. Demanding recognition for their unions, these men contended that it was the "privileged castes" who, instead of promoting a peaceful and understanding relationship between labor and capital, had propelled "resentment and hatred" among social groups. Male white-collar employees defined themselves as the most productive class because they promoted solidarity, understanding, and dependency among employers and employees; by contrast, the oligarchies wanted to bring violence and the laboring classes wanted to produce chaos. White-collar men could thus bring democracy to the nation because they could consolidate a democratic social order characterized by peace and generosity. But for some of these white-collar employees, "cultural ignorance" was the major obstacle to such democratic order, as it had pitted the Colombian people against each other: the oligarchies were ignorant about the laboring classes, and vice versa. Several editorials by white-collar unions argued that because culture leads to democracy, one could not properly enjoy the benefits of democracy without the "appropriate culture," which both the laboring classes and oligarchies lacked. It was necessary to accelerate, via middle-class leadership, the other two classes' cultural progress so that a true democracy could be developed. In a word, the middle classes were, they concluded, the representation of a proper "working . . . serving people." They therefore found politically appealing ANAPO's claim that "the people" had to be hierarchically divided between "the forces of intelligence and the forces of labor."[124]

By sharing a political claim to middle-classness, some professionals, small-business owners, and white-collar employees increasingly, if reluctantly, joined ANAPO and its oppositional efforts against the FN. But such opposition did not mean merely joining forces with the laboring classes to become part of the people.[125] Nor did it mean that the middle classes were in opposition to "the people," as most studies continue to argue. Rather, they joined ANAPO to legitimize a classed and gendered claim that they had been making for a while: that they were, as middle class, the sovereign representatives of "the people." Gender further fermented a degree of commonality among otherwise heterogeneous middle-class demands. It was middle-class men, not women, who could become "the leaders in the new guard," the representatives of an entrepreneurial state, and the members of "the serving people." It is in this context that middle-class men claimed to own the right to rule in democracies—that is, to dominate over the laboring classes and the feminized, antidemocratic oligarchies.

These gendered and classed claims generated calls to heighten—not reduce—material inequalities. These professionals, white-collar employees, and small-business owners demanded a "democratic distribution of material rewards" that included "every member of the society" to replace the "undemocratic . . . oligarchical" system.[126] This democratic vision entailed a hierarchical distribution of labor, occupations, and assignments according to the specific cultural and social "conditions of each and every member of the people."[127] These middle-class men campaigned for the universal democratic right "to do what each [was] pleased and capable of doing."[128] Professionals, white-collar employees, and small-business owners were the ones most capable to "accomplish more for society." This capability, however, brought unique "social and cultural pressures," requiring them to live "according to [their] middle-class status: a demanding modern life, a required education to succeed in democratic society, a constant preparation to avoid falling behind, a comfortable house to live well so that [their] children grow up in a healthy environment." Given this, they were entitled to "receive more."[129]

The working classes, by contrast, although part of "the people," could live "the simplest of lives with working-class salaries" because of their cultural interests, needs, merits, and roles in society. They faced no "social, cultural, political pressures" for a "better standard of living"; they wanted to lead "simple . . . uncomplicated lives" and did not have to live "beyond their means." Furthermore, working-class men did not care about the "cultural role of the family provider," which put "significantly less" pressure on them. Because the working class could "enjoy the little . . . and ingenious pleasures of life," lower incomes would not necessarily be a problem.

This demonstrates how the shared discourse of the middle class as a sacred force of democratization and sovereign representative of "the people" both facilitated a degree of consent and provided the conditions for the material reproduction of classed and gendered privilege. This explains why, whether through state-sponsored programs, ANAPO-supported congressional bills, private service companies, cooperatives, political organizations, or union struggles, the middle class materialized educational opportunities, better labor conditions, expansive recreational activities, state monies, private credit, homeownership, and small-business ownership.

As appendix figures 5 and 6 show, this translated into what was seen as "middle class budgets." To maintain "happy families," about 20 percent of middle-class men's income had to be committed to the most important "investment in middle-class lives: education . . . [which] secures the future of the children as it allows them to become somebody in life."[130] Unlike the working classes, who "put education to sleep," and the elites, who used education to perpetuate privilege, the middle class appreciated how education was "the most important investment of life," improving one's human capital for market competition. It allowed one "to beat everybody else up in the competition of life."[131] Around 10 percent needed to be spent for "help around the house" because of the demands of "modern lives," in which, with the careful supervision of a middle-class mother, all family members needed to find a "welcoming home." For similar reasons, another 15 percent had to be spent on housing (rental or ownership), because a "house [was] not just a house but a nest of democracy . . . a home where men [could] find a private place away from the busy life of modernity . . . where happiness could emerge. . . . and the future of democracy could consolidate." Owning a house was preferable because middle-class men "work[ed] hard to own things."[132] Private ownership demonstrated social worthiness, because owners would be sure to protect "what [was] privately owned." Ten percent had to be dedicated to transportation and to leisure time in order to "recover the necessary energy to continue with the labor routine." Another 10 percent needed to be dedicated to health-related issues. And the rest of the income, if possible, should be placed in savings.

These markers of the material inequalities that led middle-class men to embrace ANAPO also contributed to their claim for gender inequality. Middle-class women were seen as the principal economic tacticians for making families happy in the home made possible by independent men. They were responsible for ensuring cleanliness, nutrition, children's economic rectitude, and domestic harmony.[133] Middle-class men imagined themselves as those who could theorize the different aspects of a middle-class family's budget, and women as those who could materialize it "on the ground" by carefully managing family finances. This heteropatriarchal partnership further distinguished the middle class from the elites and working classes unable to comply with such economic and social values. Unlike "elitist women" who promoted "luxuriant or superfluous consumptions of goods," middle-class women partnered with their spouses to own a home and provide a family life, an investment in their "personal wealth for a better economy" and an "individual self-affirmation for a better society."[134]

Yet in a moment of economic difficulty during the second half of the 1960s, middle-class men struggled to fulfill their masculine obligations. Some in state development offices, for instance, complained that "marriage [was] the worst business in life," producing neither "economic profit [nor] any benefits."[135] Others protested that their salaries were too low to implement a middle-class budget. Small-business owners, white-collar employees, and middle-class professionals were happy to hear that Rojas Pinilla understood how frustrated they could feel when there were neither "credit lines to produce business [nor] enough earnings to provide housing, education, and hygiene for their sons and wives."[136] But rather than sounding "too political," middle-class men blamed women's participation in the labor market for their economic woes. State professionals claimed that this "level[ed] salaries down."[137] Service-sector employees concurred, asserting that "the more women arrive[d] to offices, the less income [men would] enjoy," as companies preferred "cheap labor regardless of professional preparation."[138] To solve this "economic maladjustment in modern societies," some middle-class men advocated sending women back home, going to great lengths to explain that, unlike working-class machista men, they wanted to "save [their] women the trouble of laboring more and be[ing] really exploited." Marriage, by keeping middle-class wives at home, would produce "a future of [middle-class] prosperity."[139] And yet economic reality hit these men—and their masculinities—hard. They soon realized how critical women's salaries were to maintaining a middle-class budget.[140] This translated into a gender and class dilemma: while women's salaries could help secure middle-classness, they would challenge middle-class masculinity, tarring it with the dependency associated with the economically castrated working-class other. This is why the ideal middle-class budget celebrated heteropatriarchal partnership, in which women's labor was defined as "help." It delegitimized employed middle-class women's critical contributions to family finances and thus the attainment of middle-class status. Women should appreciate, men concluded, "the opportunities that society provid[ed] them: to *help* their husbands move the family forward."[141]

And Rojas Pinilla agreed, as he proclaimed in his presidential nomination speech, that he had given women the right to vote because he knew that they were "the irreplaceable moral axis of the home, the family, and the fatherland."[142] Such gendered demands secured the right to rule in democracy and representation of "the people" as a prerogative of middle-class men.

7

A Real Revolution,
a Real Democracy

As some professionals and white-collar employees in Bogotá opposed the
FN and joined ANAPO, many others soon found themselves on "the left side
of history."[1] During the late 1960s and 1970s, they began to discuss relentlessly what they now remember as one of the most important questions that
their generation had to engage: How could they be part of a petit bourgeoisie
and yet, in seeming contradiction, want to participate in revolutionary movements? Marta Jaramillo, who in the early 1960s had secured a job as a professional at INCORA thanks to the Alliance and later in the decade was hired as
a professor at UNAL, remembered this discussion as vital for her life:

> I had always thought that I was part of the middle class. . . . Then I
> realized that I was part of the petit bourgeoisie. It was the 1960s and
> the world was politically boiling. I read the old guy—Marx—and I realized
> that I was, in fact, as petit bourgeois as one could get! Later I joined the
> Comandos Camilistas, engaged in liberation theology, and dreamed of
> a revolution. . . . we knew all too well, but perhaps too few dared to rec-
> ognize it, [that] we were petit bourgeois. We read Marx, Lenin, Mao,
> the Bible . . . and we discussed the so-called petit bourgeoisie's "vices"
> and "virtues," what we should, and should *not*, do for the revolution. . . .
> I then became a woman from the left. At first, I was very naive . . . but
> then I radicalized myself.[2]

Most petit bourgeois whom I interviewed in 2005 and 2010 also remembered the 1970s—a period that in their recollections loosely ranged from the mid-1960s to the late 1970s—as a decade of important political awakening, passionate debates, new political horizons, class consciousness, and gendered emotions. Their memories were inflected by the massive criminalization of dissident voices under Uribe Vélez's regime, which figured their revolutionary pasts as "terrorist threats" to democracy. These self-identified petit bourgeois wanted to reclaim—*reivindicar*—what they had done as vital to histories of democracy in Colombia. They narrated their participation in revolutionary movements because, in the present, nobody wanted to see how they had desired "to make society more democratic." They recalled participating in different sites of left activism as formative because they became "politically consequential individuals" for society. They were part of a larger collective struggling for "the most important political ideals that any decent society should achieve: equality, solidarity, equal distribution of wealth, in a word . . . true democracy."[3]

In this context, these dissident memories sought to relink the left, broadly understood, with a democratic past in Colombia. When asked whether it was at all worth it, most petit bourgeois responded, as did Marta Espinosa:

I would not change a bit about what I lived! I would not be who I am had I not experienced, and participated in, the 1970s. I supported armed rebellions. This does not mean I would support armed rebellion now, but back then it was the only possibility we had. But do not get me wrong, this is not the only thing I did. . . . We wanted a real democracy. We struggled every day for a society where our sons and daughters could have more economic opportunities, where everybody could have more access to the wealth of the nation, where everybody could have more autonomy in their lives. If we in Colombia are at all democratic, it is thanks to all the things we did back then.[4]

Yet because these petit bourgeois men and women attached many political hopes to this decade, they simultaneously remembered these years, relying on gendered and classed language, as a moment of frustration and disillusionment. For Hernando Rincón, a former militant in a Maoist group, the "fatal mistake" was "an ideological confusion . . . [and] fragmentation" produced presumably by the emergence of "cultural questions"—such as "feminists' concerns"—which destroyed the "ideological precision" needed for what the revolution was supposed to do: create "more spaces for the proletariat, who wanted to have access to the fruits of their labor . . . to their land . . . to the wealth they produced."[5] For some petit bourgeois women, by contrast, although the left opened some spaces for "women's questions," it was mainly men's "intolerance and dogmatism" on these issues that derailed a "true revolution."[6] Still for others, "the political error" was an armed struggle that privileged violence over politics, which translated into a celebration of "the warrior over the urban cultured man" in the leadership of revolutionary movements.[7] Leonardo Betancour, an agronomist and former member of the Partido Comunista de Colombia, Marxista-Leninista (PCC-ML), recalled how "the political error" was to think armed struggle an "irreversible . . . part of Colombia's history," to think it "an absolute . . . that the oligarchies . . . would not allow change to happen otherwise."[8] Thus, these petit bourgeoisie remembered this moment as a missed opportunity for revolutionary change in which they misunderstood the role of the popular groups in historical events such as the 1977 *paro cívico*, which showed how "there was no need whatsoever to combine all the forms of struggle."[9] Indeed, for some of these men and women the 1970s was a revolutionary moment that could have been but never really was.[10]

These memories raise crucial questions. Why did professionals and white-collar employees remember these years as a drastic shift from a middle-class status to a radical petit bourgeois position? What did it mean to be petit bourgeois during revolutionary times? What happens when we put these experiences of radicalization at the center of the Cold War and revolutionary politics? Amid the current political polarization and a peace agreement in Colombia, the left's revolutionary projects of the 1960s and 1970s have been explained, with few exceptions, through one-dimensional, moralistic narratives of romance, failure, and defeat.[11] On the one hand, invoking objectivity, some have reduced the complexity of left political ideas, experiences, and projects to an undifferentiated evil, often referred to as "terrorism," that has sentenced Colombia to years of unending violence.[12] In this dominant narrative, petit bourgeois who participated in left activism are depicted as villains who became foolishly enamored with armed rebellion and perpetuated illegitimate and unnecessary violence against the FN's "reasonable" liberal democracy, which, compared to dictatorships elsewhere in Latin America, provided spaces for democratic dissent.[13] Indeed, the left, broadly understood, often gets essentialized as a "mismatch" with, and "dismissive" of, the practices of democracy.[14] On the other hand, some scholars historicize the left in Colombia during the second half of the twentieth century as a failure for not creating the conditions for a coherent cross-class, national-popular bloc to challenge a dominant form of bipartisan liberal capitalism.[15]

As a result, we remain stuck in a narrative of predictable defeats and inevitable disappointments, of romanticized heroes and unidealistic villains, of melancholic histories of what historical actors should have been—and done—but never really were or did, of fights between David and Goliath, and, above all, of ahistorical evils and transcendental goods.[16] And although this chapter is very much part of recent studies on the Cold War in Latin America and the Global Sixties, it also argues against a prevalent assumption running through these studies that posits political radicalization as a product of radicalization itself. In a tautological and circular explanation, there is an inclination to understand a revolutionary temporality as generating successive forms of radicalizing events. Yet simultaneously there is an assumption that such radicalizing events ignited the radicalization and polarization of society during the 1960s and 1970s. On this argument, we quickly and confidently turn to charge the FN and its exclusionary politics as *the* main cause of political radicalization toward the left. Yet if, as shown in the previous chapters, the FN's social policies were a productive rationality of rule that gained both a fragile yet important level of legitimacy and a degree of political opposition among certain members of the middle classes, how do we explain that only some of them ended up mobilizing as part of a left-leaning radical political project that questioned the hierarchical vision of democracy promoted by these development programs and state policies?

By focusing on class and gender subjectivities, I invite us to understand this political radicalization—understood as moving toward the left of the political spectrum, joining revolutionary parties, participating in street protests, politically committing to the masses, proletarizing oneself, embracing (in some cases) feminist positions, and participating in armed rebellions—as a dialectical process. I develop my arguments in two ways. First, I offer a multidimensional explanation—one that combines structural conditions, a discussion of the political inspirations of a transnational left, and a focus on gendered and classed subjectivities—for why and how some professionals and white-collar employees reconfigured themselves as part of a radical left political struggle that they referred to, consciously and unconsciously, as petit bourgeois. Second, I focus on the experiences of flesh-and-blood petit bourgeois women and men who were profoundly inspired to become selfless and thus chase a common desire to "make democracy a reality by improv[ing] the lives of everyone."[17] I historicize the rationality and meanings behind the actions they took, the demands they made, the political ideals they discussed, and the struggles they engaged in to create a "true democracy."[18] I demonstrate how, far from being limited to armed rebellion, professionals and white-collar workers infused desire with interest and consolidated extensive petit bourgeois activism, which sought to materialize what was called "revolution" or "real democracy." Within little less than a decade, many of those charged with bringing about proper democracy for the Americas posed one of the most radical challenges to the very sociopolitical order that had empowered them in the first place. Yet, my task is not to recuperate these petit bourgeois as romanticized protagonists who, together with popular groups, fought for a unified and transcendental good.[19] Rather, what I am after is a history in which one might see how petit bourgeois women and men resignified the meanings and practices of democracy while universalizing their particular classed and gendered visions of change *within* different and new left revolutionary movements.

Becoming Petit Bourgeois Revolutionaries

As major events such as the Cuban Revolution inspired notions of political change, influenced new revolutionary movements, and shaped the emergence of insurgent groups in different parts of the country, FN administrations institutionalized a series of policies that sought to repress political dissidence, oppositional parties, and confrontational styles of politics. By the second half of the 1960s, the FN was increasingly practicing counterinsurgent and surveillance policies against those dissident groups who were categorized as threats to the consolidation of "two-party constitutionalism."[20] These conditions played an important role in the political radicalization of society, as the FN monopolized and closed the spaces for exercising legal politics while expanding paramilitary forces—legalized in Decree 3398, implemented in 1968, and converted into legislation by Law 48 of the same year—to conceal the very exclusion of oppositional groups.[21]

Some of these repressive measures exacerbated a series of unintended contradictions provoked by the FN's development programs under the Alliance. As we saw in chapter 5, during the first half of the 1960s the very operation of development programs such as the Alliance was supposed to put professionals, as conscripts of democracy, into intimate contact with those considered the main causes of polarization, violence, and class hatred: oligarchies and laboring classes. Yet these class encounters simultaneously provoked unforeseen contradictions and frustrations.[22] Professionals presumably found what they were not supposed to find. Oligarchies, rather than embracing a modernizing role, were becoming the source of backwardness, underdevelopment, and poverty, "an overwhelming reality" that professionals had neither the appropriate knowledge to understand nor the experience to overcome. Some of these professionals turned to their diaries and ethnographic notes to remember this intimate moment of radicalization, describing their constant clashes and conflicts with other classes who, they insisted, behaved in an "unpredictable way."[23] Professionals were, in a word, at odds with themselves because it was suffocating to comply with the democratic role that they were supposed to put into practice when both laboring classes and elites reacted "capriciously."[24] While attempting to educate those patronos, professionals were haunted by class questions produced by the very development programs they were participating in: "What sort of education is necessary to instill a feeling of national service . . . a sense of . . . national belonging . . . a social sentiment for the greater good, a feeling that they are also part of the nation. . . . Why do they work against their nation, country, the society to which they belong?"[25] As Ana Agudelo, a social worker working for IFI and trained in CMC, wrote in a report in the mid-1960s: "It is assumed that in our country we do not have any form of slavery . . . that we live in modernity, but the truth is that there are patronos who exploit workers, as they pay neither minimum wages nor overtime. We cannot let this happen if we want to pride ourselves as a country where social justice matters. These patronos are the worst members of Colombia— infamous, cruel, ruthless, detestable, *despiadados*."[26]

To be sure, some historians would be quick to point out that these frustrations, and their concomitant class struggles, show what was clear all along: these development programs seeking to create social peace emerged for the sole purpose of obscuring the oligarchical power behind the FN, with its exclusionary and anticommunist political order. Professionals were merely realizing that was the case. But radicalization was neither politically inevitable nor merely the product of an outside polarization fashioned by a decade of exclusionary politics and radicalizing events. Rather, along with the repressive policies, some professionals' political radicalization sprang from the very class encounter—an encounter that the Alliance sanctified— with popular sectors and oligarchies. The political rationality that underwrote both the FN's social policies and development programs undercut their very goals: promoting the harmonious—that is to say, hierarchical— coexistence of classes in fact ignited class struggles. Thus, contrary to what most studies argue, this middle-class radicalization materialized within, rather than without, the FN and its development programs.

It is at this level of classed and gendered subjectivity that professionals experienced a privileged alienation, one that intimately shaped their political radicalization.[27] As state representatives and the celebrated example of democracy, some professionals contemplated the fact that they could "go on with [their] life," continuing to enjoy the privilege of being and doing what was expected of them. They could be happy with "helping the miserable human beings hidden in the mountains of the Andes."[28] After all, their lives were "not bad," as they had decent salaries and an overall level of respect in society. Indeed, these professionals considered "looking away" from "a reality of poverty" that they had discovered through development programs because taking a more radical and critical stand would mean sacrificing their very middle-class status: "the wine days, the reading days, the teaching days, the thinking days . . . the money, the house, the savings, the possibility to get married . . . the family days will be over."[29]

Yet as they consented to their professional task, they also felt alienated from what they were supposed to do: they could neither discipline the oligarchies into modern elites nor discipline laboring classes into human capital owners. In daily contradiction with their classed privilege, the "overwhelming reality of poverty" proved impossible to ignore.[30] Carlos Restrepo, a sociologist, described in his detailed diaries, a personal form of privileged rethinking and self-critique, the doubts and anxieties of this class conundrum. As a student, then a professor of sociology at UNAL, and soon a member of the Communist Youth (JUCO), Restrepo wrote with evident despair that the search for an ideal (perhaps the ideal of being the representative of democracy) was an overwhelming, if impossible, task. But it was this ideal that gave him a privileged status that he began to describe as too simple in comparison to what was around him. He did not want to be a "faithful lover of the FN."[31] Restrepo was alienated from himself because he was afraid of becoming a failure as a man if he remained oblivious to the material realities of the country. Instead he wanted to become "a man superior to all others," one who, as a "radical of consciousness" in society, could play an important role in materializing social justice.[32] He thought of himself as somebody who wanted to overcome his former alienated middle-class self—imagined now as "mind-numbing, domesticated, tedious, monotonous, sentimental, politically docile, and feminine" because it would not have a role in changing society—while searching for a clear masculine superiority and class distinction to resolve what he referred to, rather generally, as "all the problems that affect man."[33] He now began to imagine a masculinized and radicalized identity that he defined, perhaps reluctantly, as petit bourgeois.

Professionals were not alone in these experiences of radicalization. As service unions consolidated in the second half of the 1960s, private companies across the service sector, while supporting the FN administrations and their surveillance efforts in the mid-1960s, also expanded measures to prevent further unionization among white-collar employees. These companies worried that "dangerous ideas" were now finding adepts among "naive members of the middle classes." It was "astonishing [and] shocking" to see that, as these service companies complained in classified letters to state intelligence offices, "collaborators . . . with bright futures ahead of them" decided to embrace "infertile ideologies that [would] destroy the office as we know it." Thus, it was important to develop a program of political surveillance in order to corner those categorized at public meetings as "unfit elements for the organization" and behind closed doors as "hostile . . . aggressive, and unproductive unionists."[34]

Along with a call to tighten up a "scientific" process of selection, the most common practice in this company surveillance was to dismiss white-collar employees categorized as "dangerous elements for the organization . . . deserters of their own interests." After being celebrated as members of a community of shared interests, white-collar employees were now receiving dismissal letters claiming quite the opposite: they were "obstacles for the development of our company and our services . . . unfit elements for our family company . . . unproductive . . . dangerous . . . hostile people for teamwork."[35]

Thus at the level of everyday subjectivity, these repressive measures entered into open contradiction with the celebration of the service sector as the representation of democratic labor relationships. Take, for example, Antonio Díaz's story, an employee at Colseguros. In a letter he sent to the human relations office soon after his dismissal at the end of the 1960s, Díaz expressed anger and frustration against what he suggestively called "the hypocrisy of the *clase patronal*." Such hypocrisy, one might infer, was due to what Díaz thought the service sector should represent in a "democratic society." He deemed the different spaces for participation and communication promoted by Colseguros merely "a distraction . . . to keep [white-collar employees] happy . . . to avoid a conflict, [one] that is not convenient for the company."[36] Díaz made clear that he was doing what a white-collar employee in a service company was supposed to do. He was a "team member" with the "company's goal at heart," who had served customers to the best of his abilities and produced insurance policies for the company's benefit, because this would benefit him as well. Thus, his union participation by no means contradicted his work in the service sector. Evoking what he learned at countless workshops, he made clear how a union of service workers could typify corporate teamwork: "Unionists show commitment, exhibit flexibility, treat others with respect, share benefits, and care about others."[37] For white-collar employees such as Díaz, repressive measures revealed the putative community of shared interests to be "a conflict of interests." Díaz began to see his interests as in fundamental contradiction to those of his employer, a class other he now defined as the "clase patronal."[38]

But this political radicalization was also shaped by structural and material conditions provoked by the FN's political economy. While during the first half of the 1960s the unemployment rate remained in the single digits, by 1970 13.1 percent of the economically active population was unemployed.[39] Countless letters sent to different presidents of the FN suggest that white-collar employees and professionals grew frustrated with their unsatisfied desire to achieve the material conditions required for becoming middle class. But such frustration was mediated by the sanctification of the middle classes as representatives of democracy, which further provoked dissatisfaction. Middle-class women and men complained that they could not find jobs suitable to their class and gender expectations. In a letter sent to Carlos Lleras Restrepo in 1968, for instance, Ramón Arévalo, an engineer educated at a private university, shared his frustration with the president over not being able to find "a decent job." It was becoming too common, Arévalo wrote, to live among "social injustices." After years of hard work in college against all odds, Arévalo told the president what he thought was quite obvious: "Colombia [was] not a democracy." If it were, Arévalo continued, "fifteen years of education"—five years for elementary, five for secondary, and five for college—should at least present "better economic opportunities for the future." But the antidemocratic reality worked against the dignity of "the most productive members of the nation."[40] He had no home to own, no professional incentive to pursue, no material conditions to support a family. With impatience, Arévalo concluded his rather long letter by offering an implicit political threat: "Fifteen years of education and an investment of 250,000 pesos represent for me an uncertain future. With no job, what do you want me to do Mr. President? Do you think that it would seem fair to join others like me to make things different in society?"[41]

Whether Arévalo acted on his political call is unclear, but complaints like these became common in the second half of the 1960s. The oligarchies, the clase patronal, increasingly became a political other. And for some members of the middle class who joined oppositional parties, certain events further "clarified" a political decision to join movements on the left. As shown in the previous chapter, ANAPO had gained electoral momentum, partially due to the support of middle-class organizations. On the night of April 19, 1970, when votes were being counted for the election of the next president, Gustavo Rojas Pinilla, the main leader of ANAPO, seemed to be on the road to victory. Or so radio broadcasts informed the public. That night, on Carlos Lleras Restrepo's order, transmission of the partial electoral results was abruptly canceled. The very next morning, the president announced that, after receiving uncounted votes from isolated places in the country, the newly elected president was the official FN Conservative candidate, Misael Pastrana. In Bogotá, Rojas Pinilla received majority support with 251,456 votes, while the new president secured 236,303 votes.[42]

Thus, the night of April 19 crystallized a major political disappointment among some members of the middle classes. It is crucial to emphasize, however, that such disappointment did not originate in the event itself. Rather, some professionals and white-collar workers, as part of their experiences in development programs during the 1960s, had already defined the oligarchies as a political other in fundamental opposition to a proper democracy; this event became the supreme manifestation of how "the oligarchies . . . [were] antidemocratic." The event represented how the FN, far from making possible a middle-class rule, as it had been promising since 1958, was "in bed with oligarchies' interests" and thus reveled in this group's "intransigency to democratize the nation." In the words of those middle-class people who participated in ANAPO, the fraud of the elections represented a political reality in which the middle classes would become neither a "new leading class" nor the sovereign representatives of "the people." Indeed, among some professionals and white-collar employees, this election day made clear that "the oligarchies would prevent the consolidation of any meaningful change," a conclusion that turned political participation in oppositional groups or reluctant attitude toward armed rebellion into a belief in the "mandatory need" to make the revolution by any means necessary. It is in this particular context that urban guerrilla groups such as the 19th of April Movement (M-19) became politically relevant and attractive.

Knowledge Becomes Petit Bourgeois Subjectivity

It was due to this process of privileged alienation, material frustration, and political disillusionment that for some professionals and white-collar workers the left—broadly understood—began to make sense. But let's be clear. This process of radicalization worked the other way: it was also an encounter with a transnational left that ignited professionals and white-collar workers to question their classed and gendered identities as representatives of democracy. Nowhere were these mutually inclusive practices of radicalization more clearly experienced than in what most of the social actors whom I interviewed fondly remembered as study groups where dense, foundational texts of the old and new left were deeply discussed. Everyday readings and discussions in city cafés, private and public university campuses, state offices, party meetings, street protests, and union halls became a political practice through which these professionals and white-collar employees further questioned their middle-class role as conscripts of democracy while redefining themselves—consciously and unconsciously—as part of a radical petit bourgeoisie. In a word, the production and discussion of knowledge became a question of subjectivity.[43]

Marx's thought, broadly conceived, became inspirational for understanding what was going on in white-collar employees' daily lives, just as those realities were provoked by a critical reading of what Marx had to say about labor relationships in society. White-collar employees began to wonder whether they had suffered from a "major ideological confusion": Were they, like factory workers, exploited by "grand capitalists . . . and clases patronales"? Or were they "salaried commercial workers" who suffered exploitation indirectly? Were they, unlike workers, the owners of their own labor?[44] By reading select parts of *Capital*, white-collar employees located themselves as service workers, not employees, who did not "produce surplus value directly," as factory workers did, but rather had the price of their labor determined by the value of their labor-power. They saw themselves as participating in the exploitation of workers' labor by reducing the cost of the value of their own labor-power—the exertion, expenditure of energy, wear, and tear that such labor involved. Their wages therefore did not reflect the amount of profit that they helped the capitalist to realize but rather indirectly contributed to the exploitation of workers.[45] They were also exploited because, according to their reading of Marx, "surplus value" was produced through the alienation and domination of any human productive activity. Service—redefined, after reading Marx, as a labor proper—was part of such productive activity. It was service labor that was also sold to, and exploited by, capital.

Thus, white-collar workers appropriated Marx to reconfigure new class and gender subjectivities. They located themselves in the "middling position in society." This made them different from both the industrial proletariat and the clase patronal.[46] And if that was the case, they could play a crucial role in changing labor relationships. It was their masculine task to liberate themselves from this middling political position and join forces with those "exploited groups against the clases patronales." As "true men . . . conscious of [their] role in society," they needed to struggle for the end of "any manifestation of forms of exploitation."[47]

As professionals encountered "the overwhelming reality of poverty," they indeed struggled over how to become politically committed to radical social change while maintaining a "scientific" distance necessary to do their jobs. The reading of different professionals' journals and diaries suggests that they found in Marx a way to satisfy the masculine desire to balance "the two men fighting in the life of the best professional": the man of science and the man of politics.[48] As some of these professionals began to join political parties on the left—from the Communist Party and Marxist-Leninist movements to Trotskyist and Maoist organizations—they pondered how they should continue their work as state representatives. Some evoked a letter that Engels wrote to Laura Lafargue in 1884 in which he argued that when one was a "man of science," it was also crucial to develop a political ideal.[49] Rather than seeing professional work and political commitment as separate, professionals now defined their jobs as political practice. As many of them continued to work for a development state in the 1960s and 1970s, they argued that they had to arm themselves with "scientific thought, rational action, and coherent politics" to understand the causes and consequences of poverty. They said that as true petit bourgeois men, they would overcome a feminized professional identity by embracing their jobs as a political obligation to change the social order. Many of these professionals argued that their lives, as Marx dictated, had to be lived "empirically and in praxis."[50]

But such inspiration simultaneously raised questions of classed and gendered subjectivity. Carlos Restrepo, for instance, offers a revealing, if contradictory, reading of Marx's thought during the late 1960s. He expressed his intellectual and masculine satisfaction in finding in Marx a means to address his frustration as a petit bourgeois professional still working with development programs: "I only have to embrace my profession [which] requires bravery, virility, and political commitment. And to do this I just need to do what I know best: to think. Marx is on my side . . . Marx is practice."[51] Yet reading Marx also exacerbated further his doubts about his role as part of the petit bourgeoisie. In his professional diaries, Restrepo mentioned a text by the Chilean political scientist Marta Harnecker that argued that, according to the *Communist Manifesto*, there were three classes in society: the bourgeoisie, the petit bourgeoisie, and the proletariat.[52] The petit bourgeoisie, as Restrepo noted, was destined to sink into the proletariat because, given the structural conditions of capitalism, social classes were groups of individuals who could appropriate somebody else's labor as a result of one's location in the economic structure. Thus the petit bourgeoisie, oscillating between the other two classes, had a diminutive capital, forcing it to undergo proletarianization. Harnecker, Restrepo wrote, thought of this class as profoundly conservative, as a "petit" manifestation of the bourgeoisie, and thus it tried to get away from "revolutionary groups." Yet Restrepo found these arguments unconvincing. He highlighted—literally—the core of Harnecker's argument and put a question mark in the margins where Harnecker emphasized the petit bourgeoisie's conservative role.[53] Restrepo wrote three question marks next to Harnecker's definition of classes and asked, "Is it only a matter of ownership. . . . Where am I in this society that would not let me do much. . . . Who am I???"[54]

Although it is difficult to draw definite conclusions, it seems plausible that, at least at first, professionals such as Restrepo had some difficulty finding themselves in Marx. Yet as Marxism was becoming common sense, they forced themselves to read harder. Restrepo became convinced that the more productive part of Marx was the theorist's assignment of a critical role to those who wanted "to think and live in practice."[55] Throughout the 1970s, professionals such as Restrepo found that, given their uneasy position in Marxist explanations of class belonging, their role was to transform the world around them through praxis. And to do so, they needed to think critically about the society that they belonged to. Thinking and doing, rather than opposite tasks, needed to become part of the "consciousness of those who [were] neither bourgeois nor proletariat." In what seems to be an answer to his own questions regarding Harnecker's reading of Marx, Restrepo himself reclaimed Marx's famous eleventh thesis on Feuerbach to legitimize a classed revolutionary role in society: "before I met Marx sociology was about explaining the world; after reading Marx I can see that the point [was] not only a scientific explanation of the world but also the need to transform such reality."[56]

In this context, other professionals also found partial answers by engaging with Louis Althusser's *Reading Capital*. Mimeographed by *Banda Roja*, a JUCO publication, in 1969 in Spanish translation, Althusser's text, these professionals recalled, was amply distributed in state offices, university campuses, cafés, neighborhoods, development offices, and union halls.[57] It was read as reaffirming males' gendered identification as petit bourgeois men who, in contrast to a feminized middle class, imagined as maintaining itself in the "metaphysical abstraction of their unproductive lives," devoted themselves to the "concreteness and practicality of revolutionary thought."[58] The French theorist invited professionals to ponder that *Capital* was to be read not only by the proletariat but also, and perhaps more important, by "educators, salaried employees, researchers, engineers, physicians, professors, and professionals in general."[59] And the petit bourgeoisie had to read *Capital* because, as a class, they needed to be "thirsty for knowledge," knowledge to be concretely used to explain the specific mechanisms and material conditions through which capitalist society worked.[60]

Given these questions, subjective experiences, and readings, transnational events such as the Cuban Revolution became critical political inspiration for reconfiguring newly defined petit bourgeois gendered identities. Cecilia Serrano, trained as a social worker but employed as a teacher in a private school, offers a case in point. Her professional notes and diaries indicate that Che Guevara's ideas were of some influence soon after she resigned her teaching position at a private school and got involved in literacy programs in poor neighborhoods in Bogotá. After hours of teaching working-class kids and mothers, Serrano would join discussion groups in which university students, state professionals, and white-collar workers pondered their role in a changing society.[61] Che's *Guerrilla Warfare* was a book that, among several other readings, she borrowed from a close friend. Drawing on the Cuban model for revolution, she summarized the book in her professional notes by highlighting three main points for revolutionary change in Latin America. First, she described the possibility that "people's forces can win a war against the army." Second, she recounted that it was not "necessary to wait for all conditions favorable to revolution to be present," as "the insurrection itself can create them." Finally, she reported that "in the underdeveloped parts of America, the battleground for armed struggle should be the countryside."[62]

Although it is difficult to limn how exactly Serrano interpreted *Guerrilla Warfare*, she elaborated the oligarchies' role in Latin America as a way to legitimize both her participation in revolutionary politics and the need to participate in armed struggle to bring about "meaningful change." Her language is quite telling: Serrano, following Che's arguments, noted how the oligarchies wanted to maintain a "feudal system," in which an alliance between the "bourgeoisie and landowners" would maintain a "traditional society" that oppressed "the masses of Latin America." Such descriptions resonated with the frustrations and everyday class struggles that she experienced as a teacher, which caused her to complain about the oligarchies as an obstacle to progress and democracy.[63] Although it would take a couple of years for Serrano to join FECODE and, in the mid-1970s, M-19, her professional diaries attest that for her the very notion of oligarchy—the class other—was reimagined through Che's writings, and a new concept would become more common among these professionals in criticizing society: the "bourgeoisie."[64] Indeed, Che and the Cuban Revolution further fostered a classed identity through which professional women such as Serrano saw a possibility for working for radical change as members of a petit bourgeoisie. Cecilia wrote in her professional diaries that her role as a "rational being" would make a difference because, unlike the bourgeoisie, her own class, now defined as petit bourgeoisie rather than middle class, had the important role of becoming the "consciousness of a society." Che was a good example of this consciousness, a man whose class privilege had been "put at the service of revolutionary change in Latin America."[65] To be a petit bourgeois woman meant to think "collectively," to politicize society by making "people aware" of their "exploitative status."

Yet, it is important to emphasize that this was not the only reading of the Cuban Revolution. In a moment when armed struggle was becoming a central question, a group of self-identified independent professors at UNAL thought it important to make clear that, as Che had said during the 1950s, "Cuba would not be Guatemala." While most scholars have read Che's prediction as an invitation to support armed struggles as the only option for making a revolution in Latin America, given the reactionary role played by US government in the region, these professors found inspiration in this prediction to legitimize themselves as leaders of a "revolutionary society." According to their gloss, in Cuba, unlike in Guatemala, the revolution had been made neither by peasants nor by workers but rather by a "radicalized petit bourgeoisie" who had resigned their "social conditions as a class" to produce critical knowledge and revolutionary teaching that questioned the ruling ideas of an "old . . . feudal society" so that a new and revolutionary one could emerge. A radicalized petit bourgeoisie—imagined to be embodied by gendered and classed figures such as Fidel Castro, a lawyer, and

Che, a medical doctor—would be the political gift of Latin America to the world.[66]

For other professionals and white-collar workers, it was the productive amalgamation of Catholicism and Marxism that proved crucial to rethinking themselves as petit bourgeois revolutionaries. The new Conference of Latin American Bishops (CELAM), which was created in 1955 and held its first general conference in Medellín in 1968, opened space for radical young priests who legitimized "the option for the poor" while questioning the Catholic Church's preoccupations with the interests of the elite.[67]

Pope Paul IV made such vision of society quite clear when in front of crown in Bogotá he said, "We wish to personify the Christ of a poor and hungry people." He also asked the "men of the ruling class to detach [themselves] from the stability of . . . [their] position which is, or seems to be, a position of privilege, in order to serve those who need your wealth, your culture, your authority."[68]

Although such a political call echoed the Alliance, by 1968 many professionals and white-collar workers understood it as a radical call to change society. They claimed to know that the ruling classes were not willing to, as the Pope said, "be more sensitive to the voices crying out for bread, concern, justice, and a more active participation in the direction of society."[69] Thus, some of these petit bourgeois women and men began to appropriate liberation theology. They said that, as petit bourgeois, they were definitely "not part of the people," but they had "Christian ideals" that allowed them to make "a radical difference in society."[70] In fact, virtually all these individuals remembered how they went to alternative masses given by Golconda (a group of radical priests), discussed the Bible in study groups, and realized that they could liberate not only the poor but also themselves by playing a role in revolutionary change. Indeed, such experience proved liberating because it was God's mandate to labor for social change. Or, as Marta Jaramillo recalled, citing Camilo Torres Restrepo, it was emancipating to know that "the duty of every Christian is to make the revolution."[71] These religiously inspired professionals and white-collar employees began to carry around and discuss two really thick books: "the Bible and the 'other Bible'—*Capital*."[72] And in so doing, they saw themselves as radical petit bourgeoisie, committed members of society who, through religion, would prepare both the "resurrection of the people," who, like Jesus Christ, had been crucified by the reality of poverty and thus were in need of *concientización* as a revolutionary force.

Camilo Torres Restrepo, a former university professor to many of these professionals, became a gendered and classed inspiration as the proper embodiment of a radical petit bourgeoisie who would resuscitate and raise the consciousness of "the people." Torres Restrepo joined the ELN in 1966 and was killed soon thereafter by state forces. To these professionals, Torres Restrepo exemplified what Jesus had once said: that "the truth will set you free." That truth—referred to by these professionals as "scientific exactitude"—was part of the Christian life and could be found by the petit bourgeoisie through a careful quest for knowledge, solidarity, and love.[73] For this reason, petit bourgeois professionals and white-collar employees appropriated what they considered one of the most important mandates of the Catholic religion: "Love your neighbor as yourself." The discourse and practice of revolutionary love for and solidarity with the poor provoked a major change in how this faction of the petit bourgeoisie understood their revolutionary duties.[74] They could not stay in a privileged role unaware of the reality of poverty, because that would be sinful in God's eyes. In adopting this rhetoric, these petit bourgeois women and men furthermore created gender and class adversaries—the *prójimo*, the poor, and those in need and the elites and the oligarchies, the sinners par excellence as they produced poverty—as the constitutive others who allowed these professionals and white-collar employees to define themselves as radical petit bourgeoisie.

Proletarianization Does Not Happen Overnight

But if Catholicism became the source of legitimation for a classed radicalization, other white-collar employees and professionals created a religion of sorts to reimagine themselves as part of the revolutionary change. Given the class frustrations and political disappointments provoked by development programs, members of a petit bourgeoisie found inspiration in one of the most important transnational discussions during the 1960s and 1970s throughout the old and new left: the question of proletarianization and the role of the vanguard party in revolutionary change. Everywhere, from the Communist Party to Maoist groups, from guerrilla movements to liberation theology, from Trotskyist positions to countercultural politics, one finds countless references to these questions. The PCC-ML, a Maoist political party founded in 1965 that perhaps most decisively promoted the practice of proletarianization in Colombia, "recognized" from the beginning that most of their members, at least in its urban cells, were of a "petit bourgeois background," thus giving the political party an "imperfect and faulty social makeup."[75] The Communist Party complained that they were becoming a vanguard party supporting "workerism without workers." Other political organizations protested that the "petit bourgeois origin" of their revolutionary members had produced some "deficiencies" and "deviations" in the consolidation of a "proletariat leadership for the revolution."[76] Trotskyist groups discussed whether the petit bourgeoisie should compose, along with a worker leadership, the "cuadros del movimiento." Urban guerrilla organizations such as the M-19 also worried that the presence of "too many petit bourgeois members" would put the military preparation for a revolution at risk.[77] In all these discussions, these members seemed to recognize their petit bourgeois identity while readily denying its very role in revolutionary change.

As professionals and white-collar workers searched for partial answers to their class frustrations and anxieties, these actors found themselves in a new transnational discursive conjuncture, in which the political imperatives of the new left—articulated by figures as diverse as Che Guevara, Mao Tsetung, Frantz Fanon, and God—dictated that it was the proletariat, rather than the petit bourgeoisie, who would be the fundamental revolutionary subject. This paradox of considering oneself middle class—and thus imagining oneself as playing a democratic role as part of development programs—while yearning dearly to hold onto the idea of the proletariat as the source of legitimacy for a revolutionary horizon provoked among these professionals and white-collar employees a classed, unconscious *desire* to become and represent the proletarian class.

Indeed, the category and practice of proletarianization, the very denial of being petit bourgeois, and the desire to become proletariat were part and parcel of a larger project of class politics for legitimizing a role for the petit bourgeois as a revolutionary force within a multiplicity of left movements. It is at the core of this effort through which petit bourgeoisie women and men dedicated themselves to make the very concept and identity of being petit bourgeois a political insult—indeed a taboo—whose classed and gendered power resided precisely in the careful denial of what was widely evident.

Thus personal archives are replete with manuals on how *not* to be petit bourgeois, which translated into an intense disciplinary practice. In daily discussions, left political parties, unions, and organizations constantly asserted that to be revolutionary, the petit bourgeois needed to develop a "new moral . . . a new ethical and political being" as a proletarian. Precisely because most members of these left parties saw themselves as part of the petit bourgeoisie, this task of transforming their classed selves was defined as the most revolutionary of all. If a revolution were to succeed, they needed to normalize their putative class deviation and legitimize their revolutionary potential. The teaching material produced for different left political parties, university work-study groups, plays, and movies suggests that it was mandatory to eradicate "*the original sin* of every revolutionary . . . to overcome any trace, mark, or print of a petit bourgeois custom, habit, or pattern," because those "vices" prevented the petit bourgeoisie from becoming proper revolutionaries.[78] As some petit bourgeois members of both the old and new left envisioned their own proletarianization in the late 1960s, "Proletarianization does not happen overnight. It is a struggle between revolution and counterrevolution. We need honesty, endurance, patience, persistence, resolution, willingness, high doses of revolutionary ideology, and a great revolutionary virility. It is not easy to eradicate the petit bourgeois vices from our minds and our bodies. . . . And such struggle is composed of small battles, but reading Mao and his *tres permanentes* will help us take a proletarian position."[79]

Karl Marx, Vladimir Lenin, Camilo Torres Restrepo, Frantz Fanon, Che Guevara, Paulo Freire, and, above all, Mao Tse-tung became the sources of political education for this classed disciplinary project of adopting what this petit bourgeoisie considered the genuine virtues, thoughts, and practices of the so-called proletariat. In so doing, the proletariat became a desire of classed and gendered exclusionary otherness through which petit bourgeois subjects would be able to claim hierarchical political recognition and social distinction as proper revolutionaries, usually associated with a vanguard force. To do so, these professionals and white-collar workers imagined themselves as fleeing what was referred to, following the German poet Bertolt Brecht, as the "seven capital sins of the petit bourgeoisie."[80] These sins, soon part of a shared economy of desires within the left, were performed in public spaces, constantly examined in teaching materials, endlessly discussed in everyday conversation, and continuously practiced in the bedroom.

Those capital sins, associated with notions of femininity, were the source of classed inspiration on how to behave as an *authentic proletariat.* The first and perhaps most important sin was the putatively feminine petit bourgeois "preoccupation with . . . thinking [and the tendency to follow] the subjectivity of abstraction." By implication, the masculine petit bourgeois— the imagined proletariat-to-be—had to distinguish himself from other classes by his "practicality, thingness, concreteness, and objectivity of experience."[81] In a twist on the common gendered distinction between thinking and doing, now it was a feminized petit bourgeois who would prefer to abstract—rather than experience, as the properly masculine revolutionary subject would—the conditions of revolutionary change. To avoid such a capital sin, it was mandatory, as Mao dictated, to navigate the masses "as a fish swims in the sea," to experience the purported concreteness of proletarian life.[82]

All the following capital sins of the improper and thus feminized petit bourgeois emanated from this foundational distinction between abstraction and concrete experience: *laziness* (the preference to stay behind a bureaucrat's desk instead of finding the practical truth with the proletariat), *pride* (to think of oneself as different from others and thus not being able to "go down" to work with the masses), *silence* (to think, rather than experience, social injustices and thus to avoid doing anything practical about it), *luxury* (embracing consumption excess rather than the "material scarcity" so central in the life of the masses and hence in the coming revolution), *greed* (losing one's "brain . . . what [one] think[s] . . . for the benefit of money"), and *envy* (to "resent the life of others" and not be content with one's own life).[83]

Instead of these cardinal sins, proper masculine petit bourgeois subjects would embrace the purported objective virtues of the proletarian revolutionary class—"simplicity, plainness, austerity, scarcity, material-driven decision-making, and objectivity."[84] Hence, at the core of this disciplinary process of proletarianization the petit bourgeoisie, as a class seeking self-praise as radical revolutionaries, imagined the proletariat as an excluded other, relentlessly represented in its hierarchical alterity. In so doing, the very political desire to proletarianize oneself meant to legitimize— unconsciously, no doubt—a masculinized, petit bourgeois hierarchical position within these new processes of radicalization. And such hierarchy was protected by the fact that, like a taboo, petit bourgeoisie identity had to be treated as *the* repressed secret.

It is in this context, then, that Mao's theories of the peasant as a revolutionary force, Fanon's vision of the countryside rather than the cities as a source of revolutionary energy, Torres Restrepo's decision to join the ELN, and God's mandate to serve the poor were associated with a proper process of proletarianization. Indeed, along with the frustration provoked by FN's policies, this self-identified petit bourgeoisie saw the political decision to join the "people's cause . . . hold guns, and change society" as the most important classed sacrifice for "the superior interests of the revolution." They would leave, once again, their "middle-class ways . . . [their] city behind . . . [their] classrooms . . . their vices of only thinking"—now all manifestations of the "bourgeois order"—to become part of a larger "unified . . . undivided mass working together for the revolution."[85] At last, they thought, they would become proletariat—politically well-prepared actors representing as a vanguard force "the people."

Yet once men encountered the proletariat—in this case, peasants in guerrilla movements such as the FARC—they soon found themselves demasculinized. Such an experience reminded them of who they really were: an urban petit bourgeois. There was no taboo any longer. They were told that they did not have the political preparation for a true revolution, called by peasants "little dolls . . . little ladies . . . playing to be revolutionaries." As one recalled, "We merely were *niños pequeños burgueses* with some ideas but no practice in the revolution. When we complained, they told us we were lady *burguesitas*. They treated us like we were women with no strength." And precisely because of this connection between revolution and masculinity, those women who joined rural guerrilla movements had the hardest time of all. Peasants told them that they were "little . . . small . . . petit bourgeois women" who had to "behave like real men" to keep up with the revolution.

Such experiences made evident the need to reconsider the desire to proletarianize and join the guerrillas as a part of political radicalization. Those ambivalent about joining the guerrillas learned through friends' stories, some important books, and tales about executions carried out for antirevolutionary behavior that a proper petit bourgeoisie needed to develop via a means besides proletarianization. Others would insist that armed rebellion remained critical, given the oligarchies' intransigency and the limited democracy of the FN, but they now emphasized that it was urban rather than rural guerrillas who would play a leading role in creating the conditions for a revolution. The M-19 became a group to either participate in or support.

Education as a Common Good

By the late 1960s and 1970s this political radicalization—as hierarchical and contradictory as it was—materialized a massive petit bourgeois activism that one might characterize as a social movement of class politics. Petit bourgeoisie women and men took to the streets; went on hunger strike; organized multiple protests; practiced politics in universities, public schools, and office spaces; and engaged in literacy programs sponsored by either development offices or movements on the left.[86] One of the most important aspects of this activism was the question of education and the role of knowledge in society. As a partial response to the political radicalization of petit bourgeois women and men, Pastrana's administration began to implement policies for the reconfiguration of education as the condition for a competitive society. Luis Carlos Galán Sarmiento, minister of education for Pastrana's administration, evoked Rudolph Atcon in proposing changes in how education was envisioned in democratic societies. Defining his project as a *reconquista* of educational institutions that had been plagued by "the obscure forces of Marxism [and] foreign influences of communism," Galán Sarmiento envisioned a (neo)liberal model in which universities, schools, and other educational institutions could maximize the human capital of the nation and multiply it for the benefit of the nation's wealth. Education, Galán Sarmiento contended, should not be seen as a "paternalistic gift by the state" but rather as a product of "individual hard work, [as an] economic investment into a future . . . [as] the most important equalizer of society." As such, education, concluded the minister, should be seen as the motivation to improve the economic appreciation of one's human capital in a "mercilessly competitive society."[87]

Anticipating present-day discussions, petit bourgeois women and men challenged this vision of education and offered a critique of what they described as "an imperialistic and bourgeois education."[88] For them, development programs recast educational institutions as "business enterprises" in which "economic profit, job parameters, and individual success rule[d]."[89] Such education, they asserted, "celebrate[d] exploitation . . . economic profit, and capital accumulation for the benefit of the few."[90] They, as educators, were being forced to teach members of society how to be either "exploiters . . . or exploited." This was "an elitist education" because individuals would see it as an investment in earning capacities and future profit. Such profit-driven education was producing "an army of workers" whose sole source of livelihood would be the sale of their labor-power and whose wages, given industry's dependency on their labor, were less than the value of the goods that they would produce. They asserted that education was legitimizing exploitation by securing the values of a bourgeois status quo: appropriation of workers' surplus value, profit accumulation, and individualization of economic success.[91]

In this context, teachers affiliated with FECODE, professors in the Asociación de Profesores Universitarios (ASPU), professional unions in state development offices, teachers participating in street protests, community activists working in outreach programs in popular neighborhoods, and urban guerrilla militants in literacy programs all fought hard throughout the 1970s to redefine education and knowledge as public and common goods. They demanded that education be practiced as not an individual privilege for the few but a collective right for all, through which all members of society could foster capacities for citizenship in a "real democracy." Education, as a common good, would integrate the creativity, humor, participation, and political dreams of all. It could sustain and promote the production of scientific knowledge about the nation so that, as Marx had taught so many of these women and men, orthodox wisdom could be questioned and social reality changed. It would consolidate the right to imaginative labor for all and not just the speed of learning of a competitive few. Indeed, this would be a "revolutionary and liberating education" because it would fight against the perpetuation of an imperial, dependent status in knowledge production by "overcom[ing] the mechanical transfer of US experiences" and consolidating the "national knowledge" needed to "observe, explicate, change, and act in society."[92] Furthermore, via this education "men could become *misfit* for the bourgeois system," questioning the mentality of individualized success, defined as economic profit. These petit bourgeois women and men fought hard for a "humanist education," one through which, as Freire advocated, all members of society could educate themselves beyond the need to sell their labor and instead develop the capacity and commitment to control their lives with a sense of equality, reciprocity, and solidarity.[93] They demanded education as a common good, speaking truth to the bourgeoisie's power and knowledge in criticism of a system of domination. Education, they asserted, had to be a critical tool for emancipating "every single member of society" from economic domination and thus reaching a "real [and] true democracy."[94]

Educating the Proletariat

These demands were quite transformative, expanding crucial spaces for political participation and discussion. Petit bourgeois men and women institutionalized new research initiatives outside academia, rethought school and university curricula, founded in factories after-school programs sponsored by guerrilla groups such as m-19, propagated street theater, expanded literacy programs, established outreach programs, produced movies and documentaries about the realities of poverty, volunteered in community centers, and participated in educational programs in labor unions and peasant organizations.

Yet as petit bourgeois invested themselves in these actions, they faced new difficult questions. Who should emancipate whom in a humanist education? How should the masses—the proletariat—be taught to become proper revolutionary subjects? Who should represent whom in the production of "critical knowledge/education"? What was the role of public institutions such as universities and schools in this process? It was in trying to answer these questions that a vision of education and knowledge production as central to the materialization of "real democracy" was hierarchized as a gendered and classed possession of a revolutionary petit bourgeoisie. On university campuses, for instance, these questions intensified struggles about the role of the United States in the production of knowledge in society. By the second half of the 1960s, the Alliance had become the target of constant criticism regarding a profit-driven education and the elitization of knowledge. Since the fierce opposition in 1966 to John Rockefeller III's attempted visit to unal's campus, some professors—who, it is worth noting, had been hired thanks to the expansion of development programs—found it imperative to carry out detailed research to discern the connection between US development offices and the consolidation of different disciplines across the university. And they found out that "the US [was] all over them." They reluctantly recognized in several research papers that all the university disciplines had been, in one way or another, "breathing, eating, and surviving with US money."[95]

It is in this context that some young professors in different disciplines at unal accused some of their former mentors of supporting imperial policies and thus of fundamentally opposing a vision of education as a common good and as productive of revolutionary knowledge. Important intellectuals such as Fals Borda—who, as we saw before, played a fundamental role in the so-called professionalization of society—were now being questioned for their financial and institutional ties with US development organizations. Those "pro-empire" professors were temporarily expelled from the university because, with presumably US-driven modernization theory as their main inspiration, they were seen as the main obstacles to a "true public and independent university." Against their mentors, these new professors argued that such imperial influence would make students at best "anticritical technicians" and at worst "assistants to international experts" who wanted to apply knowledge produced in the North within "completely different social, economic, and cultural conditions."[96] These professors argued that this imperial dependency would by definition put them, as petit bourgeoisie, at a "lower status" in a worldwide geography of power/knowledge, as they would be only "mimickers," rather than producers, of knowledge. What "the gringos [had] to say," they argued, would be seen as universally "applicable" to any geographical location because there was no authentic production of knowledge outside the North to challenge the hegemony of its generalizations. It was therefore necessary to reclaim the production of knowledge in public universities, which, above all, could change society.

Those self-identified independent professors at UNAL, who as we saw earlier took inspiration from Che's motto "Cuba would not be Guatemala," went a step further by elaborating on the notion of "imperial difference." Contrary to their experience in Europe and the United States, the bourgeoisie in Latin America could not play a revolutionary role because they had failed to act as a universal class in promoting the conditions for a modern society to emerge, co-opted instead by "imperial interests." As a consequence, the petit bourgeoisie would have to "substitute" for the bourgeoisie to fight against North American imperialism and the antimodern conditions of Latin American societies. These independent professors defined the public university as the place where Latin America could "give the most important political gift to the whole world: a revolutionary petit bourgeoisie."[97]

In this way petit bourgeois men and women collectively envisioned themselves as engaged in a class struggle against a powerful and anxious bourgeoisie for "the hearts and minds of the Colombian proletariat."[98] By producing revolutionary knowledge to educate those destined to make the revolution, petit bourgeois women and men viewed themselves as those who could foster the authentic conditions for "real democracy" to emerge. As so many petit bourgeois women and men believed, this revolutionary task consisted of "engaging in a fight to the death against the bourgeoisie [for] the proletariat soul" so that the proletariat could "remain faithful to himself as proletariat."[99]

Tracing this radicalization of the middle class into a petit bourgeoisie allows us to see a certain degree of classed and gendered commonality otherwise invisible across the multiple divisions within the left at this time. These professionals put the proletariat—variously referred to as the "working masses," the popular classes, the peasantry, and the laboring groups—

at the center of real, revolutionary change. Some professionals in the PCC argued that, given their dominated position, the proletariat could not question a bourgeois order. The proletariat remained in this exploited position because they did not know that they were trapped by a dominant bourgeois ideology. Therefore, the proletariat could not embrace a revolutionary consciousness until a bourgeois status quo and its ruling social ideas were questioned. Yet if the proletarian masses found themselves trapped in bourgeois ideology and the bourgeoisie benefited from this, who would be able to break such an unproductive circle? The answer went without saying and played a fundamental role in legitimizing the notion of the petit bourgeoisie's classless belonging to a vanguard party.

Such a belief crossed left party divides. Other professionals, belonging to the Movimiento Obrero Independiente y Revolucionario (MOIR), a Maoist political group founded in 1968, advocated in partial disagreement with the PCC for a "popular, anti-imperialist, and scientific education" at the service of the proletariat.[100] They argued that if education were to be revolutionary, it would have to embrace what these petit bourgeois men saw as the proletariat's authentic (masculine) interests and dispositions: concrete practice rather than abstract knowledge, materiality rather than theoretical thought, proletarian particularities rather than social universals, impulsiveness and spontaneous political decision-making rather than careful and structured deliberation. Yet the MOIR's vision concurred with the PCC in arguing that the proletariat—as those who were supposed to be concerned with the materiality of the revolution rather than with thinking about it—remained in a feminine, sentimental, and natural stage, unconscious of their exploitation and hence susceptible to the bourgeoisie's power. These petit bourgeois women and men thus naturalized a hierarchical opposition between on the one hand science, knowledge, and political training, associated with a feminized bourgeois education, and on the other the practical, masculine, political role of the proletariat in the revolution. In these visions of revolutionary change, the proletarian masses themselves needed to undergo a process of proletarianization by detaching themselves from the bourgeois values that kept them dominated and embracing a scientific and proper proletarian ideology.

Petit bourgeois men needed to educate workers and peasants to embrace their virile revolutionary predispositions: "objectivity" (the political realization of the conditions of exploitation), "vigor" (the physical and mental virility to fight exploitation), "solidarity" (the male trait seeking unity and cohesion among peers), "political preparation" (the masculine dynamism to prepare oneself for the struggle with the oppressors), "power of decision" (the vital leadership to organize and unify interests), and "camaraderie" (the muscle to stay together under any circumstance). Only then, petit bourgeois men contended, could working-class men and peasants stop treating themselves as "if they were *señoritas*" and overcome female values and inclinations such as "political spontaneity, impulsiveness, false consciousness, and frivolity," which prevented them from becoming "a revolutionary force."[101] In the process, petit bourgeois men desired their proletariat—always defined as a potential masculine revolutionary force and yet eternally discussed for his inadequacies and as not yet ready to fully embody a revolutionary consciousness—as the classed and gendered other to be morally uplifted, politically trained, and socially masculinized to make a "real democracy" possible.

Yet other petit bourgeois educators, mostly associated with Trotskyist groups, disagreed with this pedagogy. Several members of university professors' and schoolteachers' organizations (FECODE, ASPU, Asociación Distrital de Educadores [ADE], and Asociación de Profesores de la Universidad Nacional [APUN]) appropriated Antonio Gramsci to contend that "the exploitation of the masses" happened not only through violence but also through consent.[102] It followed from this that a revolutionary struggle had to happen within the "superstructure." Thus rather than reducing revolutionary education to a "curriculum for proletarianization," they, who held "an advanced position" in society, needed to teach the proletariat to be "critical thinkers for a revolutionary society."[103] Petit bourgeois men could not waste all their precious time and sophisticated thinking in "competing" with workers and peasants over the "radicalism of slogans," whether on the streets, in popular organizations, or in poor neighborhoods.[104] A revolutionary education had to move away from "verbal radicalism," which confused the scientific path toward real democracy with its "noisy, superficial, and sentimentally driven discussions."[105] Neither the proletariat's proper revolutionary education nor real democracy would come from those unable to distance themselves from their material experiences, an inability they dubbed "cerebrelización estomacal."[106] This destined the proletariat to, at worst, "pile pamphlets, recite Marx or Mao, follow a political spontaneity, [and] scream on the street in favor of the revolution" or, at best, parrot a "vulgar economism."[107] Thus the petit bourgeoisie, given "objective differences" of class experience, needed to be educated in revolutionary knowledge to explain what the proletariat could not understand: "the tricks, myths, ideology, fetishes, [and] illusions of capital." The petit bourgeois would be "revolutionary educators" because they were objectively in a better position to know the potential universality of a proper revolution and to transform the proletariat from an imperfect—trivial, particular, feminine, materialist, and simple-minded—person into a revolutionary masculine man.

Another group of professionals, professors, and teachers across university campuses and schools categorized this latter vision of revolutionary education as "frigid and privileged."[108] Some had been expelled from universities. Others had returned from joining up with rural guerrillas and were eager to become activists in the cities. Yet others had received degrees from public and private universities and wanted to put into practice their acquired knowledge. This group claimed that those who wanted to remain "safely in the privacy of a university classroom" would be untouched by "revolutionary reality," which would make academia's knowledge an "elitist and imperialist production." Such knowledge production would bring the petit bourgeoisie closer to the "bourgeois sanctuary" than "the proletarian trench." By claiming a gendered understanding of "the fathers of revolutionary thought"—Marx, Mao, Torres Restrepo, and Gramsci—this group of professionals, professors, and teachers claimed to encounter, again, the "real popular classes."[109] These professional women and men eagerly embraced an identity as committed petit bourgeois—variously referred to as activist researchers, intellectual revolutionaries, revolutionary men of science, and militants—seeking to transform, following Gramsci's idea of hegemony, the popular classes' "common sense" into a "good sense" that could realize an alternative social order. They wanted to transform the popular classes' embedded, incoherent, spontaneous beliefs into the best source of political inspiration by putting scientific techniques and knowledge production at the service of a popular cause and engaging in political teaching to clarify revolutionary aims and provoke political reflection among members of working-class unions, peasant organizations, urban communities, school classrooms, and literacy programs.[110]

During the 1970s, these pedagogical desires led to the formation of a research methodology called *investigación acción participativa*, the publication of political magazines such as *Alternativa*, the formalization of educational initiatives with peasant associations such as the Asociación Nacional de Usuarios Campesinos (ANUC), and the expansion of literacy programs organized and supported by M-19. Orlando Fals Borda and anthropologist Víctor Daniel Bonilla, along with others, founded in the early 1970s the Rosca de Investigación y Acción Social (Circle of Research and

Social Action [RIAS]).[111] La Rosca sought to connect thought with action and produce knowledge useful for a revolutionary cause. Such methodologies became common among teachers in the classroom and activists in literacy programs. In contrast to the other left sectors interested in education discussed earlier in this chapter, these committed petit bourgeois wanted to challenge the epistemological assumptions behind the proletariat's role as revolutionary subject. Radicalizing some of the claims made by LMMC during the 1960s, these professionals saw themselves as "nationalizing"— what some today would call provincializing—Marxism, because the left suffered from an "intellectual colonialism" that caused them to recite Marxist clichés without critically appropriating the epistemological and political challenge proposed by "the old guy."[112] They argued that he had provided the tools for thinking about how capitalism's political economy was by no means natural but rather the product of a certain configuration of power relationships. By anticipating the emergence of postcolonial readings in the 1980s, these committed activists, educators, and researchers, in an ample variety of educational venues, proposed decentralizing knowledge from "the normal sciences . . . political parties of the left, [and] the formality of the academia" to reinsert popular groups into knowledge production and educational processes.[113] Critically appropriating Mao, they saw this as an opportunity for consolidating a "*ciencia propia*, an insurgent science, a science for the humble" that avoided needless theoretical sophistication and celebrated practical effectiveness. Such insurgent science sought to discover the voices of the proletariat and the "culture of the people," silenced by either the economic situation or the bourgeoisie, in order to recuperate critical stories and struggles from the past for the masses' future struggle with the dominant class.

It is through the various classed and gendered discussions of education recounted above that some female professors, teachers, and activists challenged what counted as revolutionary education and knowledge. These women argued against "proletarianizing educational curricula" because this would nevertheless leave "patriarchal culture" unquestioned.[114] These petit bourgeois women, mostly affiliated with Trotskyist segments of the left and M-19, wanted to provide a "democratic education for full democracy" in which every form of domination and oppression could be questioned so that the proletariat could open spaces for thinking and acting differently in truly democratic societies.

In late 1976, for instance, these petit bourgeois women wrote two extensive mimeographed letters to "different voices of the Left" complaining that their own voices were silenced. They argued that revolutionary education was "male in composition and male in focus," and that thus disregarding half the population prevented a proper "liberating and universalizing education." These women elaborated how the education proposed by Maoist and Communist petit bourgeois men followed a "Catholic, authoritarian, and dogmatic" model in which "productive thinking" and "critical knowledge were not possible."[115] This model was religious because it always invoked a God of sorts—Marx, Lenin, Mao, Trotsky, Fidel, Che, Camilo—in response to friendly challenges. As these women paraphrased such invocations, "How could we dare to know more than Mao or Marx about revolutionary matters? Do we dare to think something new about education and revolution?"[116] These female educators argued that such restrictive religious models would transform revolutionary education into "a thought police institution" that inspired "the death of bodies, ideas, and minds" rather than change of the bourgeois status quo.[117]

In contrast, these women appropriated Freire's concept of banking education to propose a more "productive education for a revolutionary society," one in which students—always imagined as proletarian—were seen not as empty vessels to be filled with revolutionary information but rather as active participants in their own education, a pedagogical model that would allow them to change the social, political, and economic structures that sustained "their individualities, their affective lives, their environment, their domestic relationships, and their quotidian lives."[118] Such humanist education would mean not uniformity but rather a critical dialogue of ideas and feelings in which the diversity of arguments and social visions could energize the revolution that they were looking for. The women also argued that education should be predicated not on the destruction of social groups but on the production of new values, sentiments, and desires. "To change others," they proclaimed, one must "change oneself."[119] The bourgeois status quo had oppressed proletarian women into embodying "masculine values" such as "rivalry, incivility, and indifference," which prevented them from speaking with one voice as women and critiquing the bourgeois status quo. These proletarian women succumbed, furthermore, to the most insidious masculine and patriarchal value of all: "the idea that women lack power."[120] By changing how "women and men relate[d] to themselves, to children, and to things," revolutionary education would make these proletarian women more like petit bourgeois women.[121] Proletarian women were exploited and dominated within the prevailing sexual division of labor because, as women, they were unaware of the "bourgeois model" of womanhood that maintained their domination and hence of their potential role as a revolutionary force that could question this sexual division of labor.[122]

This redefinition of revolutionary education and knowledge production ignited a strong response among petit bourgeois men, despite their formal disagreements on how to make a revolution, who joined forces to disqualify women as revolutionary educators and knowledge producers. As women increasingly participated in the expansion of the left, some men appropriated Althusser's distinction between revolutionary attitudes and positions to categorize their female counterparts as "prepared for bourgeois education" but unqualified for a revolutionary one.[123] These petit bourgeois men contended that like proletarian men, petit bourgeois women had a feminine attitude that allowed them to embrace proletarian values but not a proper proletarian position, which left them ill equipped to teach the proletariat how to become revolutionary subjects.[124] Some men went so far as to blame this counterrevolutionary situation on women's sentimental tendencies, which prevented them from "digest[ing] and process[ing] the hard, highly theoretical texts" indispensable for achieving a proletarian position for themselves and for transforming the proletariat's instincts into revolutionary positions. Knowledge, they said, was foreign to women's "immediate instincts and interests."[125] Men thus claimed the position of sovereign representative who possessed the knowledge needed to transform and masculinize the workers' natural instinct for revolution into a developed proletarian consciousness.

Some went so far as to say that Colombia was not yet historically ready to address issues of feminism: "in matters of revolutionary education, everything has its time and place ... Colombia is neither Europe nor the United States when it comes to women's problems."[126] Despite all the criticisms of the United States and Europe as imperialist, these petit bourgeois men assumed that there "material disparities [had been] resolv[ed]" and thus that women there could dedicate themselves "to chang[ing] things beyond an economic sphere." But because Colombia, like the other nations of Latin America, was an "underdeveloped country par excellence," revolution had to focus on economic issues instead: "the proletariat cares for material conditions, he is interested in securing bread, land, shelter, clothes ... then he [will] get worried about everything else."[127] Hence women's questions had to be delayed until "another epoch of humanity comes," a moment when Colombia looked structurally like the United States and Europe, when a proletarian class was masculinized enough to embrace those demands. Others said that women, as a counterrevolutionary force, could only promote "the worst bourgeois deviations." Not only would an emphasis on "women's questions" educate the proletariat in "abstract" values, but it would provoke an "ideological diversionism" that would implement an "antiproletarianization . . . Europeanization, [and] proimperialist education."[128] These counterrevolutionary and countervirile values would prevent women from fulfilling the mission of a revolutionary and humanist education of the masses: "to penetrate the uncultivated land of the proletariat and to get his culture pregnant with proletarian activities so that a revolution could blossom."[129]

Delegitimizing the Bourgeoisie

Petit bourgeois men and women also united in an unprecedented interrogation of the bourgeoisie's role in society, what I call a *subversive epistemology*. Such epistemology—a lively combination of dissident teaching and critical knowledge production—was disseminated in books, magazines, manifestos, pamphlets, political banners, lesson plans, guerrilla training, art pieces, position papers at professional conferences, speeches at party meetings, ethnographic reports for state development offices, and theater scripts.

This project was at once transformative and hierarchical. One of its most important manifestations regarded questions of land distribution. As many professionals who had worked with peasants through INCORA underwent radicalization, state policies regarding rural development and land distribution gained new political traction. After four years of disinterest in agrarian reform under Guillermo León Valencia, his successor, Carlos Lleras Restrepo, sought legitimacy among peasants by supporting the creation of ANUC in 1968. At first, ANUC remained within the bounds of the official state policy to consolidate a rural society of small landholders. Soon, however, the association was radicalized from below.[130] For instance, Trotskyist employees advanced a vision of landownership without bosses— *tierra sin patrones*—as official policy at ANUC's national meeting in 1971. Multiple Maoists groups argued that ANUC policy should instead be predicated on ownership for those who worked the land—*tierra para el que la trabaja*. This became official at ANUC's second meeting, in 1972 in Sincelejo. In response, Misael Pastrana supported the Chicoral Pact of 1971. This agreement between Liberal and Conservative elites ended the possibility of a land distribution. For those working in rural development programs, the pact represented yet another manifestation of the oligarchs' antidemocratic vision.

Thus despite, or precisely because of, the pact, many state professionals still actively discussed the so-called agrarian question, most advocating the vision of land for those who work it. Among these professionals, agronomists were important. Their association, the Asociación Colombiana de Ingenieros Agrónomos (ACIA), supported ANUC's call for land invasion. Yet they proposed their own vision of how land distribution would effect social change. They questioned the "communal enterprises" promoted by the Chicoral Pact because these secured "the exploitation, subjugation, and oppression" of the peasants, who were both isolated from the collective land struggles and bureaucratized by a bourgeois state.[131] In 1973, for instance, Eudoro Álvarez, an agronomist and former president of INCORA's professionals' union, maintained that the communal enterprises were predicated on large-scale production in which peasants could at best remain "vassals of a landowning class."[132] Agronomists published and distributed scientific treatises, based on extensive statistical data, denouncing unequal land distribution.[133] Colombia, they insisted, was not a democracy, because communal enterprises protected "feudalism and imperial exploitation."[134] Yet agronomists also criticized those who advocated for land without bosses because this would further individualize peasants, depoliticize their organizations, and promote social change based on spontaneity rather than political awareness.

Agronomists joined forces with peasants' Maoist leaders within ANUC. But they also departed from the Maoists in grounding "real democracy" in the materialization of a "middle peasant" who could destroy both the latifundio (the manifestation of feudal oligarchical power) and the minifundio (the individualization of landownership). Both were antitechnical and thus exploitative of the peasants, counterproductive for the nation, and profitable only for the landowners. The minifundista peasant had no resources to use more technology, and the latifundista had no interest. Thus it was the middle peasant—sometimes suggestively called an entrepreneur—who could improve agricultural development by expanding modern technology, which would increase economic production, respect for private property, and national economic reinvestment. As Carlos Naranjo and Hector Julio Ruiz, two ACIA leaders, concluded in a paper presented at the agronomists' professional conference in late 1971, only then could a true democracy "destroy the landowning regime, liberate the land from monopoly, and create a prosperous, modern, and technical agriculture [in which] the land [could be owned] by those who work it."[135] Perhaps ACIA distanced itself from Maoist positions in ANUC because the middle peasant could both protect private property and promote agronomists as those who could teach how to cultivate the land for an advanced, technology-driven rural development. Agronomists could also frame themselves as those able to raise the political awareness of peasants, who remained "temporally confused" in their analysis of the social situation. It was this twin process of agricultural training and consciousness raising that would bring the middle peasant as a culmination of revolutionary change in the countryside.

This is why some agronomists joined with other petit bourgeois professionals to work closely with ANUC and—as they tried to educate the proletariat to be proper revolutionary actors—to produce explanations, ideas, and language questioning what they referred to as bourgeois democracy. Despite their different visions of revolutionary change, these men and women collectively declared the bourgeoisie to be in fundamental contradiction with the representation of "the people" and, above all, invalid as democratic rulers. To this end, RIAS published several pamphlets of comics based on careful research that sought to "orient workers and peasants in the current political movement."[136]

These comics were a larger project of classed and gendered politics. *Alternativa*, a magazine founded in 1974 with the support of Fals Borda and Gabriel García Márquez by and for the petit bourgeoisie, proposed a struggle against "the ideological concentration of information in the hands of those who wanted to retain, illegitimately, political and economic power."[137] The magazine wanted "to counter the systematic disinformation . . . falsehood . . . [and] deception in the media through practical, political, and pedagogical measures," thus dismantling the mechanism by which "the people [were] cheated and fooled."[138] As the magazine's slogan regularly reminded its readers, the petit bourgeoisie must "dare to think" and thereby begin to struggle for the hearts and minds of the masses and simultaneously prepare them to develop a "critical spirit and new popular beliefs."[139]

Petit bourgeois women and men delegitimized the bourgeoisie through interlocking, though sometimes contradictory, gendered and classed critiques. The political comics of RIAS questioned INCORA as a product of a landowning bourgeoisie, denounced the electoral process as a sham, criticized the consolidation of the two traditional political parties as an exclusionary political process, and reclaimed popular heroes from Colombian history. And the FN became *the* manifestation of an antidemocratic oligarchical rule.

All these petit bourgeois productions—some used by broad swathes of the left—argued that the bourgeoisie had historically failed to create the conditions necessary for the emergence of capitalism and democracy. Appropriating Marxist analysis, they elevated the bourgeoisie in Europe as an all-powerful, sovereign, and masculine force that overcame feudalism when they came to power in the eighteenth century and embraced their revolutionary and democratic role.[140] By bringing together peasants and workers under a common goal, this bourgeoisie had created the conditions for the emergence of the rule of law, the institutionalization of some basic rights for "the people," and society's movement away from "systems of bondage"[141]—nothing less than a "democratic revolution" that emancipated peasants and workers from a feudal system of domination. As committed professionals and activists, petit bourgeois women and men criticized the Colombian bourgeoisie for failing in light of this European experience and perpetuating instead a violent system of subjugation, oppression, and exploitation, the most-cited example of which was the "incomplete" independence process of the early nineteenth century. After the Spanish colonizers' departure, as these petit bourgeois women and men elaborated, the Colombian bourgeoisie failed to embrace leadership in consolidating a unified and harmonious political community and instead sought to secure the continuance of an antidemocratic order that benefited themselves as a class.[142] An unsuccessful transition to capitalism and an anemic internal market left the nineteenth-century Colombian bourgeoisie perpetuating a traditional system of exploitation and colonial conditions of corruption, defending their individual interests at the nation's expense. Rather than transcending their class interests and becoming a democratic, hegemonic, and universal class, the Colombian bourgeoisie remained particular and feminine in their political and social roles (figure 7.1).

With such knowledge production about the past, the petit bourgeoisie conjoined their political project to the consolidation of a real democracy. Consider, for instance, the case of Alberto Otalora, a sociologist working for ICT and a member of M-19 engaged in literacy programs in Bogotá's poor neighborhoods. In his teaching lessons as part of literacy programs, Otalora sought to explain "the failures of Colombian history," intimately associated with "the lack of a true and real democracy."[143] Since the mid-1970s, he thought that exposing to "the working masses the antidemocratic lies of the oligarchies [was] the most revolutionary task of all." He complained that the bourgeoisie wanted to convince "the distracted masses" of its putative "democratic role" by framing independence as the most

Figure 7.1
Unreachable
independence.
CRPA, *Rescate*,
1975, profesores
facultad de
ciencias, UNAL.

important event in history, in which "all members of the Colombian nation became free . . . [and] democracy triumphed."[144] Relying on this "fake history," the bourgeoisie had taught the proletariat to believe that "Colombia [was] a democracy." But "history" itself, he lectured, did not lie. The independence movement made no difference whatsoever to the oppressed classes; in contrast to Europe, in nineteenth-century Colombia the bourgeoisie had embodied an "estirpe colonial [colonial lineage]" that prevented them from embracing democracy.[145] Instead, they maintained their power by excluding and repressing the working masses. Uninterested in the nation's well-being, this bourgeoisie maintained elitist colonial domination: "the oppressed classes" went "from being under the joke of Spanish colonial rule to the oppression of the oligarchies."[146] Therefore, Otalora concluded, independence demonstrated "the lack of political will" among the bourgeoisie for bringing "real democracy to the nation."[147]

But what is quite interesting about these powerful critiques of the bourgeoisie as democratic rulers is how they were sustained via gendered premises. In almost every illustration used in political comics, magazines, or teaching lessons, the bourgeoisie—whether categorized as a landowning class, an urban oligarchy, or city bankers—appeared as powerful yet infantilized and feminized (figure 7.2). A good example is an illustration published in *Alternativa*'s first issue in 1974 alongside Gabriel García Márquez's political explanation of the 1973 coup in Chile, which mainly associated the United States with violence and repression underwritten by a Chilean national bourgeoisie. The United States, Márquez said, was a counterrevolutionary, illiberal, reactionary, antidemocratic, and violent force that promoted neither self-determination nor national sovereignty.[148] Yet the illustration accompanying Márquez's analysis was as telling. The United States, embodied by Richard Nixon, was depicted as a fat and hybrid, even androgynous, person breastfeeding Augusto Pinochet. Rendering the United States as a feminized, breastfeeding man suggests how it nurtured, sponsored, and cultivated violence via its support of the military, while the infantilized Pinochet, as representative of the bourgeoisie's interests, was cast as illegitimate, antidemocratic, and submissive because he relied on the imperial care of the United States. Both the United States and Pinochet—and, by proxy, the bourgeoisie—were thus depicted as unfit to rule in true democracies.

This allowed petit bourgeois men to imagine themselves as those who, in contrast to an improper bourgeoisie, could exercise the right to rule in real democracies, defend national sovereignty, and properly represent "the interests of the masses." Far from abstractions, these critiques articulate what was at stake in everyday struggles as part of a redefinition of "real democracy." These were the inspiration "to teach imperialism" and thereby reveal to the proletariat both "the true role of the United States, its multiple forms of exploitation . . . and oligarchical power manifested in the two-party political system." For instance, Rene Sánchez, an agronomist and member of M-19 involved with its literacy programs, wanted the proletariat to see what they could only "experience empirically."[149] Drawing on the methodologies proposed by RIAS and the education methodologies of Germán Zabala, a leader of Golconda, he was convinced that the proletariat had experienced "imperialism, class exploitation, poverty, oppression, and violence" but

Figure 7.2 Illustration for
Gabriel García Márquez,
"Chile, el golpe y los
gringos," *Alternativa*,
February 15–28, 1974, 4.

could not recognize this ideologically as such. As his lesson plans and informal syllabi from the second half of the 1970s indicate, Sánchez divided his
teaching into two parts, for each of which he had two in-class exercises. In
the first part—on the theme of imperialism—he asked his putatively proletarian students to identify on a map of the Americas the United States, "the
imperial force par excellence"; the countries in Latin America with dictatorial governments; the countries that could call themselves "democratic";
and, finally, "Cuba, the only independent nation in Latin America."[150]

The proletarian students, presumably after an explanation by Sánchez,
were also asked to locate the places where the United States, as an "imperialistic force," had promoted "antidemocratic regimes." Sánchez wanted his
students to realize how the United States—which had historically expropriated natural resources, exploited human labor, and economically benefited

national bourgeoisies—was the first to blame for the "underdeveloped condition of Latin America." The second in-class exercise assigned by this petit bourgeois activist on the theme of imperialism involved a map of "foreign investment," intended to teach "the working masses" the link between Colombia's poverty and the wealth expropriated by "US corporations."[151] By uncovering covert imperialism or retelling the history of the US government in Latin America, these professionals interrogated the United States as a source of democratization for the region. Anticipating current analysis of the Cold War, they showed how the United States was one of the most illiberal forces in the region, as it fundamentally contradicted democracy and peace, supporting instead dictatorship and militarization.

But behind these lessons was a more fundamental question that people like Sánchez thought essential to teach in different educational venues: "Why, in this country, [were] some people so rich and some people so poor?" Contrary to what some professionals had taught as part of development programs in the 1960s, petit bourgeois women and men now contended that the problem was threefold. First, "the foreign domination and the feudal conditions" created by the bourgeoisie had destined for Latin America "economic stagnation in production and the ruin of the majority."[152] Second, "the unequal distribution of wealth" allowed only few members of society to enjoy the nation's available resources. Third, prosperity and poverty were "intimate bedfellows." And it was this poverty that people such as Sánchez wanted to put in front of the "proletariat's eyes." By recounting stories of peasants' and workers' everyday exploitation, the petit bourgeoisie argued that, rather than a matter of individual effort, desire for economic improvement, cultural disposition, personal tenacity, or religious beliefs, underdevelopment—or poverty—was a "defining . . . structural condition in a bourgeois democracy."[153] As so many of these committed petit bourgeois women and men lectured in numerous educational venues, "exploitation forms the foundation of a bourgeois democracy": "the rich become rich because they exploit the labor of those at the bottom of society," and the "unpaid labor of workers and peasants . . . produces the wealth . . . [that] the exploiter class expropriates."[154]

Although petit bourgeois women participated in producing these critiques, they also sought to delegitimize the bourgeoisie as democratic rulers through feminist teachings and knowledge production. If education and knowledge, as common goods, were meant to question a "bourgeois status quo" as a dominant ideology, they thought it essential to demolish, "in the same struggle," what was at the core of bourgeois democracy: "a patriarchal culture."[155] The story of Cecilia Serrano, again, is quite telling. After joining M-19, she embraced her new role as a "committed teacher" in literacy programs. She appropriated Simone de Beauvoir and Elena Gianini Belotti to argue that a bourgeois status quo created "natural attitudes" toward female and male children before they were even born. Evoking Beauvoir in her lectures, Serrano contended that women were created rather than born. "There [were] not certain magic conditions that determin[ed] the traditional difference in character between men and women," Serrano wrote in her professional diaries while reading Belotti's *Little Girls*.[156] And if that was true, one needed to question how the bourgeoisie had taught proletarian women and men to think of their "anatomy . . . and biology [as] destiny" via an educational system that emphasized "the difference of the sexes." Serrano pointed to a common exercise in teaching Colombian children to read and write: "my mother takes care of me, I take care of my mom. My mom loves me. I love my mom. My mom is patient. My mom is pure love."[157] While she herself might have used such exercises as a schoolteacher in the 1960s as part of the Alliance, after joining M-19 she now found them quite problematic for at least two reasons: their reproduction of a bourgeois ideology in which motherhood was intimately tied to female identity and the domestic sphere, and their predication of motherhood on the celebration of private ownership. Such naturalization defined women as either mothers or "submissive women who [did] not want power [and instead] want[ed] to remain quiet in the privacy of the home while their bourgeois husbands [went] out and appropriate[d] the surplus value of the proletariat's labor"; in this rendering, "happiness [was] family . . . family [was] happiness."[158] Yet this model was in fact a means for the bourgeoisie to sell its status quo to society and maintain its domination. This powerful ideology was consolidated, Serrano asserted, at the level of everyday life, the proletariat, particularly women, bombarded with "bourgeois messages about the role of women at home . . . [and] the role of the patriarchal family . . . to appropriate the surplus value of women's labor."[159]

It was at this everyday level that Serrano thought it necessary to challenge these ideas, by demystifying "the lives of boring bourgeois women." Again citing Belotti, she opened her lectures by emphasizing that in-class exercises were intended not as an accusation but as a spur toward proletarian consciousness that would end the reproduction of these bourgeois myths and allow the situation of domination to be changed. She defined bourgeois women as "empty vases . . . decorative couches at home . . . frivolous . . . silly, unproductive, private, reactionary, [and] dependent" who cared only for money and satisfying their "husband[s'] desires." She rescued stories of working-class women's everyday lives, which were quite distant from those of women "at the top of society." On one occasion, for instance, she taught a story called "What Does Your Wife Do?," which featured two working-class men talking about their "frustrated family life." The story began by describing the "hard labor of working-class women in any part of Colombia." She would get up early to fix breakfast for her husband and children and then go to work as a maid in a "family house in the city" or a worker in a factory. She would quickly return home to cook dinner for the family. Over the weekends, the story concluded, she would do laundry while her husband spent time with friends in a bar. Serrano thought that these stories would resonate among proletarian women, allowing them to realize how different their lives were from the bourgeoisie's. And in so doing she aspired to make evident proletarian women's double exploitation.

But Serrano wanted to move proletarian women away from the "bourgeois values" to which they presumably had already succumbed. Bourgeois women were complicit with this exploitation, as they refused to acknowledge domestic labor, instead selling to society the ideal of a "frivolous and unproductive woman." Indeed, Serrano concluded, the wealth of the nation was the product not only of male workers' surplus labor but also of "female workers and workingwomen at home," a double exploitation that secured "the concentration of wealth" in bourgeois democracy. The best way to overcome this double exploitation was by inviting proletarian women to embrace a different role for themselves. In a word, Serrano wanted to teach "true proletarian women . . . how to live in a true democracy."[160]

Health as a Common Good

As part of a larger effort to control the middle classes' radicalization, in 1976 President Alfonso López Michelsen issued Decree 148, which classified doctors, physicians, nurses, nutritionists, dentists, and specialists working for the Instituto Colombiano de Seguros Sociales (ICSS) as public servants. There was nothing particularly new about this effort. López Michelsen drew on the 1968 constitutional reform enacted during Lleras Restrepo's administration that allowed state professionals, as public servants, to be hired and removed by the executive. In response, on September 6, 1976, professional physicians working for the ICSS who were members of ASMEDAS, ASDOAS, ASDINCOS, and ASOBAS began what would become one of the longest strikes in Colombian history.[161] For fifty-two days, doctors, dentists, nurses, ophthalmologists, nutritionists, social workers, and general medical personnel took to the streets, closing medical offices and picketing hospitals across Bogotá.[162] At the strike's beginning, they limited their demands to salary increases, better working conditions, more educational opportunities, and proper management of ICSS's resources.[163]

López Michelsen responded to these demands by further criminalizing the protest as an "illegal" mobilization, for it was impossible for professional middle-class physicians to protest the very state for which they worked. Within a week of the strike's start, the president addressed the nation in a televised speech, asking Congress to grant him extraordinary executive powers to restructure the ICSS, the necessity for which, he argued, was proven by the participation of professional unions in this organization. Management of clinics, health centers, and hospitals would have to be shifted from ICSS to the Ministry of Health. Through editorials in the major newspapers and public threats to dismiss strikers from their jobs, the government defined these radicalized petit bourgeois as "selfish, greedy, and unprofessional," willing to violate their pure, postpolitical vocation as state representatives and join "obscure [and] foreign forces," spreading death by privileging their own individual interests over the common good and the will of "a democratic majority."[164] The material resources that they demanded for better compensation, the government argued, could instead be invested in better and more expansive health services for the working masses. Thus, for the government the strike was "unjust, illegal, and criminal."[165]

It was in this context that physicians—some of them former members of UNCLAMECOL, MOCLAM, and ANAPO—soon called for a more expansive redefinition of democracy. As Eduardo Arévalo Burgos, ASMEDAS's president, put it during the strike's second week before thousands of white-coated physicians in the Plaza de Bolívar: "This may well be an illegal movement, but it is a movement for a just cause."[166] What did Arévalo Burgos mean by "just cause"? In a word, the redefinition of health's role in "a real democracy." During the strike, physicians articulated four interlocking questions. If the ICSS was to benefit a democratic majority, why did "poor people die more often than rich people?" Why could the bourgeoisie have access to better medical care than the proletariat? Was Colombia a "sick, uncultured, and undemocratic country" because it was underdeveloped, or was Colombia underdeveloped because it was sick and uncultured? And lastly, what was the democratic role that physicians should play in society?[167]

In demanding answers to these questions, physicians wanted to strip "the facade of the bourgeois democracies," in which both a market economy and a market-driven vision of society were forwarded as the way to allocate national resources, produce unmatched production of wealth for all to enjoy, and create unprecedented liberty for all members of society. This falsely suggested that medical personnel would be "totally free" because they would become "the bosses of themselves, with neither schedule nor fixed arrangements." It also suggested that they would become entrepreneurs of themselves by owning their labor-power and that, as "truly free men fashioning [their] lives as [they] would see fit," they should receive grants rather than wages.[168]

This was, these petit bourgeois women and men noted in their political posters, "the lie at the core of the bourgeois democracy." They critiqued labor relationships within the state. Rather than being "free men" receiving grants in a bourgeois democracy, they would have their labor-power reduced to a commodity to be bought or sold in a self-regulating market. This would make them similar to "workers working in a factory," preoccupied with financial gain and productivity and evaluated according to "a rubric of efficiency," which would construe more time spent with patients as "less productivity and less efficiency." Patients would become goods to be sold and consumed, while medical care would be commodified and exploited for the benefit of a bourgeoisie seeking better financial returns on its investment.[169] Drawing on Marx, physicians pointed to the bourgeoisie's definition of health as both commodity and profit-seeking endeavor as explaining why "Colombia was poor, uncultured, and underdeveloped," since considering health services only in terms of profit meant that the possibility to "live, survive, and reproduce oneself in society" would soon become "a luxury . . . a privilege" that only few members of society would be able to afford.[170]

For others professional physicians, appropriating Michel Foucault's ideas of power, the problem was that in such a commodified understanding of health, human beings—who were presumably a harmonious combination of "souls, bodies, and minds"—and their livelihood—the most important target of healthcare—would become nothing but "commodities enslaved to the rule of the market." In angry manifestos, they argued that the commodification of health would lead "human beings [to] attach price tags to their bodies to see how much they [were] worth." By this metric, "bourgeois livelihood" would intrinsically have more value—economic and otherwise—in a market-driven society, as the bourgeoisie would have the purchasing power needed to care for themselves; by contrast, the livelihood of the poor, without the means to compete in a market-driven society, could be dismissed as "worthless." Yet other physicians, inspired by Fanon's redefinition of the physician as political activist, emphasized that "Colombia was a sick and uneducated country because it was poor" and that it was poor because it did not have access to healthcare.[171] And another group, evoking both Foucault and Marx, argued that the bourgeoisie would continue to invest in workers' health only the amount needed to ensure the production of surplus value and the avoidance of resistance and protest.[172] Responding to López Michelsen, these petit bourgeois contended that the bourgeoisie were "the most criminal of all" because they had propagated the "death of the working masses," the exploitation of the proletariat, and the perpetuation of poverty.

Physicians worked hard to legitimize themselves as those who, unlike the bourgeoisie, were fighting for "a life worth living for."[173] In so doing, they laid claim to a vision of democracy in which healthcare was defined as a social right, an imperative for humanity, and a public good. For them, healthcare was the sine qua non for the material reproduction of a "healthy democracy . . . characterized by social justice [in which] everyone could develop their full potential."[174] As with considering education a common good, this redefinition of healthcare was at once subversive and hierarchical. Most, but certainly not all, physicians embraced the need to move away from the commodification of the patient as a client with a particular purchasing power. In contrast, they proposed understanding the patient as a democratic citizen with the right to enjoy health services. These women and men demanded that if Colombia wanted to become "a healthy nation," patients should be defined as citizens, as "patient[s] of rights against the tyranny of the bourgeoisie."[175]

Thus these medical practitioners—from nurses and general practitioners to dentists and psychologists—believed that health should become more collective in its conceptualization and more expansive in its objectives. The state needed to provide the conditions for the working masses' mental, social, and physical well-being by extending the quality and quantity of healthcare. The state should promote a preventive, rather than curative, medicine, as the former was more beneficial, inclusive, and cheaper, the latter more exclusionary, affordable only by the bourgeoisie. In this way, physicians attempted to place "a humanist medical ethics" at the core of real democracy, in which health, as a public good, would create "the objective circumstances and basic economic needs" for the working masses to secure livelihoods as members of a democratic society—access to economic resources, proper housing, decent employment, good working conditions, preventive health, education, and industrious recreational activities—and create the conditions for "all-encompassing human development"—participation in the political process, access to meaningful jobs, liberty to make important life decisions, opportunities to create a sense of community, development of social consciousness, and promotion of cultural practices.[176]

Yet physicians also defined themselves as those who, given their "ethical, physical, mental, and social superiority," needed to, in their medical language, "normalize" and "cure" the working masses to be proper citizens for such a democracy. Here, as elsewhere, gender played into claims to the right to rule, as male physicians suggested that only "true men" could prepare "the proletariat's masculine bodies . . . souls, and spirits" for real democracy. Finding masculine inspiration in Salvador Allende, Frantz Fanon, and Che—all of whom were doctors who had shed their class privileges after political awakening—some male physicians proposed a "humanist ethos" to change "the weak morality with which doctors perform[ed] their professional duties and their lack of social consciousness so that [they could] take care, protect, and defend weak working masses from the bourgeoisie."[177]

From the beginning of the strike of 1976, the leaders of Colombia's most important working-class organizations—the Conservative Colombian Workers' Union (UTC) and the Liberal Colombian Confederation of Workers (CTC)—expressed doubts about these demands. Both organizations were represented on the ICSS's board of directors, and both considered male physicians part of the bourgeoisie, with "privileged jobs" and "fat bank accounts."[178] For some male physicians, these were "ignorant charges" or "major misunderstandings"; for others, they proved that the working class had succumbed to bourgeois values and government manipulation. Male physicians wrote and published manifestos—one titled "The Truth about the Strike," another called "My Dear Working Class, Please Listen to Us"—during the strike to refute these claims among their "working-class brothers."[179] Questioning the numbers presented by María Elena Jiménez de Crovo, the minister of labor, who had stated that in 1976 most ICSS doctors earned between 30,000 and 50,000 pesos a month, ASMEDAS argued instead that a full-time doctor earned on average 18,000 pesos monthly.[180] Most doctors, they said, worked four-hour shifts at the institute while "going from one office to the next offering services and working late in order to make ends meet." It was unfair to consider them as part of a "lazy bourgeoisie."[181] Yet these physicians also quite clearly understood that they were "not particularly proletarian." As Miguel Escobar wrote to López Michelsen, there was no doubt that they were part of "what Marx called the petit bourgeoisie."[182] This led them to ask the working masses, imagined as a masculine force, to realize that what was at stake in the strike was much more than better labor compensation; it was "the health of the nation, the future of the ICSS . . . the working class's health."[183] Although it is difficult to draw final conclusions about the efficacy of these arguments, it seems that at least working-class leaders were not convinced. Jorge Tofiño, the UTC's vice president, declared during the strike's second week that physicians sought "to put an end to *seguros sociales*, which represent[ed] one of the great conquests achieved by the people."[184] For Tofiño, the working classes, not "greedy professionals," owned the institute. Thus the working-class leader argued, echoing López Michelsen, that the strike was a protest against the working classes. What was needed, Tofiño asserted, was more resources and better coverage, which could not happen if those resources were allocated for professionals' compensation.[185] There were no "proletarian demands" in the strike, as these physicians were not factory or industry workers but rather "petit men [*hombrecitos*] . . . merely serving in the tranquility of the offices." The unstated assumption was that those who belonged to the service sector were not laboring, as they were part of a "lazy bourgeoisie." Furthermore, this distinction was couched in gendered language: Tofiño assumed that service-sector work—in this case, healthcare—was to be performed by women or "petit men," while "real labor" would be undertaken by "true men working in the industries moving the nation ahead."[186] Tofiño and working-class men also pointed with consternation to the "women on the streets protesting along with doctors." For them the very presence of women, figured as "little bourgeois women pretending to be revolutionary," delegitimized the physicians' strike.[187]

This is why throughout the strike many male physicians tried to justify "the presence of women" in the streets. They had to come to terms with the fact that not all male physicians supported the strike. As they desperately asked at all-male union meetings, "How is it that vigorous women are here with us [while] men quietly remain in the privacy of their offices?"[188] In answering this question, some male physicians reappropriated service and care for a revolutionary masculinity: female physicians were "behaving like real men" by participating in the protests, abandoning feminine traits of "political passivity and inaction." Others, however, thought that female physicians could not embody the masculine trait of deriving "supreme enjoyment in serving others" because they were now "too calculating and too rational"; in a reversal of traditional gender roles, men were now the ones who could embody "sentimental preoccupations with feeling, serving, and curing the proletariat." Male physicians echoed the government's general critique of the medical strike by arguing that female strikers merely wanted to promote particular demands: they wanted "to improve their salaries." Those arguments served to naturalize the idea that women could not defend the "health of the nation," because they needed to be universalized—masculinized—to struggle against the working classes and the bourgeoisie for the right to rule.

Male physicians also argued that their "working-class brothers," because they were "uncultured and sick," could not see the importance of "universal demands." The proletariat, like female physicians, could only see particularities, not a larger cause. To male physicians, the proletariat did not have "a healthy manhood," a "fit body," or "emotional intelligence." They were unable to realize that the inequalities in which they were immersed were not natural.[189] This situation was caused by what Eduardo Díaz, an ICSS physician, called "the proletariat's taxonomical abnormality"—a tripartite composition of a soul, mind, and body—that prevented proletarian men from seeing how they benefited from male physicians' demands.[190] A lack of concern with health had caused the development of "submissive and passive souls" among working-class men, who thus, in a "kind of feminine attitude," remained unaware of more "universal demands . . . beyond immediate and material ones."[191]

For these same physicians, also sick and abnormal were the bourgeoisie, among whom they included those colleagues not participating in the strike. They were "behaving like women" in remaining "private, discreet, and quiet."[192] They were contracting yet another deadly counterrevolutionary virus that only "deformed men" could acquire: that of the "violent strikebreaker."[193] These "malformed, sick bourgeois men" developed that female tendency to exchange money for services in the benefit of the bourgeois order. Indeed, such malformed men suffered from "an allergy toward strikes" and, behaving like women, preferred "to sow discord" among those fighting for a just cause. In the heat of the strike, male physicians spent quite some time satirizing such deformed, feminized men, "sick people who need[ed] immediate treatment to be able to live in democracy."[194] These "fake men" needed to be taken to the emergency room for a reality check. The psychologist, they wrote in one of these satires, would diagnose them with hysteria—"feeling unreal or detached from your surroundings"—because they had that female tendency to follow what others (i.e., the bourgeoisie) say.[195] The neurologist would detect a tendency to experience frequent "nervous breakdowns . . . just like those women suffer," which prevented them from serving and caring in order to save lives. The otolaryngologist would diagnose these men with yet another female-related disease: the inability to pay attention to what was important in life. The ophthalmologist would find them suffering from "political apathy," that female disposition to ignore reality in hopes of utopian futures. But it was the sexologist who would have the hardest time providing the final diagnosis. After a long consultation, during which these malformed men do not notice "a beautiful nurse," the sexologist would conclude that those sick, violent strikebreakers could not have "things clear in life . . . their sexual drive was lacking, and their relation with women left much to be desired." They tended "to repel women and develop an interest for bourgeois men." The cardiologist would only have to ask, "Where is your heart?" to make his diagnosis, as these deformed men would be "too rational [and] too calculating" to understand humanity and thus ready to sell their "souls to the bourgeoisie."[196]

Female physicians, while joining their male colleagues to question the vision of healthcare as commodity, challenged what humanist ethics meant and what health as a right entailed. Nurses, social workers, and female doctors working for the state—for ICSS, the Ministry of Health, and the Instituto Colombiano de Bienestar Familiar (ICBF)—contended that if health was all about curing "the souls, bodies, and spirits" of the working masses, then it was petit bourgeois women, not men, who could best embody the most important part of humanist ethics: "to protect, to serve, and to love the proletariat."[197] Female physicians wanted to relink service and care with a feminine petit bourgeois revolutionary identity. If life, they asserted, was the main goal of healthcare, then women could practice it best. As Lilia Forero, a nurse at ICSS, put it, "What would a man know about the reproduction of life?"[198] Hence, it was women, with all their natural instincts and professional preparation, who could create the healthy conditions for the emergence of "a life worth living for."[199]

Other female physicians asserted that if health were to be more than a commodity, women's bodies could not be "objects owned by the market, the state, the family, and men."[200] They wanted to make women's sexual, economic, and bodily autonomy fundamental to health as a common good. They demanded the extension to women of better access to sexual health, reproductive choices, childcare, and improved maternity conditions. If health could prevent and cure poverty, proletarian women's bodies, not men's, needed to be the main target of health services.[201] Health as a common good should entail, these female physicians asserted, access to information about sexuality; workshops on the mental, physical, and emotional consequences of sexual practices; access to birth control; pregnancy testing; postpartum care; and sources that would allow for informed decisions on reproductive questions. Letters to state officials and presidents, memorandums to union representatives, and daily discussions attest to how female physicians worked hard to expand, with state resources, unofficial "informational centers" across the city where proletarian women could discuss their "family experiences, marital problems, their challenges in raising children . . . [and] their conditions of marriage."[202] Domestic violence—a "widespread problem that proletarian women suffered," they said—needed to be seen as a threat to the nation's health, as it prevented proletarian women from becoming productive members of society. These demands could materialize a definition of health in which "women's decisions, bodies, and hopes [were] not owned by their husbands" and "women could be real women in the fullest meaning of the term."[203]

Female physicians disagreed on how such demands could be materialized, however. For some, education was the answer, because the problem was that "proletarian women were ignorant about health." Thus physicians proposed that proletarian women be educated on how to embrace a "modern, productive, and caring role as mothers, workers, and members of society" and on how to exercise the right to do whatever they pleased with their bodies.[204] Yet for so many others, the question was about economic opportunities. Following a specific reading of Marx, they argued that policies and programs for health should first focus on women's economic independence before educating them to become full members of society. Economic independence would truly grant them the right to choose, as they would not have to be in unwanted relationships for economic reasons. Thus, as part of their redefinition of health as a common good, some female physicians demanded for proletarian women better job opportunities, healthcare services, and material compensation.[205]

Indeed, like female professors, teachers, and activists, these female physicians produced a subversive knowledge and practice, theirs intended to include health in what they called *vida plena*. This heteronormative vision had at least three main elements. First, these women, as part of their left political radicalization and contacts with feminist movements in Bogotá, wanted to redefine sexuality as pleasure and thereby delink sexuality from reproduction. But this required "demystifying" proletarian women's beliefs about "traditional myths that falsified sexuality as dangerous custom." They argued that proletarian women alienated themselves from their own bodies and in the process became "ignorant and naive" about their own sexuality. Physicians and professionals in general, however, were to blame, because sexuality had become a taboo hidden in "complicated medical terminology" that caused proletarian women to continue to see their bodies as "sacred, untouchable, inaccessible, [and] indifferent." In dialogue with Foucault, these women often said that society regulated women's sexuality via repression. Men experienced sexuality as a healthy and celebrated activity, while women had to experience it as "something unhealthy and illicit."[206] These female physicians complained that the problem was not just that sexuality was not discussed among proletarian women but that sexuality was perceived as dangerous and thus in need of repression. And it was this myth that female physicians needed to debunk, the educational endeavor's second element. To improve, proletarian women had to learn that "neither men, nor family, nor God could own our bodies." The third educational element was to stress that it was a woman's right to decide whether she wanted "to bring babies to the world." They no longer wanted maternity to be a "painful and suffering experience," but this required improving women's material realities, including men in child-rearing, and overcoming violence in "proletarian houses."[207]

White-Collar Employees: Democracy as Conflict

On February 25, 1976, thousands of white-collar bank employees in Bogotá went on strike for over a hundred days, including twenty days of hunger strike. Some of these employees took over eleven churches across the city. Certainly, these bank employees, along with others in the service sector, demanded better salaries, access to housing, labor stability, health services, and educational opportunities—demands they made as part of middle-class organizations. Yet by protesting the state's implementation of *tribunales de arbitramento*, which usually benefited employers and criminalized the right to protest, these bank employees claimed the right to assemble, protest, strike, and collectively bargain at the core of any real definition of democracy.

Such demands were intimately shaped by liberation theology in which personal autonomy and collective cooperation, solidarity with the *prójimo* (neighbor), had to be central to any definition of democracy. For so many of these employees, furthermore, the self—"a consequential individual"—and society—a larger collectivity that one belongs to—had to function together to radicalize democracy.[208] This was only possible when public assembly and direct action were made the norm for any manifestation of democracy, because they allowed one to be "politically consequential within a larger good."[209] Drawing on their encounter with the left, these white-collar workers demanded better pay because this would make labor a question of enjoyment or love, not of force and exploitation. In true democracies, labor was not an asymmetrical contract of exploitation with capital but a service for a larger good. Evoking Marx, they maintained that only then could labor be emancipated from alienation, as every laborer would be defined not by what they were but by what they did for the society as a whole.

Men often assumed that such emancipation from labor as a class attribute would be hierarchically organized according to gender. Once white-collar men were freed from labor, women would experience through them improved material compensation at work or rewards at home. Women simply needed either to be patient and exert more "individual effort" to catch up with male colleagues, who were paid more because of their "greater effort to get things done," or to develop "support personalities" for their husbands.[210] And as did their counterparts in teaching and development offices, male white-collar employees considered "female demands" a distraction from the real emancipation of labor, a manifestation of "a feminine lack of union consciousness."[211] Others argued that such "untimely demands . . . for women's liberation" should be set aside for the moment: since "machismo [was] a feature of bourgeois order," "women's demands" risked creating a "division of the sexes" in the fight to achieve public assembly. And others simply deemed women's demands "antirevolutionary" because they promoted "the oppression of men."[212] Only revolutionary men could exercise "a vanguard position to transform bourgeois society" and eventually change the "machismo" that radical women complained about. In a word, white-collar employees sought to claim public assembly—defined as the possibility to materialize a society defined by personal autonomy and collective cooperation, conflict and solidarity, negotiation and direct action— in a proper democracy as a gendered prerogative of men.

Yet women participated in the strike, joining their male comrades to redefine public assembly and the role of labor at the core of advancing democracy. Women questioned, however, the traditional gender roles assigned in these political gatherings. In the middle of the strike, for instance, white-collar employees decided to organize an "empty pots" protest to represent society's labor injustices. Men requested that women be present to make "as clear as possible" that men could not be men because poverty got in the way: "men labor[ed] but had no money to support their families," leaving women with "neither food nor a kitchen where to cook." Women responded that they wanted to protest against social injustices because they also were laborers and breadwinners. These women also pushed for their male comrades to include in their demands opportunities to close "the gender gap" in domestic tasks and parenting to give women time for public assembly.[213]

Women also took issue with men's monopolization of the right to protest. Striking white-collar women sought to reclaim what they suggestively called "the right to the street" while inviting men to embrace the "right to the house" and the need to "balance work and life." Indeed, they claimed that a "real democracy began at home."[214] They were questioning the distinction between private and public spheres as well as what could be said and done in public assembly. This is why these women highlighted how, during the strike's first three months, few wanted to talk about "the gender inequalities in remuneration in the service sector." This was not a new struggle, but in the 1970s white-collar women asserted that "the difference in pay between women and men in the same position and of the same preparation [had] gotten abysmal."[215] They complained that their male colleagues were behaving like "authoritarian oligarchs" by "repress[ing] women's human rights" and ignoring "the most basic norms of justice." These women highlighted how they had "labor[ed] hard to become somebody in society." They were not performing a "natural female activity" but rather laboring in "one of the most difficult jobs in society: to satisfy clients."[216] They invited their male colleagues to understand that "women need[ed] equal pay not just to buy makeup and look like pretty little girls in offices for men's contemplation" but "to get [their] families ahead." Thus alongside the demands for public assembly, the right to protest, and the right to the street needed to be included the fight for recognition and fair compensation of women's labor. These claims were also accompanied by demands about office sexual harassment, claims for the need to make reproductive labor equal among men and women, requests for affordable and quality childcare. Unless these demands were met, they concluded, a democracy predicated on personal autonomy, collective cooperation, solidarity, and care for each other was indeed a chimera.[217]

What happens when we put the mass petit bourgeois activism described in this chapter at the center of the Cold War and revolutionary politics? I have attempted to demonstrate how during the 1970s radicalized petit bourgeois women and men advanced a multiplicity of demands that reconfigured the meanings, practices, and rationalities of living in "a real and true democracy." Although this vision was hierarchical—indeed, precisely because these radicalized petit bourgeois claimed the right to rule in democracy for themselves—it posed a radical challenge to what was coming to be seen as a "viable" democracy promoted by the government administrations of the 1970s and consented to by other members of the middle class. These two visions of democracy entered into open struggle in the second half of the 1970s, and particularly in the 1977 nationwide general strike. This is the story I will tell in the book's last chapter.

8

Democracy: The Most Important Gift to the World

I think that democracy has been the most important gift
middle-class people . . . have given to the world.

—ALEJANDRO HURTADO, interview with author

James Ferguson has argued that scholars have become accustomed "to a debate pitting triumphalist accounts of the global spread of 'free-market' capitalism (decreeing the end of history, or telling us the world is flat) against critical accounts of that same ascendency that tell a formally similar story but with the moral polarity inverted."[1] For Latin America, scholars often see neoliberalism's triumph as the inevitable product of "shock therapies" implemented by military regimes and crafted by US-trained economists.[2] Neoliberalism is mostly depicted as an imperial imposition (or, at least, a calculated strategy disseminated globally from Europe and the United States) that Latin American societies had to either comply with or reject. These studies also presuppose a teleological, clear-cut transition from state-led development to free-market absolutism, unwittingly affirming the very political economists' predictions for neoliberalization.[3] Most scholars thus criticize neoliberalism as an antidemocratic global ideology benefiting the financial elites, who sought a "social order aimed at the generation of income for the upper income brackets, not investment in production nor, even less, social progress."[4] Therefore, they see it as "bad for poor and working people."[5] In these accounts, neoliberalism ineluctably leaves behind a middle-class society, via a process of dedemocratization, for a society divided between homogenous elites and the working classes, one of which the middle class must join in either embracing or resisting neoliberal policies, respectively.[6] Such a foundational narrative yet again entangles democracy and the formation of the middle classes, as neoliberalism readily appears as the opposite of an authentic democracy.[7]

In this chapter I offer an alternative narrative by explaining how during the 1970s and early 1980s, in a context in which a fragile but important neoliberal rationality of rule began to take shape, a "proper" middle class and a radical petit bourgeoisie entered into open conflict over which of their hierarchical visions of democracy should prevail.[8] In so doing, I seek "to slow down reasoning" on the social foundations of neoliberalism so that I can explain the historical process through which a particular definition of the middle class—the one that we now identify as natural to a "global middle class"—began to gain normativity and legitimacy as the representation of an early iteration of neoliberal democracy while eclipsing other visions of middle-class democracies as irrelevant, exotic, and impracticable.[9] This allows us to think the emergence of a neoliberal democracy not as the product of a unilinear movement away from the development programs of the late 1950s and 1960s but rather as a contradictory, if uneasy, outcome of these programs. Middle-class women and men, far from being elite pawns, performed substantial political work during the 1970s to naturalize the equivalence between a particular neoliberal definition of democracy and middle-classness. These middle-class people unevenly but significantly made neoliberal democracy their own.

A Neoliberal Democracy

Since the early 1970s, a select group of male Colombian political economists trained at the University of Chicago, Stanford University, MIT, and the University of California learned monetarist and neoclassical economic theory and became presidential advisers, high-ranking officials in state development offices, and central policymakers.[10] As several historians have argued, the three presidential administrations of this decade supported, to different degrees, neoliberal policies.[11] They moved from ISI to emphasize coffee exports and to more generally diversify markets through export-oriented development. They promoted tight control of public debt, "healthy" unemployment rates, the decentralization of fiscal policy, and further privatization of state programs. Despite some major disagreements, these administrations' economists shared a fundamental assumption: the state had a "strategic" role to play in transforming Colombia's inward-looking, isolated economy into a global one spearheaded by a "sophisticated and worldly middle class."[12] More important, the various development programs of the 1970s—Misael Pastrana's Four Strategies, Alfonso López Michelsen's To Close the Gap, and Julio César Turbay Ayala's National Integration Plan—gradually consolidated a fragile neoliberal rationality not just due to political economists' wisdom but also because neoliberalism's specific vision of the middle class helped address two fundamental sources of anxiety and fear since the late 1960s and 1970s: the political radicalization of a petit bourgeoisie and the middle class's mobilization toward populist and oppositional movements such as ANAPO.

This implementation of neoliberal rationality included three interlocking projects. First, policymakers, economists, politicians in transnational organizations, and intellectuals in universities in Colombia—particularly the Fundación para la Educación Superior y el Desarrollo (FEDESARROLLO) and UNIANDES's Center for Economic Research (CEDE)—intensified a critique on "the vices" of state centralism and contrived markets while advocating "the virtues" of finances and market forces.[13] These economists and policymakers revitalized modernization theories to pathologize—and thus delegitimize—petit bourgeois radicalization as the product of a presumably Latin American failure to live in democracy. Second, various development initiatives of the 1970s sought social legitimacy for a neoliberal definition of democracy by addressing some demands made by the middle classes in the late 1960s. Third, drawing on the legitimation provided by this new neoliberal rationality and the support of a part of the middle class, national administrations, particularly Julio César Turbay Ayala's, attempted to silence the radical petit bourgeoisie through an eclectic repertoire of violence, institutionalized in the Security Statute of 1978.

Pathologizing a Radical Petit Bourgeoisie

As early as 1970, Jerome Levinson, assistant director of the USAID mission in Brazil during the 1960s, and Juan de Onis, a journalist working with the United Press International and the New York Times, published a detailed report of how the Alliance had lost its way, mobilizing arguments that would shape the perception of a "destabilizing" Latin American middle class throughout the decade and beyond. From its inception, they asserted, the Alliance had suffered from an "excessive idealism and overoptimism" in assuming that by channeling capital into Latin America economic growth and political development would follow.[14] Alliance policymakers wrongly assumed that a proper middle class already existed who could transform economic aid into economic growth and, by extension, a cohesive three-class society.[15] Thus, the Alliance had "yielded more shattered hopes than solid accomplishment, more discord than harmony, more disillusionment than satisfaction."[16] Levinson and de Onis argued against those who, following "conventional wisdom," continued to blame material inequalities in Latin America on "hereditary oligarchies of extraordinary wealth," which corresponded "neither to the political realities, since aristocratic families [had] not run Latin American countries for a long time, nor to the complex economic and social conditions of Latin American development."[17] For Levinson and de Onis, it was important to stress that "the destabilizing . . . disruptive, antidemocratic element" was not "the marginalized groups," who, tormented by "disease and illiteracy," had neither "the capacity for autonomous [political] action" nor the energy "to initiate and organize a campaign" except for "limited" political agendas with "local objectives such as a land invasion."[18]

Rather, these marginal groups and their "conditions of desperation and misery" were only a "*potential* force" for preventing a liberal, pluralist, and market-driven democracy in Latin America if galvanized by "the dissident members of the core society," comprising students, engaged professionals, social workers, and "middling sectors" "motivated by compassion, opportunism, or nationalist frustrations."[19] This destabilizing middle class had thwarted the Alliance's "most noble and dramatic . . . goal": to impose political reconciliation and social harmony as a requirement for economic liberalization. Instead of facilitating "cooperation . . . and cohesion" among different social groups, the dissident middle class was exacerbating struggle.[20]

Likewise, for top policy advisers, elite intellectuals, and former presidents of Colombia, the middle class was a "repressive . . . antidemocratic, and dictatorial-driven force."[21] "No matter how exhaustively one look[ed] for a middle class in Colombia," political scientist Fernando Cepeda Ulloa advised President López Michelsen in 1976, "it [was] difficult to find one" because "the half-formed traditions of this 'middle element'" were not made from the same stuff as in modern Western democracies, whose middle classes were marked by "free enterprise, secularization . . . achievement-motivated society . . . entrepreneurial robustness, competition . . . and social responsibility."[22] Unlike the middle classes of the global North, the Latin American middle sectors had "little useful legacy or tradition to draw on" in creating a true democracy.[23] Lacking entrepreneurial rationality, professional competence, and apolitical decisiveness—features associated with masculinity—these middle sectors (Cepeda Ulloa was careful not to refer to them as classes) were preordained to embody a sentimental, feminized irrationality that would promote at best a "democracy of the mob," as they were getting too close to the "chaos of the masses."[24] Drawing on the very modernization theory studies that had inspired the Alliance, these policymakers now argued that these radical middle classes, feminized, weak, ambiguous, and dependent, had succumbed to "the ideologies of the peasants and workers."[25] Since then, the Alliance has been categorized in policy circles and academic discussions as a colossal failure precisely because the middle classes could not become a proper democratic force.

Reconscripting the Middle Classes: Toward a Democratic Neoliberal Subject

Such abnormalization of the middle classes was much more than an excuse for counterinsurgent or anticommunist programs. It productively shaped a neoliberal rationality, used by different administrations to legitimize a gradual transition to a liberalized economy: it was neoclassical economics that could create the middle-class society that development programs had presumably failed to foster. And far from being an abstract discussion, such legitimation soon translated into the partial reorganization of who should represent a democratic state—imagined now as postpolitical and postideological—for a market-oriented society. Different administrations throughout the 1970s, drawing on Lleras Restrepo's constitutional reforms of the late 1960s, increased attacks on the legal status of unions for state professionals, whom they classified as public employees and thus able to be hired and removed by the executive. A militarized state—that is to say, the armed forces—began to play a substantial role in state policies, issuing several decrees to restrict political mobilization and delegitimize the right to protest, assembly, and association. General Luis Carlos Camacho Leyva, Colombian defense minister from 1978 to 1982, put it quite simply: social protest was "the unarmed branch of subversion."[26] These administrations implemented a state of emergency to criminalize collective bargaining, public assembly, and protest because, it was argued, such rights risked "a democratic state" and forced "society as a whole on the path of dictatorship."[27]

Motivated by transnational fears of a radicalized middle class, high-ranking state officials argued that state professionals—the "middleman . . . the face of the state"—were "anarchizing" state tasks and were on the verge of seizing the state.[28] The three presidential administrations of the 1970s argued that the state was "besieged from within."[29] Lleras Camargo, fearful of what professionals could achieve, urged the government to "do away with the enemies of the state" through "blood and fire."[30] Fernando Landazábal Reyes, commander of the Brigada de Institutos Militares, argued that universities, schools, and state offices had become homes for "communist proselytism" and that thus professors, teachers, and professionals had to be treated as "agents of subversion."[31] These professionals were dangerous because, unlike popular groups, they worked toward "the subversion of the intelligence" via their "unprecedented power" to communicate ideas.[32]

But what is critical to underscore here is the productivity of the discourses that legitimized these repressive measures.[33] The task was to criminalize "politics and ideology" in state activities in particular while elevating a neoliberal rationality as a manifestation of professional objectivity. In other words, if the enemy of the state was by definition political, these administrations argued, then "the face of the state" needed to be "beyond politics" in order to create the essential precondition for a liberalized economy: a postpolitical and postideological society.[34] These administrations invoked transnational discussions of liberalized economies to proclaim the importance to democracy of a professional who knew, and could put into practice, the motto "To govern is to administrate."[35] On these goals USAID, UNESCO, and the United States Information Agency collaborated more intensely with private universities such as UNIANDES, PUJ, the UTB, and INCOLDA. What was needed now was a professional who could safeguard "objectivity and professionalism," triumph over "politicization . . . ideologization . . . and extremist influences in state activities," and prevent the "dissolution of [the] democratic state" happening elsewhere in Latin America.[36] Such professionals would transform a "state of subversion . . . a populist state"— the source of economic inefficiency and political anarchy—into an orderly, postpolitical state dedicated to "the administration of social relations" and thus national economic productivity.[37]

At the core of this revision of who should represent state rule rested yet another crucial aspect of what would soon be seen as neoliberal democracy: education as an economic investment. This particular definition of education was by no means new, drawing heavily on the notion of human capital produced by the Alliance. But the administrations of the 1970s challenged the demand by some professionals in universities and educational programs that education be considered a right and a common good, celebrating instead a vision of democracy in which education was a financial investment in one's human capital to become a competitive actor in a market-driven society. Thus for these administrations the problem was not only that the school system was run by an improper and abnormal middle class that was propagating "the obscure forces of Marxism [and] foreign influences of communism" but also that education was defined as a common good.[38] Luis Carlos Galán Sarmiento, the first minister of education in Pastrana's administration, and Rodrigo Lloreda, the minister of education under Turbay Ayala, both insisted that defining education as a common good would thwart equality by admitting students who needed to exercise neither "effort [nor] determination nor purpose," eliminating any incentive or initiative to be productive or to independently explore opportunities to improve one's material conditions. Members of society would thereby enter into a stage of "economic laziness," a perpetual "human capital depreciation." Worse still, this would hinder the expansion of the nation's wealth—measured in terms of economic growth and human capital—by preventing competition.[39]

The foundational assumption here was that an education conceptualized as a financial investment in one's human capital would spread throughout society "middle-class values," would foster a society that was "more achievement-motivated . . . more self-reliant" and thus capable of developing "greater initiative in problem-solving situations." The products of such an education would be able to "adapt themselves more easily to changing circumstances, assume supervisory responsibilities more quickly, and [be] ready for competitive economies."[40] This is exactly what López Michelsen envisioned with his To Close the Gap development program: "a country with an expansive middle class that embodied new values, new aspirations, and new national economic authenticity, a democratic society in the sense that there are no privileges other than those of intelligence, merit, and personal effort."[41]

Throughout the 1970s the government also sought to subsume some middle-class professionals, white-collar employees, and small-business owners under neoliberal rule via state programs. The reorganization of housing policy is a case in point. As part of the Four Strategies development plan—which sought to normalize income distribution, increase agricultural production, and expand foreign exports—President Misael Pastrana envisioned urban development as the engine of economic growth. In this he was following the advice of Lauchlin Currie, an economist trained at Harvard University. The future of democracy, modernity, and economic growth, Currie assumed, resided in well-planned urbanization, the expansion of the service sector, and an inclusive process of industrialization.[42] He proposed that Pastrana develop a macroeconomic strategy in which housing construction would become "the leading sector" for economic growth.[43] On the one hand, housing construction, as a labor-intensive sector of the economy, would supply well-paying jobs for both peasants who had recently migrated to the city in search of better opportunities and workers who had already been looking for higher-paying jobs in urban centers. On the other, housing construction would trigger expansive production of goods in related industries, which would in turn create new job opportunities and hence a healthier economy.[44]

But for this to happen, a new and presumably better housing finance system was needed. Currie was convinced that without credit and private investment, the construction sector could not take off. Drawing on decades of economic advising, the Harvard economist fashioned what soon became an everyday form of class distinction: the constant purchasing power unit, or Unidad de Poder Adquisitivo Constante (UPAC). Currie argued that the main reason that middle-class people, a social group that he imagined as a leading force for democratization, hesitated to deposit money in private savings accounts was the lack of profit. Currie asserted that in a context in which a currency's purchasing power was falling, inflation would negate the effects of any interest rate assigned to any amount of money deposited in a bank, decreasing the real value of money. To rectify this, Currie recommended institutionalizing private savings accounts with a constant interest rate in which the money could adjust itself daily with respect to changes in the currency's purchasing power. This would make the middle class more likely to deposit into savings accounts and, in turn, give banks private capital to use for mortgage loans. Such loans would satisfy what Currie understood as the middle-class desire par excellence—to own a home—and would further channel private capital into the expansion of a housing industry, its related expansion of job opportunities, and demand for goods in affiliated industries.[45]

Currie pleaded with major private banks to participate in UPAC. These private financial institutions did not hesitate to join the effort. As a result, in May 1972 Pastrana called a state of economic emergency to issue Decrees 677 and 678, aimed at establishing a new financing system for housing construction. The former decree formalized the Fondo de Ahorro y Vivienda (FAVI); the latter institutionalized "housing and savings corporations" (CAVS) and stipulated that the savings and housing mortgage system, for a fifteen-year term, would adjust according to changes in the currency's purchasing power. In turn, Decree 1220 of July 1972 established UPAC. State intervention granted these housing and savings corporations an economic advantage over other forms of bank savings accounts and mortgage loans. In the process, private home loans and private savings accounts began to gain legitimacy over other forms of public housing and savings strategies, such as cooperatives.[46] In a very short time these private CAVS collected enough capital to support their operations and secure construction investment, with significant economic profits for bank owners.[47]

As a policy, UPAC responded to middle-class demands made since the second half of the 1960s, but in so doing it further conscripted the middle class as the normative economic subject for a market-driven democracy.[48] Moreover, Currie remained convinced that the possibility of achieving development—a sense of economic well-being—depended on "a [new] state of mind."[49] Thus, contrary to presumably economistic understandings of underdevelopment of the 1960s, Currie thought it crucial to distinguish between human needs—"biological . . . physical necessities for food, shelter, and health"—and social wants—"much more complex [cultural] needs that can be more or less satisfied by certain kinds of interpersonal relations and thwarted by others"[50]—because "if we [did] not know our real needs and motivations, it [was] very possible that the desired fulfillment [would] not yield the satisfaction expected." This distinction would allow policies to target economic growth measured not so much by "the possession of things" as by the development of a new "human [economic] personality."[51] It was simplistic, the Harvard economist continued, to assume that "goods [had] some inherent power to yield utility or satisfaction"; such a belief would develop in social actors a "pervasive sense of deprivation" and a mere desire to impress with "the possession of [more] things."[52] Appropriating Erich Fromm's argument that economic happiness "could not be defined in terms of the adjustment of man to the needs of society but on the contrary on the adjustment of society of the needs of man," Currie thought that economic growth needed to be measured by the "potentialities of the individual," a "revolution in values" in which motivations, needs, and desires were redefined as related to a new, and presumably more democratic, economic personality.[53]

It was this "new economic personality" that soon became linked with a gendered middle-class subject. Corporación de Ahorro y Vivienda (Davivienda), perhaps the most important CAV, founded in 1972, offers a crucial example. Drawing on demands by small-business owners in the late 1960s, Currie defined the urban middle class as "wealth producers" because the housing industry, as the economy's leading sector, ultimately depended on the middle class's desire for private savings accounts and homeownership. Without this desire, there would not be the private capital needed to reactivate the housing industry and incentivize market competition. Nor would there be expansive employment opportunities for the working classes, as the middle class would not demand the construction of neighborhoods to develop their cultural vitality, independence, and, of course, personal and property security.[54] The middle class thus embodied a universal, democratic economic personality because their interests and desires could benefit society as a whole; the working class, by contrast, was considered particular, their role limited to building houses, earning an income, and satisfying an interest in "possess[ing] things," which did not initiate a whole democratic chain of economic events. This hierarchical division of tasks would secure an "escalation of benefits" according to each class's role in the "highly organized market" of a vertically defined economy: middle-class people first had to materialize their supposedly better position to own new "decent" homes—a reality literally built on working-class labor—to then be able to make available the houses that they had previously owned for the enjoyment of their working-class others.[55]

This foundational classed assumption generated multiple gender and class discourses that exacerbated—and legitimized—an unequal distribution of private and public resources. A careful reading of a significant number of the applications submitted to Davivienda throughout the 1970s and early 1980s suggests how this corporation defined middle-class men as the ideal democratic subject in a market-driven economy and thus as rightfully entitled to mortgage loans, conversely delegitimizing working-class men as unproductive economic beings unworthy of home loans. Bringing into conversation multiple treatises on the role of savings, credit, and investment in economic growth as well as social psychology studies, Davivienda, with the support of FAVI, declared with pride that unlike working-class families, "middle-class [ones] really care[d] to own not just a house but a home in order to be productive members of society."[56] The legitimation worked in a circular manner. Working-class families could not be proper economic subjects because they were mostly ignorant of how credit, private savings accounts, and profitable investments—in a word, UPAC—could "democratiz[e] society."[57] And they were ignorant of this because working-class men were dominated by certain familial, cultural, historical, and social conditions preventing them from becoming proper economic subjects.

It thus comes as no surprise that throughout the 1970s and early 1980s Davivienda approved over 90 percent of the loans to families that it considered middle class.[58] In so doing, Davivienda, along with other CAVs, both distributed material resources allowing for the middle class's social reproduction and hypostasized a middle-class economic subjectivity as the precondition for accessing those resources. Hiring private consultants from private universities, international organizations, and marketing offices, Davivienda claimed to have developed a scientific system for identifying "the typical and average *ahorrador*" for UPAC. The organization's multifaceted and intense applications asked potential homeowners endless questions about income levels, number of children, personal hobbies, the importance of personal savings accounts, the influence of family in money-saving practices, how wives could steer husbands' desires for homeownership, and, of course, the role of credit.[59] Although it has proven impossible to see how Davivienda tabulated and measured potential homeowners' answers, the rationality behind how it distributed resources was clear: "The typical and average ahorrador of UPAC [was] a married man between 35 and 45 years of age who [was] located in the middle sector of society and want[ed] to live in a middle-sector neighborhood, whose income [was] more than 10,000 but less than 20,000. . . . He [had] two children, he achieve[d] professional studies, [had] the habit of *ahorrar* thanks to a long interest in doing so passed on from earlier generations . . . and he also [knew] what UPAC [was]."[60]

This describes the figure whom Davivienda glorified as an *ahorrador feliz*, a happy middle-class man who, by fulfilling his desire for a private savings account and his own home, transformed into an ideal neoliberal subject: a competitive individual private property owner. Middle-class men secured an economically productive masculinity, which ensured that they would view homeownership not as an alienated monetary transaction or an immediate satisfaction, or right, derived from collective social struggle but rather as the product of "individual effort, life planning, efficiency, a self-actualizing economic process, and hard work."[61] So many of Davivienda's advertisements and policies throughout the 1970s echoed the sentiment that "your happiness depends exclusively on yourself. . . . You are what you own. . . . You are unique, you are your credit, you are your home. . . . You are your family. . . . These are the advantages of owning a home. . . . These are the advantages of being a true man."[62]

The qualities of this true man were based on assumptions about the gender roles proper to homeownership. For Davivienda, the ahorrador feliz was in a heterosexual partnership and had two children—one of each gender—living in a "perfect home."[63] The economic success of this unit depended on a hierarchical distribution of roles among family members (figure 8.1). The proper middle-class father would provide the home in which he would teach his children the values of "positive leadership, competition, security, trust, and economic endurance."[64] Middle-class women would "sacrifice themselves to allow their husbands to take risks [to] overcome themselves economically and provide a home." Once the home was established, women could transform children into economic assets by teaching proper economic values—"competition, flexibility, confidence, efficiency, strength, vitality"—that would ensure that they were always ready to compete "to improve themselves."[65]

When López Michelsen came to office in 1974, his political economy advisers wanted to dismantle UPAC. The administration soon backed off, realizing that the program was already very much part of the everyday lives of so many middle-class people and had proven quite profitable for private banks.[66] But even if López Michelsen disagreed with Pastrana on this, both of their administrations shared a neoliberal rationality lionizing the middle class as the benchmark of a proper democracy. López Michelsen, following Miguel Urrutia and Rodrigo Botero's advice, aspired to make Colombia "the Japan of Latin America," which required fully dismantling ISI. In this context, López Michelsen's administration fought for an integrated salary, a reform called for by small-business owners since the late 1960s that would make workers responsible for paying some of their own labor benefits. The president asserted that this would "close the social gap" and make Colombia more democratic by expanding employment, provoking competition, diversifying the market, and strengthening economic productivity. An early version of supply-side economics, this policy assumed that the more difficult the material conditions faced by workers, the better the chance that they would "fight the conditions of poverty" and thus become middle class. Echoing small-business demands, López argued that, as a legacy of

Figure 8.1 A happy middle-class family. "La casita roja de Davivienda," *El Espectador*, February 5, 1977, 7A.

archaic and colonial economies, "salaries with too many benefits" had created a "paternalist dependency" that destroyed productivity by eliminating
the need for competition. These salaries seduced childlike workers, much
like "aboriginal peoples" in colonial times, with "little mirrors and beads,"
satisfying immediate needs while sacrificing a more prosperous economic
future.[67] The privileges afforded to a few workers, the president continued,
disadvantaged most. An integrated salary, by contrast, would create a more
competitive workforce and a more harmonious relationship between labor
and capital, allowing workers to become more independent by enriching
their human capital and competing for opportunities supplied and demanded by a democratic market.[68]

Although workers protested such labor proposals throughout the 1970s
and early 1980s, preventing their implementation for at least another decade, the rationality behind them proved quite productive. It provoked an
unprecedented proliferation of managerial and organizational discourses
in offices across the service sector, which further naturalized as the classed
and gendered subject of proper neoliberal democracy the independent
middle-class male entrepreneur with no other "boss" than himself. This
rhetoric was by no means new, as this book's first part makes amply clear,
but it is striking how different service offices—private insurance companies,
health-related services, and financial agencies—further mobilized 1960s
managerial theories to glorify the service sector as the incarnation of what
all these companies began to refer to as a "postindustrial society," which
they understood as a society that had overcome the division between capital and labor. As the tertiary sector expanded its role in the economy during the 1970s, these service companies further proclaimed their employees'
classed and gendered distinctiveness—as those who *serve*, not labor—to
delegitimize factory workers and union members as "industrial remnants,"
a feminine and backward past, an obstacle to a neoliberal society.

Democracy Must Be Protected from Politics

As these discourses and policies of the 1970s presidential administrations
celebrated the middle classes, some professionals, white-collar employees,
and small-business owners began to question their political inclination
toward oppositional populist movements and to mobilize instead for neoliberal rule. As with the Alliance, certain middle-class women and men
embraced their conscription in order to lay claim to the right to rule in a

neoliberal democracy. They would prevent the consolidation of both "oligarchical rule" and "proletarian dictatorship"—what in the previous decade these middle-class people had often defined as the "democracy of the few" and the "democracy of the many," respectively.[69] By appropriating the notion of social cohesion, they reconfigured one of the most important political claims that they had made during the second half of the 1960s. In a balanced social cohabitation of classes, the middle class, rather than being located socially, politically, and economically over the elites and working classes—as they claimed when participating in ANAPO—would now be located *in the middle* of a hierarchically integrated three-class society in which anyone would get the chance to enjoy "a just economic well-being" according to what each individual offered to society.[70]

This fit with the prevalent definition of a postpolitical and postideological democratic society. In struggle with a radical petit bourgeoisie, middle-class individuals fervently fought for such a vision. At issue was nothing other than a hierarchical reordering of proper politics. These middle-class people now embracing neoliberalism collectively sought to "depoliticize" democracy as an administrative task to maintain hierarchical "social cohesion."[71] Many professionals working for the state continued to teach workers and peasants to become proper members of a democracy predicated on a competitive economy. Yet although still drawing on development programs from the 1960s, these professional women and men during the 1970s promoted more forcefully a notion of economic success as the product of personal effort and a competitive individual determination. Poverty, they argued in their reports, was the product of not "structural conditions," as the radical petit bourgeoisie were claiming, but rather the lack of "an economic individual spirit to improve oneself." They asserted that "the poor masses" could not "pull themselves out of poverty" because "the hard realism of poverty's way of life" prevented them from developing an individual disposition to take "ownership over their own economic beings." Among these professionals, economic success began to be reduced to a question of psychological competence, a finance-driven personality, and a social accident. Indeed, the possibility to overcome material inequalities in society was increasingly defined as an individual project precisely because poor people also had human capital to create their own wealth. Thus individuals were to be accountable for their own economic marginalization unless they embraced what was seen as "new middle-class attitudes and mentalities."[72]

Other white-collar employees and small-business owners wanted a middle-class social order that would cohesively but hierarchically distribute roles while recognizing the importance of "individual effort, labor understanding, professional preparation, and private capital" in cementing democratic rule and generating "a new concept of men." Such new men would replace "misleading, unrealistic, authoritarian ideology [and] political ineptitude" with a "government of the most capable"; violent social polarization with a cohesive three-class society; "social dependency" with individual liberty; and an "amorphous state" with a market-driven one in which "individual initiative" would reign.[73] These were powerful ideas reshaping multiple antiunion discourses among some service-sector employees and small-business owners. In an increasingly politicized environment, they found it imperative to distinguish themselves from the unionized and politicized working class. Some white-collar employees thus struggled against colleagues advocating for a democracy predicated on conflict and solidarity. To the former, unions were merely "bureaucratic machines" interested only in political objectives, not the common good. Unions vulgarized service-sector employees by imposing external constraints upon self-regulated individuals and by perpetuating an antagonistic capital-labor relationship. These white-collar employees thus worked "to get rid of unions" in office jobs because their "personal freedom . . . and independence [were] at stake." Unlike in factory work, these associates argued, unions were neither necessary nor desirable; they would destroy the very possibility of being "middle-class people" who respect "the parameters of democracy."[74]

Likewise, small-business owners embraced López Michelsen's development plan for "massive productive employment" and an integrated salary, given how it fulfilled their demands in the late 1960s.[75] In so doing, they fought hard to legitimize what one might call the democratization of exploitation. They attacked the prospects of minimum wage increases, as counterproductive for a competitive economy, because continued inflation would prevent increased real income and consumption for workers. A raise in the minimum wage would only force the nation's democratic and masculine forces, its small-business owners, to squander more capital in support of "fewer and fewer workers and more and more privileges." Not raising the minimum wage was much more "economically viable," as it would teach workers to "forjarse por si solos" and to more democratically share with their working-class brothers the material scarcity of resources. Cheap labor was indeed democratic, small business asserted, because it would not force them to fire workers and would thereby secure "better and more harmonious labor relationships." What was needed instead was a proper expansion of employment opportunities by "maximizing" resources and "rationalizing" the workforce, so that more workers could be included in a competitive economy. The workforce would participate in an all-inclusive exploitation project called democracy, which would incentivize workers to innovate and compete for scarce resources, become independent, and work toward self-advancement, presumably all crucial prerequisites for economic growth.[76]

By seconding López Michelsen's idea that Colombia could become "the Japan of Latin America," small-business owners also asserted that "the size of industries matter[ed]." They found inspiration in the British economist E. F. Schumacher's *Small Is Beautiful* (1973).[77] An organization's small scale promoted virile independence and proper free-enterprise attitudes because it prevented the separation of ownership and investment.[78] Small was efficient, creative, enjoyable, self-reliant, self-determining, decentralized, and masculine, while large organizations produced impersonality, insensitivity, and a concentration of "abstract power"—the very source of unionization.[79] Smallness would allow workers and small-business owners to work "flexibly and harmoniously as a unified force."[80] Smallness fostered democratic labor relationships that would allow "the use value of working-class people" to contribute to democracy, materialize an "economic advantage" in the international market, and consequently expand small and medium industries, which would produce more "cost-effective" jobs.[81] In this way, small-business owners claimed a classed and gendered superiority: unlike "immoral . . . antidemocratic, feminine, anticompetitive, promonopoly, and careless big industrialists," they knew how to exploit labor more efficiently by including more people in a competitive economy. This powerful classed and gendered abstraction of working-class labor pivotally backed small-business owners' claims to legitimately represent the "entrepreneurial people" in a neoliberal democracy.

As appendix figures 11 and 12 show, these political demands were also accompanied by significant economic rewards. Whether through political organizations such as cooperatives, unions, partially privatized state programs, larger organizations such as MOCLAM, UNCLAMECOL, FEDEPROCOL, and ACOPI, or state-sponsored but privately supported programs such as UPAC, these middle-class people further consolidated their access to educational opportunities, better labor conditions, recreational activities, state monies, and home- and small-business ownership (see appendix map 1). Despite, or precisely because of, difficult economic conditions, middle-class people were able to crystallize a classed legitimation of their right, as representatives of "the people," to specific material privileges. This was because, according to middle-class women and men, rights in a democratic society needed to be earned, distributed, and validated through competition, which could secure democratic rule of the "most competent in society."[82] In struggle against those deemed oligarchies and working groups, many women and men began to intimately equate individual privilege with collective rights as members of the middle class. These middle-class rights were further equated with democracy, and democracy with a presumably all-powerful market that allowed "anybody to become somebody in life." In such societies, they insisted, "the market dictate[d] the will of the people."[83] This legitimized middle-class women's and men's claims to such rights because neither the oligarchies—"the sons of privilege . . . lineage, and kinship"—nor the working classes—"the sons of dependency, passivity, [femininity,] and violence"—could promote a proper entrepreneurial democracy.[84] According to this logic, democracy—rather than a question of political conflict, social mobilization, or public assembly (which was the vision that a radical petit bourgeoisie was fighting for)—should be predicated on an asymmetrical distribution of rights according to gendered and classed notions of marketable entrepreneurship: self-sufficiency, self-appreciation, self-optimization, education as investment, human capital flexibilization, and individual economic independence.

This entrepreneurial definition of democracy was gendered. As inflation reached 33.1 percent by 1977, middle-class families struggled to maintain social status in a discursive context in which they were supposed to be enjoying specific economic rights as the representatives of the people in a proper democracy. Women's labor was now seen as pivotal for the middle class being able to socially reproduce itself. As women further participated in state development offices as professionals or as white-collar employees in service companies, they challenged the association between entrepreneurial democracy and middle-class masculinity by demanding political recognition as holders of the right to rule; as they argued, it was thanks to them that their families could compete and thus earn rights/privileges as a members of the middle class, in a market-driven society. And yet again, as in the late 1960s, middle-class men redefined women's contributions to family finances as "help," not labor, in a gendered partnership.

General Strike and the Formation of an
Entrepreneurial Democracy

This social and political legitimacy among the middle classes was at stake when, after several months of careful organization, the four most important working-class union confederations—the Conservative UTC, the Liberal CTC, the Communist Confederación Sindical de Trabajadores de Colombia (CSTC), and the Confederación General de Trabajo (CGT)—called for a twenty-four-hour general strike to begin at midnight on September 14, 1977.[85] In the face of galloping inflation and low real salaries, the Committee for the National Strike issued a memorandum to López Michelsen contending that it was incredible to see the government ignoring workers' demands for wage increases when there was plenty of revenue from the coffee export bonanza. The extensive resource monopolization and uneven economic development that characterized Colombia, the committee asserted, had allowed only "a privileged few" to benefit from this economic boom.[86] These unions demanded a 50 percent across-the-board wage increase to compensate for the high cost of living.[87] They also pushed for price controls on essential commodities, more low-cost housing opportunities, improved public services, and an end to the state of siege and the martial law more recently in effect since 1976. The rights to collective bargaining and protest for state professionals and white-collar employees were also central, as well as a new nationwide education statute for teachers. They requested the demilitarization of university campuses and more money for public higher education institutions. They also called for stopping state policies aimed at reorganizing ISI, along with policies that violated the rights of physicians. They advocated land reform for peasants and an eight-hour workday and minimum wage increase for transportation workers.

As these requests suggest, the strike proposed an interlinked chain of classed and gendered demands encompassing the interests of different historical actors—workers, peasants, teachers, professors, students, professionals, and white-collar employees—different left political parties, and even some sectors of the Conservative Party. This does not mean, however, that these historical actors rescinded their previous demands for a unified front against López Michelsen. Rather, for middle-class participants this strike was a struggle over which of their hierarchical visions—and attached gendered and classed subjectivities—should define a proper democracy, a struggle that had been ongoing since the late 1960s. There were those who, by not participating in the strike, claimed to represent "the will of the people . . . the democracy of the several, the will of the majority" as the proper and masculine "leaders of the public good."[88] Take, for instance, some male professionals affiliated with ASMEDAS and UNCLAMECOL who deemed their colleagues participating in "the pointless strike" "criminals, delinquents, [and] lawbreakers" for killing "objectivity and professionalism."[89] What was at stake was the political invalidation of their colleagues' redefinition of democracy, which to these "apolitical" professionals was a "politicized, proselytized, and biased" vision in fundamental contradiction with a government of "the most capable and most accomplished." Their colleagues' support for the strike caused declassing and feminization. They were embracing the antidemocratic values of both the popular classes (politics, violence, ineptitude) and elite minorities (privilege, luxury, and exploitation) and were thus disqualified from representing "the people" in a postpolitical and postideological democracy.[90]

Some service-sector employees likewise rejected the strike, while others sympathized with some demands (particularly the salary raises) but not the method of the protest. For this latter group, the strike was antidemocratic because it did not conform to a gendered and classed definition of public assembly. The strike was a "terrifying" spectacle of "the violence of the few," which destined its participants to "eternal poverty."[91] Owners of small and medium industries echoed some of this discourse by embracing López Michelsen's calls to fire workers participating in the protest, an act that under a state of emergency would bring no penalty for unfair dismissal. Again mobilizing demands that they had been making since at least the late 1960s, small-business owners claimed to be at a loss over why workers and their unions, instead of making an individual effort to "pull themselves out of poverty . . . [had found] in politics and violence the sanctuary for their economic incompetence." This was an antidemocratic strike, as it did not represent "the entrepreneurial people of the country."[92]

The López Michelsen and Turbay Ayala administrations shared a twofold response to such mobilization. First, they further empowered middle-class men and, to a lesser degree, women by revalidating a proper middle class as the representatives of "the people" in a postpolitical and postideological society. A few days after the general strike began, President López Michelsen announced on national TV and radio that all that he wanted to create via his development programs was the social, political, and economic conditions for "a middle class to become the true democratic force in the country."[93] He found it puzzling that certain "political groups" were unsatisfied with his policies, since he merely wanted to realize a society in which "60 to 70 percent of the population could be part of a middle class." López Michelsen insisted that such an enlarged middle class could prevent "dangerous events [like] the strike from ever happening again" because it would end "that rancid elitist character that has shaped Colombian society since time immemorial."[94]

Turbay Ayala did not hesitate to follow suit. Throughout his presidential campaign and term (1978–1982), he frequently participated in UNCLAMECOL conferences, ACOPI political conventions, and white-collar service-sector union meetings, and he meticulously responded to letters from middle-class people. A few months before his election, for instance, he attended an UNCLAMECOL meeting to speak "before the most powerful class in any democracy." He wanted to be clear that his "thirty-five-plus years of service" had been dedicated to "the class he [had] proudly emerged from" and the one that he would like "to bring to the presidential palace" for a government by those "who [were] most capable, work[ed] hard to get ahead every day, and want[ed] to live in peace."[95] Employing 1970s middle-class discourses, Turbay Ayala asserted that it was men like himself who could embody such a democratic disposition. He did not come from a lineage of "rancid . . . oligarchical . . . aristocratic surnames"—those who, Turbay Ayala contended, had monopolized the presidency since time immemorial—but rather from "individual effort and the desire to become somebody in life."[96]

Second, these administrations also addressed, directly and indirectly, the radical petit bourgeoisie's demands for better material conditions—as long as these demands remained within the parameters of proper middle-classness and a proper definition of democracy. Thus, most radical petit bourgeois women and men enjoyed access to material benefits unavailable to most working-class groups because they could claim to be part of a proper middle class. A couple years after the strike, for instance, an agreement between Turbay Ayala's administration and FECODE was reached, called the Teachers' Statute. It required teachers to have at least a bachelor's degree in education (until this, many teachers had only attended normal school). It created a categorized pay scale in which ranking depended on the number of professional degrees in hand and years of experience. It institutionalized a disciplinary code that was supposed to offer job security, as now teachers could not get fired for "political reasons."[97] But this agreement was only possible because it was predicated on the shared belief that competition would bring individual economic success, meritocracy would depoliticize teachers' unions, and performance evaluations would prevent political proselytizing in the classroom. A similar agreement was reached with doctors working for the state in 1981. Drawing on a couple of decades of hiring policies geared toward selecting "apolitical" candidates, Turbay Ayala formalized a new code for professional ethics aimed at restoring the "lost privilege of doctors in Colombian society."[98] University professors and state professionals also secured salary raises. White-collar employees reached partial agreements with banks and service companies for internal competition packages intimately tied to salary incentive programs. And radical petit bourgeois men, and to a lesser extent women, enjoyed the access to homeownership made available by UPAC. Looking back on the 1970s, Roberto Solano, for instance, felt compelled to offer what he considered an important confession: "At that moment few of us would have acknowledged this, but I will not lie now: many of us had bought houses with UPAC or had mortgages to pay. We had credit cards, too. . . . My wife and I were committed to the revolution. . . . We went from our middle-class neighborhoods to make a difference in poor neighborhoods. But we also needed to make sure that if the revolution did not happen we would at least have a house to live . . . and look how things turned out."[99]

What this testimony suggests is how a radical petit bourgeoisie partially participated—willingly or unwillingly—in legitimizing a larger neoliberal rationality in which the middle class could be seen as representing "the people" in a postpolitical, postideological, and market-driven democracy. Gender legitimized this participation. Radical petit bourgeois men and those who advocated for an entrepreneurial democracy, despite their profound disagreements, joined forces to silence women's demands for equal pay for equal work, crucial in several mobilizations throughout the 1970s and at the core of the 1977 strike. In fact, unequal pay was a gendered condition required for neoliberal rule to be possible at all. Female teachers, for example, complained that the Teachers' Statute did not account for the fact that with "all the family obligations falling on the women's shoulders," there was little time for them to professionalize and "rise in the pay scale."[100] Turbay Ayala's administration responded with a neoliberal maxim: "When one wants to achieve something, one can. It is up to them to take advantage of the opportunities."[101] Some male teachers echoed this, claiming that women tended to "make up barriers where there [were] none."[102] Female white-collar employees' demands for equal pay were also dismissed, service companies claiming that competition would rectify "such inequities," presumably because in a competitive environment each individual would receive an income according to "the effort that a particular individual put into what needed to be achieved."[103] Women simply needed to be patient and exert more "individual effort" to catch up with their male colleagues, who were paid more because of their "higher effort to get things done."[104] The demands of female professors and development office professionals for sexual, economic, and bodily autonomy were equally deemed political and hence criminal. And radical petit bourgeois women's feminist demands continued to be dismissed by their male counterparts as untimely or political distractions. In the process, the right to rule in democracies was defined as a masculine prerogative.

From State Representatives to Enemies of the State

These gendered exclusions also suggest that the radical petit bourgeoisie's more challenging demands to redefine democracy were silenced, categorized as political and thus as illegitimate, criminal, and antidemocratic. The López Michelsen and Turbay Ayala administrations appropriated transnational discourses on the abnormalization of the middle class, informed by the National Security Doctrine, in order to legitimize an ample, if eclectic, repertoire of violence in a concerted effort to silence—now literally—the radical petit bourgeoisie's visions of democracy. Turbay Ayala's government institutionalized a state of emergency and promulgated the Security Statute of 1978 as a way to eradicate any potential threat to "the will of the people." The rule of law central to democracy was suspended to defend a democracy predicated on a proper middle class. These multiple forms of violence aimed at not only the surveillance and annihilation of an abnormal middle class but also its active normalization. A militarized state practiced such pathologization through a hierarchical demarcation of a proper middle class with the right to represent "the people" in democracies and an improper petit bourgeoisie with the right to be silenced: legally incarcerated, rightfully tortured, justly disappeared, and, if necessary, lawfully killed. These multiple forms of violence created not only a distinction between inhuman and human, as some scholars argue, but also classed and gendered subjects in need of disciplining into hierarchically distributed roles in a proper democracy. If the middle class was forsaking its role as the social glue for a neoliberal democracy, a militarized state assumed it necessary to exercise violence to normalize the middle class—what several high-ranking military personnel, evoking Lleras Camargo's arguments of the early 1970s, called the democratic need to "spread blood and use fire."

Thus, far from undermining democracy, the inclusionary repertoire of repressive practices authorized by the Security Statute sought to democratize society by transforming a radical, improper, and abnormal petit bourgeoisie into a postpolitical, postideological, heteropatriarchal middle class who could represent "the people" in an entrepreneurial democracy.

Radical petit bourgeois recalled those years as extremely difficult. "It was a normal day in the late 1970s," Cecilia Serrano remembered, "when they came to get me."[105] She was in her apartment in Palermo, a middle-class neighborhood, fixing something for breakfast before work:

> They stormed their way through my apartment. I was scared but not surprised. The people from the organization [M-19] had already told us this would happen. But you are never prepared for this. The first thing I saw was a military boot. . . . They knew who we were. They went straight to find books, and they found some of my teaching I used in my classes: Marx, Mao, Torres, Freire, and Portelli. For them, all of this was evidence of something wrong. At the moment I began to ask myself why they came for us. . . . Yes, we were part of a military organization, but what I did was educate the masses. But at the moment I realized how much they wanted to get to us, they got the books and ripped them apart. . . . They handcuffed and blindfolded me, got me in a jeep. . . . We drove around the city for hours. . . . They took me to a military battalion in Puente Aranda. I met interrogation rooms, those rooms that everybody talked about but nobody wanted to be in.[106]

And it was there, Serrano remembered, where she experienced "the repressive forces." They focused on her literacy teaching, trying to get her "to confess that it was Marx who inspired [her] in [her] teaching, that [she] was propagating communism." To get information about the leaders of revolutionary organizations, different forms of torture were employed in which psychologists and physicians—middle-class professionals themselves— played an important role, the former to break "the minds of the prisoners" and the latter to determine how long "detainees could endure physical pain."[107] What was at stake in this violence was the normalization of a gendered middle class. Serrano, for instance, remembers how the interrogators told her that she "was a good woman who had gotten corrupted, [who] could have been somebody important in life," and that if she "thought of [her]self as very *macha*, then they would treat [her] as such" to "see if [she] could endure violence as a man." Marta Jaramillo recalled similar appeals to gendered middle-classness during her torture:

They said that my husband and my kids were in other interrogation rooms. They played a recording where you would hear children screaming as if they were being tortured. I could not help but think that they were my children. I despaired, but I tried to control myself. It could not be my children, I said to myself. But you never knew for sure. And after this they began to say that I was the worst mother, a soulless and heartless mother because I did not want to save my children. They told me that I had abandoned my kids, that I did not care about them, that I was going to let them die. . . . They felt so powerful when they kept telling me I was a whore who preferred what I did over what could happen to my children. I was the worst mother ever. They also said that my partner had already confessed because he was a faggot and he had enjoyed having sex with men and thus had confessed. . . . I was going to give in. But I was strong. And, in retrospect, I perhaps made a mistake by provoking them. I told them I could take care of them. There were three guys in the interrogation room. And that infuriated them. They wanted to destroy who I was. And they threatened me that if I thought I was very machista they could dominate me by penetrating me. With sex, they said, they would control me. I could not stand this anymore. I began to scream. If they thought I was a hysterical . . . crazy woman, well, I was going to behave like one. I did not stop screaming until I was taken to a cell. I guess my hysteria worked.[108]

Torture practices were needed to transform radical petit bourgeois women—"whores," *machas*, improper mothers, masculinized with abnormal families, enemies of the state—into proper middle-class mothers as the defenders of heterosexual families/homes and as professional representatives of the state. And for so many women, such psychological torture soon transformed into physical violence, defined by masculine domination. "I was raped," Marta Espinosa painfully remembered,

because I was not weak. They thought they could get to me. And they said that they wanted to control me with sex. They pointed a gun directly at my head. But right there I did everything in my power to suspend any feelings. Two of them kept asking, while penetrating me, if I enjoyed it. I did not want to say anything. I was completely silenced, but I didn't want to show any suffering. I didn't want to give them that. And they kept telling me I wasn't a woman because I wasn't enjoying it. When they finished with their business they asked me again if I had any energy left to plot against the government, to behave like a macho, to be crazy enough to continue spreading communism. I turned around to face them and watched them in silence. . . . That day I thought about what else I could do to be able to resist this violence. And for me the answer was to keep doing what I was doing.[109]

Middle-class men also remembered this state violence as a gendered and classed experience. Rene Sánchez recalled:

They got me at night . . . and I had left a meeting in an apartment at the Centro Nariño neighborhood. That was not a political meeting, but they were following us. They blindfolded me and got me into a jeep. They began to hit me hard in my testicles. They knew about my family. . . . My family was my weakest point. They said I had a bright future ahead of me. . . . They asked why, if my brother had become a good doctor, I could not follow his example. They took me to one of the torture centers. I didn't know at the moment, but I think it was the [*escuela de caballería*] in Usaquen or the Cavernas de Sacromonte. There, things got bad for me. I was committed, I would not break. I told myself that I had to be a man. They beat my head hard, I fell unconscious. . . . They wanted to destroy our ideas. . . . Our ideas were dangerous. . . . They told me I was playing as a revolutionary, that I was a petty bourgeois child, that I should stop playing with dangerous ideas. They said that if I believed myself to be a little worker [*obrerito*] I should endure like one. And as I did not say anything, they pointed a gun to my head and put a stick in my anus several times. They destroyed me. They asked me if I was enjoying it. . . . They said I was a faggot. You can never forget this . . . but I am here.[110]

Violence had to normalize a radical petit bourgeois—a child, a little worker, a feminized body—into a proper middle-class man, a proper doctor, a homeowner, an economically productive member of society. And if they did not comply then, it was just democratic to eradicate such improper petit bourgeois radicals. Thus, these women and men remembered how military forces killed and disappeared many of their comrades committed to social change. "They are not here to tell their stories," one noted, but "I am sure they would join me in saying that this is what democracy looked like for many of us."[111]

Yet during the late 1970s and early 1980s, the many radical petit bourgeois jailed indeterminately pending military trial—the men mostly at La Picota, the women mostly at El Buen Pastor—continued to resist, reinventing themselves as makers of "a real democracy" in prison. They wanted to re-member these difficult years as a moment not only of suffering and victim-ization but also of "powerful resistance," with "jail spaces" transformed "into political trenches and tribunes" for their visions of democracy.[112] They read out loud lengthy letters they sent to family members, friends, significant others, lawyers, and comrades to highlight how they fought back against a violent state by "enjoy[ing] every single part of the struggle."[113]

Gender and class also shaped this resistance. Against their identifica-tion by the militarized state as "common delinquents," these petit bour-geois women and men claimed to be "the expression of the people . . . the directors, the leaders, and guiders of the feelings of the marginalized and silenced."[114] They were, in a word, "revolutionaries." But, as in protests throughout the 1970s, this imagined leadership role assigned to them by the very revolution that they wanted to bring about made them both part of the people and hierarchically separate. In the process they created an-other gendered and classed other to avoid what they usually referred to as their "social and political death" as social actors in imprisonment. Marx was yet again an inspiration, allowing these petit bourgeois to define their "lower-class" prison mates as the lumpenproletariat, those members of society structurally excluded from organized socioeconomic conflict and thus from the development of proletarian consciousness. In their letters from jail, the radical petit bourgeoisie detailed these lumpenproletarians as "the human scum of Colombian society," "persons of dubious origins, vagrants, lubbers, full of vices, the embodiment of attitudes defined by treason, submission, and degenerated pride for humanity." These figures, not the petit bourgeoisie, were the "common criminals, apolitical obstacles to a potential revolution with neither economic nor political productivity, for whom violence [was] the rule."[115] These criminals, not them, were the source of danger; they did not comply with "the normal rules of society," as "men dress[ed] like women, and men flirted with men."[116] As female politi-cal prisoners noted, compared to the common criminals they came "from a different world . . . the world of discussion, a world of ideas, a life a little bit more complicated."[117] Their task in imprisonment was to "humanize what was inhuman."[118] And in the course of describing these common criminals, both women and men once again pointed to the oligarchies as the "true criminals of society," who behaved as "industrial delinquents exercising a millenarian oppression."[119]

These common criminals, as the gendered other to the petit bourgeois political prisoners, hierarchically enabled the latter to critically participate in movements for human rights and redefinitions of peace in general.[120] The petit bourgeois political prisoners subsequently published several reports on torture practices to raise social consciousness about the militarized state, wrote letters to international organizations on "the truth about what was happening in Colombia," and produced brief yet powerful analyses of the United States' political and economic support for an "oligarchical [and hence] criminal democracy." They sought to demonstrate how the peace promoted by the oligarchical state was based on violence and torture. In so doing, they placed this oligarchical state in fundamental contradiction with peace.[121] But some of these radical petit bourgeois defended revolutionary violence as still necessary to break this contradiction and thus reach "real peace," which they defined not as a matter of security—as did the militarized state—but rather as a question of social justice, the equal distribution of the nation's wealth, and the collective ownership of the means of production.

Those who self-identified as properly middle class responded critically to these demands. Some embraced the state's violent practices by simply looking away. "That [was] not my business," one UNCLAMECOL member wrote, echoing sentiments expressed by fellow members in editorials and letters; "I [was] not interested in politics . . . besides if they [were] in trouble it [was] because they [had] done something," another emphasized.[122] Still others elided the violence as "just a conspiracy by some people" who "torture[d] themselves to discredit the government," as "instead of working they [had] free time to torture themselves." "When one [was] busy becoming somebody in life," they concluded, "there [was] not time to fall into dangerous matters."[123] Others thought the repression justified, claiming that "those unworthy to belong to a democracy" always sought to "blame others for their own misery instead of becom[ing] useful citizens. . . . One gets what one deserves."[124]

And yet others, professional psychologists and physicians, directly participated in the torture of a radical petit bourgeoisie. It is here that one can see how a proper definition of democracy associated with a specific notion of middle-classness began to gain legitimacy through different forms of violence. In a very difficult conversation, Pedro Garzón, a social and clinical psychologist from PUJ, told me that he had been hired by the armed forces "to break criminals' mindsets." He conceded that it was tough to "see people like [him] in interrogation rooms . . . educated people . . . people of good origins . . . that lost track of themselves." And because these were people who had to know better "than other members of society," Garzón thought his job was even more important as he could use his professional competence "to help raise awareness of how wrong these educated people were in their doings." But at first Garzón preferred to avoid describing how specifically he performed such a task by generally claiming that "violence" was part of his job description as a professional. Indeed, violence, he insisted, had nothing to do with politics. Rather, violence was a detached, objective action he was well prepared to perform. In his mind, there was no need whatsoever to justify what he did—or take any individual responsibility—since he, as an "honorable . . . professional man," wanted to redeem "peace, democracy, and public order." Thus, he claimed that people like him represented "the will of the majority," which endowed him with righteousness as a perpetrator of violence and cruelty, always defined as professional endeavors: "Democracy needed people like us. . . . We were defending the people. . . . We were defending the mandate of a majority, of the people, that is democracy. . . . We were professionals."

Thus it is no accident that Garzón, unlike other radical petit bourgeoisie women and men, remembered the 1970s as a decade of "endless economic possibilities, a constant quest for social tranquility . . . and professional advancement."[125] But such romantic memories are predicated on the silence—or legitimation—of violence and cruelty as conditions for the proper hierarchization of democracy. Furthermore, what Garzón's memories suggest is precisely that these members of the middle class were not just complicit collaborators with different manifestations of state violence but active participants who depended—directly or indirectly—upon such violence to make a claim to middle-classness. These different practices of violence were integral to a definition of peaceful democracy: as political enemies, the assumption went, a radical petit bourgeoisie—and its vision of democracy—had to disappear for a neoliberal society centered on a proper middle class to exist. Struggling with those who saw peace as a question of social justice and economic distribution, these middle-class men and women defined protests as "political . . . criminal activities" performed by "the few . . . disposable members in society" that disturbed the tranquility that a democracy was supposed to bring about. These middle-class women and men also collectively fought for the supremacy of a vision in which the development of individual talent could materialize a legitimate—that is to say, hierarchical—democracy. These middle-class women and men, furthermore, made a concerted effort to define peace as violence because peace would create the conditions for a society in which politics could function as administration, private property could become the measure of social worthiness, rights could become undistinguishable from class privileges, labor exploitation could become justified in the name of economic opportunities for all, state tasks could be pursued as an entrepreneurial activity, democracy could mean self-exploitation, and education could be an asset in the inescapable economic competition for capital accumulation. Along the way, the middle class became the archetype of peace as violence, cohesive society as a classed hierarchy, and democracy as a dictatorship of capital.

Epilogue

A Class That Does (Not) Matter: Democracy beyond Democracy

The middle classes have yet again become *the* answer to the ills of democracy in our globalized present. For some, this middle class would counter the negative aspects of globalization by preventing wealth concentration at the national level and disciplining democratic development worldwide. For others, a Western-inspired middle class of entrepreneurs, investors, professionals, and avid consumers could "tip the scales away from extremist belligerence in the Muslim world."[1] And for still others, this middle class could restore imperial leadership for the United States, which as a middle-class nation par excellence would be the exemplar for less democratic countries.[2] At the core of this shared belief, we accept that a two-class society is the manifestation of an antidemocratic form of domination characterized by the struggle between two classes (a small oligarchy and the growing poor), which is marked by political instability, political radicalization, and economic inequality. Democracy, we are told, is in crisis. Conversely, we imagine an ever-expanding middle class as a response to such dedemocratization, as the only possibility to create—or return to—a democratic society beyond class domination.

It is in this context that scholars tend to locate a two-class society as the struggle of our times and thus in imperative need of critical appraisal. In contrast, the study of the middle classes is perceived as less important precisely because such study would get us away from what is considered the authentic manifestation of class domination and material inequalities.[3] We cannot succumb, the argument goes, to the myth of the middle classes, a myth that only disguises the real class struggle in neoliberal societies. Indeed, it is a class that does not matter for a historical explanation of the multiple forms of domination. In the process, democracy, and its intimate association with a middle class, remains under the monopoly of the sacred because any historical critique of the middle classes is perceived as an argument *against* democracy, whereas a critique of a two-class society is, almost by definition, *in favor* of a democratic society.

In attempting to break away from this framework, I have sought to illuminate the historical process through which democracy and middle-classness became ontologically identical. My task has been to demonstrate how multiple forms of class domination can be in struggle over the supremacy—or legitimacy—of what democracy is supposed to do. By focusing on Bogotá of the 1960s and 1970s, I have probed the historical definitions of democracy that we often invoke but seldom specify. This allows us to offer an important critique of democracy itself, historicized not as an ideological chimera of total emancipation and social harmony or as a transcendental norm but rather as an effect of competing discourses, collective subjectivities, and social conflict through which different historical actors, by claiming middle-classness, attempted to naturalize and legitimize class and gender hierarchies as part of democracy. Such an approach also enables a fundamental reconsideration of the assumption that class hierarchies and gender stratifications are irreconcilable with the meanings and practices of democracy. To put my main argument succinctly, the formation of the middle classes was democratic *precisely because, and not despite of,* those middle-class women and men who sought to perpetuate multiple hierarchical forms of gendered class domination. Competing class stratifications and contested gendered hierarchies, far from violating the materialization of a true democracy, were constitutive of the multiple struggles for democracy during the twentieth century's second half.

Rather than rehearsing the details of this argument, in this brief epilogue I want to dwell on how this critique of democracy matters in a current historical moment when we are forced to worship a middle-class society as democracy's future. These hierarchical definitions of democracy from the 1960s and 1970s should not be seen simply as antecedents for more recent iterations of neoliberal rule but rather as part of thick gender and class genealogies mobilized by different historical actors to legitimize particular visions in a highly contested struggle over how peaceful and democratic societies should be organized. Take, for instance, the much-celebrated Peace Colombia program, reached in February 2016 between the United States and Colombia. Presumably a replacement for the fifteen-year Plan Colombia, a military, counterinsurgent, and anti-drug-cartels program, this new initiative established US$450 million in aid, approved by the US Congress in May 2017. Yet not only does the program still provide aid for society's further militarization, but it also positions, via what are called "Economic Support Funds," the middle class as central to peace, as did development programs such as the Alliance in the 1960s and neoliberal programs in the 1970s. At the White House ceremony formalizing the program in early February 2016, President Barack Obama announced that if Colombia was near collapse almost two decades ago, when the Plan Colombia was launched, it was now on the brink of peace because a middle-class society was at last materializing. But it was President Santos who more forcefully connected this vision of peace, happiness, hope, and democracy to the consolidation of a middle class. Sharply distinguishing between a violent past and a peaceful future, the Colombian president said that "we have gone from the worst economic recession in our recent history to being leaders in economic growth in Latin America. . . . We are also leaders in job creation, in reducing poverty, and in strengthening our middle class."[4]

In October 2, 2016, 50.2 percent of Colombian voters rejected the peace agreement between the FARC and Santos's administration. Some have already categorized this as the "Colombian problem," a manifestation of a "magic realism," as it is incomprehensible how certain social actors refuse peace. Others, mobilizing a dominant narrative in the histories of Colombia, have said that the oligarchies, though divided, won once again by blocking a peaceful future. Yet when we frame these political realities as transnational questions, they emerge as part of a larger discussion about the contested definitions of democracy and peace. Although the agreement centered on "rural questions"—the crucial demands for land distribution and political recognition—the idea of an urban middle class shaped the multiple, if polarizing, responses to the agreement's meaning for Colombian society at large. Uribe Vélez proclaimed that ratification of the peace agreement would cause the middle classes to suffer the most, both because they would pay higher taxes to finance the armed conflict's end and because a dubious but all-powerful movement aligned with Fidel Castro and Hugo Chávez—the so-called *castro-chavismo*—would seize the country. Although some quickly dismiss these as sophisms to which many "ignorant people" succumb, they legitimize a definition of peace and democracy. According to this definition, the peace negotiations usher in the negation by radical populism of a Colombia comprised of an ever-growing middle class allowed to work hard for a better future and to secure tranquility against a "terrorist threat" through society's militarization. Uribe Vélez and his supporters envision a middle-class society as the product of legitimate forms of violence meant to destroy improper political and economic subjects: others—guerrilla members, unproductive unionists, lazy peasants who want to "steal" land from "good-faith landowners," critical thinkers—who prevent a proper peaceful and hierarchized democratic society. They want a society in which foreign investment reigns freely, exploitative jobs expand, militarized social relationships rule, and everybody knows—and venerates—a proper gendered and classed ordering. This is a socially cohesive society in which classes can peacefully and hierarchically coexist. Others add to the peace accord's dangers a gendered question, claiming that it sanctified a "confusing gender ideology" that would destroy the family, imagined as the embodiment of a proper heteropatriarchal middle class and thus the bedrock of any viable democracy. As one of the self-identified middle-class women whom I interviewed put it, "In Colombia, if the 'yes' wins [in the plebiscite] democracy will be over . . . the family as we know it will be destroyed."[5]

Santos's government worked hard to demonstrate, through statistics and passionate speeches, how the slow but remarkable expansion of the middle classes in the last decade has been a specific result of his policies. Santos legitimized the peace accord by asserting that "middle-class citizens" would directly benefit from armed conflict's end, security and peace allowing the expansion of productive business, foreign investment, employment opportunities, and educational prospects. One only has to read Santos's development program, Everyone for a New Country, to see how his administration wants a middle-class society as the basis for what is dubbed the postconflict era, in which a social market economy and free enterprise could prevail.

In all my recent conversations, middle-class women and men in Bogotá were eager to say, "All of us want peace. . . . All of us want democracy."[6] One might just reject this as trite, but I find it more politically consequential to see what they imagine as peace and democracy. As I have demonstrated in this book, what gets sacralized as proper middle-classness in democracy is a society in which politics is defined as administration, poverty is explained away as stemming from lack of competitive individualism and competent leadership, a hierarchical social cohesiveness gets celebrated as the condition of a peaceful society, and a free market appears as the legitimate organizer of social hierarchies. This dominant definition of democracy and peace is historically anchored in the violent occlusion and forgetting of other definitions of radical middle-classness that privileged conflict, equal distribution of resources, education as a right, and public assembly as constitutive of democracy.

Thus, a critical history of the urban middle classes contributes to our current struggle for a peaceful society in two ways. It modifies critical accounts that depict Colombia's middle classes as if in a historical bubble, touched only sporadically or recently by violence and mostly indifferent to what happened in rural places, an urban group without ideology or distinctive political identity, historical actors ever deferent to elite interests and hence to a political order not particularly theirs. For instance, Gonzalo Sánchez, the director of the Centro Nacional de Memoria Histórica (CNMH), has argued that "collective action against atrocities is mostly undertaken by the victims themselves, while most citizens consider it to be unrelated to their lives and interests."[7] The armed conflict has lasted for over five decades because it "remain[s] anonymous to a wide public," which gives rise to "an attitude that, if not passive, is indifferent to [the majority of victims] and is further fed by a comfortable perception of the country's political and economic stability."[8] Thus Sánchez concludes, as do so many others, that the armed conflict—along with its political, social, and economic causes— is alien to the urban population, imagined as predominantly middle class.

Thus although there has been ample discussion of how different historical actors have contributed to and participated in the perpetuation of armed conflict—elites, imperial countries, multinational corporations, armed groups, the military, the media, and the state—the middle classes seem shielded by the assumption that they lacked political interests of their own and were thus walled off from what *really happened* in Colombia. They have merely followed the oligarchies' interests. Thus, the middle classes, the argument goes, have lived in a different reality; when some decided not to vote for the peace agreement, the assumption goes, they were merely minding their own business.

Although exactly how class subjectivities and political interests shape responses to the peace accords merits more careful analysis, such narratives let the middle classes off the hook at the very moment when they are asked, in the name of a peaceful future, to step outside their putative historical bubble and become aware of what happened in the rural and marginalized locations in the country. Such explanations reproduce what anthropologist Alejandro Castillejo defines as historical injury, granting the middle classes

a moral superiority and ethical distinction that allow them to avoid collective responsibility for a hierarchical definition of democracy that partially
created the conditions that fostered an armed conflict.[9] Certainly, as Sánchez
himself argues, this should not dilute concrete legal accountabilities, but
we should reflect on how middle-class people, far from passive or isolated
actors in the history of power relations in Colombia, played a foundational
role in producing the very hierarchies that legitimized the different forms
of violence inflicted on those whom middle-class women and men have
historically considered as ineradicable others of democracy. Indeed, once
we criticize democracy from the middle, we recognize the histories of
a normative middle class that through a complex process of exclusions,
distinctions, exploitations, and inequalities was legitimized as the core of
a hierarchical vision of democracy, a vision that excluded other historical
actors in Colombia from equal access to material resources as well as social
affirmation, cultural difference, and political recognition.

   With this in mind, a rejection of the peace accords by some—but by no
means all—middle-class women and men begins to make sense. As one
middle-class interviewee bluntly put it, "Do you really think that the peasants, neither educated for modernity nor eager to develop their human
capital nor prepared to live outside their rural settings, could really lead
this fantastic, geographically diverse country?"[10] Or as another middle-
class man, who reluctantly accepted the peace accord, put it, "This violence
has nothing to do with me, I rather live in a peaceful society. . . . so anybody
can progress."[11] Another raised the specter of "a guerrilla member, a terrorist . . . somebody who has spent no time in a classroom govern[ing] a
country like Colombia," a situation that he compared to left governments
elsewhere in Latin America: "Have you seen Evo Morales in Bolivia or
Maduro in Venezuela. . . . They are not educated. . . . They can get almost
anything with no effort, no hard work . . . and those people like us who have
worked hard will have to give everything up. . . . It is the end of democracy
as we know it."[12] In this specific sense, I want to conclude that, far from
passive actors ever co-opted by an oligarchical rule, an assumption that
perpetually reverberates in our historical explanations, the middle classes
must assume a collective historical responsibility for the materialization of
a proper—that is to say, hierarchical—political order we are obsessed with
calling democracy.

   Thus, if *Makers of Democracy* accomplishes anything, it ought to invite
us to disentangle democracy from a very specific definition of the middle
class. Amid a perceived global crisis of democracies in which all-powerful

capitalist oligarchies consolidate, middle-class society seems the absolute for democracy's future—as the only possibility to imagine a political horizon. And herein lies the power of the notion of a middle-class society. It acts as a totalitarian gift of democracy, a political fantasy of a harmonious but hierarchical society, which, by comparison to other social orders, appears properly—and irresistibly—democratic. Thus, I would like to conclude with a provocation. If, as this book has demonstrated, the transnational formation of a middle-class democracy during the 1960s and 1970s was marked by unequal relationships and shifting class and gender hierarchies, why do we continue to imagine a middle class as the celestial—transcendental—prerequisite for a different political organization of society? This is a provocation to take democracy—associated with a gendered middle-class society—beyond itself so that we can produce epistemological change, embrace previously unimaginable language to envision a different society, generate political possibilities for challenging the exploitation created by the inexorable calculus of globalization and neoliberal capitalism, the names given to a hierarchical definition of democracy predicated on a particular demarcation of middle-classness. My task has been to approach democracy agonistically so that democracy can be imagined—and practiced—otherwise.

Appendix

Occupation by Economic Sector (percentage), 1965

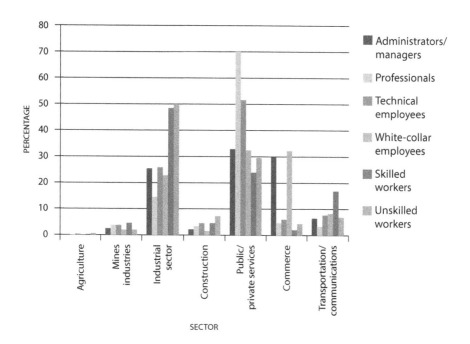

Figure App.1 Arias Osorio, *Bases para la integración*, 39. This is based on a sample of five hundred people in Bogotá.

Years of Formal Education (average), 1965

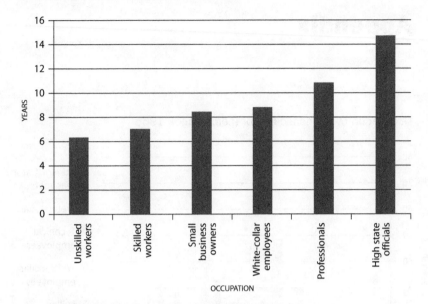

Figure App.2 Parra Sandoval, "Clases sociales," 172. Sample of two hundred "heads of household," mostly men. For Parra Sandoval occupation defined class. Lower class: unskilled and skilled workers; middle class: small-business owners, white-collar employees, and professionals; higher class: high officials and professionals.

Gender Distribution in Higher Education, 1951–1985

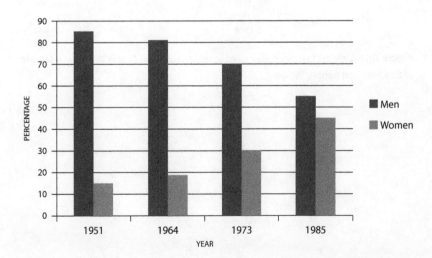

Figure App.3 Flórez, *Las transformaciones*, 94–95; Rodríguez, *El sistema*, 19. Rodríguez argued that 86.4 percent of those entering higher education came from a middle-class background, while 2.6 percent came from "lower classes."

Education Level / Average Income (pesos), 1967

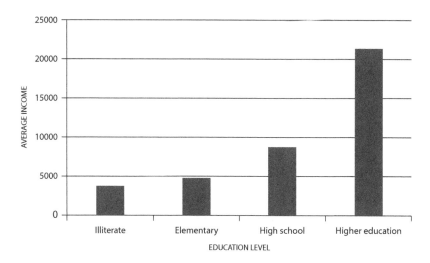

Figure App.4 CEDE, *Estructura*, 73, 149, 155, 231. This study was based on 294 household surveys in Bogotá.

Expenses, 1967–1968, Monthly Income (percentage) I

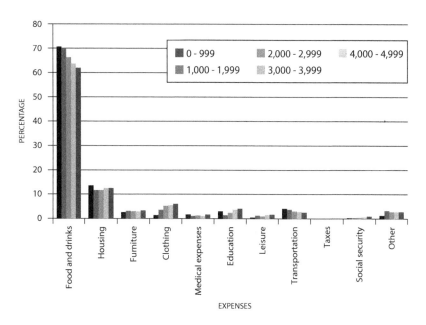

Figure App.5 CEDE, *Estructura*, 73, 149, 155, 231. This study located the middle classes in the average of 5,000–12,000 pesos per quarter (income average for a period of three months).

Expenses, 1967–1968, Monthly Income (percentage) II

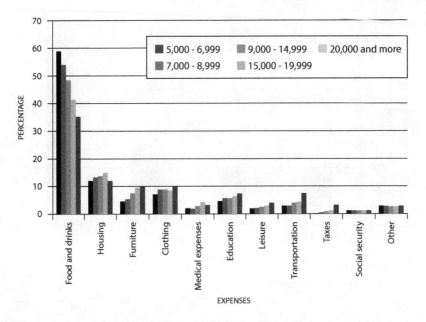

Figure App.6 CEDE, *Estructura,* 73, 149, 155, 231.

Previous Activities of Small-Business Owners, 1968 (percentage)

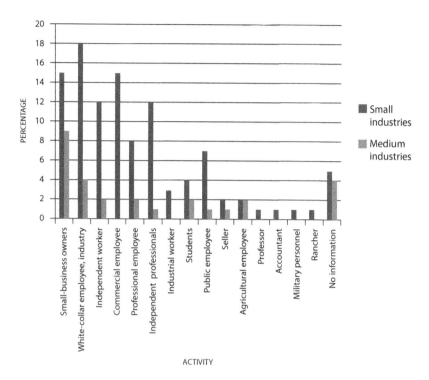

Figure App.7 Corporación Financiera Popular, *Diagnóstico*, 5. Surveys carried out among owners in small and medium industries by the OAS in 1968. A sample of 127 small and medium industries in Bogotá and other cities in Colombia.

Loan Applications / Loans Approved, 1964–1972

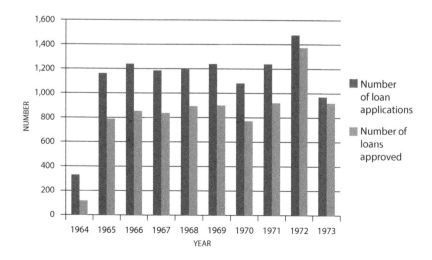

Figure App.8 RLCPMI, *Reunión*.

Amount of Money Allocated in Loans for Medium and Small Industries, Colombia, 1964–1972

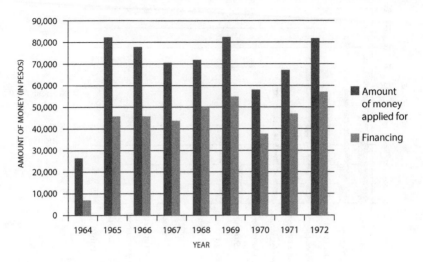

Figure App.9 RLCPMI, *Reunión.*

Self-Classification, 1976

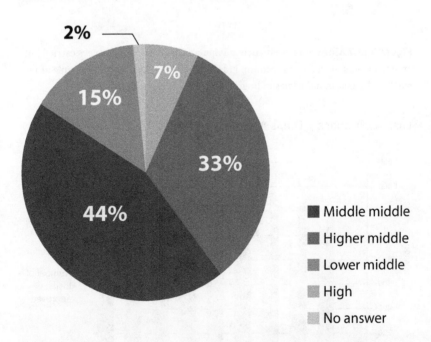

Figure App.10 UNCLAMECOL, survey tabulated in 1976 but collected in the previous years mostly from Bogotá. Eighty percent of the respondents were men and 20 percent women.

Middle-Class Budget, 1977–1979

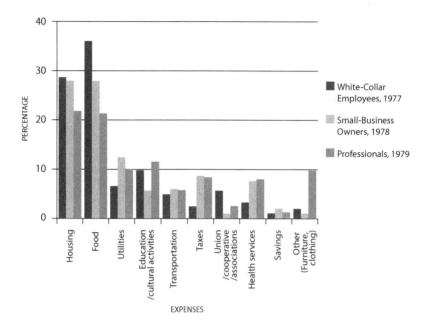

Figure App.11 Union newspapers, several personal archives, UNCLAMECOL, and ACOPI.

Middle-Class Income (Pesos), ca. 1975–1979

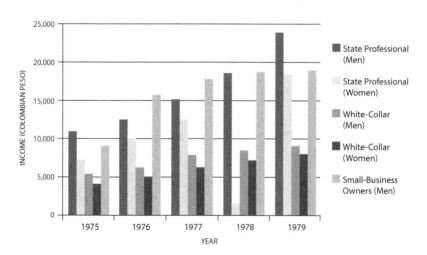

Figure App.12 Payrolls for the four service companies under study (white-collar employees); several state archives, payrolls, CVs, and pay stubs (professionals); and ACOPI (small-business owners).

Class Division by Neighborhood, 1972–1980

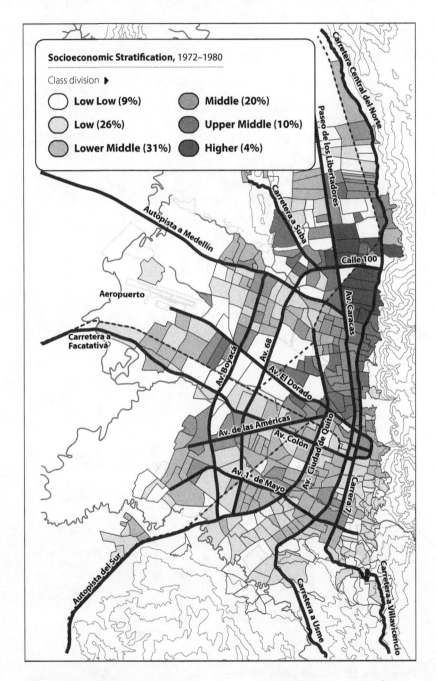

Map App.1 UNCLAMECOL-tabulated survey, 1976–1977, DANE; Arias, *Estudio*.
Map prepared by Rafael Puyana.

Notes

Introduction

1 Fukuyama, "Future of History," 60; Fukuyama, *Political Order*, 445.
2 Fukuyama, "Future of History," 61.
3 Fukuyama, *Political Order*, 445.
4 Fukuyama, "Future of History," 56.
5 Huffington, *Third World America*; Temin, *Vanishing Middle*.
6 Luce, *Retreat of Western Liberalism*.
7 Hacker, *The Great Risk Shift*.
8 Nasr, *Forces of Fortune*, 110–114.
9 Pew Research Center, *A Global Middle Class*.
10 Luce, *Retreat of Western Liberalism*.
11 Acemoglu and Robinson, *Economic Origins*, 258; *Semana*, "Colombia." For a recent statistical description of class distribution in Bogotá, see Angulo et al., *La década*.
12 Uribe Vélez, "Manifiesto."
13 Interview with Hernando Bahamón Soto.
14 Interview with Hernando Bahamón Soto.
15 Badiou, "Twenty-Four Notes," 29.
16 Žižek, *Ticklish Subject*, 187; Moretti, *Bourgeois*, 21.
17 Vivas Pacheco, "Colombia."
18 Therborn, "Class," 28.
19 James Scott, *Two Cheers*, 84–85.
20 Paley, "Introduction," in *Democracy*, 3–20.
21 Chakrabarty, *Provincializing Europe*. There is a revival of studies reclaiming the middle classes as the product of Europe and the United States. See Piketty, *Capital*, 21–22; Sitaraman, *Crisis*, 53–105, 201–220; Moretti, *Bourgeois*, 1–24.
22 López (with Weinstein), "We Shall Be All," 1–11; Paley, "Introduction."
23 Paley, *Democracy*.
24 Desmond Arias and Goldstein, "Violent Pluralism," 5.
25 Desmond Arias and Goldstein, "Violent Pluralism," 5.
26 Desmond Arias and Goldstein, "Violent Pluralism," 27. For similar arguments, see Zeiderman, *Endangered City*, 129–130.
27 Desmond Arias, "Conclusion," 258.

28 Inglehart and Welzel, *Modernization*; Pandey, "Can There Be a Subaltern Middle Class?," 322, 326–327.

29 Ekbladh, *Great American Mission*; Rabe, *Most Dangerous Area*; Gilman, *Mandarins*; Rabe, *Killing Zone*; Rabe, *John F. Kennedy*; Taffet, *Foreign Aid*; Latham, *Modernization as Ideology*.

30 Escobar, *Designs for the Pluriverse*, xiii.

31 Rabe, *John F. Kennedy*, 82; Escobar, *Encountering Development*. For a different reading, see Field, *From Development*.

32 Rabe, *John F. Kennedy*, 82.

33 Williams, *Understanding*, 190–211.

34 Grandin, *Last Colonial Massacre*, xvi; Rabe, *Killing Zone*; Fontana, *Por el bien del imperio*, 15; E. Torres Rivas, *Revoluciones*, 111, 167–168.

35 Coronil, "After Empire," 248.

36 Mignolo, *Local Histories*; Mignolo, *Darker Side*, 47, 213–251; Castro-Gómez and Grosfoguel, *El giro*; Dussel, *Politics of Liberation*, 452, 549–552; Escobar, *Territories*, 20.

37 This is how Michael Jiménez's influential article posed the problem. Jiménez, "Elision of the Middle Classes," 207–228. Following Jiménez, the recent iteration of middle-class studies has legitimized the interest in this topic as a need to fill out a historiographical void.

38 For "enduring episteme," see Mudimbe, *Invention of Africa*, x.

39 Chasteen, *Born in Blood and Fire*, 9. On this point, I draw on Said, "Politics of Knowledge"; Lee, *Unreasonable Histories*, 1–21; Spivak, "How Do We Write"; Robinson, *Black Marxism*.

40 Adamovsky, *Historia*; Parker, *Idea of the Middle Class*; Barr-Melej, *Reforming Chile*; O'Dougherty, *Consumption Intensified*; Gilbert, *Mexico's Middle Class*; Owensby, *Intimate Ironies*; Walker, *Waking*; López and Weinstein, *Making*; Parker and Walker, *Latin America's Middle Class*; Carassai, *Argentine Silent Majority*; Cosse, "Clases medias"; Visacovsky and Garguin, *Moralidades*; Sánchez Salcedo, *Los empleados*; García Quesada, *Formación*; Vrana, *This City Belongs to You*.

41 Grandin, "Living in Revolutionary Time," 23, 24.

42 Grandin, "Living in Revolutionary Time," 23, 24, 28, 29. This argument has a thick pedigree across the Americas. See Nun, *Latin America*, 363; León de Leal, "Las clases medias"; O'Donnell, *Modernization*; Guillén Martínez, *El poder*; García, "Las clases medias."

43 Grandin, *The Last Colonial Massacre*, 14, 169–198, and "Living in Revolutionary Time"; Archila, *Idas y venidas*, 421–430; Sánchez, *¡Huelga!*; Fontana, *Por el bien del imperio*, 377–405, 503–509; Torres Rivas, *Revoluciones*, 138–141, 176–179.

44 As an exception, see Cosse, "Clases medias."

45 Grandin, "Living in Revolutionary Time," 12–13, 23; Archila, *Idas y venidas*, 428, 429; Adamovsky, *Historia*; Pécaut, *Crónica*; Sánchez, *¡Huelga!*, 275–315, 317–358;

Carassai, *Argentine Silent Majority*, 3–4, 268–269; García, "Las clases medias"; Vrana, *This City Belongs to You*.

46   Safford and Palacios, *Colombia*, x; Escobar, *Territories*, 20.

47   Joshi, *Fractured Modernity*, 181; Watenpaugh, *Being Modern*, 303–308. In his influential work on Brazil, Owensby invited scholars to think the ideal of the middle class as a productive myth for certain people who identified themselves as middle class in the first half of the twentieth century. Yet he located this ideal as a reality outside Latin America. Owensby, *Intimate Ironies*, 8.

48   Derrida, *Specters of Marx*.

49   This argument is inspired by Zuleta, *Elogio*; Eley, *Forging Democracy*; Paley, *Democracy*; Spencer, *Anthropology*; Joan Scott, *Fantasy*.

50   My transnational approach is informed by Shukla and Tinsman, *Imagining Our Americas*.

51   Sick, "El concepto," 21–54; Maza, *Myth of the French Bourgeoisie*, 4.

52   Sitaraman, *The Crisis*, 12–52.

53   Foucault, "Is It Really Important to Think?," 172.

54   Butler, "Performativity Social Magic," 113–128; Bourdieu, *State Nobility*, 1–7; Hall, *Familiar Stranger*, 16.

55   Stoler and McGranahan, "Refiguring Imperial Terrains," 7; Farnsworth-Alvear, *Dulcinea*, 24–33.

56   Heiman, Freeman, and Liechty, "Charting," in *Global Middle Classes*, 13; Wacquant, "Making Class," 39–64.

57   Foucault, "What Is the Enlightenment?," 54.

58   This approach is informed by Parker, "All-Meaning Middle," 13–29; Heiman, Freeman, and Liechty, "Charting," in *Global Middle Classes*, 1–29; Joan Scott, *Fantasy*, 45–67; Butler, *Psychic Life*; David Scott, *Stuart Hall's Voice*, 85–114.

59   Joan Scott, *Fantasy*, 1–67.

60   Joan Scott, *Fantasy*, 19.

61   Adamovsky, "'Clase media,'" 115–138.

62   Adamovsky, "'Clase media,'" 135–136; Garcia Quesada, *La Formación*, 413.

63   Joan Scott, *Fantasy*, 49, 5.

64   Butler, *Notes*, 1–23; Chatterjee, *Lineages*, 140–153; Olson, *Imagined Sovereignties*, 1–17.

65   Stoler, "Colonial Archives," 87–109.

66   Stoler, *Along the Archival Grain*, 19–53.

67   Stern, *Battling*, xxviii.

68   David Scott, *Conscripts of Modernity*.

69   See note 34.

70   Joseph and Spenser, *In from the Cold*; Zolov, "Expanding," 48, 51; Archila, *Una historia inconclusa*; Green, *We Cannot Remain Silent*; Pensado, *Rebel Mexico*; Guerra, *Visions of Power*, 14, 17; Gould, "Solidarity under Siege," 349.

71   Laclau, *On Populist Reason*, 17; Chatterjee, *Lineages*, 140–143.

72 Here I follow Wolford, *This Land*; Degregori, *How Difficult*; Mallon, *Peasant and Nation*.

73 Hudson, *Colombia*, li; Jiménez Burillo et al., *La búsqueda*.

74 Gutiérrez Sanín, *El orangután*, 7; Hylton, *Evil Hour*, 8; Moncayo, *El leviatán*.

75 Palacios, *Between Legitimacy and Violence*, 228; Bushnell, *Making*; Pearce, *Colombia*, 207; Jaramillo Vélez, *Colombia*, 3–50; Zubiría Samper, "Dimensiones," 230; Melo, *Historia mínima*.

76 Hylton, *Evil Hour*, 11–12.

77 Archila, *Idas y venidas*, 346–347; Hartlyn, *Politics*; Sánchez, "Bajo la égida," 253; Salazar, "Nostalgia y aspiraciones"; Palacios, *Between Legitimacy and Violence*, 228; Moncayo, "Hacia la verdad," 145–146, 151–152.

78 For "critical fissure," see Guillén Martínez, *El poder*, 445–469; Zubiría Samper, "Dimensiones," 224–230.

79 García, "Las clases medias," 37–38. Such an argument has proven foundational; see Palacios, *Between Legitimacy and Violence*, 180; Murillo Posada, "La modernización," 278; González, *El poder*, 324; Tirado Mejía, *Los años 60*; CNMH, *¡Basta ya!*

80 Bushnell, *Making*, 285.

81 Historians have naturalized this narrative as the historical context—indeed, as historicity itself—to which every history of the second half of the twentieth century must refer. As I show elsewhere, such a narrative is a historical and political product of a petit bourgeois identity in the 1970s and 1980s. See López-Pedreros, "The Class and Gender of De-coloniality."

82 I draw on Weinstein, *The Color of Modernity*, 192–221; Yarimar Bonilla, "Ordinary Sovereignty," 152–165. This is a collective effort: Britto, "Marihuana Axis"; Roldán, *Blood and Fire*, and "Acción Cultural Popular," 27–44; Karl, *Forgotten Peace*; Calvo Isaza and Parra Salazar, *Medellín*; Garzón, *Del patrón-estado*; Farnsworth-Alvear, *Dulcinea*; Braun, *Assassination of Gaitán*; LeGrand, "Legal Narratives of Citizenship."

Chapter 1. A Bastard Middle Class

1 Koner, "Neighbors," 88.

2 Koner, "Neighbors," 88

3 Koner, "Neighbors," 89.

4 Guzzardi, "Crucial," 98.

5 Guzzardi, "Crucial," 98–99.

6 Guzzardi, "Crucial," 98.

7 Guzzardi, "Crucial," 215.

8 Stoler, "Intimidations of Empire," 5–7.

9 For surveys of US policies toward the postcolonial world, see Hanhimäki and Westad, *Cold War*; Latham, *Right Kind of Revolution*.

10 Harry Truman, "Inaugural Address, January 20, 1949," 297.

11 NARA59, Record relating to Colombia, Intern.Tech.Assit., 250/63 104 12–3 (1955–59).

12 NARA59, Record relating to Colombia, Intern.Tech.Assit., 250/63 104 12–3 (1955–59).

13 NARA59, Record relating to Colombia, Intern.Tech.Assit., 250/63 104 12–3 (1955–59).

14 NARA59, Record relating to Colombia, Intern.Tech.Assit., 250/63 104 12–3 (1955–59).

15 Reports, Missión.Colombia, Miscellaneous, Subject files (1952–59), US Mission to Colombia, 1948–1961, NARA469.

16 In this context the notion of "the culture of poverty" emerged as a transnational discussion. Rosemblatt, "Other Americas."

17 Romero Sánchez, "Ruralizing"; Corcoran, "Infrastructure."

18 Kennedy, Depart.State.publication7164, InterAmerican.series, March 1961, Off .Public.Services Bureau of Public Affairs, 4.

19 Kennedy, Depart.State.publication7164, InterAmerican.series, March 1961, Off .Public.Services Bureau of Public Affairs, 4–5.

20 Taffet, *Foreign Aid*, 5.

21 Grandin, *Last Colonial Massacre*, 10; Coronil, "After Empire," 248.

22 David Scott, "Political Rationalities," 1–22.

23 On development, see Ferguson, *Anti-politics Machine*; Cooper and Packard, *International Development*; Mitchell, *Rule of Experts*.

24 John F. Kennedy, Department of State publication 7164, 4, 5.

25 Tech.Assist.Colombia, 1956, UNA, TE 322/1col-s0175-0310-06.

26 Comm.Organ.Develop, Colombia (Colo, 250), 1956, UNA S 0175-03334-02.

27 Letter from William H. Olson to José Ricaute García, August 5, 1959, Prog .Rurales.Desarr.Comunidad, Proj.Colombia IV and Colombia XXV, Min.Agriculture, STACA.

28 NARA469, House.Programs, project.IV.Colombia XXV.Missión.Colombia, Off .Chief.Subject.Files (1952–59).

29 This reading is influenced by Wilder's critique of "colonial humanism." Wilder, *French Imperial Nation-State*, 43–145.

30 UNA, Notif.Com.Nacional.Reforma.Pública.Colombia, Comm.Org.Devel. Bogotá, December 13, 1956, Col.Technical.Assist.Program (250) S 0175-03334-02.

31 OASAR, Proced.organ.clase media.

32 Pan-American Union and Crevenna, *Materiales*.

33 OASAR, Proced.organ. ES.PS.

34 OASAR, Proced.organ. ES.PS.clase media.

35 CEPAL, *El desarrollo social*, 95–96.

36 Bryson, "Introduction," 6.

37 Bryson, "Introduction," 7–8.

38 Bryson, "Introduction," 7.

39 Bryson, "Introduction," 7–8.

40 Gillin, "Some Signposts for Policy," 24, 26.

41 Bryson, "Introduction," 6.

42 Bryson, "Introduction," 10.

43 Guzmán Campos, Fals Borda, and Umaña Luna, *La Violencia*; Gillin, "Some Signposts for Policy," 18.

44 PA, Letter Poston to Lleras Camargo, 12, December 1960.DSP.CE.1960–1961.

45 Fluharty, *Dance of the Millions*, 191.

46 US Department of State, *Intervention*, 36.

47 US Department of State, *Intervention*, 41–45; Adams, "Social Change in Guatemala," 276.

48 Ivor Bulmer Thomas, "Conclusions de la age session de l'INCIDI," 480–481.

49 US Department of State, *Intervention*, 41–42.

50 US Department of State, *Intervention*, 36.

51 Gillin, "Some Signposts for Policy," 14, 18, 57.

52 Draper, *Castro's Revolution*; Draper, *Castroism*. Draper criticized, among others, Mills, *Listen, Yankee*.

53 Draper, *Castro's Revolution*, 11.

54 Draper, *Castro's Revolution*, 21–23.

55 Draper, *Castroism*, 57.

56 Draper, *Castro's Revolution*, 49, 43–44.

57 Draper, *Castroism*, 125.

58 Novás Calvo, "La tragedia," 76.

59 Hugh Thomas, "Middle Class Politics," 259.

60 Hugh Thomas, "Middle Class Politics," 261–263.

61 Johnson, *Political Change*, ix.

62 Johnson, "New Armies," 14; Alba, "The Latin American," 50–51.

63 Johnson, "New Armies," 14; Johnson, *The Military*, 150–152.

64 Johnson, "New Armies," 14.

65 Johnson, "New Armies," 97.

66 Johnson, "New Armies," 98.

67 Johnson, *The Military*, 149–154.

68 Johnson, "New Armies," 98, 2.

69 *Hanson's Latin American Letter*, no. 1024, November 7, 1964.

70 Laserna, *Estado*, 92; Guillén, *El poder*.

71 Geithman, "Middle Class Growth," 55.

72 JFKL, Memorandum, Schlesinger to Kennedy, March 10, 1961, Schlesinger Paper, Wh14, "Latin America, Report 3/10/61," 1.

73 JFKL, Memorandum, Schlesinger to Kennedy, March 10, 1961, Schlesinger Paper, Wh14, "Latin America, Report 3/10/61," 2.

74 JFKL, Memorandum for the President from Arthur Schlesinger, March 14, 1961, 115-008.

75 JFKL, Department of State from Schlesinger to Kennedy, 1961, first part is on the current crisis in Latin America, 2, 121-033.

76 Bagley, "Political Power," 82–84.

77 Safford and Palacios, *Colombia*, 324.

78 Bagley, "Political Power," 82.

79 Karl, *Forgotten Peace*, 33.

80 Partido Liberal Colombiano, *Programa;* Gallón Giraldo, *Quince años.*

81 PA, Letter Lleras Camargo to Poston, December 12, 1960.DSP.1960–1961.comercio .exterior.

82 ESAPAR, Camilo Torres Restrepo, "Una educación para el mundo," 1961.

83 Taffet, *Foreign Aid*, 149.

84 Rojas, "La Alianza," 98.

85 Helg, "La educación," 135–158. See figure 2.4.

86 Henderson, *Modernization*, 323–347.

Chapter 2. An Irresistible Democracy

1 CINVAR, ACMTC, December.1954–July.1955; APAR, letter from Valencia to his mother.February.1955.

2 Here I am inspired by Ferguson and Gupta, "Spatializing States," 981–1002.

3 Smith, "Observations," 3, 4, 10.

4 Smith, "Observations," 3, 4, 10; Lipset and Solari, *Elites.*

5 Smith, "Observations," 5.

6 Smith, "Observations," 3.

7 Smith, "Observations," 12.

8 Smith, "Observations," 14.

9 Reichel-Dolmatoff, "Notas sobre la clase media en Colombia (una réplica al Dr. T. Lynn Smith)."

10 Reichel-Dolmatoff, "Notas sobre la clase media en Colombia (una réplica al Dr. T. Lynn Smith)," 48.

11 Reichel-Dolmatoff, "Notas sobre la clase media en Colombia (una réplica al Dr. T. Lynn Smith)," 51, 53, 54.

12 Aristotle, *Politics* IV.11.1295b4–6.

13 Aristotle, *Politics* IV.11.1296a7–9.

14 Lipset, "Some Social Requisites," 75; Lipset, *Political Man*, 31; Hoselitz, "Economic Growth."

15 Lipset, "Some Social Requisites," 83.

16 Johnson, *Political Change*, 180.

17 Johnson, *Political Change*, 181.

18 Johnson, *Political Change*, 182; Alba, "La nueva clase media," 781–789.

19 Johnson, *Political Change*, 182.

20 Johnson, Bushnell, and McAlister, "An Interview," 653.

21 Johnson, *Political Change*, 194.

22 Johnson, *Political Change*, 194–195.

23 Johnson, *Political Change*, 10.

24 Germani, *Política y sociedad*, 241; Di Tella, *El sistema político argentino*, 118–121.

25 Germani, *Política y sociedad*, 245–247.

26 Guzmán Campos, Fals Borda, and Umaña Luna, *La Violencia*.

27 PA, Public Letter from Alberto Lleras Camargo to the Professionals of Colombia .DSPCRL.Feb.15.1960.

28 PA, Public Letter from Alberto Lleras Camargo to the Professionals of Colombia .DSPCRL.Feb.15.1960.

29 PA, Public Letter from Alberto Lleras Camargo to the Professionals of Colombia .DSPCRL.Feb.15.1960.

30 For an expanded argument on this selection process, see López, "Conscripts of Democracy," 177–195.

31 Atcon, *Latin American University*, 6.

32 Atcon, *Latin American University*, 127.

33 ESAPAR, Nannetti.Administración.Directores.DI.Jul.2.1962.1.

34 ESAPAR, Nannetti.Administración.Directores.DI.Jul.2.1962.1.

35 ESAPAR, Duverger and Tannembaum.CEP.CP.1962.1.

36 ESAPAR, Mora y Mora.Publ.RH.Serie.admin.personal.[1963].1–2.

37 ESAPAR, Mora y Mora.Publ.RH.Serie.admin.personal.[1963].1–2.

38 VGPRPAR, Gabriel Isaza, SE.tugurios.3073364C718.ICT.Dec.1966.3.

39 ESAPAR, Ruth Argandoña, La neutralidad.pública.PC.PD.1963–1964.3.

40 ESAPAR, Buen funcionario.MAP.1964–1967.3.

41 ESAPAR, Fals Borda, El liderazgo rural.SD.Nov.1962.1.

42 ESAPAR, Fals Borda, El liderazgo rural.SD.Nov.1962.1.

43 ICTAR, Caroline Ware, Lideres.mañana.Apuntes.adiestramiento.SG.GSG.DP.

44 CINVAR, Caroline Ware, Material.entrenamiento.AC.1957.

45 CINVAR, Caroline Ware, Material.entrenamiento.AC.1957.

46 CINVAR, Caroline Ware, Material.entrenamiento.AC.1957.

47 ICTAR, Caroline Ware, Lideres.mañana.Apuntes.adiestramiento.SG.GSG.DP.

48 ICTAR, Caroline Ware, Lideres.mañana.Apuntes.adiestramiento.SG.GSG.DP.

49 ESAPAR, Fals-Borda, El liderazgo rural.SD.Nov.1962.1.

50 ESAPAR, Torres Restrepo, problema.estructuración.sociología.latinoamericana .MC.IAS.1961.2.

51 ESAPAR, Torres Restrepo, problema.estructuración.sociología.latinoamericana .MC.IAS.1961.2.

52 ESAPAR, Torres Restrepo, problema.estructuración.sociología.latinoamericana .MC.IAS.1961.2.

53 ESAPAR, José Joaquín Salcedo, Conclusiones.congreso.interuniversitario.desarrollo .comunidad.MC.IAS.1963.4.

54 ESAPAR, José Joaquín Salcedo, Conclusiones.congreso.interuniversitario.desarrollo .comunidad.MC.IAS.1963.5.

55 CINVAR, Gutiérrez de Pineda, Endoculturación.sociólogos.antrópologos .SE .105a/9.PV.2.

56 CINVAR, Gutiérrez de Pineda, Introducción.antropología. SE.105a/1.PV.19 60.1–4.

57 CINVAR, Gutiérrez de Pineda, Introducción.antropología.SE.105a/16.PV.8–9.

58 CINVAR, Gutiérrez de Pineda, Introducción.antropología.SE.105a/16.PV.8–9.

59 Fals Borda, *Soluciones sociales*, 5–7, and *Campesinos de los Andes*, xiii, xviii, xix.

60 ICTAR, Material.entrenamiento.profesional.progr.vivienda.urbana.rural.SG.GSG .DP.1957–1959.

61 ICTAR, Material.entrenamiento.profesional.PV.urbana.rural.SG.GSG.DP.1957–1959.

62 ICTAR, Material.entrenamiento.profesional.PV.urbana.rural.SG.GSG.DP.1957–1959.

63 VGPRPAR, Gutiérrez de Pineda, Los.problemas.culturales.hombre colombiano .Charlas.ICT.Jul.2.1963.11.

64 VGPRPAR, Gutiérrez de Pineda, Los.problemas.culturales.hombre colombiano .Charlas.ICT.Jul.2.1963.11.

65 VGPRPAR, Gutiérrez de Pineda, Los.problemas.culturales.hombre colombiano .Charlas.ICT.Jul.2.1963.11.

66 ICTAR, Material.entrenamiento.profesional.PV.urbana.rural.SG.GSG.DP.1957–1959.

67 UNA, Propuesta.establecimiento.depart.selección/comisión de recrutamiento .profesionales.servicio.estado, febrero 9, 1959, progras.apoyo.técnico, (250), S-0175-0334-02.

68 ESAPAR, Lucrecia Tello-Marulanda and Matilde González, Mujeres.administ-rando.justicia.Sem.admin.AP.IAS.Aug.1962.2.

69 ESAPAR, Lucrecia Tello-Marulanda and Matilde González, Mujeres.administ-rando.justicia.Sem.admin.AP.IAS.Aug.1962.4.

70 ESAPAR, Lucrecia Tello-Marulanda and Matilde González, Mujeres.administ-rando.justicia.Sem.admin.AP.IAS.Aug.1962.2.

71 IFIARC, Carmen Torres Media, Progr.relac.humanas.orientación.OD.RP.1964.2.

72 Fals Borda, *Soluciones sociales*, 5.

73 IFIARC, Relaciones humanas.OD.RP.1963.2.

74 ICTAR, Apuntes.adiestramiento.SG.GSG.DP.1957–1959.

75 CINVAR, Apuntes.clase.Apuntes.entrenamiento.ICT.1957–1959.

76 CINVAR, Apuntes.clase.Apuntes.entrenamiento.ICT.1957–1959.

Chapter 3. The Productive Wealth of This Country

1 Drinot and Knight, *The Great Depression*.

2 Interview with Alejandro Hurtado.

3 Interview with Alejandro Hurtado; AHPA, Solicitud [1965].

4 Interview with Alejandro Hurtado.

5   For a historiography see Brando, "Political Economy," 103–111; Avella et al., "La consolidación del capitalismo moderno"; GRECO, *El crecimiento económico*; Robinson and Urrutia, *Economía colombiana*; Safford and Palacios, *Colombia*, 312–315.

6   Brando, "Political Economy," 99.

7   Kalmanovitz, "Colombia: La industrialización a medias," 71. For works on state/government failure, see Krueger, "Government Failures"; Brando, "Political Economy," 14–15, 16, 98–99.

8   Brando, "Political Economy," 111, 16.

9   Topik and Wells, *Second Conquest*; Kalmanovitz and López Enciso, *La agricultura*; Drinot and Knight, *The Great Depression*.

10 Brando, Political Economy.

11 Ocampo and Ros, *Oxford Handbook*; Bertola and Ocampo, *The Economic Development*; Grandin, *Empire's Workshop*, 6–7.

12 CEPAL, *El desarrollo*, 99–100.

13 Henderson, *Modernization*.

14 Henderson, *Modernization*, xiv, xv; GRECO, *El crecimiento económico*.

15 Benjamin Spiro Associates, *Credit*.

16 DANE, *La importancia*.

17 BP, *Small and Medium Industry*, 2; DAP, *Programa*, 11.

18 CEPAL, *El desarrollo*, 99–100; DANE, *La importancia*, 12.

19 Kilby, "Preface," v.

20 Hagen, "Transition in Colombia," 112, 124; see also Safford, "Significación."

21 Hagen, "Transition in Colombia," 125.

22 McClelland, "Achievement Motive," 110.

23 McClelland, *Achieving Society*.

24 Schultz, "Investment in Man," 109; Schultz, "Human Capital," 1–17.

25 In his proposal for a Latin American University, Atcon followed Schultz's notion of human capital. Atcon, *Latin American University*.

26 De la Cadena, *Indigenous Mestizos*, 4; de la Cadena, *Formaciones*, 16–27; Wade, *Race*, 124–125.

27 Schultz, "Investment in Man," 110.

28 Schultz, "Investment in Man," 110.

29 UNALAR, Lipman, "Las clases sociales y la economía colombiana," 111.

30 Lipset and Solari, *Elites*, viii.

31 Hirschman, *Strategy of Economic Development*, 14–19; Cardoso, *El empresario*, 35–39.

32 Lipset, "Values," 23; Hoselitz, *Sociological Aspects*, 62.

33 Lipman, *Colombian Entrepreneur*, 23; Fals Borda, *La educación*, 20.

34 Lipman, *Colombian Entrepreneur*, 37, 52.

35 Hagen, *On the Theory*, 96–122; Schaw, *Bonds of Work*.

36 Laserna, *Estado*, 95.

37 Lipset, "Values," 23; Hagen, "Transition in Colombia."

38 Gutiérrez de Pineda, *La familia en Colombia* and *Familia y cultura en Colombia*.

39 See also Parsons, *Antioqueño Colonization.*
40 Gutiérrez de Pineda, *Familia,* 21.
41 Gutiérrez de Pineda, *Familia,* 136–137.
42 Gutiérrez de Pineda, *Familia,* xv, 236.
43 Gutiérrez de Pineda, *Familia,* 367; Hagen, *El cambio social.* Fals Borda also said that Antioquia witnessed the emergence of "a rural middle class, the first in the country, and perhaps in all Latin America as well." Fals Borda, *Subversion and Social Change,* 96.
44 Gutiérrez de Pineda, *Familia,* 367.
45 Gutiérrez de Pineda, *Familia,* 41.
46 Gutiérrez de Pineda, *Familia,* 42.
47 Gutiérrez de Pineda, *Familia,* 166–168.
48 Gutiérrez de Pineda, *Familia,* 169–172.
49 Gutiérrez de Pineda, *Familia,* 272–273, 225–352.
50 Gutiérrez de Pineda, *Familia,* 374.
51 Gutiérrez de Pineda, *Familia,* 374.
52 Gutiérrez de Pineda, *Familia,* 384–385.
53 Gutiérrez de Pineda, *Familia,* 403–404.
54 Gutiérrez de Pineda, *Familia,* 404–409.
55 Kalmanovitz and Rivera López, *Nueva historia,* 285–308.
56 UN, Tech.Assist.mission.Colombia TE 322/1col, Resolution 73, June 8, 1962, S 0175-0310-06, UNA.
57 Staley and Nanjundan, *Economic Research*; Davenport, *Financing.*
58 BP, *Small and Medium Industry,* 2.
59 BP, *Small and Medium Industry,* 2.
60 BP, *Small and Medium Industry,* 2.
61 ACOPIAR, Letter from Staley, Davenport and Morse to Eduardo Nieto Calderón .ES.pequeña.mediana empresa.Estudios1960–1964.Sep.15.1962.
62 ACOPIAR, Letter from Staley, Davenport and Morse to Eduardo Nieto Calderón .ES.pequeña.mediana empresa.Estudios.1960–1964.Sep.15.1962.
63 ACOPIAR, Letter from Staley, Davenport and Morse to Eduardo Nieto Calderón .ES.pequeña.mediana empresa.Estudios.1960–1964.Sep.15.1962.
64 For allocation of loans, see appendix figures 8–9.
65 ACOPIAR, RE.FI.1964–1966.2.
66 ACOPIAR, RE.FI.1964–1966.2.
67 CGAIMAR, Requisitos.minimos.prestamos.DCI.1966.
68 CGAIMAR, Requisitos.minimos.prestamos.DCI.1966. Loans usually lasted from one to ten years with a 10 to 15 percent interest rate on an annual basis.
69 CGAIMAR, Requisitos.minimos.prestamos.DCI.1966.
70 CGAIMAR, Solic.informes.SIV.CIS.1966.
71 CGAIMAR, Solic.informes.SIV.CIS.1966.
72 CGAIMAR, Solic.informes.SIV.CIS.1966.
73 CGAIMAR, Solic.informes.SIV.CIS.1965.

74 CGAIMAR, IVI.supervisión.CIS.DCI.1967.
75 CGAIMAR, IVI.supervisión.CIS.DCI.1967.
76 CGAIMAR, IVI.supervisión.CIS.DCI.1965.
77 CGAIMAR, Rafael Pardo, IVI.supervisión.CIS.DCI.1965.
78 CGAIMAR, IVI.supervisión.CIS.DCI.1965.
79 CGAIMAR, Los negocios.Colombia.CIS.DCI.1965.
80 CGAIMAR, Los negocios.Colombia.CIS.DCI.1965.
81 CGAIMAR, Seminarios.crédito.orientado.CIS.DCI.1965–1967.
82 CGAIMAR, Seminarios.crédito.orientado.CIS.DCI.1965–1967.
83 CGAIMAR, Seminarios.crédito.dirigido.CIS.DCI.1966.
84 CGAIMAR, Seminarios.crédito.dirigido.CIS.DCI.1966.
85 CGAIMAR, Seminarios.crédito.dirigido.CIS.DCI.1966.
86 CGAIMAR, Seminarios.crédito.dirigido.CIS.DCI.1966.
87 ACOPIAR, INCOLDA, Empresario.moderno.ES.pequeña/mediana empresa.ES
    .1960–1964.5.

Chapter 4. Beyond Capital and Labor

1 Flórez, *Las transformaciones*, 101–128; Jaramillo and Cuervo, *La configuración*,
   114–117, 213–225; Palacios, *Between Legitimacy*, 220; see also figure 1.
2 Interview with Jorge Ortiz.
3 Marx, *Economic*; Heiman, Freeman, and Liechty, "Charting," in *Global Middle
   Classes*, 22–27.
4 Brennan, "Latin American Labor History," 360. As exceptions see French,
   "Laboring," 328; Parker, *Idea of the Middle Class*; López, "It Is Not Something,"
   151–170; Porter, *From Angel to Office Worker*.
5 Heidi Tinsman argues that working-class labor histories in Latin America have
   mainly focused on production rather than consumption. Tinsman, *Buying into
   the Regime*, 14.
6 Heiman, Freeman, and Liechty, "Charting," in *Global Middle Classes*, 21.
7 Economic histories mostly ignore the role of the service sector. Kalmanovitz and
   López Enciso, *La agricultura*; Robinson and Urrutia, *Economía colombiana*.
8 Drucker, *Landmarks of Tomorrow*, 98.
9 Schultz, "Investment in Man," 16.
10 Ratinoff, "Algunos," 5–26.
11 Ratinoff, "Algunos," 7, 25.
12 UNALAR, Williamson, unpublished paper.
13 UNALAR, Williamson, unpublished paper.
14 UNALAR, Williamson, unpublished paper.
15 UNALAR, Williamson, unpublished paper.
16 UNALAR, Lipman, "Las clases sociales y la economía colombiana," 311.
17 UNALAR, Lipman, "Las clases sociales y la economía colombiana," 315.

18 UNALAR, Lipman, "Las clases sociales y la economía colombiana," 78.
19 UNALAR, Lipman, "Las clases sociales y la economía colombiana," 78. By creating a sharp distinction between an old and a new middle class, C. Wright Mills strived to restore a proper middle-class masculinity away from the monotony of the office work and closer to revolutionary politics. Mills, *White Collar*.
20 Salazar, *Study*, 76.
21 Salazar, *Study*, 76.
22 UNESCO, *La vida laboral*, 45, 78.
23 Salazar, *Study*, 76.
24 Salazar, *Study*, 58.
25 First quote is from Salazar, *Study*, 58. Second and third quotes are from CAFAR, ACD.Sep.12.1964t.
26 CAFAR, ACD.Sep.12.1964t.
27 COLARCH, ACD.Apr.10.1961.
28 For the role of scientific management in the experience of factory labor, see Arango, *Mujer*; Farnsworth-Alvear, *Dulcinea*; Mayor Mora, *Ética*.
29 COLARCH, ACD.May.11.1962.
30 Alianza para el Progreso (n.d.), Annex: Cuadro C, p. 3.
31 Barnard, *Dilemmas of Leadership*.
32 Maslow, *Motivation*.
33 COLARCH, ME.ORH.1961–1965; CAFAR, Sem.vinculación.laboral.OP.1966.
34 COLARCH, Memorias.seminarios.selección.ORH.Feb.15.1963.
35 BRAR, MS.OP.1961.
36 COLARCH, Memorias.seminarios.selección.ORH.Feb.15.1963.
37 COLARCH, Memorias.seminarios.selección.ORH.Feb.15.1963.
38 COLARCH, MS.ORH.Sep.1961.
39 COLARCH, MS.ORH.Sep.1961.
40 COLARCH, MS.ORH.Sep.1961.
41 COLARCH, MS.ORH.Sep.1961.
42 COLARCH, Código.ética.ORH.1962.11.
43 Flórez, *Las transformaciones*, 116–125.
44 CAFAR, ME.OP.1966.1–2.
45 COLARCH, Colseguros.empresa.pionera.ACD.Mar.4.1962.2.
46 COLARCH, ME.ORH.1966.1–2.
47 CAFAR, PS.OP.1964–1965.
48 COLARCH, IS.ORH.1959–1963.5.
49 COLARCH, IS.ORH.1959–1963.5.
50 COLARCH, IS.ORH.1959–1963.5.
51 CAFAR, letter Arcesio Guerrero to ORH.OP.Nov.11.1966.1. These conclusions on hiring preferences come from a reading of 4,000 CVs in the companies' archives under study, about 174 CVs per year. For statistical descriptions of these hiring policies see https://www.aricardolopezpedreros.com/.
52 CAFAR, PS.OP.1964–1965.

53 COLARCH, MP.ORH.1963.12.

54 CAFAR, CAFAM.familia.OP.1965.4.

55 COLARCH, MP.ORH.[1963].11.

56 AAR, MP.OP.[1964].5.

57 BRAR, MS.ORH.

58 COLARCH, MP.ORH.[1963].11.

59 CAFAR, CAFAM.familia.OP.1965.3.

60 COLARCH, MP.ORH.1963.13.

61 CAFAR, CAFAM.familia.OP.1965.3.

62 CAFAR, CAFAM.familia.OP.1965.3.

63 CAFAR, CAFAM.familia.OP.1965.4.

64 AAR, MP.OP.1964.9.

65 COLARCH, ACD.Mar.4.1962.2.

66 COLARCH, ACD.Mar.4.1962.2.

67 COLARCH, Info.conf.selección.ORH.1963–1965.

68 COLARCH, Info.conf.selección.ORH.1963–1965.

69 COLARCH, Info.conf.selección.ORH.1963–1965.

70 COLARCH, Info.conf.selección.ORH.1963–1965.

71 COLARCH, MP.ORH.1964.21.

72 COLARCH, ACD.June.12.1961.

73 COLARCH, MP.ORH.1963.21.

74 COLARCH, MP.ORH.1964.17.

75 BRAR, *Revista Relaciones*, V1.10l.2, Apr.1963.4.

Chapter 5. In the Middle of the Mess

1 Henderson, *Modernization*, xiv, xv.

2 For quote see Safford and Palacios, *Colombia*, 297; Henderson, *Modernization*, 342–343. Following the Lebret report of 1958, Robert Dix estimated the size of the middle class at about 15 percent of Colombians. Robert Dix, *Colombia*, 56. According to the census of 1951, which grouped together independent employees, white-collar workers, and professionals, the middle class could comprise almost 45 percent. Workers comprised 32 percent. And in 1964 the percentage of the middle class increased to 52 percent. See Archila, "El Frente Nacional," 212; see figure 1 and https://www.aricardolopezpedreros.com/.

3 Interview with Alberto Valencia.

4 Palacios, *Between Legitimacy*, 179–180.

5 Palacios, *Between Legitimacy*, 171.

6 Palacios, *Between Legitimacy*, 226.

7 Henderson, *Modernization*, xiv, xv.

8 Henderson, *Modernization*, xiv, xv, 342. See appendix figures 2 and 4.

9 González, *Educación*, 110–111.

10 Flórez, *Las transformaciones*, 90.

11 Flórez, *Las transformaciones*, 90.

12 Arias Trujillo, *Historia de Colombia contemporánea*, 311–362.

13 Safford and Palacios, *Colombia*, 307.

14 Interview with Marta Jaramillo.

15 Interview with Marta Jaramillo.

16 MJPA.

17 In his study on UNAL students in 1961, Williamson reported that 80 percent of the students considered themselves part of the middle class. The lower middle class was reported at 5.4 percent, the upper middle at 7.6 percent, and the upper class at 6.7 percent. Williamson, *El estudiante*, 13–16.

18 Interview with Marta Jaramillo.

19 Interview with Marta Flórez.

20 Interview with Marta Flórez.

21 Interview with Alicia Perdomo.

22 Interview with Alicia Perdomo.

23 APAR; see figure 4 in the appendix.

24 Interview with Alicia Perdomo.

25 Interview with Alicia Perdomo.

26 Interview with Alicia Perdomo.

27 APAR, Untitled.paper.[1962].3–4, 7–8; APAR, Mujer.hoy.[1963].

28 APAR, PN.[1960].

29 APAR, PN.[1960].

30 APAR, PN.[1960].

31 APAR, PN.[1960].

32 ICTAR, Eval.lab.SC.DSS.SA.1963–1965.

33 ICTAR, Letter José Tarazona to Arturo Bernal, DSS.SA.Feb.11.1962.

34 ICTAR, Letter José Tarazona to Arturo Bernal, DSS.SA.Feb.11.1962.

35 ICTAR, Letter José Tarazona to Arturo Bernal, DSS.SA.Feb.11.1962.

36 ICTAR, Letter José Tarazona to Arturo Bernal, DSS.SA.Feb.11.1962.

37 ICTAR, Letter José Tarazona to Arturo Bernal, DSS.SA.Feb.11.1962.

38 ICTAR, Eval.lab.SC.DSS.SA.1963–1965.

39 ICTAR, RTC.IN.DI.ST.1961–1962.

40 CVPAR, RTC.AR.DP.ST.1961–1964.

41 ICTAR, RTC.IN.DI.ST.1961–1962.

42 ICTAR, RTC.IN.DI.ST.1961–1962.

43 IFIARC, Notas.encuentros.JD.GG.Feb.15.1959.2–3.

44 Here I am inspired by Stoler, *Along the Archival Grain*, 57–102.

45 IFIARC, Inf.material.fábricas.Bogotá.DEE.ST.1963–1965.

46 IFIARC, Inf.material.fábricas.Bogotá.DEE.ST.1963–1965.

47 IFIARC, Inf.material.fábricas.Bogotá.DEE.ST.1963–1965.

48 IFIARC, Info.prof.industrias.automotriz.Bta.DEE.ST.1961–1963.

49 IFIARC, Info.prof.industrias.automotriz.Bta.DEE.ST.1961–1963.

50 IFIARC, Info.prof.industrias.automotriz.Bogotá.DEE.ST.1961–1963.

51 IFIARC, Info.prof.industrias.automotriz.Bogotá.DEE.ST.1961–1963.

52 IFIARC, Info.prof.industrias.automotriz.Bogotá.DEE.ST.1961–1963.

53 IFIARC, Info.prof.industrias.automotriz.Bogotá.DEE.ST.1961–1963.

54 IFIARC, Info.prof.industrias.automotriz.Bogotá.DEE.ST.1961–1963.

55 IFIARC, Info.prof.industrias.automotriz.Bogotá.DEE.ST.1961–1963.

56 IFIARC, RTC.metalúrgico.Bogotá.DEE.ST.1961–1963.

57 IFIARC, Notas.campo.cementos.DEE.ST.1959–1963.

58 IFIARC, Notas.campo.cementos.DEE.ST.1959–1963.

59 IFIARC, Visitas.campo.automotriz.Bogotá.DEE.ST.1961–1962.

60 IFIARC, Conf.profesionales.acero.Boyaca.DEE.ST.1963.

61 IFIARC, Conf.profesionales.acero.Boyaca.DEE.ST.1963.

62 IFIARC, Eval.personal.OP.1959–1963.

63 IFIARC, Eval.personal.DP.ST.1961–1963.

64 IFIARC, letter Jesús Antonio Toro and Gabriel Millamarín to Alfredo Vanegas .DP.ST.Sep.7.1963.

65 IFIARC, letter Jesús Antonio Toro and Gabriel Millamarín to Alfredo Vanegas .DP.ST.Sep.7.1963.

66 IFIARC, letter Jesús Antonio Toro and Gabriel Millamarín to Alfredo Vanegas .DP.ST.Sep.7.1963.

67 Interview with Alberto Valencia.

68 Interview with Alberto Valencia.

69 Interview with Alberto Valencia.

70 AVPA, Report.trabajo.campo.[1958].

71 AVPA, Report.trabajo.campo.[1958].

72 Interview with Alberto Valencia.

73 ICTAR, Notas.trabajo.campo.material.entrenamiento.AR.ST.1959–1961.

74 ICTAR, Notas.trabajo.campo.material.entrenamiento.AR.ST.1959–1961.

75 ICTAR, Notas.trabajo.campo.material.entrenamiento.AR.ST.1959–1961.

76 ICTAR, Notas.trabajo.campo.material.entrenamiento.AR.ST.1959–1961. See also STACAR, MA.RE, veredas.cundinamarquesas.SD.PRD.1959–1963.

77 ICTAR, Notas.campo.Quiroga.AR.ST.1958–1965.

78 ICTAR, Notas.campo.DV.ST.1960–1966.

79 ICTAR, Informes.eval.trabajo.DP.SG.1959–1963.

80 ICTAR, Informes.eval.trabajo.DP.SG.1959–1963.

81 ICTAR, Eval.laborales.SC.DSS.SA.1963–1965.

82 ICTAR, Eval.laborales.SC.DSS.SA.1963–1965.

83 ICTAR, Eval.laborales.SC.DSS.SA.1963–1965.

84 ICTAR, Notas.campo.Quiroga.AR.ST.1958–1965.

85 ICTAR, Notas.trabajo.campo.material.entrenamiento.DP.SG.1959–1961.

86 ICTAR, Notas.trabajo.campo.material.entrenamiento.PRU.DPG.ST.1959–1961.

87 ICTAR, Notas.trabajo.campo.material.entrenamiento.PRU.DPG.ST.1959–1961.

88 ICTAR, Notas.trabajo.campo.DV.PRU.ST.1961–1966.

89 INCORAR, NTC.EN.SA.1960–1965.

90 Interview with Clemencia Casas.

91 Interview with Clemencia Casas.

92 Interview with Clemencia Casas.

93 Interview with Jorge Ortiz.

94 Interview with Jorge Ortiz.

95 Interview with Margarita Delgado de Ortiz.

96 Interview with Margarita de Martínez.

97 Interview with Margarita de Martínez.

98 Interview with Margarita de Martínez.

99 Interview with Isabel Delgado de Téllez.

100 Interview with Isabel Delgado de Téllez.

101 COLARCH, Concursos.internos.ORH.DA.1963.

102 COLARCH, Concursos.internos.ORH.DA.1963.

103 COLARCH, Concursos.internos.ORH.DA.1963.

104 COLARCH, Concursos.internos.ORH.Requisitos.1964.11.

105 COLARCH, Concursos.internos.ORH.Requisitos.1964.12.

106 COLARCH, Concursos.internos.ORH.Requisitos.1964.12.

107 COLARCH, Julio Vaca.DA.ORH.1963.2.

108 COLARCH, Julio Vaca.DA.ORH.1963.2.

109 COLARCH, Jorge Franco.DA.ORH.1964.1–4.

110 COLARCH, Jorge Franco.DA.ORH.1964.1–4.

111 COLARCH, GP.ORH.1961–1965.

112 COLARCH, GP.ORH.1961–1965.

113 COLARCH, GP.ORH.1961–1965.

114 CAFAR, Sem.servicio.cliente.OP.1964.

115 CAFAR, Sem.servicio.cliente.OP.1964.

116 COLARCH, GP.ORH.1962–1966.

117 COLARCH, GP.ORH.1962–1966.

118 BRAR, Carlos Salcedo.GP.OP.1964–1967.

119 BRAR, Jorge Pineda.GP.ORH.1964–1967.

120 COLARCH, José Ramirez.GP.ORH.1962–1966.

121 COLARCH, Grupo.discusión.GP.ORH.1961–1965.3.

122 COLARCH, Grupo.discusión.GP.ORH.1961–1965.3.

123 COLARCH, Hernán Pulido.GP.ORH.1962–1966.

124 COLARCH, Hernán Pulido.GP.ORH.1962–1966.

125 COLARCH, GP.ORH.1962–1966.

126 COLARCH, GP.ORH.1962–1966.

127 COLARCH, GP.ORH.1962–1966.

128 COLARCH, GP.ORH.1962–1966.

Chapter 6. A Revolution for a Middle-Class Society

1 MOCLAMAR, CCB.SC.Sep.1959.3.

2 MOCLAMAR, CCB.SC.Sep.1959.5.

3 PA, Letter Vasco Vejarano to Fernando Londoño.MG.Nov.27.1961; PA, CCCME .Declaración.principios.clase media.colombiana.MG.1961.1.

4 MOCLAMAR, MOCLAM, Organismo.servicio.intereses.clase.media.SC.1963.2–3.

5 MOCLAMAR, MOCLAM, Organismo.servicio.intereses.clase.media.SC.1963.2–3.

6 MOCLAMAR, CCCME, Declaración.principios.clase media.colombiana.MG.1961.4.

7 MOCLAMAR, MOCLAM, Organismo.servicio.intereses.clase.media.SC.1963.2–3.

8 Adamovsky, *Historia*; Gilbert, *Mexico's Middle Class*; García Quesada, *Formación*; Guillén Martínez, El poder; Torres Rivas, *Revoluciones*, 136, 176.

9 Archila, *Idas y venidas*, 421–422; Sánchez, *¡Huelga!*

10 Palacios, *Between Legitimacy*, 180; González, *El poder*, 324; Pécaut, *Crónica*; Tirado Mejía, *Los años*, 60.

11 Archila, *Idas y venidas*, 131–142.

12 MOCLAMAR, CCB.SC.Sep.1959.12.

13 MOCLAMAR, CCB.SC.Feb.1961.21.

14 MOCLAMAR, Manifesto.SC.1963.4.

15 MOCLAMAR, Manifesto.SC.1963.4.

16 MOCLAMAR, CTCC.SC.Jan.1962.11–14.

17 MOCLAMAR, CTCC.SC.Jan.1962.11–14.

18 MOCLAMAR, CTCC.SC.Jan.1962.11–14.

19 MOCLAMAR, CTCC.SC.Jan.1962.11–14.

20 MOCLAMAR, CTCC.SC.Jan.1962.15.

21 MOCLAMAR, CTCC.SC.Jan.1962.15.

22 MOCLAMAR, CTCC.SC.Mar.1962.28–35.

23 RMPAR, Letter Régulo Millán Puentes and Vasco Vejarano to Guillermo León Valencia.Dec.1962.2.

24 MOCLAMAR, CCB.Com.trabajo.exterior.SC.BR.Feb.19.1962.3.

25 MOCLAMAR, CCB.Com.trabajo.exterior.SC.BR.Feb.19.1962.3.

26 MOCLAMAR, CCB.Com.trabajo.exterior.SC.BR.Feb.19.1962.3.

27 MOCLAMAR, CCB.Com.trabajo.exterior.SC.BR.SC.July.1964.

28 MOCLAMAR, CCB.Com.trabajo.exterior.SC.BR.SC.July.1964.

29 MOCLAMAR, CCB.Com.trabajo.exterior.SC.BR.SC.Mar.1962.3.

30 MOCLAMAR, CCB.Com.trabajo.exterior.SC.BR.SC.Mar.1962.3.

31 MOCLAMAR, SECB.SC.Sep.1963.7–9.

32 MOCLAMAR, SECB.SC.Sep.1963.7–9.

33 Interview with Régulo Millán Puentes.

34 Interview with Régulo Millán Puentes.

35 RMPAR, Por la clase media.1963.

36 RMPAR, Una clase vibrante.1964.

37 RMPAR, Una clase vibrante.1964.

38 RMPAR, Una clase vibrante.1964.
39 RMPAR, Democracia.1963.
40 Interview with Régulo Millán Puentes.
41 Interview with Régulo Millán Puentes.
42 MOCLAMAR, CCB.Secretaría.clase media.SC.1964.
43 MOCLAMAR, CCB.Secretaría.clase media.SC.1964.
44 MOCLAMAR, CCB.GuillermoLeónValencia.SC.Sep.1964.
45 MOCLAMAR, CCB.Vida democrática.SC.Jan.1965.
46 MOCLAMAR, CCB.Vida democrática.SC.Jan.1965.
47 MOCLAMAR, CCB.Vida democrática.SC.Jan.1965.
48 LMMCA, Carta a la nación.[1961].
49 Interview with Fernando Agudelo.
50 LMMCA, Editorial.NSP.May.1964.1.
51 LMMCA, Israel Guerrero, Nuestra.lucha.NSP.May.1964.
52 LMMCA, Israel Guerrero, Nuestra.lucha.NSP.May.1964.
53 LMMCA, Israel Guerrero, Nuestra.lucha.NSP.May.1964.
54 LMMCA, Israel Guerrero, Nuestra.lucha.NSP.May.1964.
55 LMMCA, Antonio Vega.Orgullo profesional.NSP.Aug.1963.8.
56 Interview with Germán Giraldo.
57 Interview with Germán Giraldo.
58 Interview with Germán Giraldo.
59 GGPA, La.importancia.nuestro.país.[1965].
60 Interview with Germán Giraldo; interview with Clodomiro Rodríguez.
61 CRPA, Discurso.inaguración.Congr.Bolivariano.contadores.Jul.24.1964.
62 CRPA, Discurso.inaguración.Congr.Bolivariano.contadores.Jul.24.1964.
63 CRPA, Discurso.inaguración.Congr.Bolivariano.contadores.Jul.24.1964.
64 CRPA, Discurso.inaguración.Congr.Bolivariano.contadores.Jul.24.1964.
65 CRPA, Discurso.inaguración.Congr.Bolivariano.contadores.Jul.24.1964.
66 Interview with Guillermo Ramírez.
67 Interview with Luis Torres Castro.
68 Interview with Emilio Guzmán.
69 ANEBRE was founded in 1964, first in Medellín and then in Bogotá.
70 ANEBRAR, AN.May.1966.1.2.2.
71 ANEBRAR, AN.May.1966.1.2.2.
72 ANEBRAR, AN.May.1966.1.2.2.
73 ANEBRAR, AN.May.1964.1.2.4.
74 COLARCH, RAS.July.1965.3.1.3.
75 ANEBRAR, AN.May.1996.1.2.4.
76 COLARCH, RAC.Aug.1967.3.4.1.
77 COLARCH, RAC.Aug.1967.3.4.1.
78 COLARCH, RAC.Aug.1967.3.4.1.
79 ANEBRAR, AN.May.1966.1.2.2.
80 Interview with Alejandro Hurtado.

81 Interview with Alejandro Hurtado.

82 ACOPIAR, CI.PU.Nov.1965.

83 ACOPIAR, CI.PU.Nov.1965.

84 ACOPIAR, Roberto Carbonell, Tributación.milimétrica.DS.DP.

85 ACOPIAR, CI.PU.Nov.1965.1.

86 ACOPIAR, CI.PU.Nov.1965.1.

87 ACOPIAR, CI.PU.Nov.1965.1.

88 ACOPIAR, Petición.año.nuevo.PT.DP.Dec.1965.

89 ACOPIAR, Petición.año.nuevo.PT.DP.Dec.1965.

90 ACOPIAR, CI.PU.Nov.1965.1.1.3.

91 ACOPIAR, CI.PU.Nov.1965.1.1.3.

92 ACOPIAR, CI.PU.Feb.1966.2.4–5.3.

93 ACOPIAR, CI.PU.Feb.1966.2.4–5.3.

94 ACOPIAR, CI.PU.2.3.3.

95 ACOPIAR, CI.PU.2.3.3.

96 ACOPIAR, CI.PU.2.3.3.

97 ACOPIAR, CI.PU.2.3.3.

98 ACOPIAR, CI.PU.May.1966.2.7.12.

99 ACOPIAR, Empresas.modestas.SE.Apr.1966.

100 ACOPIAR, Colombia Industrial.SE.PU.Nov.1975.12.

101 ACOPIAR, Colombia Industrial.SE.PU.Nov.1975.12.

102 ACOPIAR, Colombia Industrial.SE.PU.Nov.1975.12.

103 ACOPIAR, Colombia Industrial.SE.PU.Nov.1975.12.

104 AHPA, El futuro de la nación.

105 AHPA, El futuro de la nación.

106 AHPA, El futuro de la nación.

107 ACOPIAR, Estadocantinero.PR.VA.

108 ACOPIAR, Estadocantinero.PR.VA.

109 UNCLAMECOLAR, Aristobulo Forero, Democracia.para.pueblo.Oct.1971.

110 UNCLAMECOLAR, La clase media.contribuye.democratización.pais.AH.3.

111 LMMCA, Guillermo González, Manifestaciones.antidemocráticas.NSP.Dec.1964 .7–8.

112 LMMCA, Guillermo González, Manifestaciones.antidemocráticas.NSP.Dec.1964 .7–8.

113 LMMCA, Juan Vargas, Llamamiento.cordura.NSP.Oct.1964.1–2.

114 LMMCA, Juan Vargas, Llamamiento.cordura.NSP.Oct.1964.1–2.

115 LMMCA, Juan Vargas, Llamamiento.cordura.NSP.Oct.1964.1–2.

116 LMMCA, Juan Vargas, Llamamiento.cordura.NSP.Oct.1964.1–2.

117 LMMCA, Más.capaces.NSP.Dec.1964.7–8.

118 Ruiz Novoa, "Resucitar," 28.

119 Ruiz Novoa, "Resucitar," 28.

120 ACOPIAR, Estado.cantinero.PR.VA.

121 ACOPIAR, Estado.cantinero.PR.VA.

122 *La Nueva Prensa*, February 26, 1965, 61.
123 UNCLAMECOLAR, Discurso Gustavo Rojas Pinilla; Ruiz Novoa, "La reforma," 92.
124 Ruiz Novoa, "La organización," 136.
125 Ayala Diago, *La explosión*.
126 FEDEPROCOLAR, JDN.PR.Sep.12.1965.1–13.
127 PA, Letter Gabriel Castaño to Lleras Camargo.AD.SG.Oct.3.1961.1–19.
128 PA, Letter Gabriel Castaño to Lleras Camargo.AD.SG.Oct.3.1961.1–19.
129 FEDEPROCOLAR, Oscar Duque, Minutes.conferencia.tripartita.CF.VG.Feb.1967 .1–15.
130 ANEBRAR, AN.May.31.1966.2.4.4.
131 ANEBRAR, AN.May.31.1966.2.4.4.
132 ANEBRAR, AN.May.31.1966.2.4.4.
133 UNCLAMECOLAR, Nucleos.familiares.MNF.NF.[1977].1.
134 UNCLAMECOLAR, Nucleos.familiares.MNF.NF.[1977].1.
135 ICTAR, José Manual Sandoval, Familia.moderna.RL.SA.Oct.17.1977.
136 UNCLAMECOLAR, Discurso.Gustavo.Rojas Pinilla.
137 UNCLAMECOLAR, Discurso.Gustavo.Rojas Pinilla.
138 *Asociación*, August 1967, 2.
139 *Asociación*, August 1967, 2.
140 *Asociación*, August 1967, 2.
141 *Asociación*, August 1967, 2.
142 UNCLAMECOLAR, Discurso.Gustavo.Rojas Pinilla.

Chapter 7. A Real Revolution, a Real Democracy

1 Ghodsee, *Left Side of History*.
2 Interview with Marta Jaramillo.
3 Interview with Alberto Otalora.
4 Interview with Marta Espinosa.
5 Interview with Hernando Rincón.
6 Interview with Marta Jaramillo.
7 Interview with Carlos Restrepo; interview with Arcadio Benavides; these memories evoked Arenas, *La guerrilla*.
8 Interview with Leonardo Betancour.
9 Interview with Leonardo Betancour.
10 Interview with Roberto Solano.
11 For exceptions see Archila, *Una historia inconclusa*; Aguilera Morales, *Subjetividades*; Aguilera Peña, *Contrapoder*.
12 Gaviria, *Sofismas*.
13 Posada Carbó, *La nación*; Caballero Argáez et al., *Cincuenta años*. The following studies are published in *Contribución*: Duncan, "Exclusion," 254–256;

Giraldo Ramírez, "Política," 473–480; Brands, *Latin America's Cold War*, 82, 97; Pécaut, *Guerra*.

14   Vanegas, *Todas son iguales*, 384–437. For a critical reading, see Beverley, *Latin Americanism*, 95–109.

15   Hylton, "Experience of Defeat," 23–24; González, *Poder*, 366; Delgado Guzmán, "El experimento," 121–140; Bergquist, "La izquierda colombiana." For an expansion of this argument, see López, "De debilidades, fracasos y paradojas."

16   Vega Cantor, *Gente muy rebelde*, 30.

17   Several interviews.

18   On this point, I have found inspiration in Ghodsee, *Left Side of History*.

19   Vega Cantor, *Gente muy rebelde*, 30.

20   Palacios, *Between Legitimacy*, 170–213.

21   Palacios, *Between Legitimacy*, 190.

22   CCPA, Notes.

23   CCPA, Notes.

24   CCPA, Notes.

25   IFIARC, Notas.campo.cementos.DEE.ST.1959–1963.

26   IFIARC, Actas.visitas, SG.DA.MT.Feb.11.1965.

27   I am drawing on David Scott, *Stuart Hall's Voice*, 85–115.

28   CRPA, Diaries.1969.

29   CRPA, Diaries.1969.

30   CRPA, Diaries.1969.

31   CRPA, Diaries.1969; CRPA, Diaries.1970.12, 21–23.

32   CRPA, Diaries.1969.

33   CRPA, Diaries.1969.

34   COLARCH, ICP.ORH.Mar.4.1967.2.

35   COLARCH, ICP.ORH.Apr.29.1969.7.

36   ADPA, Letter Antonio Díaz to office of HR.May.11.1968.1.

37   ADPA, Letter Antonio Díaz to office of HR.May.11.1968.1.

38   ADPA, Letter Antonio Díaz to office of HR.May.11.1968.1.

39   Urrutia, *Winners*, 107.

40   PA, Letter Ramón Arévalo to Lleras Restrepo.238.SP.Jan.15.1968.2.

41   PA, Letter Ramón Arévalo to Lleras Restrepo.238.SP.Jan.15.1968.2.

42   Safford and Palacios, *Colombia*, 331.

43   Mace, "Ways of Reading."

44   CLPA, Notes.1966–1968.

45   ANEBRAR, AD.DS.May.15.1966.

46   ANEBRAR, AD.DS.Apr.12.1967.

47   ANEBRAR, AD.DS.Apr.12.1967.

48   CRPA, Notes.1969–1970.12, 21, 22, 23.

49   CRPA, Punto de partida.1968.

50   CRPA, Diary.1970, 12.

51   CRPA, Diary.1969, 11; Diary.1970, 12, 21–23.

52 CRPA, Marta Harnecker, Concepto.Marxista.Clases.Sociales.1969.2; CRPA, Marx y Engels, The Communist Manifesto.1965.42–43.

53 CRPA, Marta Harnecker, Concepto.Marxista.Clases.Sociales.1969.2; CRPA, Marx y Engels, The Communist Manifesto.1965.42–43.

54 CRPA, Diary.Dec.1969.

55 CRPA, Diary.Dec.1969.

56 CRPA, Diary.Dec.6.1970.

57 CRPA, Louis Althusser.Leyendo el capital.1969.JUCOROJO.3–8.

58 CRPA, 1969.

59 CRPA, 1969.

60 CRPA, 1969.

61 Interview with Cecilia Serrano; CRPA, NT.1969

62 CSPA, Guevara, Guerrilla.Warfare.NT.[1964–1967].

63 CSPA, NT.[1964–1967].

64 CSPA, NT.[1964–1967].

65 CSPA, NT.[1964–1967].

66 CRPA, Profesores independientes.DC.N1.[1975–1976].

67 Calvo Isaza and Parra Salazar, Medellín.

68 Lernoux, Cry of the People, 37.

69 Lernoux, Cry of the People, 37.

70 RSPAR, PN.1968–1971.

71 Interview with Marta Jaramillo.

72 Interview with Marta Jaramillo.

73 MJPA, PN.[1969–1971].

74 ICTAR, Profesionales.servicio.estado.ND.DP.GSG.SG.1968–1971, 2.

75 PCC-ML, Combatiendo, 45.

76 PCC-ML, Combatiendo, 91.

77 M19AR, Encuesta.EC.1975. This analysis is informed by Robinson, Black Marxism, and Rancière, Proletariat Nights.

78 CRPA, PCC-ML.Proletarización.1969.

79 PCC-ML, Combatiendo, 69, 253.

80 CRPA, Carlos Duplat, Siete.pecados.capitales.pequeños burgueses.[1969].

81 CRPA, Carlos Duplat, Siete.pecados.capitales.pequeños burgueses.[1969].

82 CRPA, Mao Tse-tung, Las Tres Permanentes.[1971].

83 CRPA, Carlos Duplat, Siete.pecados.capitales.pequeños burgues.[1969].

84 PCC-ML, Combatiendo; CRPA, Moral revolucionaria.moral burguesa.[1969].

85 RSPA, Diary.1972.

86 For such description, see Aguilera Morales, Subjetividades; Archila, Idas y venidas.

87 CRPA, Una educación.economia.moderna.material.discusión.1972.5; Ministerio de Educación Nacional, Proyecto de ley.

88 CRPA, Plan.Univer.democrática.APUN.1972; M19AR, Educación.masas.CE.1975; FECOCAR, CI.July.21.1973.6.

89 CRPA, Plan.Univer.democrática.APUN.1972.

90 FECOCAR, CI.July.21.1973.6.

91 M19AR, Educación.masas.CE.1975.

92 M19AR, ¿Qué somos y qué debemos hacer? CE.[1976].

93 FECOCAR, Declaración.princ.educativos.DP.VA.Aug.1974; Paulo Freire, *Peda-gogía del oprimido.*

94 M19AR, ¿Qué somos y qué debemos hacer? CE.[1976].

95 CRPA, Análisis.Rockefeller.1969.1–5.

96 CRPA, Análisis.Rockefeller.1969.1–5.

97 CRPA, Profesores independientes.DOCUMENTO N1, signed as Juan sin miedo, [1975–1976].

98 CRPA, Profesores independientes.DC.N1.[1975–1976].

99 M19AR, ¿Qué somos y qué debemos hacer? CE.[1976].

100 CRPA, Profesores MOIR.Avance.Profesoral.1976(1).Nov.1976.5.3.

101 RSPA, Educación.masas.[1974].

102 CRPA, Convocatoria.prof.universitarios.1976.Nov.5.1976.

103 CRPA, Profesores.independientes.Agonia.academia.1972(2).Apr.3.1976.

104 CRPA, Profesores.independientes.Agonia.academia.1972(2).Apr.3.1976.

105 CRPA, Profesores independientes.Documento.1975.6.1975.

106 CRPA, Profesores independientes.Teoría.no.volumen.pamfletos.1976(2).Apr.3 .1976.4.

107 CRPA, Profesores independientes.Politizar.Universidad.1976.Apr.3.1976.5.

108 M19AR, Cuadros.preparados.CE.1974.

109 Victor Bonilla et al., *Causa popular*, 17–18.

110 Victor Bonilla et al., *Causa popular*, 17–18.

111 Rappaport, *Intercultural Utopias*, 86–87. Elsewhere I expand these arguments; see López-Pedreros, "Class and Gender of De-coloniality."

112 Victor Bonilla et al., *Causa popular*, 18.

113 Fals Borda, *Ciencia propia*, 113.

114 M19AR, Papel.hacia afuera.CE.15.1975.

115 CRPA, Nosotras las maestras.1976(2).Sep.4.1976. 4. For a study on feminist move-ments in Bogotá, see Gómez, *Dinámicas.*

116 CRPA, Nosotras las maestras.1976(2).Sep.4.1976.4.

117 CRPA, Nosotras las maestras.1976(2).Sep.4.1976.4.

118 CRPA, Nosotras las maestras.1976(2).Sep.4.1976.4.

119 CRPA, Nosotras las maestras.1976(2).Sep.4.1976.3.

120 CRPA, Nosotras las maestras.1976(2).Sep.4.1976.3.

121 CRPA, Nosotras las maestras.1976(2).Sep.4.1976.3.

122 CRPA, Nosotras las maestras.1976(2).Sep.4.1976.3.

123 CRPA, L Unita.Louis Althuser.1970.Jan.28.1970.35.

124 CRPA, L Unita.Louis Althuser.1970.Jan.28.1970.35.

125 CRPA, L Unita.Louis Althuser.1970.Jan.28.1970.35.

126 FECOCAR, Unidad.revolucionaria.SE.EP.July.1973.5.

127 FECOCAR, Unidad.revolucionaria.SE.EP.July.1973.5.

128 FECOCAR, Educación.proletaria.ES.SE.Sep.1974.5–7.

129 FECOCAR, Educación.proletaria.ES.SE.Sep.1974.5–7.

130 Molano Camargo, "El campo es leña." For a history of ANUC, see Zamosc, *Agrarian Question*.

131 Alvarez, "Empresa," 124.

132 Alvarez, "Empresa," 126.

133 Alvarez, "Empresa," 126.

134 Naranjo and Ruiz, "Problema," 15.

135 Naranjo and Ruiz, "Problema," 21.

136 RIAS, *La historia*.

137 *Alternativa*, no. 1, February 18, 1974, 1.

138 *Alternativa*, no. 19, October 28–November 10, 1974, 8, 11.

139 *Alternativa*, no. 19, October 28–November 10, 1974, 8–11.

140 AOPA, los burgueses.ayer.hoy.1976.6–7.

141 AOPA, los burgueses.ayer.hoy.1976.6–7.

142 AOPA, los burgueses.ayer.hoy.1976.6–7.

143 AOPA, los burgueses.ayer.hoy.1976.6–7.

144 AOPA, los burgueses.ayer.hoy.1976.6–7.

145 AOPA, los burgueses.ayer.hoy.1976.6–7.

146 AOPA, los burgueses.ayer.hoy.1976.6–7.

147 AOPA, los burgueses.ayer.hoy.1976.6–7.

148 Gabriel García Marquez, "Chile, el golpe y los gringos," *Alternativa*, no. 1, 1974.

149 RSPA, PN.1975–1980.[1975].

150 RSPA, PN.1975–1980.[1975]; see also Mariño et al., *Lucharemos*.

151 RSPA, PN.1975–1980.[1975].

152 RSPA, PN.1975–1980.[1975].

153 M19AR, Pongámonos.acuerdo.CE.[1976].

154 M19AR, Pongámonos.acuerdo.CE.[1976].

155 CRPA, Nosotras.maestras. *¿De qué hablamos nosotras?*. 1976(2).June1976.1.

156 CSPA, Mujer.Hoy.1975–1980; Belotti, *Little Girls*.

157 CSPA, Mujer.Hoy.1975–1980.

158 CSPA, Mujer.Hoy.1975–1980.

159 CSPA, Mujer.Hoy.1975–1980.

160 CSPA, Mujer.Hoy.1975–1980.

161 For an account of the strike, see Greco, *Unionized Professionals*.

162 ASMEDASAR, Paro.médico.PR.1976.Dec.1976.6.

163 *Acción Médica*, March 1976, 3.

164 "Cuatro inquietudes," *El Espectador*, September 19, 1976, 2-A.

165 "El monstruo por desmontar," *El Espectador*, October 5, 1976, P2A.

166 *Tribuna Roja*, no. 4, December 1976.

167 ASMEDASAR, Paro.médico.PR.1976.Dec.1976.1–3; see Vasco Uribe, *Estado*; Fergusson, *Esquema crítico*.

168 ASMEDASAR, Paro.médico.PR.1976.Dec.1976.4.

169 ASMEDASAR, ¿Quiénes somos?PR.1976.Sep.1976.2–3.

170 ASMEDASAR, *La.industralización.medicina*.PR.1976.Oct.4.1976.

171 ASMEDASAR, Miseria.pobreza.PR.1976.Nov.1976.1.

172 ASMEDASAR, Medicina.PR.1976.Nov.1976.11.

173 ASMEDASAR, ¿Quiénes.somos?PR.1976.Nov.1976.2–3.

174 ASMEDASAR, ¿Quiénes.somos?PR.1976.Nov.1976.2–3.

175 ASMEDASAR, Paro.médico.PR.1976.Oct.1976.1–3.

176 ASMEDASAR, ¿Quiénes.somos?PR.1976.Nov.1976.2–3.

177 ASMEDASAR, Miseria.pobreza.PR.1976.Nov.1976.2.

178 ASMEDASAR, ¿Quiénes.somos?PR.1976.Sep.1976.2–3.

179 ASMEDASAR, Verdad.paro.CP.AM.Sep.1976.

180 ASMEDASAR, Verdad.paro.CP.AM.Sep.1976.

181 ASMEDASAR, ¿Quiénes.somos?PR.1976.Dec.1976.3–4.

182 ASMEDASAR, ¿Quiénes.somos?PR.1976.Dec.1976.3–4.

183 ASMEDASAR, ¿Quiénes.somos?PR.1976.Dec.1976.3–4.

184 ASMEDASAR, Dirigentes obreros.piden.mitin.CP.1976.11.

185 ASMEDASAR, ¿Quiénes.somos?PR.1976.Sep.1976.2–3.

186 ASMEDASAR, Instransigencia.obrera.CP.1976.Sep.1976.2–3.

187 ASMEDASAR, Instransigencia.obrera.CP.1976.Sep.1976.2–3.

188 ASMEDASAR, Indiferencia.médicos.VA.Oct.1976.1.

189 ASMEDASAR, Miseria.probreza.PR.1976.Nov.1976.2.

190 ASMEDASAR, Eduardo Díaz, Medicina.cultura.proletaria.ES.[Dec.1976].3.

191 ASMEDASAR, Eduardo Díaz, Medicina.cultura.proletaria.ES.[Dec.1976].3.

192 ASMEDASAR, Diario.quehacer.paro.PR.1976.Sep.1976.2.

193 ASMEDASAR, Esquirolus.virulencis.PR.1976.Oct.1976.1.

194 ASMEDASAR, Esquirolus.virulencis.PR.1976.Oct.1976.1.

195 ASMEDASAR, Esquirolus.virulencis.PR.1976.Oct.1976.1.

196 ASMEDASAR, Esquirolus.virulencis.PR.1976.Oct.1976.1; ASMEDASAR, Diario.quehacer.paro.PR.1976.Sep.1976.2.

197 ASMEDASAR, No.esun.paro.mas.OP.1977.Sep.1976.1–2.

198 FEDEPROCOLAR, Lilia Forero, Cartaabierta.VA.CG.Oct.10.1976.1–2.

199 FEDEPROCOLAR, Lilia Forero, Cartaabierta.VA.CG.Oct.10.1976.1–2.

200 ASMEDASAR, Mujer.medicina.social.ES.EMS.Nov.1976.1.

201 ASMEDASAR, Letter Clementina Sánchez to Eduardo Arévalo Burgos.CR.CG.Oct.1.1976.1.

202 ASMEDASAR, Letter Clementina Sánchez to Eduardo Arévalo Burgos.CR.CG.Oct.1.1976.1.

203 ASMEDASAR, Mujer.ética.médica.ES.EMS.Nov.1976.3–4.

204 ASMEDASAR, Mujer.ética.médica.ES.EMS.Nov.1976.3–4.

205 ASMEDASAR, Economía.medicina.sociedad.ES.EMS.1976.2.

206 ASMEDASAR, Ampl.progr.educación.PR.PED.1977.3–4.

207 ASMEDASAR, Ampl.progr.educación.PR.PED.1977.3–4.

208 These descriptions are based on *El Bogotano*, May 6, 1976, 2; May 13, 1976, 9–10; May 18, 1976, 8–9.

209 *El Bogotano*, May 6, 1976, 2.

210 *El Bogotano*, May 6, 1976, 2.

211 CRPA, Profesores comunistas, Elem.análisis.crisis.Univ.Pública.1976.Nov.1976.11.

212 ASMEDASAR, Llamado.unidad.revolucionaria.1978.Oct.1978.4.

213 *El Bogotano*, May 6, 1976, 2.

214 *El Bogotano*, May 6, 1976, 2.

215 ANEBRAR, FEBOR, Angela Gonzales Montes, Algo.para.mujer.April–May.1975.4.

216 ANEBRAR, FEBOR, Angela Gonzales Montes, Algo.para.mujer.April–May.1975.4.

217 ANEBRAR, FEBOR, Aura Mejía, Falta.reconocimiento.laboral.OP.1978.1.

Chapter 8. The Most Important Gift to the World

1 Ferguson, *Give a Man a Fish*, 1.

2 Klein, *Shock Doctrine*; Vega Cantor, *Los economistas*; Estrada Álvarez, "Élites intelectuales"; Grandin, *Empire's Workshop*; North and Clark, *Dominant Elites*; Zeiderman, *Endangered City*, 21.

3 As an exception see Tinsman, *Buying into the Regime*; Offner, "Anti-Poverty."

4 Duménil and Lévy, *Crisis*, 22; Harvey, *Brief History*, 15, 19.

5 Ferguson, "Uses of Neoliberalism," 166.

6 Piketty, *Capital*.

7 Dargent, *Technocracy and Democracy*, 76, 78, 88; Flórez Enciso, "Colombia," 197–226; Torres del Río, *Colombia*, 253.

8 This argument is inspired by Tinsman, *Buying into the Regime*; Freeman, *Entrepreneurial Selves*; Boltanski and Chiapello, *New Spirit of Capitalism*.

9 Stengers, "Cosmopolitical Proposal," 994.

10 Flórez Enciso, "Colombia," 201–203.

11 Safford and Palacios, *Colombia*, 297–308, 332–334; Torres del Río, *Colombia*, 251–272.

12 FEDESARROLLO, *Serie documentos de trabajo*, June 1974, 11.

13 Shaw, *Financial Deepening*, viii.

14 Levinson and de Onis, *Alliance*.

15 Levinson and de Onis, *Alliance*, 307.

16 Levinson and de Onis, *Alliance*, 307.

17 Levinson and de Onis, *Alliance*, 23.

18 Levinson and de Onis, *Alliance*, 308, 29.

19 Levinson and de Onis, *Alliance*, 308–309.

20 Levinson and de Onis, *Alliance*, 308–309.

21 PA, Fernando Cepeda Ulloa, Infor.señor.presidenteAlfonso.López.Michelsen .DSP.SG.11.Apr.11.1976.2 1976, Secr.General, 1976, Box, 11, PA.

22 PA, Cepeda Ulloa, Clase media.inestabilidad.política, Info.señor.presidente.Alfonso.López.Michelsen.DSP.SG.2.Feb.1976.8, 5.

23 PA, Cepeda Ulloa, Clase media.inestabilidad.política, Info.señor.presidente.Alfonso.López.Michelsen.DSP.SG.2.Feb.1976.8, 5.

24 PA, Cepeda Ulloa, Clase media.inestabilidad.política, Info.señor.presidente.Alfonso .López.Michelsen.DSP.SG.2.Feb.1976.8, 5.

25 PA, Cepeda Ulloa, Clase media.inestabilidad.política, Info.señor.presidente.Alfonso.López.Michelsen.DSP.SG.2.Feb.1976.8, 5.

26 Simons, *Colombia*, 44.

27 PA, Rafael Pardo Buelvas to Alfonso López Michelsen, SG.2.Nov.12.1976.

28 PA, Rafael Pardo Buelvas to Alfonso López Michelsen, SG.2.Nov.12.1976.

29 Sáenz Rovener, "Estudio de caso," 14.

30 Lleras Camargo, "La Revolución subvencionada: El enclave marxista," *El Tiempo*, May 26, 1972, 4A.

31 Sáenz Rovener, "Estudio de caso," 14.

32 Fernando Landazábal Reyes, "Educación en manos de la subversión," *Revista de las Fuerzas Armadas*, December 28, 1981, 3.

33 ICTAR, Servicio Civil, El.problema.humano.estado.DP.GSG.SG.1974.4.

34 ICTAR, Servicio Civil, Problema.profesional.servicios.estado.GSG.SG.1974.12.

35 ICTAR, Servicio Civil, Problema.profesional.servicios.estado.GSG.SG.1974.11.

36 ICTAR, Servicio Civil, Problema.profesional.servicios.estado.GSG.SG.1974.8.

37 ICTAR, Servicio Civil, Exige.professionalismo.hoy.DP.GSG.SG.1975.2.

38 Fernando Landazábal Reyes, "Educación en manos de la subversión," *Tiempo*, January 19, 1982, 8a.

39 Ministerio de Educación Nacional, *Proyecto de ley*.

40 Blaug, *Education*, 38.

41 Alfonso López Michelsen, "Cinco reporteros y personajes de la semana," September 18, 1977, as cited in López Michelsen, *Administración López*.

42 Currie, "Advice on Growth and Development," 23–40.

43 Currie, *Operation Colombia*.

44 Currie, "Colombian Plan 1971–74," 69–72.

45 Currie, "Advice on Housing," 143–148; Giraldo Isaza, "Currie y la sociedad," 428.

46 Amy Offner argues that some of these policies made Currie, "unwittingly, a pioneer of gentrification." Offner, "Anti-Poverty Programs," 136.

47 Silva, "Housing Finance," 10.

48 Currie, "Advice on Housing," 136.

49 Currie, "Wants," 47–48.

50 Currie, "Wants," 47–48.

51 Currie, "Wants," 48.

52 Currie, "Wants," 52–53.

53 Currie, "Wants," 55, 57.

54 Currie, "La política."

55 Currie, "La unidad," 5.

56 DAVAR, MA.SO.SA.PF.1973.11.

57 DAVAR, Principios.finalidades.actividades.UPAC.SO.SA.AH.1974.1.

58 This comes from the reading of around 540 applications, five applications per month from 1973 to 1982; Sandilands, *Life*, 258.

59 DAVAR, GuiaUPAC.SO.SA.PF.1973.15.

60 DAVAR, GuíaUPAC.SO.SA.PF.1973.15; Ocampo Zamorano and Villamizar Cajiao, *El ahorro*, 353.

61 DAVAR, Aspectos.crédito.UPAC.SO.SA.AH.1973.4.

62 DAVAR, Casita.roja.Davivienda.SO.CP.1974.11–16.

63 DAVAR, Casita.roja.Davivienda.SO.CP.1974.11–16.

64 DAVAR, Crédito.vivienda.SA.HF.1976.4.

65 DAVAR, Aspectos.crédito.vivienda.SO.SA.PA.11–12.

66 Sandilands, *Life*, 258.

67 López Michelsen, "Discurso," 421–432.

68 López Michelsen, "Discurso," 421–432.

69 UNCLAMECOLAR, Inmensa.masa.clase.media.TG.May.3.1976.2–3.

70 UNCLAMECOLAR, Llegaremos.meta.final.TG.March.1978.5.

71 UNCLAMECOLAR, Llegaremos.meta.final.TG.March.1978.5.

72 ICTAR, Vladimir Mariño, Infor.labores.barrios.marginales.RT.DI.ST.1976.

73 Antonio Beltrán, "Desarrollo equilibrado," *Bitacora*, April 1974:89, 13–14.

74 COLARCH, "Sociedad.libre.democrática.ORH.Año, 14:3 July 1975, 4–5.

75 Colombia, *Para cerrar la brecha*.

76 ACOPIAR, Por.Colombia.industrial.PU.Nov.1975.11.

77 Schumacher, *Small Is Beautiful*.

78 ACOPIAR, Papel.pequeña.empresa.ES.1977.1.

79 ACOPIAR, Papel.pequeña.empresa.ES.1977.1; Schumacher, *Small Is Beautiful*, 4, 36.

80 ACOPIAR, Por.Colombia.industrial.PU.Nov.1975.17–20.

81 ACOPIAR, Por.Colombia.industrial.PU.Nov.1975.17–20.

82 UNCLAMECOLAR, Comentario.horaactual.CG.Feb.1975.5.

83 UNCLAMECOLAR, Comentario.horaactual.CG.Feb.1975.5.

84 UNCLAMECOLAR, Comentario.horaactual.CG.Feb.1975.5.

85 Pécaut, *Crónica*, 309. For a description of the strike, see Medina, *La protesta*, 123–186.

86 Julia Preston, "Colombian General Strike," NACLA, 1.

87 Torres del Río, *Colombia*, 255.

88 UNCLAMECOLAR, Clase media.democratización.AH.3.

89 UNCLAMECOLAR, Luis Díaz, Hora.actual.AH.Nov.5.1977.2.

90 UNCLAMECOLAR, Luis Díaz, Hora.actual.AH.Nov.5.1977.2.

91 COLARCH, Raúl Mantilla, Tribuna.libre.democrática.VA.ES.July.1975.9–11.

92 ACOPIAR, Pequeños.industriales.caos social.ES.1977.1.

93 UNCLAMECOLAR, López Michelsen, Programa.cinco.reportajes.AH.1.

94 López Michelsen, Programa.cinco.reportajes.AH.1.

95 UNCLAMECOLAR, Visita.presidencial.Apr.1978. CCM.

96 ACOPIAR, Discurso.presidencial.XXIII.conferencia.ACOPI.FPM.1978.1–15.

97 FECOCAR, Estatuto.docente.ED.Sept.14.1978.

98 ASMEDASAR, Normas.ética.médica.Ley 23 de 1981.RS.Feb.1981.18.

99 Interview with Roberto Solano; RSPAR, PN.[1978].

100 FECOCAR, ED.Sept.14.1979.1–2.

101 FECOCAR, ED.Sept.14.1979.1–2.

102 FECOCAR, ED.Sept.14.1979.1–2.

103 BRAR, FEBOR, Aura Mejía, Falta.reconocimiento.laboral.OP.1978.1.

104 BRAR, FEBOR, Aura Mejía, Falta.reconocimiento.laboral.OP.1978.1.

105 Interview with Cecilia Serrano.

106 Interview with Cecilia Serrano.

107 Interview with Pedro Garzón.

108 Interview with Marta Jaramillo.

109 Interview with Marta Espinosa.

110 Interview with René Sánchez.

111 Several interviews. See also Amnesty International, *Violación*.

112 RSPA, Cartas.1979–1981.

113 CSPA, Cartas.1979–1981.

114 RSPA, Cartas.1979–1981.

115 RSPA, Cartas.1979–1981; Karl Marx, *The Eighteenth*, 73.

116 RSPA, Cartas.1979–1981.

117 CSPA, Cartas.1979–1981.

118 RSPA, Cartas.1979–1981.

119 RSPA, Cartas.1979–1981.

120 Winifred Tate, *Counting the Dead.*

121 *Alternativa*, February 18, 1974.

122 UNCLAMECOLAR, Violentos.no.pasarán.OP.Sep.25.1977.1–2.

123 UNCLAMECOLAR, Violentos.no.pasarán.OP.Sep.25.1977.1–2.

124 UNCLAMECOLAR, Violentos.no.pasarán.OP.Sep.25.1977.1–2.

125 Interview with Pedro Garzón.

Epilogue

1 Nasr, *Forces of Fortune*, 110–114.

2 As examples see Huffington, *Third World America*; Vahab, *America's Shrinking Middle Class*.

3 As an example, see Madland, *Hollowed Out.*

4 White House, "Remarks."

5 María Ángel, phone interview.

6 Pedro Neira, phone interview.

7 CNMH, *¡Basta ya!*, 20. Francisco de Roux, the president of the Truth Commission created as a result of the peace agreement between the FARC and Santos's government, has argued that "the urban nation" remains oblivious to the war. This urban nation only sees the war as a movie rather than an everyday reality. See de Roux, "El pais urbano."

8 CNMH, *¡Basta ya!*, 20, 22.

9 Castillejo, "On the Question," 17–20.

10 Antonio Guzmán, phone interview.

11 Gabriel Vega, phone interview.

12 Carlos Cantor, phone interview.

Bibliography

A Note on Citations and Archives

Most of the archives that I have used for this book are bureaucratic state or private productions. I have reviewed the organizational charts of each institution during the 1960s and 1970s to see where specific documents were located at the time. In general, citations include archive name and, if available, collection, author, title, folder, box, date of composition, and page numbers. I have also used abbreviations for these citations. For example, a citation for Compañía Colombiana de Seguros, Colseguros Archive, Raúl Mantilla, Tribuna libre y democrática, Folder: Varios, Box: escritos, July 1975, 9–11 appears as COLARCH, Raúl Mantilla, Tribuna.libre.democrática.VA.ES .July.1975.9–11.

I also use abbreviations for citations of personal archives. These citations include as much of the little location indicator information available. In some cases, these archives are collections of documents stored in *baúles*, or boxes, kept in closets, cabinets, or attics. Documents from the 1960s and 1970s that at an early moment of my research, in 2004–2005, were housed at the Archivo de la Presidencia (PA) have since been relocated to the Archivo General de la Nación. I follow the organization used at the PA.

Institutional Archives—Bogotá

Archive of the Colombian-American Cooperative Technical Service in Agriculture (STACAR)

Minister of Agriculture (MA)
Programas Rurales y Desarrollo (PRD)
Reportes (RE)
Sección de Divulgación (SD)

Archive of the Inter-American Center for Housing and Planning (CINVAR)

Apuntes Clase (AC)
Instituto de Crédito Territorial (ICT)
Material de Trabajo de Campo (MTC)
Programas de Vivienda (PV)
Seminarios (SE)

Archivo Central e Histórico, Universidad Nacional (UN)

Archivo de Aerolineas AVIANCA (AAR)

Manuales de Personal (MP)
Oficina de Personal (OP)

Archivo de la Caja de Compensación Familiar, CAFAM (CAFAR)

Actas Consejo Directivo (ACD)
Material de Entrenamiento (ME)
Oficina de Personal (OP)
Políticas de Selección (PS)

Archivo de la Caja de Crédito Agrario, Industrial y Minero (CGAIMAR)

Crédito Industrial Supervisado (CIS)
Division de Crédito Industrial (DCI)
Informes de Visitas Industriales (IVI)
Supervisión de Informes de Visita (SIV)

Archivo de la Compañía Colombiana de Seguros, Colseguros (COLARCH)

Actas Consejo Directivo (ACD)
Discursos de Agradecimiento (DA)
Escritos (ES)
Grupos Primarios de Participación (GP)
Informes Confidenciales de Personal (ICP)
Informes de Selección (IS)
Manuales de Personal (MP)
Manuales de Selección (MS)
Material de Entrenamiento (ME)
Oficina de Relaciones Humanas (ORH)
Revista ACASE (RAC)
Revista ASDECOS (RAS)
Varios (VA)

Archivo de la Escuela de Administración Pública (ESAPAR)

Administración de Personal (AP)
Conferencia Empleados Públicos (CEP)
Conferencias (CF)
Conferencias Públicas (CP)
Discursos Inauguración (DI)
Instituto Administración Social (IAS)
Manuales Administración Pública (MAP)
Materiales de Clase (MC)
Programas Clase (PC)
Programas de Desarrollo (PD)

Relaciones Humanas (RH)
Seminarios Dirigidos (SD)

Archivo de la Presidencia de la República (PA)

Administración General (AG)
Comercio Exterior (CE)
Despacho Señor Presidente (DSP)
Ministerio de Gobierno (MG)
Secretaria General (SG)

Archivo del Banco de la República (BRAR)

Grupos Primarios de Participación (GP)
Manuales de Selección (MS)
Material de Entrenamiento (ME)
Oficina de Personal (OP)

Archivo del Departamento de Sociología, UNAL (UNALAR)

Archivo del Instituto Colombiano de Reforma Agraria (INCORAR)

Entrenamiento y evaluación (EN)
Notas de Trabajo Campo (NTC)
Subgerencia Administrativa (SA)

Archivo del Instituto de Crédito Territorial (ICTAR)

Arquitectura y Urbanismo (AR)
Departamento de Proyectos (DP)
Departamento de Servicio Social (DSS)
Divulgación (DV)
Gabinete Sub-gerente General (GSG)
Investigaciones (IN)
Programas de Vivienda (PV)
Proyectos Rurales y Urbanos (PRU)
Reclamos Laborales (RL)
Reportes de Trabajo (RT)
Reportes Trabajo de Campo (RTC)
Servicio a la Comunidad (SC)
Subgerencia Administrativa (SA)
Subgerencia General (SG)
Subgerencia Técnica (ST)

Archivo del Instituto de Fomento Industrial (IFIARC)

Departamento de Estudios Especiales (DEE)
Departamentos de Evaluación de Proyectos (DP)
División Administrativa (DA)

Encuentros de la Junta Directiva (JD)
Gerencia General (GG)
Ministerio de Trabajo (MT)
Oficina de Personal (OP)
Oficina Divulgación (OD)
Relaciones Públicas (RP)
Secretaria General (SG)
Subgerencia Técnica (ST)

Archivo de Virginia Gutiérrez de Pineda and Roberto Pineda (VGPRPAR)

Instituto de Crédito Territorial (ICT)
Seminarios (SE)

Corporación de Ahorro y Vivienda, Davivienda (DAVAR)

Ahorro (AH)
Campañas Publicitarias (CP)
Hogares Felices (HF)
Manuales de Ahorro (MA)
Políticas de Ahorro (PA)
Políticas Financieras (PF)
Sección Administrativa (SA)
Subdirección Operativo (SO)

Institutional Archives—United States

J. F. Kennedy Library, Boston, MA (JFKL)

Organization of American States Columbus Library and Archives, Washington, DC (OASAR)

Estudios (ES)
Publicaciones (PS)

United Nations Archive, New York, NY (UNA)

United States National Archives, College Park, MD (NARA)

Miscellaneous, Subject Files, 1952–1959 (SF1952–1959)
Record Group 59 (NARA59), Department of State
Record Group 469 (NARA469), Records of U.S. Foreign Assistance Agency

Archives of Political Organizations—Bogotá

Archivo de la Asociación Colombiana de Pequeños Industriales (ACOPIAR)

Colombia Industrial (CI)
Discursos (DS)
Discursos Presidencia (DP)
Estudios (ES)
Estudios Fomento Pequeña y Mediana Empresa (FPM)
Financiamiento (FI)
Peticiones (PT)
Prensa (PR)
Publicaciones (PU)
Reportes (RE)
Seminarios (SE)
Varios (VA)

Archivo de la Asociación de Médicos al Servicio de las Instituciones de Asistencia Social (ASMEDASAR)

Acción Médica (AM)
Campañas Publicitarias (CP)
Comunicados de Prensa (CP)
Correspondencia (CR)
Correspondencia General (CG)
Estudios (ES)
Estudios Medicina Social (EMS)
Organizaciones Profesionales (OP)
Paro (PR)
Programas Educacionales del Distrito (PED)
Resoluciones (RS)
Varios (VA)

Archivo de la Asociación Nacional de Empleados del Banco de la República (ANEBRAR)

Apuntes de discusión (AD)
Discusiones (DS)
Fondo de Empleados Banco de la República (FEBOR)
Revista ANEBRE (AN)

Archivo de la Federación Colombiana de Educadores (FECOCAR)

Circular Informativa (CI)
Declaraciones Públicas (DP)
Educación Pública (EP)
Estatutos docentes (ED)

Seminarios (SE)
Varios (VA)

Archivo de la Federación Colombiana de Profesionales Universitarios
(FEDEPROCOLAR)

Conferencias (CF)
Correspondencia General (CG)
Junta Directiva Nacional (JDN)
Presidencia (PR)
Varios (VA)
Vicepresidente General (VG)

Archivo de la Unidad de Clase Media de Colombia (UNCLAMECOLAR)

Asuntos Hoy (AH)
Materiales para Nucleos Familiares (MNF)
Nucleos Familiars (NF)
Trabajos de Congresos (TG)

Archivo del Movimiento 19 de Abril, Centro de Documentación y Cultura para la
Paz (M19AR)

Comité de Educación (CE)
Encuenstas (EC)

Archivo del Movimiento Aliado de la Clase Media Colombiana (MOCLAMAR)

Boletines de Radio (BR)
Comité Central Bogotá (CCB)
Comité Central de la Clase Media Económica (CCCME)
Comité de Trabajo y Comité Central (CTCC)
Minutas del Comité Ejecutivo Central, Bogotá (SECB)
Sección Cundinamarca (SC)
Secretaría Cultural (SC)

Archivo Movimiento de Liberación de la Clase Media (LMMCA)

Noticias al Servicio de los profesionales del Estado (NSP)

Private Archival Collections

Carlos Cruz (CCPA)
Antonio Díaz (ADPA)
Germán Giraldo (GGPA)
Alejandro Hurtado (AHPA)
Marta Jaramillo (MJPA)
Carlos Lizarazo (CLPA)

Alberto Otalora (AOPA)
Professional Notes (PN)
Régulo Millán Puentes (RMPAR)
Alberto Valencia (AVPA)

Oral Interviews—Bogotá

When requested I have used pseudonyms.

Phone Interviews, September 2016

Ángel, María
Cantor, Carlos
Guzmán, Antonio
Vega, Gabriel

Personal Interviews

October 2004

Delgado de Ortiz, Margarita
Ortiz, Jorge

November 2004

Casas, Clemencia
Delgado de Téllez, Isabel
de Martínez, Margarita
Perdomo, Alicia

March 2005

Agudelo, Fernando
Giraldo, Germán
Guzmán, Emilio
Ramírez, Guillermo
Rodríguez, Clodomiro
Torres Castro, Luis
Valencia, Alberto

June 2010

Bahamón Soto, Hernando
Benavides, Arcadio

Betancour, Leonardo
Espinosa, Marta
Jaramillo, Marta
Millán Puentes, Régulo
Otalora, Alberto
Restrepo, Carlos
Rincón, Hernando
Sánchez, René
Serrano, Cecilia
Solano, Roberto

July 2010

Garzón, Pedro
Hurtado, Alejandro

Published Primary Sources

Adams, Richard N. "Social Change in Guatemala and U.S. Policy." In *Social Change in Latin America Today: Its Implications for United States Policy*, edited by Richard N. Adams et al., 231–284. New York: Council on Foreign Relations and Harper and Brothers, 1960.

Alba, Victor. "La nueva clase media latinoamericana." *Revista Mexicana de Sociología* 22, no. 3 (September–December 1960): 781–789.

Alba, Victor. "The Latin American Style and the New Social Force." In *Latin American Issues: Essays and Comments*, edited by Albert O. Hirschman, 43–52. New York: Twentieth Century Fund, 1961.

Alianza para el Progreso. *Alianza para el Progreso*. N.d.

Alvarez, Eudoro. "La empresa comunitaria." In *La tierra para el que la trabaja*, by Asociación Colombiana de Ingenieros Agronomos (ACIA), 119–132. Bogotá: ACIA, 1975.

Amnesty International. *Violación de los derechos humanos en Colombia: Informe de Amnistía Internacional: Texto íntegro*. Bogotá: Comité de Solidaridad con los Presos Políticos, 1980.

Angulo, Roberto, Alejandro Gaviria, and Liliana Morales. *La década ganada: Evolución de la clase media y las condiciones de vida en Colombia, 2002–2011*. Bogotá: Universidad de los Andes-Cede, 2013.

Arenas, Jaime. *La guerrilla por dentro*. Bogotá: Ediciones Tercer Mundo, 1971.

Arias, Jairo. *Estudio de estratificación socio-económica de los barrios de Bogota*. Bogotá: Departamento Administrativo de Planeación Distrital (DAPD), 1974.

Arias Osorio, Eduardo. *Bases para la integración de una política de recursos humanos en el desarrollo educativo y económico de Colombia*. Bogotá: Ministerio de Educación Nacional, Oficina de Planeamiento, 1966.

Atcon, Rudolph P. *The Latin American University*. Washington, DC: Pan American Union, 1963.

Barnard, Chester. *Dilemmas of Leadership in the Democratic Process*. Princeton, NJ: Princeton University Press, 1939.

Belotti, Elena Gianini. *Little Girls: Social Conditioning and Its Effects on the Stereotyped Role of Women during Infancy*. London: Writers and Readers, 1981.

Benjamin Spiro Associates. *Credit with Technical Assistance to Small and Medium Scale Industry in Colombia: Report*. San Francisco: Benjamin Spiro Associates, 1964.

Blaug, Mark. *Education and the Employment Problem in Developing Countries*. Geneva: International Labour Office, 1973.

BP (Banco Popular). *Small and Medium Industry in Colombia's Development: A Survey and a Recommended Program*. Menlo Park, CA: Stanford Research Institute, 1962.

Bryson, Lyman. "Introduction." In *Social Change in Latin America Today: Its Implications for United States Policy*, edited by Richard N. Adams et al., 231–284. New York: Council on Foreign Relations and Harper and Brothers, 1960.

CEDE (Centro de Estudios sobre el Desarrollo Económico). *Estructura del gasto y distribución del ingreso familiar en cuatro ciudades colombianas, 1967–1968*. Bogotá: Uniandes. CEDE, 1971.

CEPAL (Comisión Económica para América Latina, Naciones Unidas). *El desarrollo social de América Latina en la postguerra*. 2nd ed. Buenos Aires: Ed. Solar, 1966.

Colombia. *Para cerrar la brecha: Plan de desarrollo social, económico y regional, 1975–1978*. Bogotá: Departamento Nacional de Planeación, 1975.

Crevenna, Theo, and Pan-American Union, eds. *Materiales para el estudio de la clase media en América Latina*. Washington, DC: Pan-American Union, 1952.

Currie, Lauchlin. "Advice on Growth and Development." In *The Role of Economic Advisers in Developing Countries*, 23–40. Westport, CT: Greenwood, 1982.

Currie, Lauchlin. "Advice on Housing and Urban Policy." In *The Role of Economic Advisers in Developing Countries*, 143–148. Westport, CT: Greenwood, 1982.

Currie, Lauchlin. "The Colombian Plan 1971–74: A Test of the Leading Sector Strategy." *World Development* 2, nos. 10–12 (October–December 1974): 69–72.

Currie, Lauchlin. "La política de vivienda." *Revista Desarrollo y Sociedad* 4 (1982): 3–9.

Currie, Lauchlin. "La unidad de poder adquisitivo constante: Una breve historia de su nacimiento." *Desarrollo y Sociedad* 6 (1989): 5–10.

Currie, Lauchlin. *Operation Colombia: A National Economic and Social Program*. Bogotá, 1961.

Currie, Lauchlin. "Wants, Needs, Well-Being and Economic Growth." *Journal of Economic Studies* 2, no. 1 (1975): 47–59.

DANE. *La importancia de la pequeña y mediana empresa*. Bogotá: DANE, 1962.

DAP. *Programa de desarrollo industrial*. Bogotá: DAP, 1963.

Davenport, Wesley. *Financing Small and Medium Manufacturing Enterprises in Latin America: Prepared for Inter-American Development Bank*. Menlo Park, CA: Stanford Research Institute, 1962.

Di Tella, Torcuato. *El sistema político argentino y la clase obrera*. Buenos Aires: Editorial Universitaria, 1964.

Dix, Robert. *Colombia: Political Dimensions of Change*. New Haven, CT: Yale University Press, 1967.

Draper, Theodore. *Castroism: Theory and Practice*. New York: F. A. Praeger, 1965.

Draper, Theodore. *Castro's Revolution: Myths and Realities*. New York: Frederick A. Praeger, 1962.

Drucker, Peter Ferdinand. *Landmarks of Tomorrow*. New York: Harper and Row, 1965.

Fals Borda, Orlando. *Campesinos de los Andes: Estudio sociológico de Saucío*. Bogotá: Universidad Nacional, 1961.

Fals Borda, Orlando. *Ciencia propia y colonianismo intelectual*. Colombia: Punta Lanza, 1976.

Fals Borda, Orlando. *La educación en Colombia: Bases para su interpretación sociológica*. Bogotá: Universidad Nacional de Colombia, Facultad de Sociología, 1962.

Fals Borda, Orlando. *Soluciones sociales para los problemas del odio y La Violencia*. Bogotá: Universidad Nacional de Colombia, 1960.

Fals Borda, Orlando. *Subversion and Social Change in Colombia*. Translated by Jacqueline D. Skiles. New York: Columbia University Press, 1969.

FEDESARROLLO. *Serie documentos de trabajo*. June 1974.

Fergusson, Guillermo. *Esquema crítico de la medicina en Colombia*. Bogotá: CIEC, 1979.

Freire, Paulo. *Pedagogía del oprimido*. Mexico City: Siglo Veintiuno Editores, 1978.

Geithman, David T. "Middle Class Growth and Economic Development in Latin America." *American Journal of Economics and Sociology* 33, no. 1 (1974): 45–58.

Germani, Gino. *Política y sociedad en una época de transición, de la sociedad tradicional a la sociedad de masas*. Buenos Aires: Editorial Paidós, 1962.

Gillin, John P. "Some Signposts for Policy." In *Social Change in Latin America Today*, edited by Richard Adams et al., 14–62. New York: Council on Foreign Relations, 1960.

Giraldo Isaza, Fabio. "Currie y la sociedad." *Cuadernos de Economia* 13 (1993): 423–438.

Gutiérrez de Pineda, Virginia. *Familia y cultura en Colombia*. Bogotá: Tercer Mundo Editores, 1968.

Gutiérrez de Pineda, Virginia. *La familia en Colombia*. Bogotá: Universidad Nacional de Colombia, 1963.

Guzmán Campos, Germán, Orlando Fals Borda, and Eduardo Umaña Luna. *La Violencia en Colombia: Estudio de un proceso social*. Bogotá: Ediciones Tercer Mundo, 1963.

Guzzardi, Walter, Jr. "The Crucial Middle Class." *Fortune* 65, no. 2 (February 1962): 88–97.

Hagen, Everett E. *El cambio social en Colombia: El factor humano en el desarrollo económico*. Bogotá: Ediciones Tercer Mundo, 1963.

Hagen, Everett E. *On the Theory of Social Change: How Economic Growth Begins*. Homewood: Dorsey Press, 1962.

Hagen, Everett E. "The Transition in Colombia." In *Entrepreneurship and Economic Development*, edited by Peter Kilby, 191–224. New York: Free Press, 1971.

Hoselitz, Bert F. "Economic Growth in Latin America." In *Contribution to the First International Conference of Economic History*. Stockholm and The Hague: Mouton, 1960.

Hoselitz, Bert F. *Sociological Aspects of Economic Growth*. Glencoe, IL: Free Press, 1960.

Jaramillo, Samuel, and Luis M. Cuervo. *La configuración del espacio regional en Colombia: Tres ensayos*. Bogotá: Universidad de los Andes, 1987.

Johnson, J. John. *The Military and Society in Latin America*. Stanford: Stanford University Press, 1964.

Johnson, J. John. "New Armies Take Over in Latin America." *New York Times*, March 8, 1964, 14, 97–99.

Johnson, J. John. *Political Change in Latin America: The Emergence of the Middle Sectors*. Stanford: Stanford University Press, 1958.

Johnson, J. John, David Bushnell, and Lyle N. McAlister. "An Interview with John J. Johnson." *HAHR* 66, no. 4 (1986): 643–666.

Kilby, Peter. "Preface." In *Entrepreneurship and Economic Development*, edited by Peter Kilby, 1–8. New York: Free Press, 1971.

Koner, Marvin. "Neighbors Who Are Neither Rich nor Poor." *Fortune* 65, no. 2 (February 1962): 88–97.

Laserna, Mario. *Estado, consenso, democracia y desarrollo*. Bogotá: Tercer Mundo, 1966.

Lebret, J. J. *Misión económica y humanismo: Estudios sobre el desarrollo en Colombia*. Bogotá: Comité Nacional de Planeación, 1958.

León de Leal, Magdalena. "Las clases medias y la dependencia externa en Colombia: Un esquema para su estudio." *Razón y Fábula* 23 (January–February 1971): 58–73.

Lernoux, Penny. *Cry of the People: United States Involvement in the Rise of Fascism, Torture and Murder and the Persecution of the Catholic Church in Latin America*. Garden City, NY: Doubleday, 1980.

Levinson, Jerome, and Juan de Onis. *The Alliance That Lost Its Way: A Critical Report on the Alliance for Progress*. Chicago: Quadrangle Books, 1970.

Lipman, Aaron. *The Colombian Entrepreneur in Bogotá*. Coral Gables, FL: University of Miami Press, 1969.

Lipset, Seymour. *Political Man: The Social Bases of Politics*. Garden City, NY: Doubleday, 1960.

Lipset, Seymour. "Some Social Requisites of Democracy: Economic Development and Political Legitimacy." *American Political Science Review* 53, no. 1 (1959): 69–105.

Lipset, Seymour. "Values, Education and Entrepreneurship." In *Elites in Latin America*, edited by Seymour Lipset and Aldo E. Solari, 3–60. New York: Oxford University Press, 1967.

Lipset, Seymour, and Aldo E. Solari. *Elites in Latin America*. New York: Oxford University Press, 1967.

López de Mesa, Luis, T. Lynn Smith, and Gerardo Reichel-Dolmatoff. *Tres estudios sobre la clase media en Colombia*. Bogotá: Imprenta del Banco de la República, 1952.

López Michelsen, Alfonso. *Administración López: Documentos, discursos*. Bogotá: Banco de la República, 1975.

López Michelsen, Alfonso. "Discurso en la instalación del V congreso Nacional de Economistas, Cúcuta 26 de Mayo 1976." In *Obras selectas*, 421–432. Bogotá: Cámara de Representantes, 1985.

Mariño S., Germán, Leonardo Pérez T., and Vladimir Zabala A. *Lucharemos: Método de alfabetización liberadora*. Bogotá: Dimensión Educativa, 1978.

Maslow, Abraham. *Motivation and Personality*. New York: Harper and Row, 1970.

Marx, Karl. *Economic and Philosophic Manuscripts of 1844*. Moscow: Foreign Languages Publishing House, 1961.

Marx, Karl. *The Eighteenth Brumaire of Louis Bonaparte*. Peking: Foreign Languages Press, 1978.

McClelland, David C. "The Achievement Motive in Economic Growth." In *Entrepreneurship and Economic Development*, edited by Peter Kilby, 109–122. New York: Free Press, 1971.

McClelland, David C. *The Achieving Society*. Princeton, NJ: Van Nostrand, 1961.

Mills, C. Wright. *Listen, Yankee: The Revolution in Cuba*. New York: McGraw-Hill, 1960.

Mills, C. Wright. *White Collar: The American Middle Classes*. London: Oxford University Press, 1977.

Ministerio de Educación Nacional. *Proyecto de ley, por la cual se dicta el estatuto general de la educación, y exposición de motivos*. Bogotá: Ministerio de Educación Nacional, 1971.

Naranjo, Carlos, and Hector Julio Ruiz. "Problema nacional agrario." In *La tierra para el que la trabaja*, edited by Asociación Colombiana de Ingenieros Agrónomos (ACIA), 15–36. Bogotá: ACIA, 1975.

Novás Calvo, Lino. "La tragedia de la clase media cubana: Los hijos y las hijas de la burguesía." *Bohemia Libre* 13, no. 53 (January 1961): 28–29, 76–77.

Ocampo Zamorano, Alfredo, and Lucía Villamizar Cajiao. *El ahorro y la gente en Colombia: Motivaciones, orientaciones y toma de decisiones para ahorros. Estudio sociológico para el Banco de la República y la Junta de Ahorro y Vivienda.* Bogotá: Estudios Científicosociales Aplicados, 1974.

Parra Sandoval, Rodrigo. "Clases sociales y educación en el desarrollo de Colombia." *Revista de la Universidad Nacional*, no. 3 (April–August 1969): 166–182.

Parsons, James. *Antioqueño Colonization in Western Colombia.* Berkeley: University of California Press, 1968.

Partido Liberal Colombiano. *Programa del Frente Nacional.* Bogotá: Editorial ARGTA, 1962.

PCC-ML (Partido Comunista de Colombia, Marxista-Leninista). *Combatiendo unidos venceremos.* Medellín: Editorial 8 de junio, 1975.

Ratinoff, Luis. "Algunos problemas de la formación y utilización del capital humano en el desarrollo reciente de América Latina: Una interpretación." *Revista Mexicana de Sociología* 29, no. 1 (January–March 1967): 5–26.

Reichel-Dolmatoff, Gerardo. "Notas sobre la clase media en Colombia." *Ciencias Sociales* 3, no. 13 (1952): 1–5.

Reichel-Dolmatoff, Gerardo. "Notas sobre la clase media en Colombia (una réplica al Dr. T. Lynn Smith)." In *Tres estudios sobre la clase media en Colombia*, edited by Luis López de Mesa, T. Lynn Smith, and Gerardo Reichel-Dolmatoff. Bogotá: Banco de la República, 1952.

RIAS. *La historia de los partidos politicos . . . la historia que nunca se ha contado.* Bogotá: Editorial El Machete, 1972.

RLCPMI. *Reunión Latinoamericana y del Caribe sobre la pequeña y mediana industria.* Bogotá: SENA, 1973.

Rodríguez, Jaime. *El sistema de bachillerato colombiano y el cambio social.* Bogotá: Universidad Nacional, 1964.

Ruiz Novoa, Alberto. "La organización de la victoria." In *El gran desafío*, edited by Alberto Ruiz Novoa, 133–146. Bogotá: Ediciones Tercer Mundo, 1965.

Ruiz Novoa, Alberto. "La reforma de nuestras estructuras." In *El gran desafío*, by Alberto Ruiz Novoa, 91–108. Bogotá: Ediciones Tercer Mundo, 1965.

Ruiz Novoa, Alberto. "Resucitar la política como mística del hombre." *La Nueva Prensa*, no. 129 (February 26, 1965): 28–42.

Safford, Frank. "Significación de los antioqueños en el desarrollo económico colombiano: Un examen crítico de las tesis de Everett Hagen." *Anuario Colombiano de Historia Social y de la Cultura*, no. 3 (1965): 49–69.

Salazar, María Cristina. *A Study of the Social Crusade in Bogota, Colombia.* 1953.

Schaw, Louis C. *The Bonds of Work: Work in Mind, Time, and Tradition.* San Francisco: Jossey-Bass, 1968.

Schultz, Theodore. "Human Capital." *American Economic Review* 51 (March 1961): 1–17.

Schultz, Theodore. "Investment in Man: An Economist's View." *Social Service Review* 33, no. 2 (June 1959): 109.

Schumacher, E. F. *Small Is Beautiful: Economics as if People Mattered.* New York: Harper & Row, 1973.

Shaw, Edward S. *Financial Deepening in Economic Development.* New York: Oxford University Press, 1973.

Smith, Lynn. "Observations on the Middle Class in Colombia." In *Materiales para el estudio de la clase media en la América Latina,* edited by Theo R. Crevenna. Vol. 6, 1–14. Washington, DC: Pan American Union, 1950.

Staley, Eugene, and S. Nanjundan. *Economic Research for Small Industry Development.* New York: Asia House, 1962.

Thomas, Hugh. "Middle Class Politics and the Cuban Revolution." In *The Politics of Conformity in Latin America,* edited by Claudio Veliz, 249–277. London: Oxford University Press, 1967.

Thomas, Ivor Bulmer. "Conclusions de la age session de l'INCIDI." *Civilisations* (Brussels), no. 3 (1955): 480–485.

Truman, Harry. "Inaugural Address, January 20, 1949." In *The Presidents Speak: The Inaugural Address of the American Presidents from Washington to Clinton,* edited by David Newton Lott, 297–300. New York: H. Holt, 1994.

UNESCO. *La vida laboral en el sector de servicios.* Washington, 1961.

US Department of State. *Intervention of International Communism in Guatemala.* Washington: US Government Printing Office, 1954.

Vasco Uribe, Alberto. *Estado y enfermedad.* Medellín: Universidad de Antioquia, 1988.

Wiliamson. *El estudiante colombiano y sus actitudes: Un análisis de psicología social en la Universidad Nacional.* Bogotá: Universidad Nacional de Colombia, Facultad de Sociología, 1962.

Journals and Magazines

Acción Médica
Administración y Desarrollo
Alternativa
Asociación
Bitacora
El Bogotano
El Espectador
El Tiempo
Hanson's Latin American Letter
La Nueva Prensa
Revista Fuerzas Armadas
Tribuna Roja

Web Sources

de Roux, Francisco. "El pais urbano no sabe lo que es la guerra." Accessed July 12, 2018. http://www.elpais.com.co/judicial/el-pais-urbano-no-sabe-lo-que-es-la -guerra-francisco-de-roux.html.

Preston, Julia. "Colombian General Strike." NACLA. Accessed February 2, 2015. https://nacla.org/article/colombia-general-strike.

Semana. "Colombia un país de clase media." Accessed February 2, 2015. https:// www.semana.com/nacion/articulo/colombia-un-pais-de-clase-media /427747-3.

Uribe Vélez, Álvaro. "Manifiesto Democrático: 100 Puntos Álvaro Uribe Vélez." Accessed July 2015. http://www.mineducacion.gov.co/1621/articles-85269 _archivo_pdf.pdf.

Vivas Pacheco, Harvy. "Colombia: ¿Un país de clase media? *La silla vacía.*" Accessed July 15, 2016. http://www.razonpublica.com/index.php /econom%C3%ADa-y-sociedad/8497-colombia-%C2%BFun-pa%C3%ADs-de -clase-media.html.

White House. "Remarks by President Obama and President Santos of Colombia at Plan Colombia Reception." *The White House: President Barack Obama.* February 4, 2016. https://obamawhitehouse.archives.gov/the-press-office /2016/02/05/remarks-president-obama-and-president-santos-colombia-plan -colombia.

Works Cited

Acemoglu, Daron, and James A. Robinson. *Economic Origins of Dictatorship and Democracy.* New York: Cambridge University Press, 2005.

Adamovsky, Ezequiel. "'Clase media': Problemas de aplicabilidad histo- riográfica de una categoría." In *Clases medias: Nuevos enfoques desde la sociología, la historia y la antropología*, edited by Ezequiel Adamovsky, Sergio Visacovsky, and Patricia Beatriz Vargas, 115–138. Buenos Aires: Ariel, 2014.

Adamovsky, Ezequiel. *Historia de la clase media argentina: Apogeo y decadencia de una ilusión, 1919–2003.* Buenos Aires: Planeta, 2009.

Aguilera Morales, Alcira. *Subjetividades políticas en movimento(s): La defensa de la universidad pública en Colombia y México.* Bogotá: Universidad Ped- agógica Nacional, Magisterio editorial, 2014.

Aguilera Peña, Mario. *Contrapoder y justicia guerrillera: Fragmentación política y orden insurgente en Colombia (1952–2003).* Colombia: Penguin Random House Grupo Editorial SAS, 2014.

Angulo Salazar, Roberto Carlos, Alejandro Gaviria Uribe, and Liliana Morales. *La década ganada: Evolución de la clase media y las condiciones de vida en Colombia, 2002–2011.* Bogotá: Universidad de los Andes, Facultad de Economía, CEDE, 2013.

Arango, Luz Gabriela. *Mujer, religión e industria: Fabricato, 1923–1982.* Medellín: Editorial Universidad de Antioquia, 1991.

Archila, Mauricio. "El Frente Nacional: Una historia de enemistad social." *Anuario Colombiano de Historia Social y de la Cultura* 24 (2010): 189–215.

Archila, Mauricio. *Idas y venidas, vueltas y revueltas: Protestas sociales en Colombia, 1958–1990.* Bogotá: Instituto Colombiano de Antropología e Historia, 2003.

Archila, Mauricio, ed. *Una historia inconclusa: Izquierdas políticas y sociales en Colombia.* Bogotá: Cinep, 2009.

Arias Trujillo, Ricardo. *Historia de Colombia contemporánea, 1920–2010.* Bogotá: Universidad de los Andes, 2011.

Avella, M., J. Bernal, M. Errázuriz, and J. A. Ocampo. "La consolidación del capitalismo moderno, 1945–1986." In *Historia económica de Colombia,* edited by J. A. Ocampo, 243–332. Bogotá: Tercer Mundo Editores.

Ayala Diago, César Augusto. *La explosión del populismo en Colombia: Anapo y la participación política durante el Frente Nacional.* Bogotá: Universidad Nacional de Colombia, 2011.

Badiou, Alain. "Twenty-Four Notes in the Use of the Word 'People.'" In *What Is a People?,* edited by Alain Badiou, Pierre Bourdieu, Judith Butler, Georges Didi-Huberman, Sadri Khiari, Jacques Rancière, Bruno Bosteels, Kevin Olson, and Jody Gladding, 21–31. New York: Columbia University Press, 2016.

Bagley, Bruce Michael. "Political Power, Public Policy and the State in Colombia: Case Studies of the Urban and Agrarian Reforms during the National Front, 1958–1974." PhD diss., University of California, Los Angeles, 1979.

Barr-Melej, Patrick. *Reforming Chile: Culture, Politics, Nationalism and the Rise of the Middle Class.* Chapel Hill: University of North Carolina Press, 2001.

Bergquist, Charles. "La izquierda colombiana: Un pasado paradójico, ¿un futuro promisorio?" *Anuario Colombiano de Historia Social y de la Cultura* 44, no. 2 (2017): 263–300.

Bértola, Luis, and José Antonio Ocampo. *The Economic Development of Latin America since Independence.* Oxford: Oxford University Press, 2013.

Beverley, John. *Latin Americanism after 9/11.* Durham, NC: Duke University Press, 2011.

Boltanski, Luc, and Eve Chiapello. *The New Spirit of Capitalism.* Translated by Gregory Elliott. London: Verso, 2005.

Bonilla, Victor, Gonzalo Castillo, Orlando Fals Borda, and Augusto Libreros. *Causa popular, ciencia popular: Una metodología del conocimiento científico a través de la acción.* Bogotá: Rosca, 1972.

Bonilla, Yarimar. "Ordinary Sovereignty." *Small Axe,* no. 42 (2013): 152–165.

Bourdieu, Pierre. *The State Nobility: Elite Schools in the Field of Power.* Translated by Lauretta C. Clough. Stanford: Stanford University Press, 1996.

Brando, Carlos. "The Political Economy of Financing Late Development: Credit, Capital and Industrialisation. Colombia 1940–67." PhD diss., London School of Economics and Political Science, 2012.

Brands, Hal. *Latin America's Cold War.* Cambridge, MA: Harvard University Press, 2010.

Braun, Herbert. *Assassination of Gaitán: Public Life and Urban Violence in Colombia.* Madison: University of Wisconsin Press, 1986.

Brennan, James P. "Latin American Labor History." In *The Oxford Handbook of Latin American History,* edited by José Moya, 342–366. New York: Oxford University Press, 2011.

Britto, Lina. "The Marihuana Axis: A Regional History of Colombia's First Narcotics Boom, 1935–1985." PhD diss., New York University, 2013.

Brown, Wendy. *Politics out of History.* Princeton, NJ: Princeton University Press, 2001.

Bushnell, David. *The Making of Modern Colombia: A Nation in Spite of Itself.* Berkeley: University of California Press, 1994.

Butler, Judith. *Notes toward a Performative Theory of Assembly.* Cambridge, MA: Harvard University Press, 2015.

Butler, Judith. "Performativity's Social Magic." In *Bourdieu: A Critical Reader,* edited by Richard Shusterman, 401–417. Oxford: Blackwell, 1999.

Butler, Judith. *The Psychic Life of Power: Theories in Subjection.* Stanford: Stanford University Press, 1997.

Caballero Argáez, Carlos, Mónica Pachón Buitrago, and Eduardo Posada Carbó, eds., *Cincuenta años del regreso a la democracia: Nuevas miradas a la relevancia histórica del Frente Nacional.* Bogotá: Universidad de los Andes, 2012.

Calvo Isaza, Óscar, and Mayra Parra Salazar. *Medellín (rojo) 1968: Protesta social, secularización y vida urbana en las jornadas de la II Conferencia General del Episcopado Latinoamericano.* Bogotá: Planeta, 2012.

Carassai, Sebastian. *The Argentine Silent Majority.* Durham, NC: Duke University Press, 2014.

Cardoso, Fernando. *El empresario industrial en América Latina: Brasil.* Mar del Plata: CEPAL, 1963.

Castillejo, Alejandro. "On the Question of Historical Injuries: Transitional Justice, Anthropology and the Vicissitudes of Listening." *Anthropology Today* 29, no. 1 (February 2013): 17–20.

Castro-Gómez, Santiago, and Ramón Grosfoguel. *El giro decolonial: Reflexiones para una diversidad epistémica más allá del capitalismo global.* Bogotá: Universidad Central, 2007.

Chakrabarty, Dipesh. *Provincializing Europe: Postcolonial Thought and Historical Difference.* 2nd ed. Princeton, NJ: Princeton University Press, 2007.

Chasteen, John Charles. *Born in Blood and Fire: A Concise History of Latin America.* New York: W. W. Norton, 2016.

Chatterjee, Partha. *Lineages of Political Society: Studies in Post-colonial Democracy.* New York: Columbia University Press, 2011.

CNMH. *¡Basta ya! Colombia: Memories of War and Dignity*. Bogotá: CNMH, 2014.

Cooper, Frederick, and Randall Packard, eds. *International Development and the Social Sciences: Essays on the History of Politics of Knowledge*. Berkeley: University of California Press, 1997.

Corcoran, David Andrew. "The Infrastructure of Influence: Transnational Collaboration and the Spread of US Cultural Influence in Colombia, 1930s–1960s." PhD diss., University of New Mexico, 2011.

Coronil, Fernando. "After Empire." In *Imperial Formations*, edited by Ann Laura Stoler, Carole McGranahan, and Peter C. Perdue, 241–274. Santa Fe: School for Advanced Research Press, 2007.

Cosse, Isabella, ed. "Clases medias, sociedad y política en la América Latina contemporánea." *Contemporánea* 5, no. 5 (2014).

Dargent, Eduardo. *Technocracy and Democracy in Latin America: The Experts Running Government*. Cambridge: Cambridge University Press, 2015.

Degregori, Carlos Iván. *How Difficult It Is to Be God: Shining Path's Politics of War in Peru*. Translated by Steve J. Stern. Madison: University of Wisconsin Press, 2012.

de la Cadena, Marisol. *Formaciones de indianidad: Articulaciones raciales, mestizaje y nación en América Latina*. Bogotá: Envión, 2007.

de la Cadena, Marisol. *Indigenous Mestizos: The Politics of Race and Culture in Cuzco, Peru, 1919–1991*. Durham, NC: Duke University Press, 2003.

Delgado Guzmán, Álvaro. "El experimento del partido comunista colombiano." In *Una historia inconclusa: Izquierdas políticas y sociales en Colombia*, edited by Mauricio Archila. Bogotá: Centro de Investigación y Educación Popular, Cinep, 2009.

Derrida, Jacques. *Specters of Marx: The State of the Debt, the Work of Mourning, and the New International*. New York: Routledge, 2011.

Desmond Arias, Enrique, and Daniel M. Goldstein, eds. *Violent Democracies in Latin America*. Durham, NC: Duke University Press, 2010.

Drinot, Paulo, and Alan Knight, eds. *The Great Depression in Latin America*. Durham, NC: Duke University Press, 2014.

Duménil, Gérard, and Dominique Lévy. *The Crisis of Neoliberalism*. Cambridge, MA: Harvard University Press, 2013.

Dussel, Enrique D. *Politics of Liberation: A Critical World History*. London: SCM Press, 2011.

Ekbladh, David. *The Great American Mission: Modernization and the Construction of an American World Order*. Princeton, NJ: Princeton University Press, 2010.

Eley, Geoff. *Forging Democracy: The History of the Left in Europe, 1850–2000*. Oxford: Oxford University Press, 2002.

Escobar, Arturo. *Designs for the Pluriverse: Radical Interdependence, Autonomy, and the Making of Worlds*. Durham, NC: Duke University Press, 2018.

Escobar, Arturo. *Encountering Development: Making and Unmaking of the Third World*. Princeton, NJ: Princeton University Press, 1997.

Escobar, Arturo. *Territories of Difference: Place, Movements, Life, Redes*. Durham, NC: Duke University Press, 2008.

Estrada Álvarez, Jairo. "Élites intelectuales y producción de política económica en Colombia." In *Intelectuales, tecnócratas y reformas neoliberales en América Latina*, edited by Jairo Estrada Álvarez, 259–320. Bogotá: Universidad Nacional de Colombia, 2005.

Farnsworth-Alvear, Ann. *Dulcinea in the Factory: Myths, Morals, Men and Women in Colombia's Industrial Experiment, 1905–1960*. Durham, NC: Duke University Press, 2000.

Ferguson, James. *The Anti-politics Machine: "Development," Depoliticization, and Bureaucratic Power in Lesotho*. Minneapolis: University of Minnesota Press, 1990.

Ferguson, James. "The Uses of Neoliberalism." *Antipode* 41 (2009): 166–184.

Ferguson, James, and Thomas Gibson. *Give a Man a Fish: Reflections on the New Politics of Distribution*. Durham, NC: Duke University Press, 2015.

Ferguson, James, and Akhil Gupta. "Spatializing States: Toward an Ethnography of Neoliberal Governmentality." *American Ethnologist* 29, no. 4 (2002): 981–1002.

Field, Thomas. *From Development to Dictatorship: Bolivia and the Alliance for Progress in the Kennedy Era*. Ithaca, NY: Cornell University Press, 2014.

Florez Enciso, Luis Bernardo. "Colombia: Economy, Economic Policy and Economists." In *Economists in the Americas*, edited by Montezinos and John Markoff, 197–226. Cheltenham, UK: Edward Elgar, 2009.

Flórez Nieto, Carmen Elisa. *Las transformaciones sociodemográficas en Colombia durante el siglo XX*. Santafé de Bogotá: Banco de la República; Bogotá: Tercer Mundo Editores, 2000.

Fluharty, Vernon. *Dance of the Millions: Military Rule and the Social Revolution in Colombia, 1930–1956*. Pittsburgh: University of Pittsburgh Press, 1957.

Fontana, Josep. *Por el bien del imperio: Una historia del mundo desde 1945*. Barcelona: Pasado & Presente, 2013.

Foucault, Michel. "Is It Really Important to Think?" In *The Essential Foucault: Selections from Essential Works of Foucault, 1954–1984*, edited by Paul Rabinow and Nikolas Rose, 170–173. New York: New Press, 2003.

Foucault, Michel. "What Is the Enlightenment?" In *The Essential Foucault: Selections from Essential Works of Foucault, 1954–1984*, edited by Paul Rabinow and Nikolas Rose, 43–57. New York: New Press, 2003.

Freeman, Carla. *Entrepreneurial Selves: Neoliberal Respectability and the Making of a Caribbean Middle Class*. Durham, NC: Duke University Press, 2014.

French, John. "The Laboring and Middle-Class Peoples of Latin America and the Caribbean: Historical Trajectories and New Research Directions." In *Global Labour History: A State of the Art*, edited by Jan Lucassen, 289–334. Bern, Switzerland: Peter Lang, 2006.

Fukuyama, Francis. "The Future of History: Can Liberal Democracy Survive the Decline of the Middle Class?" *Foreign Affairs* 91, no. 1 (2012): 53–61.

Fukuyama, Francis. *Political Order and Political Decay: From the Industrial Revolution to the Globalization of Democracy.* New York: Farrar, Straus and Giroux, 2014.

Gallón Giraldo, Gustavo, *Quince años del estado de sitio en Colombia, 1958–1978.* Bogotá: Librería y Editorial América Latina, 1979.

García, Antonio. "Las clases medias y la frustración del Estado representativo en América Latina." *Cuadernos Americanos* 1 (January–February 1967): 7–40.

García Quesada, George. *Formación de la clase media en Costa Rica: Economía, sociabilidades y discursos políticos (1890–1950).* San José: Editorial Arlekín, 2014.

Garzón, Maite Yie. *Del patrón-estado al estado-patrón: La agencia campesina en las narrativas de la reforma agraria en Nariño.* Bogotá: Universidad Javeriana, 2015.

Gaviria Velez, José Obdulio. *Sofismas del terrorismo en Colombia.* Bogotá: Planeta, 2005.

Ghodsee, Kristen. *The Left Side of History: World War II and the Unfulfilled Promise of Communism in Eastern Europe.* Durham, NC: Duke University Press, 2015.

Gilbert, Dennis. *Mexico's Middle Class in the Neo-liberal Era.* Tucson: University of Arizona Press, 2007.

Gilman, Nils. *Mandarins of the Future: Modernization Theory in the Cold War America.* Baltimore: Johns Hopkins University Press, 2003.

Gómez, Diana. *Dinámicas del movimiento feminista bogotano: Historias de cuarto, salón y calle, historias de vida (1970–1991).* Bogotá: Universidad Nacional de Colombia, 2011.

González, Fernán. *Poder y violencia en Colombia.* Bogotá: CINEP, 2014.

Gould, Jeffrey. "Solidarity under Siege: The Latin American Left, 1968." *American Historical Review* 114, no. 2 (2009): 348–375.

Grandin, Greg. *Empire's Workshop: Latin America, the United States, and the Rise of the New Imperialism.* New York: Metropolitan Books, 2006.

Grandin, Greg. *The Last Colonial Massacre: Latin America in the Cold War.* Chicago: University of Chicago Press, 2004.

Grandin, Greg. "Living in Revolutionary Time." In *A Century of Revolution: Insurgent and Counterinsurgent Violence during Latin America's Cold War*, edited by Greg Grandin and Gilbert Joseph, 1–44. Durham, NC: Duke University Press, 2010.

GRECO (Grupo de estudios del crecimiento económico colombiano). *El crecimiento económico colombiano en el siglo XX.* Bogotá: Banco de la República, 2002.

Greco, Ernest A. "Unionized Professionals in Latin America: A Colombian Case Study." PhD diss., Boston University, 1987.

Green, James. *We Cannot Remain Silent: Opposition to the Brazilian Military Dictatorship in the United States.* Durham, NC: Duke University Press, 2010.

Guerra, Lillian. *Visions of Power in Cuba: Revolution, Redemption, and Resistance, 1959–1971*. Chapel Hill: University of North Carolina Press, 2012.

Guillén Martínez, Fernando. *El poder político en Colombia*. Bogotá: Planeta, [1979] 1996.

Gutiérrez Sanín, Francisco. *El orangután con sacoleva: Cien años de democracia y represión en Colombia (1910–2010)*. Bogotá: Debate, 2014.

Hacker, Jacob. *The Great Risk Shift: The New Economic Insecurity and the Decline of the American Dream*. 2nd ed. Oxford: Oxford University Press, 2019.

Hall, Stuart. *Familiar Stranger: A Life between Two Islands*. Edited by Bill Schwarz. Durham, NC: Duke University Press, 2017.

Hanhimäki, Jussi, and Odd Arne Westad. *The Cold War: A History in Documents and Eyewitness Accounts*. New York: Oxford University Press, 2005.

Hartlyn, Jonathan. *The Politics of Coalition Rule in Colombia*. Cambridge: Cambridge University Press, 1988.

Harvey, David. *A Brief History of Neoliberalism*. Oxford: Oxford University Press, 2005.

Heiman, Rachel, Carla Freeman, and Mark Liechty, eds. *The Global Middle Classes: Theorizing through Ethnography*. Santa Fe: SAR Press, 2012.

Helg, Aline. "La educación en Colombia, 1958–1990." In *Nueva historia de Colombia*, vol. 4, edited by Alvaro Tirado Mejia, 135–158. Bogotá: Planeta, 1989.

Henderson, James. *Modernization in Colombia: The Laureano Gómez Years, 1889–1965*. Gainesville: University of Florida Press, 2001.

Hirschman, Albert. *The Strategy of Economic Development*. New Haven, CT: Yale University Press, 1958.

Hudson, Rex. *Colombia: A Country Study*. Washington, DC: Federal Research Division, Library of Congress, 2010.

Huffington, Arianna. *Third World America: How Our Politicians Are Abandoning the Middle Class and Betraying the American Dream*. New York: Crown, 2010.

Hylton, Forrest. *Evil Hour in Colombia*. London: Verso, 2006.

Hylton, Forrest. "The Experience of Defeat." *Historical Materialism* 22, no. 1 (2014): 65–67.

Inglehart, Ronald, and Christian Welzel. *Modernization, Cultural Change and Democracy: The Human Development Sequence*. Cambridge: Cambridge University Press, 2005.

Jaramillo Vélez, Rubén. *Colombia: La modernidad postergada*. Bogotá: Editorial Temis, 1998.

Jiménez, Michael. "The Elision of the Middle Classes and Beyond: History, Politics and Development Studies in Latin America's 'Short Twentieth Century.'" In *Colonial Legacies: The Problem of Persistence in Latin America*, edited by Jeremy Adelman, 207–228. New York: Routledge, 1999.

Jiménez Burillo, Pablo, Eduardo Posada Carbó, Jorge Orlando Melo, and Alejandro Gaviria, eds. *La búsqueda de la democracia 1960–2010*. Madrid: Taurus, 2015.

Joseph, Gilbert, Catherine C. Legrand, and Ricardo D. Salvatore, eds. *Close Encounters of Empire: Writing the Cultural History of U.S.-Latin American Relations.* Durham, NC: Duke University Press, 1998.

Joseph, Gilbert, and Daniela Spenser. *In from the Cold: Latin America's New Encounter with the Cold War.* Durham, NC: Duke University Press, 2008.

Joshi, Sanjay. *Fractured Modernity: Making of a Middle Class in Colonial India.* New York: Oxford University Press, 1999.

Kalmanovitz, Salomón. "Colombia: La industralización a medias." *Cuadernos de Economia* 9, no. 12 (1988): 71–89.

Kalmanovitz, Salomón, and Enrique López Enciso. *La agricultura colombiana en el siglo XX.* Bogotá: Fondo de Cultura Económica, 2006.

Kalmanovitz, Salomón, and Edwin Rivera López. *Nueva historia económica de Colombia.* Bogotá: Fundación Universidad de Bogotá Jorge Tadeo Lozano, 2010.

Karl, Robert. *Forgotten Peace: Reform, Violence, and the Making of Contemporary Colombia.* Berkeley: University of California Press, 2017.

Klein, Naomi. *The Shock Doctrine: The Rise of Disaster Capitalism.* New York: Metropolitan Books / Henry Holt, 2007.

Krueger, Anne O. "Government Failures in Development." *Journal of Economic Perspectives* 4, no. 3 (1990): 9–23.

Laclau, Ernesto. *On Populist Reason.* New York: Verso, 2003.

Latham, Michael E. *Modernization as Ideology: American Social Science and "Nation Building" in the Kennedy Era.* Chapel Hill: University of North Carolina Press, 2006.

Latham, Michael E. *The Right Kind of Revolution: Modernization, Development, and U.S. Foreign Policy from the Cold War to the Present.* Ithaca, NY: Cornell University Press, 2011.

Lee, Christopher J. *Unreasonable Histories: Nativism, Multiracial Lives, and the Genealogical Imagination in British Africa.* Durham, NC: Duke University Press, 2014.

LeGrand, Catherine C. "Legal Narratives of Citizenship, the Social Question, and Public Order in Colombia, 1915–1930 and After." *Citizenship Studies* 17, no. 5 (2013): 530–550.

López-Pedreros, A. Ricardo. "The Class and Gender of De-coloniality: The Politics of Knowledge and the Formation of a Radical Petit Bourgeoisie, 1970–1991." Unpublished article.

López, A. Ricardo. "Conscripts of Democracy: The Formation of a Professional Middle Class in Bogotá during the 1950s and 1960s." In *The Making of the Middle Class,* edited by A. Ricardo López and Barbara Weinstein, 161–195. Durham, NC: Duke University Press, 2012.

López, A. Ricardo. "De debilidades, fracasos y paradojas: Notas para pensar las historias de las izquierdas. Comentarios a propósito del artículo de Charles Bergquist." *Anuario Colombiano de Historia Social y de la Cultura* 45, no. 1 (2018): 291–312.

López, A. Ricardo. "'It Is Not Something You Can Be or Come to Be Overnight': *Empleados*, Office Angels, and Gendered Middle Class Identifications in Bogotá, 1930–1955." In *Latin America's Middle Class: Unsettled Debates and New Histories*, edited by David Parker and Louise E. Walker, 151–170. Lanham, MD: Lexington Books, 2013.

López, A. Ricardo, and Barbara Weinstein, eds. *The Making of the Middle Class: Toward a Transnational History*. Durham, NC: Duke University Press, 2012.

López, A. Ricardo (with Barbara Weinstein). "We Shall Be All." In *The Making of the Middle Class*, edited by A. Ricardo López and Barbara Weinstein, 1–25. Durham, NC: Duke University Press, 2012.

Luce, Edward. *The Retreat of Western Liberalism*. New York: Atlantic Monthly Press, 2017.

Mace, Marielle. "Ways of Reading, Modes of Being." *New Literary History* 44, no. 2 (2013): 213–229.

Madland, David. *Hollowed Out: Why the Economy Doesn't Work without a Strong Middle Class*. Berkeley: University of California Press, 2015.

Mallon, Florencia. *Peasant and Nation: The Making of Postcolonial Peru and Mexico*. Berkeley: University of California Press, 1995.

Mayor Mora, Alberto. *Ética, trabajo y productividad en Antioquia: Una interpretacion sociológica sobre la influencia de la escuela nacional de minas en la vida, costumbres e industrializacion regionales*. Bogotá: Tercer Mundo Editores, 1996.

Maza, Sarah C. *The Myth of the French Bourgeoisie: An Essay on the Social Imaginary, 1750–1850*. Cambridge, MA: Harvard University Press, 2005.

Medina, Medófilo. *La protesta urbana en el siglo XX*. Bogotá: Ediciones Aurora, 1984.

Melo, Jorge Orlando. *Historia mínima de Colombia*. Mexico City: Colegio de México, 2017.

Melo, Jorge Orlando. "Las claves del periodo." In *La búsqueda de la democracia 1960–2010*, edited by Pablo Jiménez Burillo, Eduardo Posada Carbó, Jorge Orlando Melo, and Alejandro Gaviria. Madrid: Taurus, 2015.

Mignolo, Walter. *The Darker Side of Western Modernity: Global Futures, Decolonial Options*. Durham, NC: Duke University Press, 2001.

Mignolo, Walter. *Local Histories: Coloniality, Subaltern Knowledges, and Border Thinking*. Princeton, NJ: Princeton University Press, 2012.

Mitchell, Timothy. *Rule of Experts: Egypt, Techno-politics, and Modernity*. Berkeley: University of California Press, 1997.

Molano Camargo, Frank. "El campo es leña seca lista para arder: La Liga Marxista Leninista de Colombia, 1971–1982." *Anuario Colombiano de Historia Social y de la Cultura* 44, no. 2 (2017): 137.

Moncayo, Víctor Manuel. *El leviatán derrotado: Reflexiones sobre teoría del estado y el caso colombiano*. Bogotá: Grupo Editorial Norma, 2004.

Moncayo, Víctor Manuel. "Hacia la verdad del conflicto: Insurgencia guerrillera y orden social vigente." In *Contribución al entendimiento del conflicto armado en Colombia, Comisión Histórica del Conflicto y sus Víctimas*, 107–197. Bogotá: Ediciones desde Abajo, 2015.

Moretti, Franco. *The Bourgeois: Between History and Literature*. London: Verso, 2014.

Mudimbe, V. Y. *The Invention of Africa: Gnosis, Philosophy, and the Order of Knowledge*. Bloomington: Indiana University Press, 1988.

Murillo Posada, Amparo. "La modernización y las violencias." In *Historia de Colombia: Todo lo que hay que saber*, ed. Luis Enrique Rodríguez Baquero et al. Bogotá: Editorial Taurus, 2007.

Nasr, Vali. *Forces of Fortune: The Rise of the New Muslim Middle Class and What It Will Mean for Our World*. New York: Free Press, 2009.

North, Liisa, and Timothy David Clark. *Dominant Elites in Latin America: From Neo-liberalism to the "Pink Tide."* Cham: Palgrave Macmillan, 2018.

Nun, José. *Latin America: The Hegemonic Crisis and the Military Coup*. Berkeley: Institute of International Studies, University of California, 1969.

Ocampo, José Antonio, and Jaime Ros. *The Oxford Handbook of Latin American Economics*. Oxford: Oxford University Press, 2011.

O'Donnell, Guillermo. *Modernization and Bureaucratic-Authoritarianism*. 2nd ed. Berkeley: University of California Press, 1973.

O'Dougherty, Maureen. *Consumption Intensified: The Politics of Middle-Class Daily Life in Brazil*. Durham, NC: Duke University Press, 2002.

Offner, Amy. "Anti-poverty Programs, Social Conflict, and Economic Thought in Colombia and the United States, 1948–1980." PhD diss., Columbia University, 2012.

Olson, Kevin. *Imagined Sovereignties: The Power of the People and Other Myths of the Modern Age*. New York: Cambridge University Press, 2016.

Owensby, Brian. *Intimate Ironies: Modernity and the Making of Middle-Class Lives in Brazil*. Stanford: Stanford University Press, 1999.

Palacios, Marco. *Between Legitimacy and Violence: A History of Colombia, 1875–2002*. Durham, NC: Duke University Press, 2006.

Paley, Julia, ed. *Democracy: Anthropological Approaches*. Santa Fe: School for Advanced Research Press, 2008.

Paley, Julia. "Introduction." In *Democracy: Anthropological Approaches*, edited by Julia Paley, 3–20. Santa Fe: School for Advanced Research Press, 2008.

Pandey, G. "Can There Be a Subaltern Middle Class? Notes on African American and Dalit History." *Public Culture* 21, no. 2 (2009): 321–342.

Parker, David. "The All-Meaning Middle and the Alchemy of Class." *Estudios interdisciplinarios de América Latina y el Caribe* 25, no. 2 (2014): 13–29.

Parker, David. *The Idea of the Middle Class: White-Collar Workers and Peruvian Society, 1900–1950*. University Park: Pennsylvania State University Press, 1998.

Parker, David, and Louise E. Walker. *Latin America's Middle Class: Unsettled Debates and New Histories*. Lanham, MD: Lexington Books, 2013.

Pécaut, Daniel. *Crónica de dos décadas de política colombiana, 1968–1988*. Bogotá: CEREC, 1989.

Pécaut, Daniel. *Guerra contra la sociedad*. Bogotá: Espasa, 2002.

Pensado, Jaime M. *Rebel Mexico: Student Unrest and Authoritarian Political Culture during the Long Sixties*. Stanford: Stanford University Press, 2015.

Pew Research Center. *A Global Middle Class Is More Promise Than Reality*. New York: Blackwell, 2005.

Pierce, Jenny. *Colombia: Inside the Labyrinth*. New York: Latin America Bureau, 1990.

Piketty, Thomas. *Capital in the Twenty-First Century*. Cambridge, MA: Harvard University Press, 2017.

Porter, Susie S. *From Angel to Office Worker: Middle-Class Identity and Female Consciousness in Mexico, 1890–1950*. Lincoln: University of Nebraska Press, 2018.

Posada Carbó, Eduardo. *La nación soñada: Violencia, liberalismo y democracia en Colombia*. Bogotá: Grupo Editorial Norma, 2006.

Rabe, Stephen. *John F. Kennedy: World Leader*. Washington, DC: Potomac Books, 2010.

Rabe, Stephen. *The Killing Zone: The United States Wages Cold War in Latin America*. New York: Oxford University Press, 2012.

Rabe, Stephen. *The Most Dangerous Area in the World: John F. Kennedy Confronts Communist Revolution in Latin America*. Chapel Hill: University of North Carolina Press, 1999.

Rancière, Jacques. *Proletariat Nights: The Workers' Dream in Nineteenth-Century France*. New York: Verso, 2012.

Rappaport, Joanne. *Intercultural Utopias: Public Intellectuals, Cultural Experimentation, and Ethnic Pluralism in Colombia*. Durham, NC: Duke University Press, 2005.

Robinson, Cedric J. *Black Marxism: The Making of the Black Radical Tradition*. Chapel Hill: University of North Carolina Press, 2000.

Robinson, James A., and Montoya M. Urrutia. *Economía colombiana del siglo XX: Un análisis cuantitativo*. Bogotá: Fondo de Cultura Económica, 2007.

Rojas, Diana. "La Alianza para el Progreso en Colombia." *Análisis Político* 23, no. 70 (2010): 91–124.

Roldán, Mary. "Acción Cultural Popular, Responsible Procreation, and the Roots of Social Activism in Rural Colombia." *Latin American Research Review*, no. 49 (2014): 27–44.

Roldán, Mary. *Blood and Fire: La Violencia in Antioquia, Colombia, 1946–1953*. Durham, NC: Duke University Press, 2002.

Romero Sánchez, Susana. "Ruralizing Urbanization: Credit, Housing, and Modernization in Colombia, 1920–1948." PhD diss., Cornell University, 2015.

Rosemblatt, Karin A. "Other Americas: Transnationalism, Scholarship, and the Culture of Poverty in Mexico and the United States." *HAHR* 89, no. 4 (2009): 603–641.

Sáenz Rovener, Eduardo. "Estudio de caso de la diplomacia antinarcóticos entre Colombia y los Estados Unidos (Gobierno de Alfonso López Michelsen, 1974–1978)." *Documentos-FCE-CD* 13 (July 2012): 1–37.

Safford, Frank, and Marco Palacios. *Colombia: Fragmented Land, Divided Society.* Oxford: Oxford University Press, 2002.

Said, Edward. "The Politics of Knowledge." *Raritan* 11, no. 1 (Summer 1991): 17.

Sánchez, Ricardo. "Bajo la égida de los Estados Unidos." In *Historia de las ideas políticas en Colombia de la independencia hasta nuestros días,* edited by José Fernando Ocampo, 221–258. Bogotá: Taurus, 2008.

Sánchez, Ricardo. *¡Huelga! Luchas de la clase trabajadora en Colombia, 1975–1981.* Bogotá: Universidad Nacional de Colombia, 2009.

Sánchez Salcedo, José Fernando. *Los empleados durante el régimen liberal: Acciones políticas y producción simbólica.* Cali: Universidad del Valle, 2015.

Sandilands, Roger J. *Life and Political Economy of Lauchlin Currie.* Durham, NC: Duke University Press, 1990.

Scott, David. *Conscripts of Modernity: The Tragedy of Colonial Enlightenment.* Durham, NC: Duke University Press, 2005.

Scott, David. "Political Rationalities of the Jamaican Modern." *Small Axe,* no. 14: (2003): 1–22.

Scott, David. *Stuart Hall's Voice: Intimations of an Ethics of Receptive Generosity.* Durham, NC: Duke University Press, 2017.

Scott, James. *Two Cheers for Anarchism: Six Easy Pieces on Autonomy, Dignity, and Meaningful Work and Play.* Princeton, NJ: Princeton University Press, 2012.

Scott, Joan. *The Fantasy of Feminist History.* Durham, NC: Duke University Press, 2012.

Sharma, Aradhana, and Akhil Gupta, eds. *The Anthropology of the State: A Reader.* New York: Blackwell, 2006.

Shukla, Sandhya, and Heidi Tinsman, eds. *Imagining Our Americas: Toward a Transnational Frame.* Durham, NC: Duke University Press, 2008.

Sick, Klaus-Peter. "El concepto de clases medias: Noción sociológica o slogan político." In *Clases medias: Nuevos enfoques desde la sociología, la historia y la antropología,* edited by Ezequiel Adamovsky, Sergio Visacovsky, and Patricia Beatriz Vargas, 21–54. Buenos Aires: Ariel, 2014.

Silva, Juliana. "Housing Finance in Colombia: From UPAC to UVR." Master's thesis, University of Strathclyde, Scotland, 2003.

Simons, Geoff. *Colombia: A Brutal History.* London: Saqi, 2004.

Sitaraman, Ganesh. *The Crisis of the Middle-Class Constitution: Why Income Inequality Threatens Our Republic.* New York: Vintage Books, 2018.

Spencer, Jonathan. *Anthropology, Politics, and the State: Democracy and Violence in South Asia.* Cambridge: Cambridge University Press, 2007.

Spivak, Gayatri Chakravorty. "How Do We Write, Now?" *Publications of the Modern Language Association of America* 133, no. 1 (2018): 166–170.

Stengers, Isabelle. "The Cosmopolitical Proposal." In *Making Things Public: Atmospheres of Democracy,* edited by Bruno Latour and Peter Weibel, 994–1004. Cambridge, MA: MIT Press, 2005.

Stern, Steve J. *Battling for Hearts and Minds: Memory Struggles in Pinochet's Chile, 1973–1988.* Durham, NC: Duke University Press, 2006.

Stoler, Ann Laura. *Along the Archival Grain.* Princeton, NJ: Princeton University Press, 2009.

Stoler, Ann Laura. "Colonial Archives and the Arts of Governance." *Archival Science* 2 (2002): 87–109.

Stoler, Ann Laura. "Intimidations of Empire: Predicaments of the Tactile and the Unseen." In *Haunted by Empire: Geographies of Intimacy in North American History,* 1–22. Durham, NC: Duke University Press, 2007.

Stoler, Ann Laura, and Carole McGranahan. "Refiguring Imperial Terrains." In *Imperial Formations,* edited by Ann Laura Stoler, Carole McGranahan, and Peter C. Perdue, 3–44. Santa Fe: School for Advanced Research Press, 2007.

Stoler, Ann Laura, Carole McGranahan, and Peter C. Perdue, eds. *Imperial Formations.* Santa Fe: School for Advanced Research Press, 2007.

Taffet, Jeffrey F. *Foreign Aid as Foreign Policy: The Alliance for Progress in Latin America.* New York: Routledge, 2007.

Tate, Winifred. *Counting the Dead: The Culture and Politics of Human Rights Activism in Colombia.* Berkeley: University of California Press, 2007.

Temin, Peter. *The Vanishing Middle Class: Prejudice and Power in a Dual Economy.* Cambridge, MA: MIT Press, 2017.

Therborn, Göran. "Class in the 21st Century." *New Left Review* 78 (November–December 2015): 27–37.

Tinsman, Heidi. *Buying into the Regime: Grapes and Consumption in Cold War Chile and the United States.* Durham, NC: Duke University Press, 2014.

Tirado Mejía, Alvaro. *Los años 60.* Bogotá: Editorial Debate, 2014.

Topik, Steven, and Allen Wells. *The Second Conquest of Latin America: Coffee, Henequen, and Oil during the Export Boom, 1850–1930.* Austin: University of Texas Press, 1998.

Torres del Río, César Miguel. *Colombia siglo XX: Desde la guerra de los mil días hasta la elección de Álvaro Uribe.* Bogotá: Grupo Editorial Norma, 2010.

Torres Rivas, Edelberto. *Revoluciones sin cambios revolucionarios.* Guatemala: F&G Editores, 2011.

Urrutia, Montoya Miguel. *Winners and Losers in Colombia's Economic Growth of the 1970s*. New York: Oxford University Press, 1985.

Vahab, Aghai. *America's Shrinking Middle Class*. Authorhouse, 2014.

Vanegas, Isidro. *Todas son iguales: Estudios sobre la democracia en Colombia*. Bogotá: Universidad Externado de Colombia, 2011.

Vega Cantor, Renan. *Gente muy rebelde: Enclaves, transportes y protestas obreras*. Colombia: Ediciones Pensamiento Crítico, 2002.

Vega Cantor, Renan. *Los economistas neoliberales—nuevos criminales de guerra: El genocidio económico y social del capitalismo contemporáneo*. Bogotá: Centro Bolivariano, 2015.

Visacovsky, Sergio, and Enrique Garguin, eds. *Moralidades, economías e identidades de clase media: Estudios históricos y etnográficos*. Buenos Aires: EA, 2009.

Vrana, Heather. *This City Belongs to You: A History of Student Activism in Guatemala, 1944–1996*. Berkeley: University of California Press, 2017.

Wacquant, Loïc. "Making Class: The Middle Class(es) in Social Theory and Social Structure." In *Bringing Class Back In: Contemporary and Historical Perspectives*, edited by Scott G. McNall, Rhonda F. Levine, and Rich Fantasia, 39–64. Boulder: Westview, 1991.

Wade, Peter. *Race, Nature and Culture: An Anthropological Approach*. London: Pluto Press, 2002.

Walker, Louise. *Waking from the Dream: Mexico's Middle Classes after 1968*. Stanford: Stanford University Press, 2013.

Watenpaugh, Keith David. *Being Modern in the Middle East: Revolution, Nationalism*. Princeton, NJ: Princeton University Press, 2006.

Weinstein, Barbara. *The Color of Modernity: São Paulo and the Making of Race and Nation in Brazil*. Durham, NC: Duke University Press, 2015.

Wilder, Gary. *The French Imperial Nation-State: Negritude and Colonial Humanism between the Two World Wars*. Chicago: University of Chicago Press, 2005.

Williams, Mark Eric. *Understanding U.S.-Latin American Relations: Theory and History*. New York: Routledge, 2012.

Wolford, Wendy. *This Land Is Ours Now: Social Mobilization and the Meanings of Land in Brazil*. Durham, NC: Duke University Press, 2010.

Zamosc, Léon. *The Agrarian Question and the Peasant Movement in Colombia: Struggles of the National Peasant Association, 1967–1981*. Cambridge: Cambridge University Press, 1986.

Zeiderman, Austin. *Endangered City: The Politics of Security and Risk in Bogotá*. Durham, NC: Duke University Press, 2016.

Žižek, Slavoj. *The Ticklish Subject: The Absent Centre of Political Ontology*. London: Verso, 2009.

Zolov, Eric. "Expanding Our Current Horizons." *Contracorriente* 5, no. 2 (2008): 47–73.

Zubiría Samper, Sergio. "Dimensiones políticas y culturales en el conflicto colombiano." In *Contribución al entendimiento del conflicto armado en Colombia*, 197–248. Comisión Histórica del Conflicto y Sus Víctimas. Bogotá: Ediciones desde Abajo, 2015.

Zuleta, Estanislao. *Elogio de la dificultad y otros ensayos*. Bogotá: Ariel, 2015.

Index

Botero, Rodrigo, 236

BR. *See* Banco de la República

Brecht, Bertolt, 190

Brennan, James P., 87

Brigada de Institutos Militares, 230

Bryson, Lyman, 29–30

Caja de Compensación Familiar (CAFAM), 88, 94, 99, 131, 134, 153

Caja de Crédito Agrario, Industrial y Minero (CCAIM), 63, 78, 80–81

Camacho Leyva, Luis Carlos, 230

Capital (Marx), 182, 185, 187

capitalism, 1–2, 7, 90, 158–161, 163, 166–167, 182, 184, 206, 225

Captain Courage allegory, 83–84

Casa Hurtado, 62–63

Casas, Clemencia, 129

Castillejo, Alejandro, 259

Castro, Fidel, 23, 34, 186, 257

Catholicism. *See* religion

CCAIM. *See* Caja de Crédito Agrario, Industrial y Minero (CCAIM)

census taking, 142–143, 284n2

Central Bank of Colombia (BR). *See* Banco de la República

Centro Inter-Americano de Vivienda y Planeamiento Urbano. *See* CINVA

Centro Nacional de Memoria Histórica (CNMH), 259

Centro Urbano Antonio Nariño, 147

Cepeda Ulloa, Fernando, 228–229

Chasteen, John Charles, 8

Chávez, Hugo, 257

Chicoral Pact of 1971, 203–4

CINVA, 42, 54, 56–57, 118, 124

class: democracy and, 23, 53, 61, 99, 157–162, 165–167, 216; Frente Nacional and, 110–113, 160; gender and, 55, 73, 81–82, 112–113, 125, 129–134, 138–146, 155–156, 174, 183–186, 189–212, 222, 233–236; historical, 44–45, 48; inherited, 57–58, 70, 125–126, 130; professionals and, 42, 47–51, 61, 75–79, 89–91, 95, 112–119,

123–124, 129, 134; structures, 8–18, 28, 31–32, 34, 177, 184, 206, 239–240, 256; struggles and, 128, 140, 154, 215, 258–259; two-class societies, 46, 69, 72. *See also* democracy; gender; middle class; petit bourgeoisie; professionals and professional class

class relations: ideal of, 50–52, 117–121, 123–129, 188, 191, 238–239; tension of, 57–60, 69, 95, 111, 122, 134, 145–149, 154–160, 167–169, 176–177, 258

Cohen, Lucy M., 92

Cold War, 14, 16, 174–175, 210

collaboration, 101–4, 134–136

Colombian Agrarian Reform Institute. *See* INCORA (Colombian Agrarian Reform Institute)

Colombian Institute of Administration (INCOLDA), 77, 80, 82, 94, 230

Colombian Social Security Institute (ICSS), 212–213, 216, 218–219

colonialism, 24–26, 44–45, 58, 72–73, 90, 149–150

Colseguros (Compañía Colombiana de Seguros), 86–88, 94, 96–99, 105, 129–130, 132–137, 152–153, 179

Comados Camilistas, 172

Committee for the National Strike, 243

communism: fear of, 12, 25, 90, 94, 147; involvement in, 178, 183–184, 188–189, 231; spread of, 31–34, 43, 230, 248–250

Communist Confederación Sindical de Trabajadores de Colombia (CTSC), 243

Communist Manifesto (Marx and Engels), 147, 184

Communist Youth (JUCO), 178, 185

compensation, 40, 72, 154–155, 159–161, 168–170, 214–223, 231, 240, 243, 245–246

competition, 69, 83–84, 132–134, 159, 193, 231, 236, 238, 242

Confederación General de Trabajo (CGT), 243

Conference of Latin American Bishops (CELAM), 187

Lebret, J. L., 49

Lenin, Vladimir, 190

León Valencia, Guillermo, 143, 159, 203

Levinson, Jerome, 227–228

Lewis, Oscar, 29

Liberal Colombian Confederation of
Workers (CTC), 216, 243

Liechty, Mark, 88

Lipman, Aaron, 70, 92

Lipset, Seymour Martin, 46, 69–70

Little Girls (Belotti), 211

Lleras Camargo, Alberto, 38–40, 49, 230

Lleras Restrepo, Carlos, 159, 180–181, 203,
212, 229

López Michelsen, Alfonso, 212–213, 215,
217, 227–228, 231, 236, 240, 243–245, 247

Los Alcázares, 147

machismo, 73–74, 114, 127, 222. *See also*
masculinity

Marx, Karl, 1, 68, 90, 172, 182–184, 190, 194,
199, 220, 222

masculinity, 55–58, 74–75, 92–93, 103,
120–122, 131–134, 138, 149–151, 247.
See also families; femininity; gender;
professionals and professional class

Maslow, Abraham, 95

McClelland, David C., 67, 71

Méndez Calvo, Jorge, 144

middle class: definitions of, 3–8, 10–14, 31,
143, 228–229; democratizing influence
of, 27–29, 35–40, 45–52, 58, 71, 111,
113–120, 123, 127–128, 146, 158, 226–232,
246–247, 254–261; family dynamics and,
98, 103, 112, 125, 169–170; formation of,
28, 30, 35–37, 109–110, 146; gender and,
44–45, 98–100, 115–116, 131; identity of,
9, 15–16, 86–87, 129–130, 139, 144–145,
150–156, 163–168, 172, 239–241, 242,
252–253; international distinctions of,
23, 36; petit bourgeoisie and, 174–175,
178–179, 182–186, 188, 191–192, 196,
206; as political force, 140–142, 147, 157;
professionals and, 42–43, 46, 53, 88–92,

101, 180; as revolutionary, 32–34, 37–38,
67, 165; small business and, 75–84; study
of, 28; in United States, 21. *See also* class;
democracy; families; gender

Middle Class Hour at Your Service, The
(MOCLAM), 143

military rule, 35–37, 174, 229, 247–253, 258,
260

Millamarin, Gabriel, 122

Millán Puentes, Régulo, 139, 143, 146–147

Ministry of Health, 219

MOCLAM. *See* Allied Movement of the
Colombian Economic Middle Class
(MOCLAM)

modernization, 29, 114, 123, 227, 229

Molina, Geraldo, 50

Mora y Mora, Eduardo, 51–52

Morse, Richard, 76–77

Movimiento de Liberación de la Clase
Media (LMMC), 149–150, 165, 200

Movimiento Obrero Independiente y
Revolucionario (MOIR), 197

M-19 (19th of April Movement), 181, 189,
192, 195, 199–200, 206, 208, 211, 248

Mujeres de Oficina, 154

MUNIPROC, 123, 149

Nannetti, Guillermo, 50

Naranjo, Carlos, 204

National Association of Industrialists
(ANDI), 77, 244

National Civil Service Office (ONSC), 50, 59

National Federation of Colombian Coffee
Growers (FEDECAFE), 40

National Front. *See* Frente Nacional (FN)

National Integration Plan, 227

National Popular Alliance, 15

National School of Commerce (ENC), 62

National Security Doctrine, 247

National Service of Learning (SENA), 77, 82

National Union of Accountants (UNC), 139

National Union of the Colombian Middle
Class (UNCLAMECOL), 163, 213, 241,
244–245

Turbay Ayala, Julio César, 227, 231, 244–245, 247

Umaña Luna, Eduardo, 31, 50, 114
UNAL. *See* Universidad Nacional de Colombia (UNAL)
UN Economic Commission for Latin America and the Caribbean (ECLAC), 29, 65, 75, 230
UNESCO (United Nations Educational, Scientific and Cultural Organization), 50
Unidad de Poder Adquisitivo Constante (UPAC), 231–236, 241, 246
Unión Nacional de Empleados Bancarios (UNEB), 153
unions, 87, 94, 101–4, 136–138, 149, 152–163, 167, 179–180, 216–217, 241–243
United Nations (UN), 24, 28, 40, 50, 95, 150
United Press International, 227
United States: involvement of, in Latin America, 24–40, 78, 90, 110, 150–151, 195, 209–210, 225, 252, 256–257; middle class of, 2, 14, 21
United States Information Agency, 230
Universidad de los Andes, 36, 94, 227, 230
Universidad Jorge Tadeo Lozano (UTB), 230
Universidad Nacional de Colombia (UNAL), 39, 52, 54–55, 70, 91, 178, 186, 195–196
University Movement for Community Development (MUNIPROC), 123, 149
UN Special Funds, 82
UPAC. *See* Unidad de Poder Adquisitivo Constante (UPAC)
urbanization, 11, 47–48, 64, 92, 109–112, 231, 259. *See also* industrialization
Uribe Vélez, Álvaro, 2–3, 86, 173, 257–258
Urrutia, Miguel, 236
US Agency for International Development (USAID), 60, 77, 82, 94, 227, 230
US Office of Technical Assistance (USOTA), 42

US State Department, 31–32
UTC. *See* Conservative Colombian Worker's Union (UTC)

Valencia, Alberto, 42–43, 110, 123–124, 147–148
Vallejo, Fabiola, 105
Vargas, Getúlio, 47
Vargas, Juan, 165
Vejarano, Vasco, 143
Viera Moreno, Rafael, 142–143
violence, 5–6, 17, 31, 55, 165, 174, 192, 221, 247–254, 258–259
virility, 133–134, 136–137, 197. *See also* masculinity
Volgenau, Howard, 78

Wagley, Charles, 29
Ware, Caroline, 54
Weber, Max, 17, 29, 55, 70–71, 74
Western influence, 5–7, 14–15, 18, 24–40, 46, 50, 67, 110, 149–151
white-collar professionals, 86–93, 129, 131–136, 152–155, 167, 179, 183. *See also* professionals and professional class
Williamson, Robert C., 91
women: family dynamics and, 129–130, 144, 169–170, 211–212, 223, 233–236, 242; health and, 213–221; petit bourgeoisie and, 174, 183–186, 190–192, 197–202, 208–211, 219, 248–251; in the professional class, 58–61, 80–82, 92–93, 111–117, 121–122, 125–126, 129–134; service sector and, 96–99, 104–5. *See also* gender
work ethic, 86–87, 112–117, 125–127, 134, 138, 217, 231, 238–240, 245–246
working classes, 57–58, 71, 92, 101, 111, 117–128, 133–134, 138, 177, 216. *See also* class
World Health Organization, 40
World War II, 24

Zabala, Germán, 208